HISTORY, CLASSES
AND NATION-STATES

HISTORY, CLASSES AND NATION-STATES

Selected Writings of V. G. Kiernan

Edited and Introduced by
HARVEY J. KAYE

Polity Press

Copyright © Victor Kiernan 1988
Introduction © Harvey J. Kaye 1988

First published 1988 by Polity Press
in association with Basil Blackwell.

Editorial Office:
Polity Press, Dales Brewery, Gwydir Street, Cambridge CB1 2LJ, UK

Basil Blackwell Ltd
108 Cowley Road, Oxford OX4 1JF, UK

Basil Blackwell Inc.
432 Park Avenue South, Suite 1503
New York, NY 10016, USA

British Library Cataloguing in Publication Data

Kiernan, V. G.
 History, Classes and nation-states.
 1. Europe—History
 I. Title. II. Kaye, Harvey J.
 940   D20
 ISBN 0–7456–0424–2

Library of Congress Cataloging-in-Publication Data

Kiernan, V. G. (Victor Gordon), 1913–
        History, classes, and nation-states: selected writings of
 V. G. Kiernan/edited and introduced by Harvey J. Kaye.
        p. cm.
 Essays originally published 1965–1983.
 Bibliography p.
 Includes Index.
 ISBN 0–7456–0424–2
        1. Socialism—Europe—History. 2. Social conflict—
 Europe—History. 3. State. The—History.
 4. Nationalism—Europe History. 5. Marxian
 historiography. 6. Historical materialism. 1. Kaye.
 Harvey J. II. Title.
 HX238.K54 1988   87–35336
 320.5'315—dc19   CIP

Typeset in 10½ on 12pt Sabon
by Cambrian Typesetters, Frimley, Surrey
Printed in Great Britain by Billing & Sons Ltd, Worcester

For Christopher Hill
in memory of the Garibaldi Restaurant
where we first met.

Contents

Editor's Preface   ix

Acknowledgements   xi

Introduction   V. G. Kiernan: Seeing Things Historically   1

1   History   29

2   Gramsci and Marxism   66

3   State and Nation in Western Europe   102

4   Foreign Mercenaries and Absolute Monarchy   118

5   Nationalist Movements and Social Classes   138

6   Conscription and Society in Europe before the
War of 1914–1918   166

7   Working Class and Nation in Nineteenth-century Britain   186

8   Revolution   199

Notes   233

Index   267

Editor's Preface

For the past several years we have been subject to a barrage of articles announcing the demise of Marxism and the collapse of socialism in the West. These dire prognoses of terminal illness for both the Left's major intellectual tradition and its primary political movement, however exaggerated, are not merely the fantasies of a conservative press. The writings of critical and left journalists, writers and academics responding to the poor electoral performance of socialist parties – and the tragedies and disappointments of Soviet and Third World 'socialisms' – also provide evidence that Marxism and socialism are in crisis and are being subjected to extensive rethinking. An important aspect of this reconsideration of the Left's strategies, tactics and vision is the recognition that there are problems and issues which have not been addressed adequately in the past and that, moreover, if the Left is to progress politically and make history more effectively these cannot be ignored. These issues are many and varied, ranging from the relations between the sexes to the relations amongst nation-states. Though there are many vantage-points from which they might be addressed, it is essential that they be approached historically. However contemporary the questions may seem to appear it is crucial that they be thought through in historical terms, for only in historical perspective can we perceive continuity and change and begin to appreciate the making and unmaking of the problems we confront, and of the relations that we would hope to reform, undo, or secure more firmly.

It is in light of the current discussions and debates on the crisis of Marxism and the future of socialism – and the need for historical thinking on these and such subjects as class and class struggle, nationalism and state formation and the place of force in history – that this volume of Victor Kiernan's writings is presented. For more than fifty years now he has been aggressively committed to historical study and thought, and his writings attest to the value and worth of that practice – as Antonio Gramsci wrote in the pages of his *Prison Notebooks*: 'The point is precisely that of seeing things historically'.

In the 'Preface' to my book, *The British Marxist Historians*, I apologized for having had to omit consideration of the work of two outstanding historians, Victor Kiernan and George Rudé, and I promised to make up for doing so. This is a first step in that direction and I must thank Victor Kiernan most warmly both for allowing me the opportunity to edit and introduce his writings and for his co-operation and assistance in preparing this book – including the provision of postscripts to six of the articles. Though we are not in agreement on every aspect of history and politics – what two people are? – I feel quite strongly that his writings on topics past and present represent a model to which we ought to attend. Thus, three additional volumes of his writings are also being prepared: selections of his essays on *Intellectuals, Culture and History, Poets, Politics and the People* and *Europe, Britain and the World*.

I must personally thank the members and especially the Director, Rodney Hilton, of the Institute for Advanced Research in the Humanities at the University of Birmingham, for appointing me Visiting Fellow for the academic year 1986–7, during which time the work on this book and other projects was pursued. Similarly, I must note the helpfulness of the staff of the School of History at Birmingham, and my colleagues in the Historical Materialism Group. Also, I must acknowledge the essential support of my home institution, the University of Wisconsin–Green Bay, for providing me with the sabbatical award enabling me to take up residence in England.

Numerous people have made their own individual contributions to the publication of this collection. In particular I must thank Heather Kiernan, Henry Ferns, Christopher and Bridget Hill, Tony Giddens, Ron Baba, Tony Galt, Craig Lockard, Per Johnsen, Jennifer Tillis and Joan Robb. Finally, the interest and enthusiasm – in spite of their young years – of my daughters, Rhiannon and Fiona, and the invaluable aid and support of my wife, Lorna, made the work even more a labour of love.

HJK, Birmingham
May 1987

Acknowledgements

Except for the Editor's Introduction, the articles which are collected here were originally published elsewhere. For permission to reprint them, we thank and acknowledge the following:

1 Fontana Books for 'History', originally published in D. McLellan (ed.), *Marx: The First Hundred Years* (London, 1983).
2 Merlin Press for 'Gramsci and Marxism', originally published in R. Miliband and J. Saville (eds), *Socialist Register 1972* (London, 1972).
3 The Past & Present Society for 'State and Nation in Western Europe', originally published in *Past & Present*, 31 (July 1965).
4 The Past & Present Society for 'Foreign Mercenaries and Absolute Monarchy', originally published in *Past & Present*, 11 (April 1957), and reprinted in T. Aston (ed.), *Crisis in Europe, 1560–1660* (London, Routledge & Kegan Paul, 1965).
5 Macmillan for 'Nationalist Movements and Social Classes', originally published in A. D. Smith (ed.), *Nationalist Movements* (London, 1976).
6 Grafton Books for 'Conscription and Society in Europe before the War of 1914–1918', originally published in M. R. D. Foot (ed.), *War and Society* (London, 1973).
7 Lawrence and Wishart for 'Working Class and Nation in Nineteenth-century Britain', originally published in M. Cornforth (ed.), *Rebels and their Causes* (London, 1978).
8 Cambridge University Press for 'Revolution', originally published in P. Burke (ed.), *The New Cambridge Modern History* (Cambridge, 1979), vol. 13: *Companion Volume*.

Introduction

V. G. Kiernan: Seeing Things Historically

Victor Kiernan is probably best known as a historian of modern imperialism, through such works as *The Lords of Human Kind*, *European Empires from Conquest to Collapse, 1815–1960*, *Marxism and Imperialism*, and *America: The New Imperialism*, plus two earlier monographs, *British Diplomacy in China, 1880–1885* and *Metcalfe's Mission to Lahore, 1808–1809*.[1] These books are themselves quite varied both in terms of the subjects they treat and the dimensions of imperialism they consider, extending from diplomatic and military to social and cultural history; and they are joined by numerous articles and essays in international studies taking up such diverse topics as the South American War of the Pacific, nineteenth-century imperial rivalries in Central Asia, colonial armies in Africa, the historic relationship between Portugal and Britain and the post-colonial development of India and Pakistan.[2]

Yet however wide-ranging the subjects and geographical areas dealt with in these writings on imperialism and international history, they represent merely one of the themes of modern European and world history that have engaged Kiernan's historical imagination. One might turn to the recently published *Dictionary of Marxist Thought*,[3] of which he was a co-editor, noting the entries for which he was personally responsible: Agnosticism, Christianity, Empires of Marx's Day, Hinduism, Historiography, Intellectuals, Paul Lafargue, Ferdinand Lasalle, Nation, Nationalism, Religion, Revolution,

Manabendra Nath Roy, Stages of Development, and War. But even this list does not give full account of the subjects on which Kiernan has written, for beyond the history of diplomacy and war, politics and the state, revolution and social change and intellectuals and religion,[4] he is also the author of articles on labour and the working class,[5] and literature, the arts and cultural studies.[6] Finally, he has translated three volumes of South Asian poetry and prose for publication in English.[7]

It is not, however, just the range, diversity and voluminousness of Kiernan's writings that warrant our attention, though they are truly impressive. As significant is the consistently critical perspective which he has brought to bear on the variety of issues he examines historically. Kiernan is, of course, closely identified with a distinguished generation of historical scholars that includes Rodney Hilton, Christopher Hill, Eric Hobsbawm, George Rudé and E. P. Thompson. As I have argued elsewhere, in addition to their outstanding individual contributions to their respective fields of historical study these British Marxist historians have made important collective contributions to the discipline of social history and to historical-social theory more generally.[8] Framed by the historical problematic of 'the transition from feudalism to capitalism', their studies – from the medieval to the modern – have provided the basis for the development of history from below or 'the bottom up'. Recovering the history which was made by the lower classes but not written by them, they have approached the past through the grand hypothesis offered by Marx and Engels in *The Communist Manifesto* that 'The history of all hitherto existing society is the history of class struggles', thereby developing Marxism as a theory of 'class determination'.

Clearly Kiernan has always been very much a part of this cohort as an early and active member of the Communist Party Historians' Group in the period 1946–56 and through the formal and informal relationships that were maintained after 1956 when most of them left the Party.[9] The principal formal link has been the journal, *Past & Present* (founded by Hilton, Hill, Hobsbawm and others in 1952), for which Kiernan wrote an article for the inaugural issue, and served on the editorial board from 1973 to 1983.[10] Nevertheless, it is arguable that Kiernan's scholarship stands somewhat apart from that of his fellow British Marxist historians. His writings, for all their variety, are regularly set within the problematic of the transition to capitalism and they are strongly informed by class-struggle analysis (to which the selection of essays in this volume attests); and to the extent that history from below is generally comprehended to mean having 'sympathy with the victims of historical processes and skepticism about the victors' claims'[11] then Kiernan has been working from the bottom up. Nevertheless, if history from below is understood more specifically to entail both a perspective *and* the recovery of the experiences and struggles of the labouring classes historically, then, except for a small number of his writings,[12] Kiernan has not been working in this historiographical tradition. Rather, he has been the historian of the original group who has concentrated most on what Perry Anderson has appropriately termed 'history from above – the study of the intricate machinery of class domination'; though – it should be reasserted here – always conceived in terms of the relations of conflict and struggle that determine and shape it.[13]

This chapter is offered as an introductory survey of Victor Kiernan's scholarly career as a Marxist historian and thinker. There are too many directions in which he has travelled as a writer for it to be comprehensive, but following a brief biographical sketch it will consider his work on Marxism and history, diplomacy and imperialism, classes and nation-states and culture and socialism.

V. G. Kiernan

Edward Victor Gordon Kiernan was born 4 September 1913 in Ashton-on-Mersey, a southern area of Manchester. He describes his parents as lower-middle class and his family generally as 'not political in any active sense but mostly well stored with conservative prejudices'. His parents were, however, quite religious and Kiernan was brought up an active Congregationalist, which he views as having been an important formative influence contributing to his later socialist commitments and also to his continuing scholarly interest in the place of religion in history.[14]

Kiernan was educated at Manchester Grammar School which had only recently set up a 'History Sixth form' – if it had not it would have meant his entering the 'Classical Sixth form' – and thus he notes that his choice of history was more 'accidental' than anything else. In 1931 he entered Trinity College, Cambridge to read history and was an outstanding student. A lifelong friend (in spite of their contrasting political trajectories since the 1930s), Professor Henry Ferns presents this picture of Kiernan the young scholar at Cambridge:

A visit to Mr. Kiernan was my first intellectual encounter with Cambridge University. [He] is a man of my own age. I have always thought of him, however, as senior to me. He was my first supervisor and I was *in statu pupillari* for my first term. Although we became good friends and companions, this feeling of Victor's superiority endured, and for good reason. He had achieved a first class with distinction in both parts of the Historical Tripos. In 1936 he was in his third year as a research scholar and in 1937 he was elected a Fellow of Trinity College. A list of his academic distinctions does not alone account for his authority in my mind then. He was immensely learned. He had a good knowledge of Latin, Greek, French . . . and Spanish. He knew some Italian and was acquiring a knowledge of Urdu . . . He loved music – particularly that of the seventeenth and eighteenth century. He had an intimate knowledge and love of English literature, which, like his taste in music, seemed concentrated on comparatively few artists of the first rank: Shakespeare, Samuel Johnson, and Wordsworth. If his knowledge was limited to men of the past his taste was catholic.[15]

Taking his degree in 1934 Kiernan remained at Cambridge for the next four years, first as a research scholar and then as a Fellow of Trinity. Also in 1934 he joined the Communist Party. Cambridge University of this period has provided the material for numerous reminiscences, exposés, historical studies and fictional representations, and Kiernan was very much a part of the generation of student Communists that has been the subject of so many of those writings.[16] Indeed, amongst his closest friends and comrades were John Cornford and James Klugmann, the leading figures of Cambridge Communism;[17] also Kiernan was quite close to the Canadian, Herbert Norman.[18] By most accounts these years seem to have been understood by these young leftists as 'the worst of times . . . the best of times'. The world economic depression and industrial unemployment, the rise and triumph of Fascism in Central Europe and the ever-increasing threat of a second world war (made even more evident by events in Spain), all contributed to the view that the capitalist world was going through its final crisis. Yet for these students there was also the sense that they were living through the prelude to socialist revolution, which perhaps by their own efforts they might hasten.[19]

Kiernan did not see his political commitments as being in conflict with his scholarly labours. He has always been of the opinion that his explorations of the past were, and should be, connected with his political concerns; indeed, he says that ever since his days at Cambridge he has held the view that 'History and politics are two sides of the same coin.' Confronting a world characterized by persisting overseas colonial empires, resurgent European imperial aspirations in Africa and Europe itself, and Japanese expansionism in Asia and the Pacific, Kiernan focused his research on the historical development of modern colonialism and empire-building. Especially he took up the study of Britain's relations with Asia, more specifically, Anglo–Chinese relations. Thus, he was also motivated to make contact with Asian students at Cambridge who were themselves attempting to deal with the questions of British and European imperialism and colonialism, and his activity for the Party principally took the form of working with an Indian Marxist study group organized by his friend, Herbert Norman.

The product of his Fellowship research was the book, *British Diplomacy in China, 1880–1885*. The outcome of his work with Indian students was his departure from Cambridge and England to take up school-teaching in India, first at the Sikh National College and then at Aitchison College in Lahore (in what is now Pakistan). Spending the Second World War years in India (1938–46) Kiernan continued to pursue both the study of British imperialism in Asia and political work in contact with the Communist Party of India. His historical researches led to another shorter monograph in diplomatic history, *Metcalfe's Mission to Lahore, 1808–1809*, and the mix of his political and literary interests brought him into contact with the Indian Progressive Writers' Association which had been formed in London before the war. Improving his knowledge of literary Urdu and Hindi, Kiernan was stimulated to begin a series of translations eventualy published as *Poems from Iqbal, From Volga to Ganga*, and *Poems by Faiz*.[20] He also wrote a children's novel, *The March of Time*; poetry, a collection of which was published as *Castanets*; and several stories, two of which appeared in *Longman's Miscellany*.[21] These years in India were tremendously important in shaping his later work. Pre-existing interests expanded and deepened: his study of colonialism and imperialism grew to encompass the issues of nationalism and nation-state formation, and he has maintained a lifelong fascination and concern for the politics and culture of the Indian subcontinent. But also, it is arguable that this period – living in a colonial society in contact with an intelligentsia which was, at best, ambivalent about the British war effort – must have contributed greatly to the development of his own perspective on imperialism and colonialism which is undeniably critical and yet quite sensitive to the historical contradictions of those experiences (as I will discuss).

Following the war Kiernan returned to Cambridge University for a two-year period as a Fellow of Trinity during which (amongst other studies) he wrote a 200,000-word manuscript dealing with the political and social ideas of Shakespeare's drama. Though publishers were interested in the work, he was unable to carry out the necessary revisions because he was too busy preparing courses for his first university teaching-post. (Now, forty years later, he is committed to taking up this project anew, focusing on Shakespearean tragedy.) His work with the Communist Party upon his return to Britain involved both practical political work within the University and in the town and contributions to the formation and development of the Historians' Group, the activities of which were centered on London. He was extremely active with the Group in its first few years and remained in contact following his move to Scotland and a lectureship. However, as a formal enterprise, the Group all but fell apart in 1956–7 when many of its central figures left the Party in protest at the Soviet invasion of Hungary and the failure of the British Party to break with the Soviets and reform itself.[22] Kiernan was active in the debates of the time, but he did not leave the party until 1959, hoping for changes that did not take place. Since then he has referred to himself as an 'independent Marxist' with 'no enemies on the Left'. He has joined no other party or political grouping. In 1948 Kiernan had taken up a lectureship at the University of Edinburgh in the History Department, later being promoted to Reader and then Professor before retiring as Professor Emeritus in 1977. By all accounts, his teaching responsibilities were as varied as his researches.

Before turning to consider Kiernan's ideas, another feature, or characteristic, of his erudition should be noted. In addition to important studies based on primary research, Kiernan's scholarship includes masterful works of synthesis drawing on both primary and – in some cases, mostly – secondary study.[23] Moreover, he has been recognized as an exceptionally skilful 'historical essayist', which I believe the articles in this volume illustrate. This has been accomplished through vast and extensive reading, phenomenal note-taking and file-keeping and especially, as his long-time friend, Eric Hobsbawm, has remarked, his 'encyclopaedic knowledge'.[24] In light of recent criticisms that the historical profession is failing to write in such a way as to make its studies meaningful to non-scholars, and the associated call to provide new syntheses, or 'grand narratives', out of the innumerable explorations of the past carried out during the last twenty years and more, it may well be that we should attend as much to the form and shape of Kiernan's writings as to their content.[25]

Marxism and the Necessity of History

Kiernan subscribes to the classical or Renaissance ideal of historical practice wherein scholarship is closely bound up with ethicopolitical discourse.[26] In this view history is not merely 'for its own sake' – as some conservatives have recently insinuated even as they practise otherwise – but in the words of E. H. Carr: 'To enable man to understand the society of the past, and to increase his mastery over the society of the present, is the dual function of history.'[27] Thus, history is a critical pursuit standing in dialectical relation to social and political thought. Kiernan has been quite direct about the necessity of history for perspective and imagination. For example, in the heady days of the late 1960s he wrote:

> The past is not abolished by being disregarded but turned into a dead weight of habit, stultifying the present. It is only by trying to comprehend the past rationally that we can transform it from a shapeless mass into a platform, or draw energy from it like the giant Antaeus from contact with his mother Earth. The maxim that only active involvement in the present can develop the right sense of touch for the past is a true one, but so is the converse, that only familiarity with the past can impart the right touch for the present. We cannot act on things gone by, but they continue to act on us, and past and present combine to make the future.[28]

In the more bracing experience of the 1980s, discussing the ideological inclinations of nineteenth-century historians, he points to the imperative, or at least potential, of history as critique or demystification, quoting the epigram of Paul Valery that 'History is the most dangerous product evolved from the chemistry of the intellect.'[29] The intimacy of history and politics for Kiernan must not, however, be construed as implying any tolerance for subordinating the study of the past or its findings to political expediency. He has stated his contempt for the abuse and misrepresentation of history in both the East and the West, by both the Right and the Left, because, as he warns, if history is to contribute to the comprehension and the making of *new* history, it will not do to deceive ourselves: 'Any falsification of the past must point a wrong way to the future.'[30]

Kiernan's own guide to the past has been, of course, Marx: 'A Marxist likes to suppose that all he writes, even if not written in terms of art or Hegelian geometry, is – to adapt Boswell – fully impregnated with the Marxian aether . . . I, at least, always liked to feel while writing that the Grand Old Man was within hailing distance.'[31] For Kiernan, as for his fellow British Marxist historians, Marxism is *historical* materialism (the stress is their own!). It is not to be conceived of as a system of logic or philosophy in either the Hegelian or Anglo–Saxon analytical modes. On a variety of occasions he has expressed a particular frustration with the tendency in Marxist studies towards such practice. In fact, he seems to share the general antipathy of historians towards philosophers: 'All that philosophers have discovered since the world began could be written on one sheet of paper – or so one is frequently tempted to conclude.'[32] Not a philosophical system, neither is Marxism a model to be applied to, or a formal theory to be simply fleshed out with, historical materials. What Marxism is − or at least what Kiernan interprets it to be − is *historical* theory, to be developed further in the course of historical study and revised in its light. This is not to suggest, however, that Kiernan assumes some kind of monopoly licence to have been granted to historians: 'What is of solid worth in Marxism lies in its theory of history, its theory of politics, or economics, or art, and its promise if not yet performance of a psychology and an ethic.' The main thing is that Marxist practitioners of whatever discipline think historically. Thus, in urging serious attention to the related issues of justice and morality, he writes that they should be studied 'not in the abstract but in the setting of history'.[33]

Kiernan has long been insistent that Marxist thought give priority to history over models and abstractions. Recalling the early years of the Historians' Group, Eric Hobsbawm notes that there was a tendency amongst them to allow their assumptions and expectations to determine their historical answers. To Kiernan, however, Hobsbawm gives the title 'our chief doubter', and Christopher Hill, referring to the same experiences, says of him that 'He kept us on our toes.'[34] It is quite likely that these reminiscences of Kiernan's participation refer in particular to his dissensions in the course of the group's deliberations in 1947 on the subject of the transition to capitalism, treating specifically the questions of the nature of England's mode of production and social structure in the sixteenth and seventeenth centuries, the class character of the state in that period, and thence the degree to which the English Revolution can be understood as a 'bourgeois revolution'. In short, Kiernan took issue with the thesis, offered in a document prepared for the Group by Hill, that the Tudor polity was a feudal-absolutist landowners' state. He agreed that the Tudor state was absolutist, but he held that it could not be defined as feudal because whereas absolutism entailed centralized political power and authority, feudalism was a polity characterized by dispersed powers and authorities. Moreover, the agrarian relations of production around which the social order and the state were formed in the sixteenth century were no longer feudal but much more capitalist. Regarding the struggles of the seventeenth century Kiernan proposed that rather than there having been only one bourgeois revolution there had actually been several from the fifteenth to the seventeenth century. Finally, on the related question of the characterization of the period as either feudal or capitalist, he suggested that 'merchant capitalist' seemed most appropriate to this transitional phase; indeed, Kiernan felt that too much was being made of a supposed distinction between mercantile and industrial capitalists, the former conservative and the latter progressive (a position advanced by Maurice Dobb in his book, *Studies in the Development of Capitalism*).[35]

The Group did not accept Kiernan's criticisms.[36] Forty years on, these questions continue to be debated, though our knowledge of the transition process is greatly increased and the concepts used to analyse it are arguably more refined.[37] We find that the historical evidence and current arguments do support aspects of Kiernan's dissent, especially that the development of agrarian capitalism was well under way in the sixteenth century and that the 'bourgeois revolution', though culminating in the struggles of the seventeenth century, was in fact a much longer and more complex process.[38] Yet it would appear that he underestimated the degree to which West European absolutism could be a 'feudal' state (a position which he revised in his later writings), and I would ague that, though the transitional centuries remain ill-defined, he was also mistaken both in proposing the term merchant capitalism to cover the period and in assessing merchant capital as an essentially developmental force in the process.[39] Nevertheless – perhaps even in spite of, or on account of, the rejection of his criticisms of what was to be the Group's 'official' position – Kiernan has remained actively interested in the historical problem of the transition, as evidenced in his many writings on both imperialism and nation-state formation (a point to which I shall return).

Amongst his fellow Marxist historians Kiernan is both one of the most critical and one of the most appreciative of Marx himself (though this may be due to the fact that Kiernan has seemed more willing than most to reflect aloud about Marx and the development of Marxist thought).[40] In his 1983 Marx Centennial essay, 'History' (the first of his articles included here), Kiernan surveys and assesses the development of 'historical Marxism'. He does so by situating Marx, Engels and a variety of later Marxists in their historically specific circumstances, acknowledging their personal commitments, the particular intellectual legacies available to them, and the specific international and national developments, demands and possibilities that shaped their work. In this fashion he objectively considers the bases upon which Marxist historical practice has evolved, highlighting in these experiences the ideas worth preserving, subject to further exploration and possible revision, and the problems demanding urgent consideration either because of inadequate attention in the past, or worse, intellectual corruption, or because Clio has only now thrown them up in such a form that we can properly recognize them.

Critical appreciation of Marx and Engels is evident throughout Kiernan's writings. At one moment he points to where they overemphasized the economic factor in order to secure their materialist perspective; at another, to their imperfectly successful attempts to discover the 'logic' of history which might thereafter guide them through the thickets of the past; and, at yet another, to those numerous occasions on which Marx allowed his ideas and aspirations for humanity to outrun the historical evidence.[41] At the same time, however, Kiernan maintains that it was probably this very same 'passion' which infused Marx's writings with their continuing relevance: 'The most formidable intellect cannot work at full stretch on human problems, except passionately, and all original and intense thought must be one-sided; the eye that sees every aspect of a question sees none of them vividly.' Kiernan does not hesitate to remind us that 'Marx was an amateur historian', but, of course, one whose 'mind roamed over world history at large'. Regarding his contributions to historical theory he finds Marx a great explorer: 'Much as Columbus and those who came after him convinced men once for all that the earth was round, Marx brought recognition of an order and priority of relationships among all human concerns.'[42]

Even as he pays homage to Marx, Kiernan notes that it seems unfortunate that an ever-developing body of thought should go 'under one man's name'. Amongst the things he may well have had in mind were the labours of Marx's comrade and intellectual partner, Engels; for in contrast to the many philosophers who have attributed the reductionisms in Marxism to Engels, Kiernan expresses warm appreciation (again, critical) for his efforts. Fully aware of Engel's simplification of Marx's thought following Marx's death, Kiernan sympathetically attributes this to Engels having the weighty responsibility of drawing together and popularizing his friend's ideas, which necessarily entailed simplifying them. Kiernan's appreciation is, however, not only on account of Engels's support for Marx and Marx's writings, but just as much because of Engels's own commitment to historical study, a product of which was his pioneering work, *The Peasant War in Germany*. In fact, Kiernan reminds us that it was not unusual for Engels to be pushing Marx into being ever more historical in his writing.[43]

Of those who have followed Marx and Engels, Kiernan feels the greatest affection for the Italian, Antonio Gramsci (1891–1937), whom he dubs the 'first great standard-bearer of Western Marxism'. In two articles, considering Gramsci's *Prison Notebooks* and *Prison Letters* respectively, Kiernan makes clear that his admiration is inspired by the rich political, cultural and literary content of these writings and the contributions they might make to socialist thought and practice.[44] Above all else, however, Kiernan seems to respond to Gramsci's commitment to history and his view that Marxism must be 'completely historical in spirit'. Gramsci's imprisonment for over a decade until his death kept him from carrying out any of the historical researches he outlined in the *Notebooks*, but as Kiernan states admiringly: 'All Gramsci's speculations took . . . a historical shape, and history was with him the grand interest, embracing all the rest'; indeed, 'No one has laid more stress on history as the accompaniment or vehicle of all thinking about human affairs.'[45]

Another practice of Gramsci's that Kiernan commends is his willingness to confront other intellectual traditions not merely for the sake of critique and dismissal but with the intention of learning from them and possibly even drawing out elements to be incorporated into Marxism itself. If historical materialism is to continue to develop, it is essential, Kiernan argues, that it be self-conscious and self-critical about its own inadequacies, responsive to new challenges and demands and receptive to what may possibly be garnered from competing theories: 'Marxism in other words cannot generate all its intellectual capital out of its own resources.'[46] Kiernan himself has been more than willing to be critical of Marxists whose analyses fail on historical grounds, as he is, for example, with Ernst Fischer's book, *The Necessity of Art*, in a review essay entitled 'Art and the Necessity of History'.[47] In the same spirit, he has shown himself to be warmly disposed towards non-Marxist scholars whose works have contributions to make to Marxist historical enquiry. For example, in a review essay on Braudel's *Capitalism and Material Life, 1400–1800*, he writes:

> There is also a great deal in the book for Marxists to ponder over, asking themselves whether their categories have grown flexible and subtle enough to accommodate all this multitude of facts and ideas. Their understanding of 'base and superstructure' would profit from such an exercise. Above all they might comprehend more clearly how and why mankind has mostly been standing still, instead of focusing their studies on the few 'big leaps'.[48]

Imperialism and its Contradictions

Written before the Second World War, Kiernan's first book, *British Diplomacy in China, 1880–1885*, is in one sense a traditional work focusing on the efforts and intrigues of diplomats and statesmen to secure and further their respective countries' interests in late nineteeth-century China and East and South East Asia. In another sense, however, it stands as an attempt at innovation for, as Kiernan explains, he was seeking to unravel the manner in which the politics of diplomacy are bound up with, and expressive of, economic forces, and thereby bring together the two seemingly separate fields of diplomatic and economic history. This is accomplished well, but the book is, nevertheless, marked by a duality. Within the larger work there is a second, shorter one reflecting Kiernan's Marxist-historical concerns, and therein he presents a sociological analysis of China's historic mode of production, social structure and the state, and class conflicts, influenced by the 'hydraulic' theories offered by Karl Wittfogel and others.[49] This latter 'work' is indicative of the direction in which Kiernan's post-war and later scholarship would go. Although he continued to publish in diplomatic history right into the 1960s, he increasingly came to see diplomatic affairs, in so far as his own researches were concerned, as of mostly antiquarian interest.[50]

The Lords of Human Kind appeared in 1969 and though there are evident links with his diplomatic writings, it represents a real shift, for it is a study in the historical psychology of race. Set within the process of European expansion overseas, the book surveys the attitudes of merchants and traders, diplomats and military men, and missionaries and colonial officers towards those over whom they sought hegemony. Although concerned with the view, or perspective, 'from above', Kiernan appreciates that the development of European attitudes cannot be treated in isolation. Thus, in addition to illustrating how Europeans' racial(ist) and ethnocentric perceptions of the 'outside world' were conditioned by the particulars of their countries of origin and therein by class, he shows how these views were shaped by the cultures, social structures and levels of development of the non-European peoples themselves, which were, of course, determinants of those peoples' capacities to resist, or possibly thwart (as in the case of Japan), European advances, encroachments and conquests.

The Lords of Human Kind is complemented by Kiernan's later book, *European Empires from Conquest to Collapse, 1815–1960*, published in 1982. Whereas the former treats the cultural dimension of imperial expansion, the latter is a historical sociology of Europe's imperial and colonial wars. *European Empires* looks at Europe's armies and technologies of death and their applications to killing in Africa, Asia and the Pacific, together with considerations of the ideologies and doctrines of colonialism and colonial warfare, the publicity and political consequences at home and the resistance and rebellions offered by colonial peoples. A reading of this work should cure one of any nostalgia for Europe's colonial past. Indeed, both *The*

Lords of Human Kind and *European Empires* arose out of Kiernan's mutual historical and political concerns. The first book was intended to provide a historical mirror in which Britons might reflect on their attitudes and relations with non-European peoples, which Kiernan saw as all the more urgent as Britain was ever more obviously becoming a multi-ethnic and multiracial society with all the attendant difficulties exacerbated by post-imperial political and economic decline.[51] The second book was also for the purpose of historical reflection and to draw attention to the persistence and continuity of the past in the present: 'There are, after all, good reasons for prying into the past with the historians' telescope, and trying to see more clearly what happened, instead of being content with legend or fantasy. Of all the reasons for an interest in the colonial wars of modern times the best is that they are still going on, openly or disguised.'[52]

Thus, Kiernan has also explored American history in *America: The New Imperialism*, published in 1978. In it he provides an interpretation of American history in which expansion and imperialism are conceived as central to its development. Though not offering an original thesis as to the causes of American imperialism, the book is effectively written, connecting the historically particular modes of the United States' 'march westward' and hegemonic advances globally to the changing complex of its regional and class forces and conflicts. Kiernan's observations on American history and politics, in the book and related articles,[53] are often acerbic, yet in the very same texts he exhibits and expresses a sensitivity to, and appreciation of, the tensions and contradictions which have characterized American growth and development. At the beginning of the book he writes:

America's early settlers left an England astir with progressive impulses, and might have seemed to be building in the wilderness the better society that the Levellers tried in vain to build in England. But there was always in this new land a duality, a division of the soul as deep as the racial cleavage between black and white. Aspiration towards a new life was never to succumb entirely to what our ancestors called 'the world, the flesh and the devil'. Yet these latter temptations remained potent, and imperialist hankerings – running all through America's history and at last becoming its most obtrusive feature – have been one consequence.[54]

Published in the wake of the Vietnam War, *America: The New Imperialism* joined those studies which have sought to demolish that powerful historical myth of Americans which holds that the United States has never been a 'colonial' power; but it is also made quite clear in the course of the historical narrative, as well as in an earlier article, 'Imperialism, American and European', how the development of American imperialism has contrasted historically with that of Europe: 'It lost interest overnight in its first flutter with colonialism, in a volatile fashion impossible to a Europe rancid with hereditary ambitions and vendettas.'[55] Nevertheless, foregoing direct colonialism American empire-building led the way towards *neo*-colonialism.

In line with his pronouncements on Marxism and history, Kiernan's studies in this area have not been pursued for the purpose of elaborating a formal theory of the causes of imperialism and colonialism, but they have been written in relation to the development of Marxist historical thinking on the subject. In the 'Foreword' to *Marxism and Imperialism*, a collection of articles published in 1974, Kiernan remarks that the strength of Marxist and Leninist thought has been in economic analysis, and 'In this preoccupation Marxism continued Marx's own turning away ... from a many-sided approach to history and society towards a narrower concentration on their economic structure.' This, however, was inadequate. Marxist work on imperialism had become 'most vulnerable to criticism through its comparative neglect of other motive forces, political or psychological'. In other words, Marxism had been reduced and was now being equated too much with economics and economic determinism. *The Lords of Human Kind, European Empires* and *America: The New Imperialism* can be read, then, as efforts to 'round out' Marxist investigations. Yet they are more than merely attempts to add politics and culture to economics. Although Kiernan does not attend adequately to political economy, his studies do represent, as I have indicated, explorations of the dialectical relations between class and imperialism, and thus his writings in this area (along with those on nationalism and nation-state formation to be discussed) are very much a part of the British Marxist historians' development of Marxism as a 'theory of class determination'. As Kiernan suggests:

> Modern imperialism has been an accretion of elements, not all of equal weight, that can be traced back through every epoch of history. Perhaps its ultimate causes, with those of war, are to be found less in tangible material wants than in the uneasy tensions of societies distorted by class divisions, with their reflections in distorted ideas in men's minds.[56]

Where he has spoken directly to the theoretical questions, as in 'The Marxist Theory of Imperialism and its Historical Formation', we find it has been in the fashion of his previously noted article, 'History'. That is, he brings the theory face to face with historical experience, his purpose being to separate out 'what may be of permanent value in it from what was ephemeral, or has been discounted by later history'.[57]

In the past several years Kiernan has often been invited to consider and address the *consequences* of imperialism and colonialism both for Europeans and for Afro–Asians. His assessments remain critically objective and his observations offer little comfort to either party. For example, however much his own writings attest to the brutality of conquest and oppressiveness of colonialism, he also feels compelled to state in conclusion to *European Empires* that 'Even with the aid of machine-guns and high explosives, the total of deaths inflicted on Afro-Asia by Europe must have been trifling compared with the number inflicted on it by its own rulers, in Africa chiefly through wars, in Asia chiefly through crushing revolts.'[58] Indeed, since Kiernan has consistently been attentive to the pre-existing modes of class domination amongst *both* the colonizers and the colonized, he has necessarily recognized that 'So many lands were under alien or semi-alien rule that the overthrow of thrones might be welcomed as the deliverance which Europeans professed to be bringing.'[59] (It need hardly be said that remarks such as these are not intended to absolve Europeans of their colonial histories and atrocities.)

What about the longer-term, the so-called 'developmental' consequences of European imperialism and colonialism? This is a question Kiernan himself asks, noting that 'Western thinking has usually favoured the view that colonialism, despite much that is shameful in its record, rescued backward or stagnating societies by giving them better government, and transformed them by drawing them out of isolation into the currents of the world market and a world civilisation';[60] but, of course, as he is fully aware: 'Each nation – feeling itself the strongest – has sought to impose its will on others, but to think of itself as their warden or rescuer'.[61] His own answer is historical. First, he distinguishes between the early colonialism of Spain and Portugal – when 'Europe was still too little developed to have much to bestow.'[62] – and the later north-western European imperialisms following on the Industrial and American and French Revolutions. Then he considers the differing effects of these latter imperialisms on various Asian and African peoples, for clearly the impact of European expansion on, for example, India, China and Japan was dramatically different.[63] Nevertheless, allowing for significant historical and moral reservations, it appears that Kiernan does comprehend European imperialism and colonialism as having been 'progressive', at least initially, in the developmental sense.

It is here that we encounter most directly a central characteristic of

Kiernan's conception of history, one that links him closely with Marx and Engels, perhaps more so than any of the the other British Marxist historians. I am referring specifically to his sense of history as tragedy. He aims us toward it himself with reference to imperialism when he writes: 'Conquest and occupation were grievous experiences; whatever beneficial results might ensue, the cure was at best a harsh one, like old-style surgery without anaesthetics. Only in the light of their tragic vision of history could Marx and Engels contemplate conquest as sometimes a chapter of human progress.' On another occasion, he observes that there is a 'sombre contradiction at the heart of imperialism.'[64] That is, if we subscribe to the assumption that economic development – or, 'modernization' – is preferable to the persistence of 'pre-industrial' social orders, then we are drawn inevitably to the historically 'realistic' position that north-western Europe's intrusions overseas were a required catalyst for change and development because it was the only region dynamic enough to accomplish it. This was Marx's and Engel's view and thus they welcomed capitalism's revolutionary momentum; and this is Kiernan's view – up to a point. As he reminds us, though Marx and Engels had a tragic vision of the past, they were optimistic about the future and, indeed, too ready to separate the two, crediting capitalism with too much revolutionary determination and, as a result, they failed to recognize the way in which it would compromise and incorporate pre-capitalist forces to acomplish its ends.

Kiernan, too, sees European imperialism as having been necessary to instigate change and, potentially, development, and yet he also recognizes– more so than Marx and Engels – how the tragedy was compounded. Not only did imperialism have the effect of reinforcing class power at home and abroad – this fact Marx and Engels had sadly realized; but, as Kiernan shows, this often helped to bring about the coalescence of bourgeois and aristocrat in Europe (thereby making a fatally important contribution to war and Fascism in the twentieth century) and the buttressing or calling into being of 'parasitic ruling groups' in the colonies. Thus, at the same time that Kiernan sees imperialism as having been progressive – at least to some extent, he also indicates how, in time, it was inevitably 'deforming' to both colonizers and colonized. In the end he declares that the real contribution of European imperialism 'was made less by imposing its rule on others than by teaching others how to resist it',[65] referring both to the capitalist modernization from above of Japan and the ideologies and forces of nationalism and socialism in Asia and Africa, which, I would add, have generated their own dialectics of hope and tragedy.

Classes, Nation-States and Force

In 'Notes on Marxism in 1968', Kiernan emphasizes that 'Marxist history owes much of its strength to its grasp of the importance of class'. This is not because we should expect to find fully formed class-conscious assemblages in every epoch; indeed, such moments are rare – modern Western Europe being exceptional in so many ways. Rather, it is because of the centrality of *class struggle* in the movement of history. (In this way, Kiernan aligns himself with his fellow British Marxist historians.) He suggests that there have been, broadly-speaking, only two types of class societies, each characterized by the role of the ruling class in the process of production. The first type, occurring twice in history, is where the ruling group organizes production; in its early form exemplified by the ancient civilizations of the Near East, and in its modern form by capitalism (and, we should add, state socialism). The second type, which has been much more common historically, covers the whole array of 'feudal' modes of production in which the rulers are 'parasitic' on production. Even though he provides this generic model of the latter type, Kiernan insists that the historical varieties of 'feudalism' need to be examined much more closely for they are quite distinct forms of appropriation. He especially urges further investigation of medieval European feudalism 'for it was the incubator of modern capitalism and of the whole world-civilization of today.'[66]

Kiernan himself has shown greatest interest in the European aristocracy, originally the feudal ruling class, which he explains (here distinguishing his work from that of Hilton, et al.) on these lines:

> Even if classes were likely to disappear soon, they would deserve all the light that Marxism can throw on them. They will remain embalmed in the common culture, the amalgam of values, to which every class like every race by its unique contact with life has a unique contribution to make. It is of peculiar importance . . . to scrutinise the ruling classes of the past and their cultural record: feudal ruling groups still more than capitalist, because they were more set apart and above societies they controlled, enjoyed a more unique status and privilege and commanded a kind of awe that no mill-owners however rich can aspire to, so that so far as those societies formed any meaningful whole it was the aristocracies that represented it.[67]

Then, in a brief but intriguing discussion of the characteristics of Europe's feudal ruling classes, he proffers the idea that in spite of their distance and separateness from those over whom they ruled, their experience was both unique *and* metaphoric of human experience as a whole. Following Shakespeare, he finds in the aristocracy in its declining years as a ruling class, 'incarnations of the tragic spirit we all dimly feel in the lives of all of us'.

Kiernan's most recent book. *Duelling in Social History: A Study in the Aristocratic Ascendancy*,[68] is an exploration of a practice that was charged with political and cultural significance. Originating earlier, the modern duel actually developed in the sixteenth and seventeenth centuries, a period characterized by chronic warfare; lingering into the nineteenth century and carried abroad in the course of European expansion (for example, to the United States). Kiernan argues that the duel was an 'exclusive' class practice, its moral and ideological purpose being to secure the nobility's *'esprit de corps'*. Moreover, duelling served to reduce intra-ruling-class conflicts to symbolic proportions; that is, since it was confined to individuals, as opposed to whole families and their entourages, it required only a limited number of victims. Actually it might be said that duelling reflected the development of aristocratic individualism under the influence of the age of emergent bourgeois individualism. At the same time, duels which pitted noble vs. bourgeois provided a mode of incorporation of bourgeois individuals by the aristocracy.

Kiernan's previous studies of the aristocracy are also framed by the transition from feudalism to capitalism but focus more directly on the political dimension. Twenty years before the current heightened attention to the issues of nationalism and state formation Kiernan was pursuing such questions,[69] doing so in a Marxist fashion which presented the state as class-structured but allowing for it an autonomous role in social change. His most significant writings in this area are his article, 'State and Nation in Western Europe' (chapter 3 in the present collection), and his *State and Society in Europe, 1550–1650.*[70] In these, Kiernan concentrates on the absolutist monarchy and state of the sixteenth and seventeenth centuries. Revising the position he took in the Historians' Group discussions of the 1940s, Kiernan argues that the absolutist monarchy was essentially a feudal polity 'existing primarily for the benefit of the landed nobility', which remained the dominant class but was decreasingly a 'governing class'. Still, he does see difficulties with this formulation: 'Absolutism was the highest stage of feudalism much more than the first stage of bourgeois or middle-class hegemony. To speak of the new pattern as "feudal" is, all the same, liable to many confusions; the least misleading designation for it may be "the aristocratic state" '.[71] Kiernan demonstrates how the absolutist state came to be established out of the very 'crisis of feudalism'; the absolute monarchy having secured the seigneurial order by subduing both peasant discontent and conflict within the nobility, at the same time limiting the authority of the latter in its own favour. How this was effected varied, of course, across Europe, but it did not represent a ' "freezing" of the status quo'. This is evidenced in part, he says, by the fact that the absolute monarchs themselves were quite often 'new men', though admittedly establishing themselves on 'old foundations'.[72]

That absolutism was essentially feudal, or aristocratic, was of crucial significance, for this was a formative state in the making of the modern world, and the absolutist state itself was the political crucible in which the many rich tensions of late medieval society were melted down to varying degrees, re-formed and bequeathed to the modern. Thus, however dynamic nascent capitalism was – and was to become – it was originally shaped by aristocratic states and imbued with feudal elements of which it would not so easily rid itself. It is not very difficult to see how these works are related to his writings on imperialism. As Kiernan says, the absolute monarchies did not set out to establish national states but rather 'Each aimed at unlimited extension . . . and the more it prospered the more the outcome was a multifarious empire instead of a nation.'[73] Nevertheless, inheriting territorial roots from their medieval antecedents, the absolutist polities were the embryonic experiences out of which developed the nation-state, western Europe's major political contribution to the world.

There is to be no mythologizing of the origins of national states for Kiernan. To start with, it is his contention that the State moulded the Nation (out of the existing materials of 'nationality') more than vice versa, and *State and Society* portrays at length how this process was determined by war and class conflict. Indeed, the absolute monarchies committed so much of their resources to warfare that it has often been assumed that the development of absolutist states was due mostly to 'foreign pressures'. Kiernan, however, dissents, insisting that the pressures toward inter-monarchical bellicosity were primarily internal in that there was a continuing need to turn 'outwards' the intra-class conflicts of the nobility and the class antagonisms between them and the common people.[74] The militarism of the developing absolutist states also provided an outlet for the surplus labour thrown up by the crisis of feudalism; although, as Kiernan shows in 'Foreign Mercenaries and Absolute Monarchies' (chapter 4 in the present collection), their armies depended most heavily on foreign hirelings. This had several advantages. First, however unwilling the common people were to be exploited in order to pay for the wars, they were less eager to fight in them, so foreign mercenaries were a welcome alternative for monarchs. Secondly, foreign mercenary armies strengthened the monarchs against their nobles. Thirdly, though they were more costly to employ they could be 'sent home' when no longer needed and there was no obligation to the widows and orphans of those who did not return. Fourthly, professional soldiers regularly kept up with the latest technologies of war. Finally – and perhaps most importantly – it was safer politically than arming one's own peasants and, moreover, foreign mercenaries were especially useful in suppressing rebellions, an important feature of government in the sixteenth century.

A legacy of feudalism, the absolutist state thus took on a warlike character which, Kiernan observes sadly, it was to pass on to the modern state. This was of tragic consequence, for however intimate the relationship between Mars and markets has been there was, he surmises, nothing inherent in the laws of capital that it should seek outlets in arms and conquests.[75] It might be noted in this context that Kiernan's admiration for Engels is in part attributable to the fact that he, more than Marx, was a student of war, to the point of being nicknamed 'The General' by Marx's family.[76] Kiernan himelf wrote in 1968 that 'The fortunes of Marxism must depend a great deal on its ability to illuminate the causes of war both past and present.'[77]

Kiernan's articles, 'Nationalist Movements and Social Classes' and 'Conscription and Society in Europe before the War of 1914–1918' (chapters 5 and 6 in this collection), extend his class-structured analysis of nation-state formation and the place of the military in those experiences. These too reveal how there was nothing natural or organic about nationalism and nation-states, which were in great part 'creations from above' (by the state, not a divinity). In the article on conscription Kiernan notes how compulsory service has appeared throughout history and in each episode reflects much more about the society than simply how it raises up an army. In the case of late nineteenth-century Europe he argues that conscription to the military served as a mode of educating the masses both to the political and ideological requirements of the nation-state and the regimenting demands of industrial capitalism.

In 'Nationalist Movements and Social Classes', Kiernan traces the development of nationalism as a political force from its origins in north-western Europe – England first of all; across the continent through the course of the nineteenth century; and, by way of selected countries, around the globe in the twentieth, showing how the class bases of nationalist movements varied in the different historically structured contexts. Considering the European pattern, Kiernan links its emergence in the early modern period to the growth of capitalism within the framework of the absolutist state. Undermining traditional social relations, capitalism provided for even more intense class antagonisms requiring both a stronger state apparatus and a renovated set of ideologies. In this context it was the urban middle classes that were most important to the development of nationalism: 'Patriotic feeling could bolster their self-esteem and confidence, and by identifying themselves with it they could better aspire to a leading place in a changing pattern of society.'[78] Indeed, he notes how the national revolt of the Dutch was something of a 'bourgeois revolution' and how the 'bourgeois revolutions' of England and France were imbued with nationalist fervour. Aristocrats, however, found nationalism much less convenient, for it entailed the incorporation of the popular classes into public life; and Kiernan asserts, whereas for peasants and the lower-middle classes the appeal to 'national community' was attractive, the urban proletariat originally had different priorities, though in time it too responded as it increasingly had to attend to the activities of the state and its political culture.

The revolutions of 1789 and 1848 had dramatic effects on the history of nationalism as a political force. The significance of the former is that it provided the basis for 'nationalist movements of opposition' which might be either conservative or progressive. Later, the struggles of 1848 put fear into the hearts and minds of bourgeois and aristocrat alike and thus, as Kiernan describes, national states were even 'more rapidly to be built from above with modern administrative resources', as was most definitely the case in Germany. Thereafter, with the development of socialist and Communist parties commanding working-class allegiances, 'patriotism' became 'the last refuge or reaction, and nationalist labels were favourites with right-wing parties' (for example, Franco's 'Nationalist' movement and Hitler's corruptly titled 'National' Socialists.)[79] Nevertheless as his comparative-historical narrative illustrates, nationalism remained an ambivalent force in this century, even being married to socialism in the defence of the Soviet Union in the Second World War and in the anti-colonial struggles in Africa and Asia.

Along with his work on aristocracy, absolutism and nation-state formation, Kiernan has pursued research and writing on revolutions. In the article 'Revolution' (the last chapter in the present collection), he surveys the social and political struggles from the sixteenth to the nineteenth century, highlighting the bourgeois revolutions of the Netherlands, England and France. His concern, as we should expect, is with the way class forces and conflicts shaped the course of these upheavals. Though subscribing to the view that social revolts are usually instigated by 'intensified pressure from above', and also that 'Revolutions more than anything else can only be carried forward by minorities', Kiernan does not discount the role of the popular classes. In resistance and revolt the common people contribute to the movement of history, even in defeat, to the extent that 'fear of social upheaval' determines the actions of states and ruling classes. As to the classification of the Dutch, English and French Revolutions as 'bourgeois' Kiernan's view is that 'They were not projected, fought and won by any bourgeoisie, though this class would be their chief heir. Capitalism was as yet embryonic.' Indeed, repeating a proposition he advanced in the Historians' Group in 1947, he adds that 'Bourgeois revolutions, like "bourgeois art", are made for the more or less reluctant bourgeoisie by the radical petty-bourgeoisie.' Moreover, the lower-middle classes, labourers and, in the French case, the peasantry, who did most of the fighting, did not have in mind the furthering of capitalist development.[80] Nevertheless, whatever the contradictions and ironies, these revolutions did represent 'progress', which is all the more apparent when contrasted with the absence or failure of such revolutions.

Appropriate to his tragic vision of history is Kiernan's primary work in this area, *The Revolution of 1854 in Spanish History*, published in 1966.[81] The volume is dedicated to his father, to whom he credits his initial interest in Spain, but there can be no doubt that it has also been determined by the dramatic impact which the Spanish Civil War (1936–9) had on the political formation of Kiernan's generation.[82] As a study of the 'Bienio' of 1854–6, the book is Kiernan's effort to unravel the historical origins of twentieth-century Spain and its Civil War: 'Brief as it was a great deal of history was concentrated in it; nearly all the persistent problems of modern Spain – political, economic, cultural – asserted themselves forcibly; nearly all the parties of the epoch had their roots in it.'[83] Essentially, the tragedy of the Revolution, with its grave consequences for both Spain and Europe, was the failure of Spanish liberals and, in their wake, Spanish democrats, to mobilize mass discontent or place themselves at the head of the popular struggles that presented themselves, which might have enabled them to renovate Spanish society along the lines of a bourgeois revolution. But, of course, as much of Kiernan's work reminds us, history does not operate according to formulae and we find in the disruption of 1854–6 the first interventions of the Spanish proletariat as a class, which in the shadows cast by the upheavals of 1848 represented too much of a threat to the propertied for them to risk too great a commitment to social transformation.

Culture and Socialism

Though very much the member of the original Historians' Group who went on to pursue the study of 'who rides whom and how' rather than the story of the common people, Kiernan has always set his work in the context of class relations and struggle.[84] Moreover, he has regularly called for the past to be explored from the bottom up and, as noted earlier, he has himself written several pieces in the genre.[85] The question which seems to inform these studies and concern him most – in response to which he offers a variety of historical observations – is 'What is the relationship between the struggles of the working class and the making of socialism?' His observations are as objective as ever and his assessments are far from sanguine. He notes that Marx may have been overly impressed by the 1844 weavers' insurrection in Silesia, to the point of assuming that the proletariat was innately revolutionary. Kiernan disagrees: 'There are no revolutionary classes in history, none whose intrinsic nature compels revolt.' As for the revolutionary instincts of the working class in particular, Kiernan reminds us that 'Workers everywhere have been readier to fight against the establishment of industrial capitalism than for its abolition, once firmly established.'[86] Nowhere, he says, has the identity of the working class merged with the cause of socialism to the degree or in the fashion that Marx presumed it would.

Kiernan has written several articles on the 'making of the English working class' in which he describes its development in the course of the nineteenth century in terms of a metamorphosis: whereas the early working class of artisan and proletariat was characterized by some 'vision' which enabled them to conceive of turning the world upside down, the post-Chartist working class became ever more enveloped in ' "labourism", content with what improvements could be got by trade unions, and relinquishing any design of transforming society'.[87] Depicted most concisely in his article, 'Working Class and Nation in Nineteenth-century Britain' (chapter 7 in the present collection), Kiernan's analysis is pursued in terms of a particular interpretation of Gramsci's concept of hegemony which does not reduce it to cultural domination. He allows that working-class accommodation in the nineteenth century was accomplished in part through a combination of coercion, especially in the first few decades; slow reform in response to working-class organization and demands; an apparent or merely limited share in the benefits of empire; and a variety of nationalist appeals (patriotism and jingoism). But equally

significant was the collective *self*-enclosure of the working class in
'labourism'; mirroring the geographical apartheid of class in the cities
of Victorian Britain. Kiernan depicts the working class in this period
as 'segregated, morally and physically' in the expanding industrial
towns and, mobilized out of an agricultural proletariat dispossessed of
both its land and folk arts, lacking a 'culture of its own', which had
the effect of keeping it *'incomunicado'*.[88]

Inspired by the writings of the British Marxist historians (those of
Hobsbawm, Rudé and Thompson most especially), and carried on
most fervently through the History Workshop movement, there has
been a generation of scholarly exploration of popular and working-
class experience in eighteenth- and nineteenth-century Britain,
revealing a rich variety of customs and cultural practices.[89] Kiernan,
however, is not much impressed with this 'culture'. In 1968 before
much of this work was available, he spoke of the kind of popular
activities that were being 'discovered' as 'moral lightning-rods'
channelling into the ground the energy which might otherwise be
directed against the social order.[90] Even a decade later he would say
quite bluntly that there can be no 'proletarian culture except on the
humblest level'. This might be taken to be merely an expression of an
elitist view of culture and the arts, and to some extent it no doubt is,
but he is also referring to what he sees as the labour movement's
failure to appropriate unto itself, and develop, the culture, arts and
ideas 'belonging to the common stock'.[91] He concedes that labourism
has insulated the working class against some of the worst features of
ruling-class ideology and even worse alternatives (for example,
Fascism), but, he contends, it has also inhibited the effectiveness of
socialist appeals. Indeed, Kiernan has argued that a consequence of
labourism was that 'the working class suffered from what may be
called a crippled imagination ... [and] without imagination no
audacious action is possible.'[92]

Lest he be misinterpreted, it should be stressed that however much
Kiernan seems to underestimate the working-class contribution to the
making of an at least social-democratic Britain – which admittedly is
in great jeopardy at the moment – he is not arguing that class struggle
has ever been laid to rest or suspended. Neither is he saying, in the
crudest sense, that British workers of the Victorian era suffered from
'false consciousness', for, as he acknowledges: 'The plain workman
has always known without aid of syllogisms that his employer lives
by exploiting him.'[93] What he is saying, however, is that class conflict
does not in itself make socialism, or, to put it another way: 'Socialists
are not born, in any class, but have to be made.'[94]

It should be noted that Kiernan did not join those Western

socialists of the 1960s who, exasperated by working-class 'eco-nomism' and 'reformism', projected their revolutionary aspirations onto Third World struggles, expecting peasantries to provide the basis for world revolution. He compares such notions to the eighteenth-century dream about 'noble savages'.[95] Reflecting, however, that 'No revolution has ever succeeded without massive support from the peasantry', he admonishes Marx for having failed to properly appreciate peasant revolts historically. Nevertheless, while the Third World 'may liberate itself . . . it cannot liberate all of humanity'. In the end his position is that no class on its own – neither workers nor peasants, in the developed or underdeveloped countries – is capable of bringing about socialism. European history illustrates, he says, that some form of alliance is necessary.[96]

In the language of the 1980s, does Kiernan eschew 'class politics' in favour of the 'new social movements', pluralism and middle-class alliances?[97] His call for a 'spring-cleaning' of Marxism as early as 1968, along with his historical assessments of the working class, would seem to indicate this. That, however, would be pushing his views too far. In fact, he cannot be assimilated to either orthodoxy or the new socialist revisionism. Although he is not at all optimistic about the possibility of such developments, he persists in the conviction that working-class struggle 'remains indispensable to any thoroughgoing social change,' both for the necessary strength it would provide to the socialist movement and for the sake of ensuring that its successes entailed the maximization of democracy. At the same time, his historical findings lead him to support a 'progressive alliance, including radical middle-class groups and intellectuals'.[98]

Kiernan has been especially intrigued by the place of intellectuals in history and has written often on the subject.[99] As ever, what he has to say is critical, never failing to consider the intelligentsia's traditional role of supporting the powers that be; and in the same way that he does not subscribe to the fantasy of peasants providing the socialist alternative to the Western working class, neither does he defer to those who propose the 'intellectual class' as the stand-ins. He does, however, see an essential role for intellectuals of the Left which further explains his special interest in Gramsci, who more than any other Marxist figure concerned himself with that problem. Though actually he often seems closer to Lenin on the role of intellectuals in the making of socialism, Kiernan clearly appreciates Gramsci's thought for its assertion of the crucial part that intellectuals must play both in the development of the 'progressive alliance', with the working class as its leading force and, in 'organic relationship' with the working class, in the development of socialist consciousness. Also, in spite of his own inclination to pessimism, Kiernan is most sympathetic with Gramsci's advocacy of socialist intellectuals promoting the intellectual and cultural advancement of the working class in preparation for the making of socialist democracy.[100]

As pointed out at the beginning of this introduction, Kiernan has written widely on literature and cultural studies and he has been insistent that Marxists and socialists continue to give ever greater attention to both the arts and religion. In an essay originally published in 1956, entitled 'Wordsworth and the People', he closes with the reflection that 'Marxism also has much to learn, that it has not yet learned, from poetry.'[101] (On a more general level, he has lamented that though the English amongst all Europeans are the richest in both history and poetry, they are also 'the most indifferent to both.')[102] Art ought to have a natural relationship to socialism, he says: 'After all [it] had a share in inventing the idea'.[103] These sentiments are not merely the result of his elitist opinion of working-class 'culture'; they are also linked to the view, which he shares with Gramsci, that Marxism and the making of socialism are not be to conceived of as entailing the rejection of Europe's cultural past and achievements but rather their redemption and renovation.[104]

As for the place of religion in history, Kiernan expresses ambivalence. His own studies amply reveal that religion has for the most part served as a conservative force and that the clerical and sacerdotal elites have regularly lined up with the rest of the rich and powerful. Yet he also realizes that religion has been a deep source of inspiration to movements of resistance and rebellion.[105] Indeed, Kiernan was an active student Congregationalist before becoming a student Communist, and he has wondered aloud on several occasions about the relationship between the Christian and Jewish upbringings of his comrades on the Left and their 'conversions' to socialism and Communism. A selective historical survey of the movements, institutions and individual figures that nourished the idea of a social order characterized by liberty, equality and community, Kiernan's article, 'Socialism, the Prophetic Memory', includes an acknowledgement that socialism is an unintended progeny of Christianity – one strand of the Church itself having kept alive through the centuries the vision of a true *commonwealth*. Here and elsewhere Marxists are urged to reconsider their too often one-dimensional views of religion, for in general, he states, Marxism has failed to value properly 'ideas and ideals, the emotional wants left by religion and many other things of the past, which are needed to create the will to socialism'.[106]

Yet Kiernan also warns against illusions and delusions derived from history. Echoing the Marx of the *Eighteenth Brumaire*, he concedes that because socialism is to be a 'new thing' it cannot be approached in reverse, 'eyes fixed on familiar landmarks of the past'. This may be true, but not in the obvious form in which it is presented. Kiernan's own writings illustrate that however 'new' a social formation may appear, the 'past is never mere dead rubble to be carted away'. Furthermore, as great a hindrance to the making of socialism, indeed of progresive social change generally, is the contemporary self-deception that history does not actually count for very much. Kiernan himself writes of this amnesia: 'History, it often seems, weaves everyday its lessons, and every night, like Penelope, unpicks the web, leaving men's minds as blank as ever.'[107]

Kiernan's writings assert emphatically the *necessity* of history both for perspective and critique and for remembrance and imagination; and at the same time, they attest to his own persistent dedication to objective and critical exploration and dereification of the past. His findings and conclusions may well be subjected to criticism and revision in the light of further research, but however often scholars of the Right or Left contend with and challenge Kiernan's work and arguments, they would do well to consider carefully and try to imbue their own with the kind of rigorous commitment 'to rubbing history against the grain' so characteristic of his.[108]

I argued in *The British Marxist Historians* that while Hilton, Hill, Hobsbawm, Rudé and Thompson have not been primarily strategists of socialist politics, by way of their historical practice they have been pursuing a particular political strategy. This might be comprehended as the creation of a 'historical aesthetic', and their writings seen as contributions to the formation of a critical, democratic and socialist historical consciousness. Though, as I have noted here, Kiernan's work both intersects *and* diverges in significant ways from that of his former comrades of the Historians' Group, his wide-ranging historical efforts have consistently been bound up with this project. Here I would recall the words of the German–Jewish writer, Walter Benjamin, that 'Only that historian will have the gift of fanning the spark of hope in the past who is firmly convinced that *even the dead* will not be safe from the enemy [the ruling class] if he wins. And this enemy has not ceased to be victorious'. For it might be said that while his fellow-historians have been 'fanning the spark of hope', Kiernan has been reminding us that 'The enemy has not ceased to be victorious.'[109]

Though Kiernan's own vision of history is tragic – and we might well ask ourselves if it could be anything but so – it is important that we recognize how he understands this sense of the past:

What makes tragedy is not failure in action, but the impossibility of seeing its results, so that every tragedy is a tragedy of errors; and if tragic drama ends on a note of acceptance, of turning away from past to future, this only epitomizes human experience that through storms and stresses, the strife of wills and its unguessable outcome, new beginnings are at last reached.[110]

1

History

When Engels late in life described the founders of bourgeois philosophy as adventurous minds, not cramped like their successors by specialization and narrowing horizons, and often working out their thoughts amid the noise and heat of contemporary strife,[1] he must have had in mind the founders of socialism as well. At any rate it was very true of Marx and himself. They grew up close to the main high road of modern events, exposed to the pressure of forces old and new but not yet overpoweringly complex. On one side they had in their ears the whistle of the steam-engine, on the other the snores of an elder Europe whose torpor even the French Revolution seemed to have disturbed only for a moment. They might well have an intuition, not illusory, that humanity was entering an age of ordeal and decision, and must at all costs find the right way.

They plunged into the search for it with an ardour which ensured that their ideas were many and bold, but irregularly thrown off, and left in the end in a form into which diverse meanings could be read. In his funeral speech Engels claimed for his friend, besides many minor discoveries, two vast ones: 'the law of development of human history', and the special law of capitalist development. A century later we are still far from being able to feel that we understand the human record; and Marx was no more than a self-taught and occasional historian. Yet we can say of him, what T. S. Eliot said was the mark of a great poet, that after him no one else can write without having to take account of him.

'I am one that am nourished by my victuals,' the hungry servant in Shakespeare protests to his lovelorn master, feeding on amorous fancies; a stock contrast of plebeian with aristocrat, and an expression of the common sense of humanity. This instinctive sense of the primacy of the material, with food in first place, was elaborated by writers of the eighteenth-century Enlightenment into a treatment of history as a succession of epochs each marked by its own type of economy, starting with hunting and fishing and going on to agriculture.[2] Four main stages were recognized, or 'modes of subsistence' as they were called by the brilliant 'Scottish school' of theorists, stimulated by the rapid transformation their country was undergoing as Marx and Engels were by that of western Europe. A more abrupt scene-changing in 1789 shed lurid light on the dynamics of change. It was clear that the ascendancy of a nobility was being supplanted by that of an upper-middle or business class. That this meant also an economic shift to a more positively capitalist organization was nearly as obvious.

Lenin was to point out that French historians after 1815 were finding the key to history in the tug of war of rival classes.[3] Kautsky declared that by the 1840s 'All the essential elements of the materialist conception of history had been supplied', and were only waiting to be fused together by socialist insight.[4] So much was 'Marxism' in the air by that time, Engels himself remarked some years after Marx's death, that the same conception was discovered independently by an untutored German working man, Joseph Dietzgen.[5] During the early 1840s circumstances were carrying Marx and Engels out of their somnolent Germany into France with its lively political spirit kindled by the Revolution, and England, well ahead with its machine industry. New surroundings helped to bring together their scattered sources of inspiration, and set them on the track of a way of thinking that would combine them all. It could be most readily looked for in the field of history, with its inexhaustible materials waiting to be classified and arranged, for the elucidation of the present and charting of the future. To them by now this meant a socialist future, and it was the working class they had in view as the new social force destined to give history its next great push forward.

Germany had no historians worth the name, in their opinion, because it had no national history, whereas France and England had at least made a start at writing history on rational lines, including economic history in which the Germans were most deficient.[6] Neither of the two could think of turning himself into a professional historian, carrying out first-hand research on the principles that were being worked out; their aim from first to last was to get a bird's-eye view of history, from which its broad outline and patterns of change could be mapped. For facts this meant relying on others. How much of their method they borrowed from Hegel and his 'dialectic' has never ceased to be a vexed question. One view is that Marx turned his back on the dialectic as soon as he emancipated himself from Hegelian philosophy, and only sparingly returned to it in later years.[7] A second is that he rejected it, in his reaction against idealism, for a good many years, but thereafter adopted it afresh, so that his theory of history is properly called 'dialectical materialism', even if he did not give it that title himself.[8] A third is that he and Engels never really abandoned it.[9] They seldom wrote history, or even discussed it between themselves, in the set terms of Hegelian logic. Yet it may be safest on the whole to conclude that its main concepts, resorted to more often instinctively than consciously, continued to be part of the way they thought about complex processes and interactions.

In the mid-1840s a number of essays by Marx, some published, others not, show him exploring various angles of history, with sharpening clarity. As a German he was closer to the European past than his French, still more his English, contemporaries. He noticed how obsolescent regimes are apt to undergo a reversal, and gave as an instance that absolutist government in his day favoured decentralization instead of, as earlier, its opposite, the centralism 'wherein consists its proper civilizing activity'; and it was now impeding trade and industry instead of fostering them, and turning for support away from the towns to the countryside.[10]

In the summer of 1843 he was busy studying English history, and the English, French and American Revolutions: the New World was having its share in forming his outlook. He was looking on the Civil War in seventeenth-century England as what Marxists would learn to call a 'bourgeois revolution', and was dissatisfied with its presentation by Guizot, the French right-wing liberal politician and historian. Guizot thought of the issue between Charles I and Parliament in merely political terms, he complained; and the real reason why the Revolution, and more still its 1688 pendant, could be praised by Guizot as so admirably moderate was that most of the big landlords originated from the Reformation, and were a class not in conflict but rather in complete harmony with bourgeois life. They were in fact 'not feudal but middle-class'.[11] Intensive research has not altogether confirmed this diagnosis, but its author was a historian making a very promising start.

In 1844 insurrections of weavers in factories in Silesia and Bohemia deeply impressed Marx and Engels as harbingers of revolution of another sort, and a display of class-conscious militancy. These impressionable young men may have derived from them an over-hopeful estimate of the innate revolutionariness of the proletariat; but in 1845, thus heartened, they felt ready to embark on an all-round exposition of their ideas. The result, *The German Ideology*, was a bundle of long essays, some on topics of less permanent interest than others; the first and most momentous, on the post-Hegelian philosopher Feuerbach, was in reality their 'first and most comprehensive statement of historical materialism'.[12] It is brimful of originality, along with the exhilaration of discovery. At the same time, in their minds their picture of history was a strictly objective one; their business was to set up in place of 'Utopian socialism' a 'scientific socialism' which demanded an equally rigorous study of history as its groundwork, not a propagandist mythology.

They were feeling their way towards a very broad threefold demarcation: an epoch of 'primitive Communism', or 'clan society'; a second, relatively brief but dynamic, of class division; then a synthesis of these two, socialism or classless society on a high technological level. About the number and character of stages within the second time-span, their speculations were to take many turns. What were to be known as their 'modes of production' were a more complex version of the stages chalked out by their predecessors. Each was a combination of two pairs, tools and materials making up the 'forces of production', labour power and social organization the 'relations of production'.[13] Each formed an unstable compound, to whose internal disharmonies the current of change could be traced. None could be permanent, for alterations in what we may call in sum the potential of production would affect everything else, and prompt another class to strive for the dominant position.

These salient features were most readily identified close at hand, in European feudalism and capitalism. It was not far-fetched to argue that feudalism was brought to an end by production on new, capitalist lines growing up within it and releasing new ambitions. It has been observed that the notion of productive energy straining at the leash of an antiquated framework could easily be drawn from the condition of Germany in the 1840s; 'This was certainly how things looked to liberals and industrialists at the time'.[14] As a further step, it was open to Marx and Engels to forecast that in a similar though not identical fashion industrial potential would swell to proportions which the capitalist framework would find it impossible to contain — as may well seem to be happening today.

There was always an ambiguity in the argument between two postulated strains on each system in turn: this inner tension between 'forces of production' and 'relations of production', and an outward, more visible one between ruling and subordinate classes. These two could not coincide with any exactness, and from then on Marx and

Engels – and their successors – would try to combine them with emphasis now on one, now on the other. To a man of action like Lenin it would be natural enough to think of class struggle as the 'open sesame' to history. To Marx and Engels as philosophers of history it was the other contradiction that was fundamental, and represented their basic hypothesis.

Using their words in a somewhat different sense (as, it cannot be denied, they too frequently did)[15] they tried to bring practical realities home to the German mind by asserting that 'Not criticism but revolution is the driving force of history.'[16] In the shape of revolution, and of class struggle more at large, they were stressing, now as later, the *ultima ratio* of physical force. In the shape of war, on the other hand, their aim was to minimize its significance, reduce it to mere sound and fury. Their interest was in production, not destruction. 'Up till now', they wrote, 'violence, war, pillage, rape and slaughter, etc., have been accepted as the driving force of history.'[17] They controverted this by maintaining that no martial prowess could override economic limits, and victors have had to adapt themselves to 'the stage of development of the productive forces they find in existence'; hence after the barbarian invasions of the Roman Empire 'The conquerors very soon took over language, culture and manners from the conquered.'[18]

But this was very far from being the whole story of the beginnings of medieval Europe, and the further afield they looked, the harder it proved to find situations fitting into their formula. Rome itself, the mighty ancestor with whom every European has to come to terms, offered many puzzles. The Empire, and slavery which they assumed to be 'the basis of the whole productive system',[19] had been built on conquest. On their own showing it would appear a counter-productive system, rather than an enlargement of output; for they held that Rome's decline was caused by over-concentration of landowning in Italy, with slaves replacing free farmers ruined by an influx of tribute corn from the provinces.

Imperfect success is not to be wondered at in such an enterprise, an attempt to make sense of history by finding a logic underlying its apparent confusion. In the course of it they were finding novel things to say, though none worked out with any fullness, about incidental problems they came up against, always trying to follow the precept laid down early in the work that the historian must in every case analyse 'the connection of the social and political structure with production'.[20] It was a fruitful idea, capable of many applications, that the state which arose with the cleavage between individual and community was in one way a substitute for the old tribal community, in an illusory form to be sure but with a firm foothold in the surviving sentiment of solidarity.[21] There is an explanation to be found here of why kings, as personifications of state or pseudo-community, continued for so many ages to be revered by the masses whom they took the lead in exploiting.

The thought is carried on into another, that so long as classes are indeterminate, not yet hardened into their modern distinctness, the state retains a considerable measure of independence from them all, because 'No one section of the population can achieve dominance over the others.'[22] This they held was still true of their Germany. In other words, the now habitual Marxist view of every type of state as controlled by a ruling class does not correspond with the conclusion Marx and Engels came to in the formative days of their thinking about history, however true it may be to call governments of our own day executive committees of the capitalists.

Western Europe's transition from medieval to modern may well rank as the greatest new departure in all human history. On the political side it was accompanied by the 'absolute' monarchy, whose bearings can be very variously judged. Marx and Engels referred to it often, and in a style oddly closer to what is now conventional than 'Marxist', as an autonomous power. They could do so because of their concept of the state as substitute community, which could be supposed to act and sometimes believe itself to be acting for the common good against antisocial groups. By the sixteenth century, according to *The German Ideology*, men of business had grown so strong that 'The princes took up their interests in order to overthrow the feudal nobility by means of the bourgeoisie.'[23] A variation on the same theme can be found in a sketch of Spanish history by Marx a decade later. He depicted the Comunero rebels of 1520 (one-sidedly, if we go by some recent interpretations) as defenders of medieval liberties against a ruler endeavouring to turn feudal into absolute monarchy: they failed because of hostility between nobility and towns-people – regarded by Marx as roughly equal in strength – which enabled the Crown first to defeat the rebel towns with the help of the nobles, and then to turn on the latter.[24]

Ultimately the hypothesis Marx and Engels were hammering out in 1845–6 ought, if valid, to throw light on how all thought and culture have been related to economic life. This they never fully brought their minds to bear on, though numerous and often striking pointers are scattered through their writings. In this joint work, and later on at times as well, they were laying heavy emphasis on the material substratum of the human record. They themselves were clearly impatient to break out from their native German atmosphere, bulging with nebulous or gaseous abstractions, a monstrous quantity of cerebration to every pennyworth of hard fact. They were both, moreover, lively young men with strong literary leanings and a taste for mordant satire, quite ready at times to say things startlingly in order *épater les bourgeois*.

'*Ideology*' in their title stood for a special sort of mental activity, or social psychology, set forth in their opening statement: 'Hitherto men have constantly made up for themselves false conceptions about themselves,' and they were now in need of liberation from 'phantoms of their brains' which imprisoned them.[25] Every society, that is, exhales from its collective life accepted but largely bogus notions about the way it lives. Many are purveyed by professional ideologues; this has been furthered by the separation, always emphasized by Marx and Engels, of mental from physical as division of labour advanced.[26] Ideas thus hatched, they also warned, have been taken too much at face value by later minds of similar cast. Historians have imagined the illusions of past epochs about themselves to be true – a reminder still pertinent, and followed by a sardonic comparison between the gullible scholar and the plain shopkeeper, 'very well able to distinguish between what somebody professes to be and what he really is'.[27]

Bent on brushing away all such cobwebs, Marx and Engels could dismiss 'ideology' as no more than a mechanical reflection of social life, with no vitality of its own, 'no history, no development'; they used the simile of a camera obscura, reproducing images faithfully, but upside down.[28] Even of ideology with their restricted meaning this was an inadequte account, if only because ideas with no energy of their own could not acquire the sway attributed to them. Sometimes, too, Marx and Engels, and some of their later followers much more, were tempted to see all ideas, including far more complex or subtle ones, as no more than shadows of material life, instead of looking for reciprocal interactions.

No publisher was forthcoming, and with magnificent prodigality the manuscript was abandoned, as its authors said, to the gnawing criticism of the mice. Rereading it forty years later Engels recalled that the vital first section was unfinished. It is understandable that they may have come to feel that they were getting out of their depth; but his verdict that the work only proved 'how incomplete at that time was our knowledge of economic history'[29] did it vastly less than justice. Mere fragment though it might be, it was a milestone in the evolution of historical thinking, even if scarcely any of its propositions would be repeated exactly by any Marxist today. It seems extraordinary, and is certainly lamentable, that they never found time to take it up again together. Most of their work was very haphazardly done, and this is exceptionally true of their theory of history, despite the importance they unmistakably attached to it.

Distractions followed, and in 1848 they were plunged into the maelstrom of the European revolutions; another hindrance to quiet study, but their experiences inspired several writings on the events of 1848–9 and their sequel. In all of these, history as the backcloth of politics was in evidence, and the fact that Marx and Engels owed part of their understanding of it to their share, however modest, in making it, lends point to their comments on the contemporary scene. They could find confirmation of some of their theorems in what had been happening. Austria between 1815 and 1848 had been insulated from Europe by its ultra-conservative Habsburg government, which nevertheless was powerless to hinder 'a slow underground movement' of growth in trade and industry and the commercial classes, and this 'came everywhere into collision with the old feudal institutions'.[30]

Two pamphlets by Marx were an ambitious attempt to interpret events in France from the February Revolution of 1848 to the *coup d'état* by Louis-Napoleon in December 1851. In *The Class Struggles in France 1848–50* he tried for the first time, as Engels said in a foreword to a later edition, to explain a series of contemporary events in terms of his economic conception of history. It was followed in 1852 by *The Eighteenth Brumaire of Louis Bonaparte*, a title referring to the coup that brought the first Napoleon to power in 1799. These two works display exceptional brilliance both of insight and of style; they are an intricate counterpoint of class interests and party passions, depicted with all Marx's peculiar sardonic humour and more than his usual wealth of literary allusions. *Brumaire* opens with words which have become famous: men make their own history, but not by their own free choice, because they are always clogged by the legacy of the past. 'The tradition of all the dead generations weighs like a nightmare on the minds of the living.' To Marx's eyes mankind stumbles onward half conscious, half sleepwalking or hypnotized.

Individual figures are not neglected, especially Bonaparte, always flitting through the background shades. Marx sets himself a hard task in undertaking to account for the rise of a man whom he never ceased to regard as a mediocrity, a mere political trickster. He gave great prominence to the rhythm of economic activity, as an immediate as well as long-term influence on politics; its improvement from the middle of 1848 seemed to him the reason for the recovery of conservatism in France and Europe, while renewed depression in the spring of 1851 unsettled things again and helped to give Bonaparte his chance. He was repeating a maxim of *The German Ideology* when he wrote that as in private life the historian must distinguish between romantic phrases and the real interests behind them; and in analysing the 'party of order' he made much of the cleavage that weakened it between the two royalist factions, the Legitimist representing large landed property and the Orleanist standing for big business, with high finance in the lead. Marx was strongly impressed by the gulf between town and country as revealed in these years. Bonaparte was elected President by the votes of the peasantry, the class embodying, in Marx's words, barbarism within civilization, which however he counted on, thanks to its deepening impoverishment, to become in the future an indispensable ally for the working class. Above all the classes towered a state whose vast multitude of employees gave it a semi-autonomous life, and whose hypertrophy he traced back to the days of absolute monarchy.

Meanwhile Engels was turning his attention further afield. One of several echoes of 1848–9 in his book on the Peasant War of 1524–5, which he wrote in 1850, is an allusion to the use of Czech and Croat soldiers against the German-speaking peasant rebels in Austria.[31] In a way he could think of history repeating itself. Germany's retarded development left sundry evils of 1520 still in being in 1848, like the feudal dues weighing on the countryside. He was writing 'the first Marxist work of *history*', as distinct from historical theory, and the model for much Marxist historiography of days to come.[32] It went beyond *The German Ideology* in having necessarily to reckon with ideas as active influence instead of passive reflection. Engels must have been helped by his own firmly religious upbringing; he could feel emotionally with Thomas Münzer, moving as he himself had done from religion to social involvement.[33] He could contemplate the Reformation as an early exercise in bourgeois revolution (thus providing later Marxists with another tough morsel to chew over), abortive because of the failure of the anti-feudal outbreak of 1524, failure for which he laid part of the blame on Luther.

Engels had done some fighting as well as writing in 1849, and he was to become a recognized expert on army matters. Military considerations have a prominent place in the book. He saw the levies of the nobles triumphing through their strength in cavalry, ready to charge and rout insurgents shaken by cannon-fire.[34] But above all the rising failed, in his opinion, because of the same narrow-minded localism, and the same hesitancy and willingness to compromise, as the German middle classes and their spokesmen showed in 1848–9. Here was fresh reason to think of the proletariat as the destined maker of revolution, because of its far greater concentration and the unity of action this made possible. Peasant revolt led by a disciplined party, such as Asia has given birth to in our century, was still far out of sight.

These compositions of 1850–2 were followed by a copious stream of articles on things taking place in arenas in and out of Europe. They kept for the most part to a straightforward political approach. Marx must have felt that day by day or year by year episodes are affected by too many contingencies and unpredictables to be amenable to long-range calculation: history has to be studied by two time-charts, neither of them without its importance. Pressing need for journalistic earnings prompted the articles. Still, their themes stirred his interest in historical antecedents afresh, and suggested further speculations.

In 1854 a Liberal revolution took place in Spain, with the small working class taking a hand for the first time and, after two troubled years, a counter-revolution. Marx had already made some study of the Spanish resistance to Napoleon and of the Liberal years 1820–3, he told Engels, and he was now trying to fill in the gaps, not finding it easy to hit on the key – but, he added characteristically, with his favourite *Don Quixote* a good starting-point.[35] In his prefatory sketches he dwelt on jarring class interests in the resistance, the divergence between progressives and conservatives. He shows no great enthusiasm for it as a patriotic struggle; at its first outbreak, he writes, it looked less revolutionary than anti-revolutionary, and popular sentiment, rabidly Catholic and enraged against everything modern and enlightened that France represented, had throughout a strongly reactionary flavour.[36] The rapturous welcome given to the restored King Ferdinand, bringing back with him despotism and Inquisition, elicits the comment: 'A more humiliating spectacle has seldom been witnessed by the world.'[37] No one was further from identifying *vox populi* with *vox Dei*.

1854–6 was also the time of the Crimean War, to which he devoted, with assistance from Engels on military affairs, far the bulkiest of his series of commentaries. Here we see him studying international relations, through the medium of the first grand conflict since 1815. For him the worst obstacle to European progress was tsarism, against which in 1848 he and Engels had longed for a 'revolutionary war'. Now that Britain with France as ally was at war with Russia, he was feverishly eager to see a conventional trial of arms turning into a resolute drive that would liberate both Europe and Russia from the dead weight of tsarism. It cannot be gainsaid that the relegation of war to a minor place in *The German Ideology* seems to be directly contradicted by the hopes now rested on this 'revolutionary war'. Marx grew more and more disgusted with what in his eyes was a very half-hearted effort by the Allies, a 'phoney war' likely to peter out with nothing accomplished. He was indignant at the western bourgeoisie for shirking, like the German in 1848, a duty laid on it by the 'historical mission' he attributed to each class in turn in furtherance of the great historical process. Some of his most vitriolic language was bestowed on Cobden and the Manchester School, as basely money-grubbing and pacific.[38]

Marx's serious interest in India was set alight by the debate on renewal of the East India Company charter in 1853, and then in 1857 was fanned by the Mutiny. As always, he could not help delving into the past. In Europe he had been searching for the secret of change, in Asia he was confronted by a seeming absence of that elixir of life: history's 'laws of motion' were paralysed. This strange and unwelcome phenomenon drew him to the bedrock of things, the manner of existence of the masses. He and Engels were struck at the outset by the report, first set afloat by the seventeenth-century French traveller Bernier, that there was no private landowning in India, that all land belonged to the state.[39] Immobility might be a natural consequence, they thought. Later on, with the Mutiny priming a fresh flow of information and public discussion, Marx had doubts about the alleged dearth of private property in land.[40] Land tenure in India has proved an immensely complicated subject, still being painfully disentangled.

Marx's picture in any case was of a small self-contained village, finding its own food and its own simple craft wares, a brotherhood of poverty and ignorance. The reality was less egalitarian than he supposed: but the Indian village might well be, as he surmised, a convenient footstool for autocracy. Economic and political were thus fitted together. If the state, there or in the rest of Asia, was responsible for anything useful, it might be water-control and irrigation. This was a supposition frequently considered by him and Engels, and they came near at times to endorsing what has been called the 'hydraulic theory' of the oriental state. It is most plausible when applied to China, surprisingly not mentioned in an early article on India in a list of countries whose climate might make large-scale irrigation a necessity.[41] This too remains a point of controversy; it seems likely that in most kingdoms less was done by governments, more by local enterprise, private or collective, than Marx was led to think.

His estimate of the British conquest was another weighty concession to the efficacy of war and conquest, so much pushed into the background in *The German Ideology*. If German medieval expansion had been a civilizing force in eastern Europe, as Engels maintained,[42] British expansion in Asia might be so likewise. Marx denounced the brutality and rapacity of the subjugation of India, most angrily of all during the reconquest in 1857–8 – in his journalism he had no inhibitions against confronting history as a moralist – but it did at least open the way to change. He was thinking of India being liberated by it not from bad rulers, but from old fixed grooves of social habit. This would come about at first destructively, through machine competition crippling handicrafts, then more constructively by bringing in new technology and a new mentality.

From 1856 to 1860 England was fighting its second Opium War with China. To Marx China seemed even more stationary than India, and he thought he had found the root cause in a self-sufficiency, in both food and clothing, not merely within every village but within every household. He looked forward to the equilibrium being upset by manufactured imports, forced into the country along with opium by Western military power; he was greatly overestimating the rate at which this could happen. With a keen dramatic sense, he loved to see History seizing its cue, doing things with well-timed effect like a *pièce bien faite* in the theatre. Naval attack on Canton would cause commercial collapse there, he wrote, which would rebound on Europe, lead to unemployment and spread revolution over the continent.[43] We need not take all his pronouncements in this vein literally, but it was in line with his expectation of working-class revolt as offspring of capitalist crisis.

In a more sober tone Engels was speaking for both men when in an article of 1857 he condemned British barbarities in China and poured scorn on their perpetrators' objections to unorthodox Chinese methods of self-defence, but wound up with a hopeful prediction of 'the death struggle of the oldest empire in the world, and the opening of a new day for all Asia',[44] His and Marx's historical vision was optimistic about the future, tragic when it turned to the past, as a record so dreadfully bad that any sacrifice was worth while to get away from it. Bolshevism in the years after 1917 may be said to have acted on the same conviction.

In 1857–8, with a full-scale economic crisis in prospect, Marx was busy with a voluminous outline of his long-planned *magnum opus* on economics, and it included a lengthy section on *Pre-Capitalist Economic Formations*. Evidently he felt that a thorough analysis of capitalism, the latest mode of production, required as prelude a survey of earlier modes and the relation in which they stood to one another; nothing less than a sort of X-ray photograph of world history. This task was being undertaken near the end of a decade of watchful observation of history on the march, leading further and further outwards from western Europe to the Far East. In the course of it Marx had amassed knowledge of the past whose essence he was now trying to distil. Still committed to the modes of production, he was setting himself to reckon them up and arrange them into an evolutionary pattern. One may feel that an insatiable curiosity, and the passion inherited from German philosophy for universal understanding, were carrying him too far afield; and that more might have been achieved by concentration on European history, or those phases of it well enough known to make a fairly detailed scrutiny of it practicable.

His only published statement arising from these speculations was the often-quoted one of 1859 about a sequence of four modes of production: Asiatic (or primitive), slave, feudal, capitalist.[45] As it stands it can only be called, as an editor of the *Pre-Capitalist Economic Formations* says, disconcertingly 'brief, unsupported and unexplained'[46] Eighteen years later Marx was indignant with a Russian commentator who wanted to elevate his 'sketch of the genesis of capitalism in Western Europe into an historico-philosophic theory of the *marche générale* imposed by fate upon every people'.[47] In 1857–8 he saw a common beginning in what he termed, sociologically rather than geographically, an 'Asiatic mode of production'; from this primal base, however, western Europe, but not Asia, had broken away.

The next discernible stage appeared to be slavery. This can grow within societies, through debt, crime and so on, but only on a limited scale. No inner law of mutation seems to have been responsible for it, unless it was a law of population. Marx did indeed conjecture, in orthodox enough style, that pressure of population in early Rome led to wars of expansion, reduction of opponents to slavery and consequent landlord ascendancy, ending in expropriation of the peasantry. He might have been expected to think of the patrician beneficiaries as instigating the wars, in which peasants were often conscripted to fight unwillingly. But in his view the Mediterranean city-state was organized primarily for land-grabbing: war was 'the great all-embracing task, the great communal labour'.[48] He was virtually construing war as part of a mode of production; realistically, perhaps, but leaving less originality to the concept than it had claimed at the outset. He had been coming to think of serfdom as well as slavery as ordinarily brought about by conquest: in a letter of 1856 he wrote of its growth within Polish society as an exceptional happening.[49]

He never abandoned the mode of production as the building-block of history; he and Engels went on in later years thinking tentatively of miscellaneous classifications and subspecies, 'Ancient', 'German',

'Slavonic', but the idea was less precise now than when they first hit on it, and enveloped in many obscurities. It may be deemed valuable for the epochs they were least unfamiliar with; further back in history, or further away from western Europe, its relevance is more dubious. An essential of the capitalist economy from which their inquiry set out is that the possessing class takes the lead in the relations of production; capitalists manage it themselves. A parallel might be drawn with the demesne farming practised at times in medieval Europe, and its recrudescence in eastern Europe in the early modern era; also with slavery, because it too drew the owners, the master-class, into the organization of production; and with the Asiatic (or the Inca) state, or landlords, when they directed water-control. But whereas capitalism has been the most dynamic system, water-control in China was part and parcel of the most immobile of all larger structures.

Altogether the list of these cases is not long. Within the Indian village, relations of production were limited to barter-exchange of food for craft wares, while above it stood the state, or its deputies, skimming off a good part of the surplus. In far the greater number of societies there has been the same parasitism, with no functional link between production and consumption. What confronts us is a limited number of economies surmounted by an endless array of modes of appropriation, methods by which the stronger have levied tribute from the weaker.

An uneasy feeling of something missing may have lent insistence to another thought in the *Pre-Capitalist Economic Formations*, the significance of individual energy and initiative. People after all constitute the chief force of production, and Marx was after all a man of the Romantic age with its cult of the demonic personality, who found a congenial symbol in Prometheus. Asiatic society is the most unchanging, he writes at one point, because in it 'The individual does not become independent of the community.'[50] In the birth of the individual the city, in its European guise as a political entity, not a mere agglomeration, had a crucial part to play. Marx allowed for this by recognizing, if he did not explain, the distance between urban life in Asia and that of classical Europe with its citizenship and its freedom of self-development.[51]

Lenin correctly ascribed to Marx not invention of the 'materialist conception of history' but 'consistent continuation and extension of materialism into the domain of social phenomena'.[52] If Marx performed much less of this than might have been expected from him, it was because he became so deeply engrossed with the intricate workings of the capitalist economy, and really used himself up on the task. In undertaking it he had no intention of abandoning history, the subject which has convincingly been called his 'true intellectual passion' or vocation,[53] and the only field where all his many talents could be combined. As the grand accelerator of change, capitalism was itself a historical problem, and he would have made this clearer had his strength allowed him to carry out the many-sided investigation that he projected. It was to the advent of capitalism in England that the *Formations* led up, by way of a salutary reminder that a new economic order could not be self-created, but that political authority had much to do with it, like conquest at earlier stages. Vagrants, the debris of a crumbling feudal society, had to be driven into a labour-market by penal legislation; in this way, Marx wrote, Tudor monarchy was among the necessary conditions for the establishment of capitalism.[54] From this point of view Henry VIII and Elizabeth can be said to have participated in the relations of production. In the historical summary in *Capital* the picture changes to an even darker, and perhaps less accurate one, of peasants uprooted from their holdings so as to be compelled to work for the new masters. It had the advantage of justifying the formula of *The Communist Manifesto* – reiterated in *Capital*[55] – of capitalist expropriators being in their turn expropriated by the working class, to make way for socialism.

Altogether Marx left nothing like a systematic doctrine, and responsibility fell to Engels for pulling together the ideas of both of them; a heavy as well as exacting one, because he had also to take over the mass of unfinished work on economics under which Marx had succumbed, on top of the role of adviser to the socialist movements now stirring everywhere. Considering this, what Engels accomplished in historical theory is very remarkable indeed. It is to be found in his *Anti-Dühring*, in 1878; in the study of Feuerbach in 1886 where a section of the 1845–6 joint design was worked out afresh; in the essay of 1892 'On Historical Materialism',[56] mainly concerned in a more factual way with aspects of modern European development; and in a wonderful set of letters written very late, between 1890 and 1894.

'The materialist interpretation of history is the main item in the intellectual legacy left us by Engels,' it has been said lately by a friendly critic; his comments on or continuations of Marx made him its real originator. The same critic is inclined to tax him with going too far, making the theory sound too much like a rounded whole. Still, as he notices,[57] Engels had begun long before, by coining the title 'materialist conception of history' in a review of Marx in 1859, so that there had been a quarter of a century for Marx to object if he wished; and if Marx's ideas were to survive and exert influence, it was indispensable for them to be given a somewhat more regular form, which he himself, with his perpetual dubitations and notebook-fillings and second, third, fourth thoughts on everything, would in all probability never have been able to give. Without Engels the needed systematizing would have been far worse done.

It has been rightly pointed out besides that in the handling of historic fact he was the superior:[58] his practical judgement was sounder, and he never fell into fantasies like Marx's about Palmerston and Moscow and secret agents mysteriously burrowing. It is not without relevance that Engels's life was that of a man of affairs, most of Marx's of a recluse. Engels might see less deeply or comprehensively, but also more realistically. It was characteristic of him to advise Marx to supply *Capital* with more historical illustrations. It is highly regrettable that, having to devote his limited time to the theory, he was not able to undertake further pieces of history-writing like his pioneer work on the Peasant War. Not much of his projected history of Ireland got done. More employment of this kind would have benefited him as a theoretician too, and so enriched posterity doubly.

One item among his many duties was to popularize his friend's ideas, as well as interpret them; for this he was obliged to simplify, and sometimes over-simplified. In an encomium written in June 1877 he summarized the 'new conception of history' in the words: 'Marx has proved that the whole of previous history is a history of class frictions.' He gave the familiar example of bourgeoisie supplanting *noblesse* in 1789, and added sweepingly: 'From this point of view all the historical phenomena are explicable in the simplest possible way – with sufficient knowledge of the particular economic conditions';[59] a proviso that a hundred years of diligent research since then have only inadequately satisfied.

If he was sometimes simplifying unduly, he has also been charged with the opposite fault of over-elaborating, wrapping up a historical approach too much in Hegelian formulae, under the rubric of 'dialectical materialism'. In these later years he does seem to have returned, more whole-heartedly than Marx, to Hegelian procedures, as an aid to his formidable task of gathering scattered conjectures together. Later on, if not in his own work, this did have an unfortunate effect by tying Marx too closely to Hegel, and investing Marx's method with too much of a pretentiously esoteric flavour, likely to lead to long words being mistaken for deep ideas. A very superfluous addition to Hegel came into vogue with the foisting on him of the 'dialectical triad', squeezing the flow of history into the tight corset of thesis, antithesis and synthesis. Non-Marxists not surprisingly found it hard to envisage history in so geometerical a style, as a pyramid or procession of isosceles triangles, but it had entered into Marxist orthodoxy by the time this began to percolate into countries like England.

Reliance on Hegelian aids to thinking might sometimes seem to lead Engels himself towards trust in a necessity of history of which human beings were not much more than puppets. If Machiavelli allowed too much room to Fortune, Marxism has often been found fault with for trying to impose on history a rationality foreign to it. This is of course a charge that any attempt at interpretation on any lines must expose itself to. As a counter to it the Englightenment devised a so-called 'law of unintended consequences', with Vico for one of its proponents, according to which historical events result from men's actions, but do not fulfil men's conscious designs.[60] Such a conclusion may be native to any epoch when people are impelled to consider their situation and wonder how to remedy it, but feel that much in it is beyond their limited strength.

Both Marx and Engels were quite alive to the problem, and their answers are not very dissimilar to Vico's. World history would be 'very mystical', Marx wrote in 1871, if accidents had nothing to do with it, but they were causes of 'acceleration and delay' rather than of radical changes of course.[61] In the same vein Engels wrote: 'Where on the surface accident holds sway, actually it is always governed by inner, hidden laws and it is only a matter of discovering those laws',[62] and again: 'Amid all the endless *host* of accidents . . . the economic movement finally asserts itself as necessary.'[63] These propositions may be cavilled at as taking for granted what requires to be proved, namely that there is a single final determinant, that this is the expanding energy of production, and that it carries humanity in one ultimate direction. Any invoking of 'hidden laws', shepherding us towards socialism willy-nilly, must arouse some uneasiness; and it is hard to adopt even a 'guiding thread' to history, as Marx modestly called his method,[64] without drifting into thinking of it as a 'law'. In the end judgement can only rest on a weighing-up of probability, in the light of collective experience.

As regards Engels, uneasiness must gain something from his attitude to physical science. Over many years he was collecting materials for a never completed work, published long after his death as *Dialectics of Nature*. There he invites scepticism about the dialectical principle by placing the entire universe as well as human existence under the sway of its 'laws'. He had an old soldier's liking for order and precision, and his mind might well turn with relief at times to Nature as a realm where chance could be left behind.

Knowing so much both of science and of history he could have done praiseworthy service by writing on scientific history. This is touched on here and there in *Dialectics of Nature*, but it was a generalization too many later students were to make do with that 'From the very beginning the origin and development of the sciences has been determined by production.'[65] The instances adduced, from ancient Egypt, are the needs of irrigation, town planning and war, only one of which belongs to the sphere of production.

Engels wrote odd pieces on topics of military history, for which also he was excellently qualified, but it is a great pity that he did not undertake some extended study of it, or of the 'sociology of war'. There is a prophetic ring in his remark that in modern times the effects of war have been altering, 'At least among great nations: in the long run the defeated power often gains more economically, politically and morally than the victor.'[66] But the only substantial work bearing on war that he embarked on in his later years was a study in 1887–8 of *The Role of Force in History*. This was left unfinished, as if he lost confidence in his argument, a restatement in the light of recent events of a leading thought of *The German Ideology*. It is concerned with the question, so pregnant for the growing socialist movement in Germany, of Bismarck's unification of the country by blood and iron. Engels contended that this achievement could only be temporary, because resting on bayonets instead of on economic development. Yet he held that unification was a precondition of German economic progress.[67] What he had better warrant to think insecure was the preservation, which was Bismarck's true aim, of the obsolete Prussian monarchy and social structure. Yet German industry accommodated itself to them contentedly enough.[68] When the throne collapsed it was through no revolt either of bourgeoisie or of working class, but defeat in a European war, in other words through a fresh intervention of force.

It was a penalty Marx and Engels had to pay for their failure to work out their method more comprehensively, and the fact that most of their joint or several meditations on it had never seen the light, that there was a gap between them and the next generation, a stretch of time when their thinking, so far as it was known, was largely misunderstood. It is clear that towards the end Engels was very conscious of this danger, and did his best to guard against it. He fully understood that tracing historical interconnections required detailed research in every particular case; in 1880 he was regretting that very little had yet been done. Instead vulgarizers, young intellectuals of the socialist mass movement and its fringes, were treating Marxism as a short cut, a substitute for patient investigation.[69] The main burden of his parting admonitions was a warning against crude, one-sided use of the materialist explanations which he and Marx in youth had enjoyed rubbing their readers' noses in as a means of driving out old, ingrained illusions. Ultimately the determining factor, he wrote now in a letter of 1890, is the economic, but it is not the sole force at work; and he went on to blame himself and Marx for having obscured this truth.[70]

A long letter of a few weeks later is a miniature treatise in which full allowance is made for the ability of, for instance, a legal system, which grows, if not in every detail, out of society's material operations, to react on them: it has done so very markedly by helping to shape property and inheritance, so different in France and England since the French Revolution. Due place is also given to the fact that remoter branches of thinking, like philosophy and religion, are not born exclusively from the actual condition of society, but 'have a prehistoric stock, found already in existence and taken over in the historic period'.[71] A good illustration of the shuttling to and fro of ideas is the saying in *Dialectics of Nature* that after Darwin the old notion of natural harmony was suddenly exchanged for an equally lop-sided myth of universal strife: this derived from the Hobbesian war of all against all, compounded by capitalist competition, and was now being illegitimately transferred back again from biology into sociology.[72]

By the late nineteenth century history was gaining a secure place in the universities of Europe, with economic history more and more vigorous. It was long before Marxist theory could have any influence on academic practice. At Oxbridge it was virtually unknown before the 1930s. For long it remained closely tied to the political movement, a link which brought it into greater prominence, or notoriety, than it would have had otherwise, but also subjected it to some cramping, the fate of all official doctrines. It continued to owe most of its development to individuals who were also active political workers, mostly by those with a bent for study like Kautsky, one of the direct successors of Marx and Engels, rather than the true men of action like Lenin. Another distinction can be drawn between those who wrote about specific historical topics, and those drawn to historical theory. The latter were often party leaders, who felt it their responsibility to give the movement sound guidance on theory as well as on current tactics. As Kautsky said, the materialist conception should enable socialists not only to understand history better, but to make history better.[73]

Kautsky wrote about a wide variety of eras, ancient and modern; thinkers like him were legitimate heirs of Marx and Engels in taking all history for their province, before the specialists who were coming on the scene could cut it up into private enclosures. His concern was far from exclusively with economic foundations: religion was one of his fields, and his work on Thomas More displayed an interest in the outstanding individual, as well as in the earliest socialism which had been part of Engels's theme in his *Peasant War*. Regrettably his work as a historian came under a cloud after 1917 and his collision with Lenin and lapse from grace.

In a work published in 1906 he attempted to restate and add to Marxist historical theory on a broader moral basis. It was an indigestible feature of the theory as left by its founders that it seemed to care little about ethical impulses. Marx might be deeply a moralist, but in his scheme the duties or 'missions' of progressive classes were ambiguously interwoven with pressure of blind forces. Kautsky set himself to trace the evolution of the moral feelings, and show how they flowered from social life, from the earliest times. Marx and Engels had been drawn to prehistory in their later years, under the spell of the American anthropologist Lewis Morgan whose findings they took as confirmation of their own tenets; and Kautsky held that study of it, working on the ordinary stuff of human life, brought out more patently than the record of historical times an evolutionary process within which technology interacted with religion and all the rest.[74]

He tackled a frequent misunderstanding of Marxist theory, that technology by itself determined social structures; and an objection founded on it that heterogeneous societies could be supported by the same techniques of production. His solution is not altogether clear, but he saw diversity as arising in the first place from geographical settings, 'differences in the natural and social surroundings'.[75] Morality, he allowed, like 'the rest of the complicated social superstructure', might drift some distance from its social foundations, but then it would wither before long into mere formal observance. Meanwhile the struggling masses confronted the old order with a new ethic of their own, which with their successful rise would become the moral code of a whole society.[76]

In the diffusion of Marxism from its west European cradle into other climes, one of its attractions was often its historical theory, promising revelations of their past to peoples trying to understand how it was that they found themselves where they were. In Russia there was already among historians an interest in the principles of their craft, one manifestation it has been shrewdly suggested of 'the familiar self-consciousness of Russian culture'.[77] Marxism was carried forward most notably by Plekhanov, who resembled Kautsky in being better suited to scholarship than to political storm and stress, and in being exceedingly well read over a very wide range. He too was attracted to the new science of anthropology, and he found much to discuss in primitive religion and arts.

His *Defence of Materialism* came out in 1895. Much of it was an inquiry into the ancestry of Marxist theory, starting with the French materialists of the Enlightenment and going on to French historiography after the Revolution and Napoleon, and thence by way of Utopian socialism and German idealism to 'modern materialism'. This was for him very definitely 'dialectical materialism', sharply distinguished in another work of the same time from the simply 'economic' version, which he associated with figures as oddly assorted as Thorold Rogers and Blanqui, with Guizot and Tocqueville for forerunners. What they did, in his view, was to pick out and make much of an 'economic factor' which, attuned to their estimate of human nature, was really only disguised idealism. Its place was with a 'theory of factors', to which every specialist added his own – religion, law, etc. – all together forming a bundle of independent variables whose orbits were impossible to chart.[78] Marxism was able to chart them by virtue of its monistic approach, its reduction of everything to a single process with one basic determinant and multiple internal exchanges.

Plekhanov felt acutely, as Engels had done, that Marx's historical teaching was in urgent need of clarification because it was being misused by 'those who utter so many follies in his name'.[79] Hence the large space devoted to it in his last work, *Fundamental Problems of Marxism*, published in 1908. He, like Kautsky, put much weight on geographical environment as governing 'the development of economic forces and, therefore, the development of all the other social relations'. This accounted for the bifurcation of the Western and Asian line of evolution, 'the classical and the oriental', from their common antecedent, 'the clan type of social organization'.[80] But as soon as specific relations of production formed, they in turn affected the further unfolding of the forces of production; so also did external relations, intercourse with other communities. It was not therefore a matter of unmediated control of social evolution, except at the most primitive level, by climate and other physical elements, as supposed by Buckle and his disciples.[81] Earlier Plekhanov had observed that the rise of the state in western Europe did not appear to be directly moulded by the system of production,[82] and now he was widening the 'decisive influence' of the political, legal, miscellaneous relations engendered by economic life on 'the whole psychology of man as a social being'.[83]

After the Revolution it was Bukharin who became the accredited spokesman of Marxism at Moscow, including historical theory though he himself was more economist or philosopher. He wrote in a very sanguine tone, with a confidence inspired by the triumph of 1917; in his estimation very little thought was required to make 'the full wealth of the Marxian method absolutely clear in comparison with all other schools and tendencies'.[84] His appeals to the 'laws' of history were loud and frequent, and he seemed disposed to equate them with those of natural science.[85] He drew no line between 'historical', 'economic' or 'dialectical' materialism; and his exposition has a somewhat pedestrian march, as though intended for elementary reading. Of historical events he says little; his illustrations are few and obvious.

Lenin found time amid the tempests of 1920 to read and warmly praise Pokrovsky's outline history of Russia,[86] one of the earliest works of Marxist history to become known in the West and to set a standard for budding historians there. Pokrovsky had been in the thick of party activity before the Revolution, and after it was the first organizer of historical studies in the Soviet Union. He held that 'The Russian proletariat must have its own interpretation of the Russian past,'[87] and in the *Brief History*, which grew out of lectures given during the Civil War, he too may have been in a measure writing down to his audience. However, he had already before 1917 traced the main lines of his approach. In this, class struggle played the same part as in the West, instead of Russia following a path of its own as Slavophil patriots had wanted to believe. What came to be most controversial was the place he assigned to merchant capital, which he thought powerful enough as early as the sixteenth century to use the tsars as its instruments for conquering trade outlets. This was certainly an exaggeration, and in his late years – he died in 1932 – he had perforce to yield much ground to Soviet critics, and to contemplate old Russia more as one form of feudalism. The debate had repercussions abroad, making it a subject of dispute whether state power could ever be wielded by merchant capital – only loosely linked with the means of production – as distinct from industrial capitalism.

In Russia the issue was less purely theoretical, because Pokrovsky's elevation of the trading class implied a demotion of the tsars from their proud eminence, and among them Peter, whom Stalin's admirers were holding up as his great precursor in the modernizing of Russia. A standard allegation against Marxism was turned against Plekhanov; by failing to do justice to the impact of exceptional individuals, it could be said, he was falling into economic determinism and compressing all events into economic grooves. This led to the further charge of making all history lead by smooth progression towards the present day; of giving it, one critic, Gorochov, declared, 'a mystical appearance', a purpose from the outset to arrange the stage for us.[88]

Stalin in power made it part of his duty to supply an official summing-up of the principles of historical Marxism. This could only make it look more complete and solid than it really was, heedless of Lenin's caution that Marx left no finished doctrine but simply 'laid the cornerstone of the science which socialists *must* advance in all directions.'[89] Stalin's 1938 treatise has a lumpish and schematic character: it admits no doubts or difficulties, and discusses few specific points of history. It was typical of its author's mechanical or bureaucratic turn of mind to choose quotations often from Engels's experiment of applying dialectics to nature, and to conclude that the study of history could be made as exact as a science like biology.[90]

A good deal worse than Stalin's formulation of history, it must be added, was his falsification of it, of recent events at least, his own way of acting on the maxim that theory can show how to make history as well as to write it. 'History is becoming clay in the hands of the potter,' Trotsky commented as he watched the Bolshevik annals undergoing their stealthy transformations.[91] But theory as well as fact suffered; Stalin, as Lukács said, was standing Marxism on its head by making it teach whatever suited his tactics of the moment.[92]

Part of the purpose of the new orthodoxy was to discredit anyone who had been Stalin's rival. Bukharin was found fault with in an authoritative textbook, in darkly scholastic language, on the ground that he made too much of external collisions and environmental influences, whereas the essence of dialectics was the unfolding of inner contradictions.[93] Another manual, published as recently as 1960, took a firm stand on the assertion, which Marx had firmly (though not in print) disclaimed, that in spite of every variation of local detail 'All peoples travel what is basically the same path,' because all history depends on 'the development of the productive forces, which obey the same internal laws'.[94] So far as it treads any terrestrial ground, this survey is almost confined to Europe, for all its pose of universality. It lays down that 'The masses are the makers of history' (not much of a compliment, considering what human history has been), with scant definition of what is meant.[95] Respect is paid to ideas and their influence,[96] but so few examples are given, here as throughout, that the statement lacks meaning. It seems on the whole that Marxist theory has made little progress in the Soviet Union, and brought little inspiration to historians in countries in its sphere. Soviet scholars have produced a great deal of good work in numerous fields, but for the most part on the simpler levels of political and economic history, not requiring many of the new ideas wanted to illumine more exacting problems.

Marxism in power, in a single embattled state, gave more importance to the state in history than Marx and Engels with their more cosmopolitan outlook had done. It was as ready to admire Richelieu as a paladin of the French nation as Peter of the Russian.[97] In a very different way something similar can be said of Gramsci, writing in the shadow of defeat as Bukharin wrote in the glow of victory, and preoccupied with the fate of his own country. In Mussolini's prisons he was not in a position to write history, but he had leisure to think about it, and he can be seen as one of the firstlings of 'Western Marxism'. He was looking beyond the defeat of his young Communist Party to Italy's shortcomings during the Risorgimento or national revival of the nineteenth century, and further back to its failure to unite in the sixteenth. In both those periods the foreign presence was the most tangible obstacle. He was curiously fascinated by Machiavelli, took seriously the concluding appeal of *The Prince* for Italy to be freed from the barbarians and believed that 'a unitary absolute monarchy' was a possibility of that age, in Italy as in France or Spain[98] – where he may have overlooked that there were already national foundations to build on.

For Marxism he made very lofty claims, as a doctrine qualified 'to explain and justify all the past', in a completely historical spirit.[99] On the other hand he was aware that at present it was still only an inchoate body of thought. Non-Marxist efforts to construct a historical sociology he dismissed as 'vulgar evolutionism';[100] Bukharin's presentation he thought not much better. It failed in his opinion to grapple with the fundamental question: 'How does the historical movement arise on the structural base?' What, in other words, is the prime driving force? He considered Bukharin too cavalier in dismissing all previous philosophers as twaddlers, and poor in his aesthetic judgements.[101] More suprisingly Gramsci had equally hard words for Plekhanov, as prone to relapses into 'vulgar materialism' and positivism, and gifted with little historical insight.[102] One puzzle he wrestled with lay in the domain of chance: the effect of errors that leaders might commit – and had lately committed in Italy – in spite of the mechanistic notion that 'Every political act is determined, immediately, by the structure.'[103] This runs counter to the axiom that every situation throws up the right man, and suggests a fruitful line of inquiry.

Marxism, which had migrated to central and eastern Europe, was returning to its western birthplace, where it might still be tied to a party but was not under the surveillance of a Marxist government. In France the Revolution, which counted for so much with Marx, had always been in the forefront of historical studies, and provided a point of entry where Marxist ideas could show themselves at their most relevant. A succession of leading scholars carried them more and more into the ascendant, though they have never gone unchallenged. More generally, Marxist thinking has done much, as a stimulus, to raise French history-writing to its present eminence. From the 1930s the English Revolution was being rediscovered by Marxists, and became one of the chief nourishers of a flourishing school.[104] Marx and Engels were firm believers in national character, as a deposit of national experience, and it is noteworthy that Marxists in Britain have turned much more to history than, as over much of the Continent, to philosophy; while as historians they have been drawn more to specific times and issues than to theory in the abstract.

Meanwhile, Marxism was finding its way into Asia, rooting itself in lands that Karl Marx strained his eyes to see from distant London, as Sherlock Holmes's mind hovered over his map of Dartmoor in Baker Street. After the post-1918 split the Second and Third Internationals both continued officially Marxist, but it was the Third that took Marxism seriously, and also made strenuous efforts to enlarge a European into a world-wide movement. India was one of its first targets; but a vigilant police made it hard for Marxist literature to enter the country, and for long after 1918 Communists were only small, scattered, fractured groups. A critical concern with Marxism and history made its appearance only after Independence. In China there had earlier been a disposition to look to Russian history, especially to times of reform like Peter's, as a lesson to a backward country anxious to catch up with the times;[105] the prompt reception of Marxism in the 1920s was in a way a sequel. But civil war, White Terror and Japanese invasion soon interrupted theorizing, and its application to the perplexities of China's past could only be taken up in earnest after the revolution. In another far-off quarter, Latin America, historical Marxism was arousing interest among intellectuals frustrated by a morbid inheritance. Of late years Marxism, or at any rate 'Marxology', has been gaining entry even into what for long was the dark continent of North America; today it abounds in young historians full of their discovery of it as a dazzling novelty.

Both the swelling current of history written under Marxist inspiration, and the volume of writing in defence of or attack on historical Marxism, testify to its vitality. Yet this theory, left so rudimentary by Marx himself, after a century both of debate and of history unrolling itself, still leaves room for manifold disagreements among adherents. All its main concepts still await more precise definition, beginning with the mode of production. Classification of societies has attained clarity only with respect to the two latest modes, capitalist and socialist. In Europe and still more outside, all earlier ones remain questionable.

Slavery, a case in point, was a common feature of ancient empires; whether Marx and Engels were right in supposing that it ever formed the basis of an entire productive system is open to doubt. Slave labour on the land, as in late republican and imperial Italy, must usually have been devoted to raising of cash crops for markets at a distance. In a debate twenty years ago on the modes and their sequence one suggestion was that if branches of production resting on slavery are the most profitable in an economy, even though forming only a minor part of the total, they entitle it to rank as a slave economy.[106] But it may be needful to draw a line between methods adapted to support of a dominant class, as slavery was in Rome, and those by which the bulk of a population lives.

In western Europe chronic change and something like an understandable succession of epochs do seem to catch the eye, with a fairly continuous tendency towards a higher level both of organization and of output. Even here, the formation of feudalism from a synthesis of Roman and barbarian has the obvious drawback that it does not show one mode arising logically from another.[107] What it does perhaps indicate is that internal stresses within a single homogeneous system (China may be the best example) have been less fruitful than the double process represented by change within both West–Roman and barbarian society during a long period of neighbourhood, ending in their creeping fusion rather than conquest of one by the other, and resulting in a structure or civilization uniquely complex and correspondingly liable to instability. But the mechanics of the all-important transition from medieval Europe to modern, or feudal to capitalist, are still among the most eagerly debated of all problems of Marxism – in Japan too, on account of analogies with its own passage to modernity in the last century.

In most or all other regions no such progression as Europe's, no onward-leading road, seems visible, only a maze of tracks losing themselves here and there. Radical alteration is very much the exception; the blessing or curse of immobility, or a perpetual *da capo*, is far more the rule. Societies have been hard to categorize in Marxist language, since they form a medley not following one after the other but scattered higgledy-piggledy. They have been loosely bundled together as 'feudal'. This rag-bag procedure can be censured with good reason, not only as clashing with the familiar usage of the term to denote the institutional structure of medieval Europe, but also as obscuring the very exceptional and mutable complex that medieval Europe was. When Charlemagne and Akbar, Genghis Khan and Montezuma, are all herded together like stray animals in a village pound, we do not really learn anything about them.

We are brought back again to the fact that what most societies have had in common is the exploitation of a majority for the benefit of a minority, by dint of armed force, or force softened into use and wont, or sanction of superstition. This is far from representing a 'mode of production' as originally conceived, since in most cases the ruling group takes no more part in production than a protection-racket in Chicago, but merely appropriates; and (as Plekhanov saw) methods of appropriation may, as in India, come and go or evolve while the productive system stands still for ages. Over the greater part of the world the dogma that the 'main historical issues' always 'relate to the development of forces of production'[108] practically reduces history to a blank.

What gives rise to change remains an equally challenging question. Marxists have usually disclaimed a 'technological' explanation, with new tools the prime mover of history, but they have often been very near to it, and they have not offered a clear alternative. Some recent writers have indeed defended the technological view, with the help of more sophisticated reasoning.[109] Marx replaced God with technology, one concludes, as 'the ultimate arbiter of history'.[110] But new tools will only transform a society if it is ready to welcome them; so that we are left to ask how this readiness has come about. A tool may turn up, it has been shown, in response to changed environmental requirement, as when in Africa the hoe replaces the digging-stick. Then the tool is 'the result and no longer the cause'.[111] But new equipment has not always in the past, or not even often, been forthcoming when needed, and this cannot be explained on technical grounds alone.

The starting-point seems as hard to find as the end of a tangled ball of string. Now that runaway multiplication of human beings is threatening to become humanity's worst of all perils, it is inevitable that some Marxists as well as others should look to population pressure as the arch-disturber of equilibrium. Marx's view of early Roman expansion might be quoted in their favour; but they are criticized for giving too little attention to the social and economic contexts within which numbers grow, or do not grow, and thus yielding to a sort of 'demographic determinism'.[112]

Much change has come about through intercourse between different communities, most abruptly through war and conquest, with no more logic than that armed force has flowed to wherever resistance was weak and booty cheap, as spontaneously as today capital flows towards the most tempting profits. By this means arts and crafts, weapons and techniques, have been carried from region to region as capriciously as seeds borne on the wind, while Turks ruled Bulgaria, Spaniards ruled Peru, Afghans Bengal. Conquest brought into being most of that swarm of 'feudal' or parasitical societies that occupy most of history. Each has had its own intrinsic quality, its local contacts and antagonisms and culture, to which Marxist scrutiny can properly be applied; but these societies have nearly always been incapable of sustained growth, sterile like hybrid plants or animals, and therefore intractable to the wider Marxist scheme of evolution.

Revolution, one of the points of departure of Marx's own study of history, has aroused the stiffest disagreements between Marxists and others. Much light has been thrown on it, but – as happens in natural science – each step forward has thrown up fresh dilemmas. One hindrance is that there have been very few revolutions, either 'bourgeois' or socialist, to compare, and scarcely any pre-modern ones that seem at home in any Marxist category. Students of the English Revolution set out by bracketing it with 1789, and explaining both in terms of productive forces bursting the integuments of an old order. But it has been hard to demonstrate this, and also, in England on the political plane, to identify the combatants as champions of older and newer classes. A 'revolutionary bourgeoisie' is far from easy to pin down even in the French case, or at any time before the nineteenth century, and then it was invariably a failure. Without it we seem to have *Hamlet* without the Prince of Denmark. Marxists have had to reconsider their analysis of revolution as the overthrow of an obsolete regime by a dynamic class bent on establishing a new mode of production on its ruins. No one willed modern capitalism; it was, so far as the people of 1642 or 1789 were concerned, a by-product. There were already capitalists, and they came out of the turmoil with power in their hands to build a capitalist order; but this is no proof that the Revolution was therefore made and managed by them.

It may be necessary to think of these upheavals as semi-accidental, in their timing being due to things like Charles I's quarrel with the Scots, or the bad harvests before 1789; and confused, because of discordance between the two vibrations shaking an old society; growth of productive forces, and friction between classes, the two things connected but each following a rhythm of its own. An obtrusive complication was the intervention of other social strata –

English yeomen and petty bourgeois, French peasants and artisans – with interests and mentality distinct from those of both the major combatants. The two tremors may not merely fail to synchronize, or reinforce each other, but may positively collide; if, for example, peasants rebel against being expropriated and turned into labourers to expedite the growth of capitalism. In such a case the class struggle which Bukharin called 'the motive force of history'[113] is a brake on it instead. We may even have to ask whether in China chronic peasant revolt was one of the reasons why history stuck fast.

Clearly one of the factors of human change is man himself, whom Marxists are often arraigned for taking too little notice of. They deny the charge, but it is true that they have thought most commonly of mankind in the mass; though it was to Winwood Reade, not any Marxist, that Sherlock Holmes owed his axiom that 'While the individual man is an insoluble puzzle, in the aggregate he is a mathematical certainty.'[114] Their bent has been towards rationalizing behaviour overmuch. Neither man nor his history is in any strict sense rational, though both may come by degrees to be rationally comprehended. But this requires more knowledge of the puzzling individual, or elite group, as an indispensable part-cause of historical change. Marx evidently had this in mind when he spoke of the absence of the individual from Asia.

All this borders on the enigma of human freedom. Marx, it is said, 'could not allow free will to those whose activity was to be explained and predicted by his theory'.[115] Marx the moralist would not have pleaded guilty to this, Marx the scientific socialist might often be constrained to. Without diving too deep into opaque waters, note may be taken of the most contentious aspect of the human dimension, the status to be assigned to 'great men'. Indifference to them, and to biography, is one reason why Marxist history-writing has sometimes been called dull. Really it has wavered between under- and overvaluation, in a way that betrays uncertainty. In its early optimistic conviction of having found the clue, its sensation of being borne on by an irresistible tide, the rise of a unique new class, Marxism felt no more need of aid from exceptional individuals than from Providence. Later on, when socialism had to come to grips with practical difficulties that often seemed insuperable, a nostalgia for great men revived. Lenin and Stalin in Russia, Mao in China – both countries where a new economy had to be built by an exertion of will, against the grain of history – loomed up larger than life as personifications of heroic effort. Marx himself, it may be added, has always been looked up to by Marxists from Engels on as a very great man.

Marxism has strengthened a willingness among most historians, which would have grown in any case, to think of all compartments of history as opening on to each other. Engels defined dialectics as 'the science of interconnections', in contrast with metaphysics;[116] but he admitted that he and Marx had not given sufficient thought to the obscure processes by which ideas come to birth.[117] Marxism has thought of successive tiers rising above the economic foundations of society: political institutions and laws, as Plekhanov said, directly governed by it, art of philosophy only indirectly, with the mediation of levels in between.[118] This has not protected it against charges like Mannheim's of '*directly* associating even the most esoteric and spiritual products of the mind with the economic and power interests of a certain class'.[119] All sorts of irregularities complicate the working model. While the 'base' may be stationary for long periods the 'superstructure' may be blown about by winds of change. Or economy may alter while ideology lags. Civilizations, Braudel has written, are 'strange collections of commodities, symbols, illusions, phantasms', all churning together.[120]

Comprehension of all this is improving, thanks to numerous explorations of the history of ideas, of the arts, of religion, of science. It is on this side, it has been noticed, that 'Western Marxism' is most proficient, and can be said to have compiled a body of writing 'far richer and subtler than anything within the classical heritage of historical materialism'.[121] The reason may well be that it has found itself cut off from any realistic prospect of socialism in power in any near future, and hence has been less taken up with practical concerns. 'Base and superstructure' is an image that goes back to Marx himself, but one that he used only a handful of times.[122] It is being felt now to be too static and rigid. A biological image, of some kind of symbiotic relationship, may be more appropriate. There is not one plane of existence on which *Homo sapiens* acts, another on which he thinks; he is a thinking creature in all his doings, and only animal behaviour can be exclusively regulated by material causes.

Not many years ago Marxist and 'bourgeois' history-writing could look as different as chalk from cheese; today they often differ much less obviously. For one thing Marxism has shed most of the old vocabulary borrowed from Hegel, though how much, if any, of his logic is still to be considered valid has not been frankly faced. The formal framework is omitted, rather than repudiated; thereby Marxism may have grown more reasonable, but less readily recognizable. It is far less closely tied to party considerations than it used to be. In Japanese universities, where Marxist historians are legion, many of them are not socialists, and some are conservatives, who simply find Marxism a useful tool.[123] It is in short no longer easy to say who is entitled to call himself – if he chooses – a Marxist.

It may be nearly as hard to say who is *not*, in some measure, so widely has the influence of Marx's more general ideas spread. Among historians nowadays only the most unlettered are ignorant of him, only the dullest have failed to learn something from him. Fairly typically, an English historian some years ago expressing his distrust of single-cause interpretations deprecated, nevertheless, 'any partisan approach that would dismiss Marxism offhand; Marx was a great thinker'.[124] More lately a Dutch historian commenced a chapter of a biography by saying: 'We are all familiar with the teachings of Marx', and know that account has to be taken of the big objective forces.[125] There was a time when Marxists were resentful of outsiders taking over some of their ideas and, as they felt, denaturing them; the fashionable 'Sociology of Knowledge' looked to them like historical materialism minus class struggle, a bowdlerizing on a par with Tate's *King Lear*. Since the embitterments of cold war years there has been a freer interchange of opinions and criticisms. It is to a great extent through the controversies Marxism has stirred up, ever since it became impossible to ignore it, that history as a science has advanced.

By and large Marxist writing has grown plainer, less esoteric, but in some directions it has been proliferating into scholastic abstruseness, or running to academic seed, through increasing detachment from practical politics. These divagations are often the more baffling because couched – like so much contemporary sociology – in a worse than Hegelian jargon, as arcane as Marx's handwriting, a language that as Lord Dundreary would say 'no feller can understand'. Recent 'structuralist' glosses of Marx seem, a critic remarks, to lose all contact with his materialism.[126] Any historical school needs fresh air from outside, but Marxist history may be in some danger of too much encroachment by theorists lacking in factual acquaintance with history. A case where the merits of an intrusion are hard to gauge is that of Althusser, with his insistence on a genuine Marxist philosophy of history, to be gathered together from elements latent in Marx's work, and his dismissal of history-writing without this as mere 'historicism' or humanism, and of Gramsci as one of the chief delinquents.[127]

Another development, to be welcomed with some caution, has taken the form of a number of ambitious attempts at wide-arching hypotheses intended to embrace whole epochs and their ramifying problems. Marx and Engels indulged in such speculation, though as a rule tentatively; and it is valuable as an antidote to the specialization forced on scholarship now, confinement to narrow areas where there may be little scope for a Marxist approach to stand out from others. Wallerstein's thesis of a 'world market' as the indispensable setting of the advance to capitalism[128] is impressive, but not always easy to square with humdrum detail. Frank's portrayal, with Latin American poverty for its backcloth, of the rise of capitalism in Europe as a cannibalistic preying on other continents, cutting short their development,[129] suffers much more from a lack of congruence with history as known to the textbook.

It may often seem that to try to interpret non-European histories on Marxist lines is as misconceived as to classify non-Aryan languages by the rules of English or Latin grammar. But this can be debated less one-sidedly and more fruitfully now that there are Marxists everywhere. Communism in the Third World has had close links with colonial nationalism and liberation movements, and this is bound to be reflected in Marxist theory; as with Christianity, new peoples taking up Marxism are making it their own, not something to be expounded to them from Europe. It was in this spirit that Cabral, the revolutionary leader in Portuguese Guinea and a pioneer of African Marxism, rejected any postulate of history beginning with class struggle, and the implication that great tracts of Africa, Asia, America had no history worth the name until they were turned into colonies: 'This we refuse to accept.[130] It is undeniable, after all, that history in the sense of migrations, inventions, cults, adaptations to environment, was going on for millennia before true classes and class conflict began.

India was the country outside Europe that Marx gave most thought to, and his articles on it, collected and republished in the 1930s, did much to rouse interest among Indian socialists in their national history. Marxists there have been less intent than in some other countries on claiming an evolution running through the same sequence of stages as Europe's, by way of a denial of European uniqueness. But many have been increasingly concerned to maintain that India was moving on its own towards capitalism, the gateway to socialism, before it succumbed to British imperialism.

Against Marx's forecast of beneficial results in the long run from this interruption or disruption of Indian history, or lack of history, it is urged that the real shortage was of enough information to allow him to discover an economic life in old India with an energy and forward movement of its own. Even so, it may be urged that foreign intervention was needed to release energy from obstructions that were holding it up, as it did, all can agree, in the case of Japan. But many Indian Marxists are not prepared to admit that their country had come to a standstill, and had to be painfully dragged back on to the narrow causeway of progress by imperialism. Their picture of pre-colonial India is one of trade and finance blooming, agriculture improving, political conditions in the wake of the Mogul empire far less chaotic than British propagandists gave them out to be. On this showing Britain, so far from jerking India forward, was thrusting it back, by cutting short its progress, destroying its manufactures, condemning it to the underdevelopment of the entire colonial world.

If the contention can be substantiated it will turn a fresh page of historical Marxism, at the expense of some of its older notions. At present no more can be said than that sufficient evidence of an indigenous Indian advance is not yet forthcoming. Meanwhile the polemics have at least thrown up novel ideas; among them, that of a special 'colonial mode of production', an economy and society combining capitalist with pre-capitalist structures, is advocated by a number of Marxists both Western and Indian.[131] Quite apart from controversial issues of the recent past, Marxist historians have been taking a very active hand in the investigation at many points of India's often enigmatic annals, and its prehistory.[132]

In China much fruitless effort was expended, as a Western scholar respectfully critical of Marxism writes, in the endeavour to categorize the national story without distorting either it, or historical material-ism, or both; the great stumbling-block being the dogma of 'a universally applicable model of progress'.[133] It seems perverse to insist on an epoch of slavery in ancient China because Marx believed there was one in ancient Europe; socialism can regard all human beings and peoples as equals without any myth of equal pedigrees. By this insistence Chinese Marxism only landed itself in difficulties, like Cinderella's sisters trying to get their feet into her slipper; a new sort of Chinese foot-binding. An embarrassment early encountered was that feudalism, in the sense of rule by feudal lords and princes, broke up exceptionally early, and yet for another couple of thousand years China failed to move on to capitalism.[134]

Early on, Marx and Engels too summarily wrote off agrarian risings in medieval Europe as 'totally ineffective because of the isolation and consequent crudity of the peasants'.[135] Chinese historians can scarcely endorse such a view of the peasant rebellions that were so striking a feature of China's past. Yet it is a puzzle how to think of them as progressive if the touchstone of progress is to be economic expansion. A promising if not conclusive answer has been found in the dictum that despite failure 'The class struggle none-theless affected the deeper undercurrents of history.'[136] Another facet of the Chinese approach which has been noted is the greater weight given to the force of ideas and of human will than in classical

Marxism. For the Chinese Revolution, with its very weak urban and working-class base, there has been little choice but to rely on faith to move mountains.

A generation ago a young Marxist historian could feel like a Columbus boldly crossing sea and oceans while timider navigators hugged their shores. Since then it has sometimes appeared to the onlooker that in order to keep afloat, historical Marxism has had to introduce so many qualifications and refinements, admit so many exceptions, that it resembles the Ptolemaic system in decline, tacking on more and more epicycles to explain anomalies.[137] Nevertheless a hundred years have gone by since Marx, and no Copernicus has come forward with a better scheme. Whatever objections it is open to, all other ways either of interpreting history or of writing it without benefit of any philosophy are open to far more. Opponents have found it easier to criticize Marxism than to defend themselves against its criticism. Fallible as they may often be, Marx's outlines, even his guesses, belong to the world of reality; his map has no fabulous continents or Mountains of the Moon, no 'seas of butter and seas of treacle'.

History has moved towards some at least of the destinations he expected, but by more roundabout routes. The time may be at hand when the economic and political spheres of his thinking, to which in his day he had to give priority, will be less helpful to our much-altered planet, at least to societies entering a 'post-industrial' era, than his illumination of the past, the conjectures comprised within his historical theory about how humanity's workaday life has been married to the arts, sciences, religions. It may be regrettable that a corpus of ideas still in the making, the work of many minds, goes under one man's name. But in Marx's centenary year it is proper to make all the acknowledgement due to an unforgettable genius.

Postscript

Agnostic ideas are spreading, Leslie Stephen wrote a century ago, 'in spite of the incessant and crushing refutations to which they are so frequently exposed'.[138] There is the same tale to be told of Marx's ideas about history, the life and soul of all his encyclopaedic range of interests. He was drawn most strongly to history and sociology, which he was far quicker than most later scholars to recognize as aspects of the same thing, and to economics. Through the first two lenses he was an observer of human beings in action; through the third, of impersonal forces coercing human beings into patterns of behaviour devised by themselves, spiders entangled in their own web.

It was congenial to his nature to move to and fro between these approaches. History, contemporary or earlier, meant most to him when he was concerned in the making of events; economics absorbed him in times, especially after the defeat of the revolutions of 1848 and their display of the frailty of human will, when society seemed incapable of change, and could only be subjected to analysis, on lines in some ways very abstract. He had a taste for mathematics, finding in it perhaps – like Wordsworth in youth with geometry – a fixed harbourage from the perpetual flux of mortal affairs, the birth and death of civilizations, languages, creeds.

Professional historians, newcomers of the nineteenth century, were elaborating ways of unearthing and heaping up facts. They were weak at interpreting them. Ranke's general ideas were often silly, Bury disclaimed any search for them. With Marx and Engels and their early disciples it was the opposite; they had no leisure for laborious research, but were seeking hypotheses to link and elucidate primary materials brought to light by others. This implies no undervaluing on their part of facts, dates, or narrative details. Engels planning a study of Irish history, Marx of Indian history, each laid a basis by compiling a meticulous chronological summary of whatever was known to have happened.

Their moment of illumination came early on with the recognition that there is always some method in the madness of history, to be looked for in material needs underlying the surface of events. The focal point at which Marx's delvings in all his fields of study converged with his practical politics was the concept of Class – like other leading ideas of his, never reduced to precise definition. History as class struggle is still much in need of thinking out by Marxists,[139] and to others can easily appear a restrictive formula, even within Europe where its claims are most assertive. At ordinary times struggle has been diffuse, sporadic. It has permeated consciousness only in the towns, those islands in the grey misty waste of rural existence, and only in towns like Europe's, first built on Mediterranean coasts, entities capable of the vitalizing spirit of political life. All through history there has been 'struggle' of a sort at work within myriads of families, but it was only yesterday that a movement of women claiming rights began; class relations have mostly been of the same muffled kind, strains and grudges within the microcosm of manor, guild, galleon.

Jotting down his thoughts, oftener than not hastily and sketchily, Marx sometimes turned classes, as others have turned nations, into persons, collective actors on the stage of history. They do have something of this character, but (with the partial exception of ruling classes or groups) only at supreme moments with any distinctness. They are aggregates of individuals, none identical and each concerned first of all with himself and his todays and tomorrows. Only an elite of any class embodies its 'historical' self, able to comprehend such mission as Marx assigned to it. Only a minority of workers have been interested in socialism. Cobden and Bright, so deeply hated by Marx for their Quakerish-capitalist hypocrisy and their opposition to the Crimean War which he hoped would shatter the throne of the tsars, were spokesmen of an elite of the new industrial bourgeoisie: their failure to carry their class with them further than the anti-Corn Law campaign was a misfortune for it and for England. Marx did, all the same, admit the importance of individual as well as of class; and to understand history we must often be alert for contradictions or frictions between the two. A peasantry like the Indian, in which individuality had no chance to push its way out of the swaddling clothes of caste and religion, except in the mythic form of a pilgrimage from life to life towards a remote heaven, might be called a perfectly homogeneous class, but it would also be at most times perfectly inert.

Dominant classes have occasionally been active participants in the economic sphere, as owners of slave plantations or feudal demesnes, or directors of water-control, or factory-owners. It might be better to limit the term 'mode of production' to these cases, instead of stretching it out across all history; and to pay more attention than Marxists have done to pre-capitalist modes of *exploitation*, far more numerous and varied. To speak of 'relations of production' when a peasant grows rice and a lord or prince eats half of it, seems a misnomer. By taking account of a habitual wide gap between economic and political structures, Marxism might make it easier to explore problems of change. It is only seldom, but then most far-reachingly, that the two have undergone simultaneous change, as in the still vexed case of Europe's translation from medieval to modern.

One of the three Asian realms that Marx took most interest in subscribes today to his teaching, and if the recent swing away from the simple certainties of Maoism liberates thinking in China – as may be hoped of the new dispensation in the Soviet Union as well – much progress in the study of Chinese history can be expected. Already the monumental *Cambridge History of China* (now at volume 13, part 2) shows Western understanding being more and more assisted by Chinese scholars, and by Western scholars who have also been at least exposed to Marxist influence. But Marx's own tentative picture of an isolating self-sufficiency carried down from the national level to that of each household finds no warrant in modern research, which points instead to a brisk exchange everywhere between village and market town, and in the last few centuries a swelling volume of internal trade.

Marx may seem to have taken a more deterministic view of history in his later years, when he could feel that he had solved at last the riddle of the capitalist sphinx. Since then the world's population has swollen monstrously, while its forests and all other natural resources have shrunk, the number of peoples involved in the world market has multiplied, electricity has put a girdle round the earth faster than Puck. With all this acceleration, the factor of accident, or the contingent, in history poses a more insistent challenge. Interactions among people and between forces of all kinds pressing on them, have proliferated incalculably. From this it can be urged that it is no longer possible, if it ever was, to identify significant currents or tendencies amid the vast welter.

Or, on the other hand, it can be argued that this very multiplication is simplifying the historian's task, by cancelling out inessentials and repeating basic themes *ad nauseam*. The trend, in other words, towards concentration of capital, overleaping of national boundaries, domination by a few centres, accompanied by the harnessing of science to power-politics and the piling up of armaments, – all this, and many of its political consequences, are unmistakably clear. History is being reduced to its crudest elements; mankind with its overflowing gifts and potential achievements is in danger of the same fate.

2

Gramsci and Marxism

When Marx died in 1883 and Engels, less than twenty years before the Great War, in 1895, they left the outlines of a 'Marxist' philosophy to be carried forward by disciples of their own like Kautsky, and by new figures in new lands like Plekhanov and then Lenin in Russia, or Labriola in Italy. This Marxism held its ground against 'revisionist' criticism in the international socialist movement before 1914, but more securely in appearance than in reality because most of its upholders were too much concerned to defend it as an established creed, too little to develop it and keep abreast of changing times. In 1914 war, in 1917 revolution, produced an immense cleavage in the socialist movement; from which time Marxism came to be identified with Lenin, Bolshevism and the Soviet Union, while the Marxism of the non-Communist parties, with Kautsky at the outset for its exponent, faded away. It faded, or grew only very patchily, in the Communist camp too, under the weight of orthodoxy now reinforced by state power or outside the Soviet Union, by allegiance to Moscow leadership. Issues between the two factions were, or seemed, clear and straightforward, and were almost exclusively practical matters of strategy and tactics. Amid vituperative controversy over these, interest in refinements of Marxism as a theory of society and history at large fell very much into the background.

Meanwhile, Marxism was spreading outside Europe, as earlier it had spread outside western Europe; but here still more one-sidedly as a guide to immediate political action, rather than a comprehensive philosophy. In India this narrowly practical – not to say philistine –

bent has persisted all along, and can be seen to have done much practical harm. Never-ceasing demands of the struggle first against the British and then against native Indian reaction, in a land of crushing poverty, made anything like abstract thinking – impossible without a certain leisure and detachment – seem a superfluity, a mere luxury, as biochemical researches would seem to a patient with a broken leg waiting to be set. Even in China, Mao's grand extension of Marxism belonged to the realm of actual struggle, the management of class war and anti-foreign resistance in the conditions of a peasant society. It must not be forgotten too that, with all its universality of vision, Marxist philosophy in conception and gestation was highly specific to western Europe, because many of the elements that entered into it – Judaism, Western Christianity, Enlightenment, Hegel – had no counterparts anywhere else. The Industrial Revolution could reproduce itself elsewhere but not this age-old intellectual and emotional travail, the Via Sacra or Via Dolorosa of the European mind.

Equally, Marxist theory originated in a specific social stratum, an intelligentsia, and has not yet travelled far outside it. It is too complex, it demands too wide a background of reference, to be reduced to popular comprehensibility without grave risk of dilution. Altogether, the very disparate growth of Communism as a political force in the world, and of Marxism as an intellectual force, has been striking, despite their never-repudiated belief in the unity of thought and action. Latterly it has manifested itself in a new guise in the appearance of movements more revolutionary – really or ostensibly – than Communism, but owning a general allegiance to Marxism. Theory and practice cannot be expected ever to be in perfect step with one another, but the gap separating them has too often been far too wide, and is still on the whole, widening. Its reduction depends on more freedom of intercourse between Marxists in and out of the Communist countries, on new relationships between socialist intellectuals and workers, and on a new and more meaningful involvement of Western socialism with the undeveloped lands.

Antonio Gramsci, who died in 1937 – he was born eight years after Marx's death – was, thanks to an intense absorption in and then forcible isolation from political life, a pioneer, the first outstanding one perhaps of a new kind of Marxism or, more exactly, of fidelity in a new age to the spirit of early Marxism, enquiring and speculative as well as purposeful, truly catholic or world-embracing, after the great schism and the onset of its rigid disciplines. He can be looked back on as the first standard-bearer of what has come to be called 'Western Marxism', but with broader and deeper implications than this title often suggests, and completely free from any tendency towards mere cloistered intellectualism. But ideas advance, like waves on an uneven beach, very irregularly. Gramsci's way forward for Marxism remained for long unknown. His prison writings on politics and history have only gradually been dawning on us since the end of the Second World War. How they might have influenced thinking if they had come earlier into circulation, one can only wonder. Possibly they would in any case have had to wait for a climate where they could be recognized as a contribution genuinely Marxist though often daringly novel, sometimes even eccentric. Now, at any rate, they are a treasure trove for us to delve into, or a rediscovered missing link, a lost generation, in the evolution of Marxism. Gramsci is a voice from the past, from beyond the tomb, and a summons to the future; he points us along one path towards a restored unity, or rather community, of socialist thinking, for Europe and the world.

When Gramsci was dying in 1937 he could not know whether anything would survive of his ten years' prison toil; a world of ideas hung by a thread, like Catullus' poems surviving for centuries in a single copy in a monastic vault. What his sister-in-law Tatiana smuggled out of the clinic in thirty-three notebooks was a chaos of notes, sketches, jottings, resembling nothing so much as the learned Professor Teufelsdröckh's six huge bags of papers in *Sartor Resartus*. The editors of a new, large and splendid English anthology[1] are to be warmly congratulated on reaching successfully the end of what must have been a dauntingly difficult task. It is no fault of theirs if the reader must often find it hard to get at Gramsci's meaning. Apart from circumlocutions meant to baffle the prison censor (who however must have been a very gullible person), Gramsci employs special terms of his own, and does not always seem to give them the same significance. His thoughts often slide to and fro, from point to point: there is always a link, but it may be a subterranean one. He is a political leader thinking of strategy, and a student of the human record, at once; analysing the structure of his Italy he is seeking materials 'for building a "train" to move forward through history as fast as possible' (p. 98). Much in the *Notebooks*, the editors remark, has 'an organic continuity' with the situation he was wrestling with before his arrest in 1926,[2] and their long and very valuable introduction mainly covers in detail the brief period of his political activity.

Corsica astonished the world by producing Napoleon, and Sardinia with no Rousseau to prophesy produced Gramsci, whose thoughts were to move about Europe as Napoleon's armies did. James Connolly, banished from political activity by a firing-squad when

Gramsci was just entering it, was born in the Cowgate of Edinburgh, another example of how enormous a leap an individual mind can make when caught up by a progressive historical movement. For Gramsci, removal to university life at Turin, the country's biggest manufacturing centre, was something like a Highlander of old days coming to Edinburgh. With his rustic background and his European culture he stood at a remarkable point of confluence of diverse epochs and social climates. Italy lay between Europe's eastern and western poles and partook of the character of both. It was itself a Europe in miniature, and every epoch that Europe has lived through was still alive on its soil, not merely buried beneath the pavements of its ancient cities. Gramsci's faculty for perceiving all kinds of social phenomena – religious, for example– as breathing realities was a reflex of this. Scottish sociology in the late eighteenth century benefited by standing at an analogous crossroad, between Highland and Lowland, feudal and capitalist, Europe and the world.

Gramsci's curiosity about his own country and its complex fabric was insatiable, and his mind often turned to obscurities of its recent history, especially of the nineteenth-century Risorgimento and the kind of national unification and independence it led to. The Risorgimento left all Italy, not simply the few districts still in Austrian hands, an *irredenta*, a land unredeemed from misery and ignorance, so unready for national existence that the advent of Fascism might seem no more than a logical conclusion. Gramsci found the fatal flaw in the cleavage between north and south, and he saw political life in his own day as still vitiated by this dichotomy of town and country, factory and plough, workman and peasant. Sardinia and Turin between them put him in a better position than almost any socialist of this century to combine an understanding of both realms, and his grand political formula was a mobilization of the peasantry under the leadership of the working class. He once contrasted Lenin, 'profoundly national and profoundly European' at the same time, with the cosmopolitan, rootless Trotsky (pp. 236–7), and he himself had a similar double identity. Rooted very deeply in Italy and its history, he was a European thinker as well.

In his political life too Gramsci stood at a turning-point. He was one of the protagonists of a brief, possibly unique, interval of opportunity for socialist revolution in Europe; then, in prison, he was one of the pathfinders of the long endeavour to advance by other routes to which Europe condemned itself by its failure to seize opportunity. In the Italy of his campaigning years after the First World War, as in other countries, the Left was so full of the conviction of revolution round the corner that it quite failed to discover what was really preparing, counter-revolution. While Communists and socialists and trade unionists wrangled, in October 1922 Fascism came to power and began stage by stage to erect its dictatorship. A streak of the hard-headed countryman in Gramsci, understanding that the correctest ideas had no weight by themselves, helped him to recognize later, if not fully at the time, that the theses his party rested on were infected by 'Byzantinism', 'scholasticism', divorce from reality (pp. 200–1).A sober realism was the keynote of the *Notebooks*, expressed in sober utilitarian language that contrasts startlingly with the many-coloured glow of his prison letters. While in Russia success hardened Bolshevik thinking into dogma, failure taught Gramsci to question, doubt, analyse over and over again. Some academy should undertake as a tribute to him the 'critical inventory' and bibliography which he envisaged of all problems that have come under debate in connection with Marxism (p. 414). Without 'scrupulous accuracy, scientific honesty', he wrote, it would be impossible to work out the general character of Marx's ideas, from the master's scattered hints (p. 382). Here was a standard of intellectual probity which from the standpoint of Stalinism, or of Maoism at its cruder levels – the doctrine that 'truth' is what serves the working class, in other words the party leadership – would have to be called academic.

Yet with him reasoning was never a bloodless, pedantic pursuit. While he warned himself of the need for 'critical equilibrium' – all scholars know, he remarks, how a theory studied with ardour takes possession of the mind (p. 383) – he recurred more than once to Giordano Bruno and the 'heroic fury' of thought that brought him to the stake. In such ardour he recognized the afflatus of a progressive historical movement. Political thinking cannot be purely objective or detached, because human will enters as a component of prediction – which 'only means seeing the present and the past clearly as movement'. 'Only the man who wills something strongly can identify the elements which are necessary to the realisation of his will'; and 'Strong passions are necessary to sharpen the intellect and help make intuition more penetrating' (pp. 170–1). All this is equally relevant to Marxist exploration of history or society or art, and much might be learned from it about how Marx or Lenin thought, or indeed about the psychology of thinking altogether.

How Gramsci's own mind worked we can often catch glimpses of, as we grope our way about the *Notebooks* amid a confusion of half-cut masonry and columns never reared; how his ideas took shape, what aims he was setting before himself. In a laborious dissection of some trivialities of a forgotten scribbler named Azzalini he pauses to remark – as if aside, to us – that the man is paltry, but 'I wanted to take all these notes, in order to try to disentangle his plot, and see if I could arrive at clear concepts for my own sake' (p. 251). Many of his sequences of thought had similar casual starting-points, like Diabelli variations; largely because his access to books was limited, but as he says in several of his letters he had a natural gift for extracting nourishment from any kind of mental pabulum or experience. Minds like his, or Marx's, can rove into the remotest-seeming realms without losing the guiding thread of purpose that distinguishes them from the pedant or dilettante.

He had found his own way to Marxism from out of a medley of contending theories, and could still take Sorel seriously enough to find in him 'flashes of profound intuition' (p. 395). This learning from scratch may have been necessary to form him into a creative Marxist: no intellectual tradition can easily be developed from within, because the adherent born and brought up to it, as Marxists have been in the Soviet Union, cannot have the same sense of its deficiencies or incompletenesses. In prison Gramsci was doubly cut off, not only from other minds but from nearly all Marxist literature: condemned to think instead of to think and act, he was also forced to think for himself. Doubtless with more books at hand he would have been a better-ballasted Marxist, not perhaps so original a one. His basis was an adequate though far from exhaustive knowledge of the Marxist classics, fertilized by a brief but intense season of political experience. This gives him a unique place among the major thinkers of the movement, as a pioneer, a scout, unencumbered with impedimenta, rather than a regular soldier. It has naturally exposed him to orthodox criticism from one side as well as anti-Marxist criticism from the other. Very often in the *Notebooks* he is raising questions, sketching projects of study, suggesting very tentative answers if any. If we have his ideas only in fragmentary form, the same is true (except for economic theory) of those of Marx, who as Gramsci stressed left no rounded philosophy but only a heap of solutions or suggestions strewn here and there over his numerous works (p. 382), mostly topical or else unfinished. It may in fact belong to the nature of Marxism, as not a system but a search, to function best in this apparently haphazard fashion, and never to arrive at codification, whatever Athanasiuses or Nicaean Councils may come and go. Gramsci risks a guess that the most significant views of any original mind should be looked for not in its direct pronouncements, but rather in its comments on extraneous issues (p. 403); a helpful idea for study of writers such as Balzac in whom professed opinion and inner feeling may be far apart, but also very possibly for approaching a mind like Marx's, too overflowing with discoveries to be able to arrange them symmetrically.

Gramsci had an awareness of the immense complexity of things, that would not come so readily to Marxists with the simpler traditional polities of Russia or China for background. One must look for answers 'within the contradictory conditions of modern society', he writes, full of anomalies and involutions (p. 279). Marxism represented to him 'the beginnings of a new civilisation' (p. 399), it opened up 'a completely new road' (p. 464), but in proportion to the magnitude of its tasks it seemed to him, as currently put forward hitherto, very unsophisticated. It had been chiefly engaged in combating religious superstitions or other crude errors, and this kept it within the confines of a banal materialism.[3] He felt, as one must still feel today, that it was insufficiently developed for anyone to be able to sum it up on a popular treatise, like Bukharin's *Historical Materialism*: any such attempt must produce an illusory appearance of unity and finality.[4] He himself might have written brilliantly the 'new *Anti-Dühring*' that once crossed his mind (p. 371), against the opponents of Marxism but also against its vulgarizers.

At times Gramsci's words point to an inclination to regard Marxism as, potentially if not actually, a self-sufficient whole. He defines Marxist orthodoxy, or emancipation from 'the old world' of ideas, as 'the fundamental concept that the philosophy of praxis (*sc. Marxism*) is "sufficient unto itself", that it contains in itself all the fundamental elements needed to construct a total and integral conception of the world' (p. 462). This sounds like a claim to monopoly of truth; it may be better understood as the more reasonable claim that Marxism, because it goes down to the deepest levels of the historical movement, has a unique capacity to amalgamate or co-ordinate what is valid in all other modes of thought; its self-sufficiency consists in this faculty of organic absorption – a very different thing from patchwork borrowing. It can mature this faculty only by wrestling with other philosophies, and learning from them. Gramsci argues strikingly that the Hegelian element in Marxism itself is not fully subsumed or resolved in it, but retains a vitality of its own, so that their relationship is 'a historical process still in motion in which the necessity for a philosophical cultural synthesis is being renewed' (p. 402). We might add the same claim on behalf of any other stream that has entered into socialism, including Christianity, which is still capable both of imparting a fresh stimulus to it and of itself putting forth new shoots.

Similarly in his frequent scrutinies of Croce he was simply

concerned to brush away metaphysical cobwebs: there was something to be learned from Croce as well, 'as a thinker whose work could be profited from in the struggle to renew Marxist thought' (p. xxiii). Marxism in other words cannot generate all its intellectual capital out of its own resources. One failing for which Gramsci took Bukharin to task was his dismisal of all earlier philosophies as mere nonsense (p. 470). The best thinker is one who discerns that there may be something in his opponent's case which it behoves him to learn and incorporate in his own – 'And sometimes one's adversary is the whole of past thought'; one thus escapes from 'the prison of ideologies in the bad sense of the word – that of blind ideological fanaticism' (p. 344). Marxist intolerance has alway been fed by lurking self-doubt, morbid fear of eclecticism or heterodoxy, an anxiety like that of Ulysses when he tied himself to the mast for fear of being beguiled by the Sirens as his ship passed their rocks. Conversely, Gramsci notes, ruling-class thought has had to take over some features of Marxism, in a form obvious and avowed, as with Croce, or more covertly; Marxists ought not to shut their eyes to the fact that their ideas have sometimes had most effect by influencing or mingling with other streams of thought.[5] It might indeed be asked whether ideas have ever existed in a state of chemical purity, and in complex modern societies they are less likely than ever to do so; ideas of all kinds may alway have been more potent when compounded, deliberately or not, with others.

Gramsci insists, none the less, that Marxism must learn to transcend both idealism, the fetishism of ideas, and crude materialism, the denial of ideas. He found these opposite systems of error embodied in two writers, Croce and Bukharin, who were important to him for partly accidental reasons. No one can be perfectly equidistant from the two poles, and it is not surprising that Gramsci has often seemed to his readers a man brought up in the watery realm of ideas and finding his way from it to the *terra firma* of economics, rather than the other way about. Prison made it in some degree harder to find this way. It would be absurd to deny that solitude and ill-health must have had some disturbing effects on his judgement, and it was only by an at times overemphatic belief in the power of thought and of thinkers that he could compensate for his own practical impotence, and convince himself that what he could still do was worth doing, and life therefore worth living. He was ready to take some philosophical terms from non-Marxist writers like Bergson or Croce, evidently feeling that the standard Hegelian-Marxian terminology, or range of octaves, was not adequate for all purposes[6] It was characteristic of him to say that in developing historical materialism one should pay more attention to the first term than the second, 'which is of metaphysical origin' (p. 465). For Marxism it can only be beneficial to have disciples starting from different points of the intellectual globe and trying to meet at an equator.

Bukharin's book happened to be one of the few Marxist writings available to Gramsci in prison. He commented on it with uniform severity; it may be noted that while he admired Labriola, the introducer of Marxism into Italy, he censured Plekhanov, whom Lenin had extolled, for the same vice of 'vulgar materialism' as he objected to in Bukharin, and found in him positivist leanings and little historical insight (pp. 386–7). Bukharin he accused of stultifying Marxism through 'the baroque conviction that the more one goes back to "material" objects the more orthodox one must be' (p. 461). This 'attempt to reduce everything to a single ultimate or final cause' belonged to 'old-fashioned metaphysics' and was really an echo of the theologians' search for God (p. 437). To translate all happenings from one level to another, more elementary one, until nothing is left but the swirl of electronic patterns, would indeed be crass reductionism. But at what point, then, are we to stop, and in what way can we hold on to the 'historical monism' which Plekhanov was trying to build, and without which history remains an incomprehensible play of independent variables? It seems only possible to say that within the sphere of human history the forces at work are multiple, and because of men's heavy prehuman inheritance are not all reducible to a single source; but they are of unequal weight, and among them one – the collective activity of material production – is weighty enough to mould or moderate all the rest.

Gramsci did not set out to investigate the 'mode of production' and its constituent parts, but he was haunted by the problem of base (or 'structure') and superstructure and their association, intimate but elastic and subtle like that of body and mind. As usual we find in his pages no complete statement, but a cluster of approaches from various angles. Only by exploring their reciprocal workings can we gauge the pressures active in any epoch, he writes (p. 177); and again, material forces and people's thoughts belong to each other as inseparably as content and form (p. 377). 'The complex contradictory and discordant *ensemble* of the superstructure is the reflection of the *ensemble* of the social relations of production' (p. 366). Here is a salutary reminder that the ideas of an age – our own, for instance – reflect its manifold discords, not in any straightforward fashion the interests or outlook of a dominant class. Looking not at any single ideology, but at the whole jarring melée of ideas, we find 'manifestations of the intimate contradictions by which society is lacerated' (p. 404).It may be added, each philosophy by itself (not excluding

Marxism) must be built on discords, many or fewer, because each class and social group (and sex), not only the social whole they belong to, suffers from disharmonies of its own, so that the individual cannot escape from its inner divisions by merging himself with any one of them. Because of this also every class, and increasingly in the measure of its energy and ambition, has a diversity of needs for beliefs or fantasies, and borrows these from a diversity of sources. Feudal Europe's ruling class was truly 'Christian' as well as rootedly militaristic.

There is besides all this the common phenomenon of declining creeds being used, so to speak, as rubble to fill the interior of castle walls between a facing of new masonry. Gramsci's test of how far ideals are authentic expressions of a society is their ability to 'react back on that society and produce certain effects' (p. 346). It may be objected that trivialities often seem to exert more influence than profounder thinking, for the time being at least. Nietzsche's worse ideas (more pedestrian as well as more unwholesome) made a greater stir than his more inspired ones. In such cases the mediocre idea, by whomever expressed, is an emanation of collective moods, themselves a fermentation of what men are already habitually doing, and serves to lend this a sanction. Nietzsche was welcomed as spreading a halo over an arms-race already being carried on by the militarists, Darwin as appearing to ratify the elimination of primitive peoples by colonialism.

Cases like these may be examples of what Gramsci on one occasion calls, very remarkably, 'catharsis' — meaning coming-to-consciousness, 'elaboration of the structure into superstructure in the minds of men' (p. 366). Here is a term too out of the way and striking to have been chosen (like some curious phrases of Gramsci) to baffle the prison censor. He may well have seen something akin to 'purgation' or release in such inventions of ideas able to set at rest people's misgivings and self-reproaches about their own behaviour. But it is tempting to read a deeper significance into the word, and take it as also, or more properly, denoting an eruption into social consciousness of some deeply buried conflict — like the unearthing of a neurosis by Freudian analysis, but with the difference that men collectively may only be willing to face their fundamental maladies when a solution to these seems to have been found. Mankind made a profound discovery about itself and its condition when Marx pointed to the new working class as the ender of all class divisions — divisions it had for ages rubbed all kinds of religious unguents into its eyes in order not to have to see. In time of revolution, as in the mimic form of tragic drama, human self-discovery is most intense and swift; hence the appropriateness of Hazlitt's epithet for the French Revolution, of 'apocalyptic'.

Gramsci was concerned to set Marxist theory apart from bourgeois sociology, a would-be science founded on 'vulgar evolutionism' and oblivious, in particular, of the change of quantity into quality.[7] But the old question remains of whether Marxism is to be considered as itself a science or 'philosophy', as something, that is, over and above its interpretation of history — as Althusser, prominently, has argued that it can and must be. Gramsci wanted it to be completely historical in spirit, but at times, if not always, he too seems to have wanted it to be something more than history. He could call it 'the science of dialectics and cognition', distinct from, though arising out of exploration of history.[8] Bukharin failed in his view to counter the argument that Marxism 'can live only in concrete works of history', because he failed to derive from these a true historical methodology, 'the only concrete philosophy' (p. 436). In another passage he called Marxism 'a doctrine of consciousness and the inner substance of society', not reducible to a system of logic for organizing historical studies. Yet he went on to speak of history and philosophy as identical.[9] To overcome this seeming discrepancy we may be obliged to take history not as the formal sequences of events, 'movements', 'waves', investigated in university departments, but as the sum total of human experience on every plane. In the meantime any adequate formulation of Marxism as a general 'philosophy' seems still more remote than as a guide to history.

Most Marxist thinkers who have been also makers of history have written about history only with reference to events close to their own time, leaving it to men like Kautsky, more scholar than man of action, to range over the ages. Marx and Engels wrote much on contemporary or recent events, and Engels occasionally went further back; Marx did so oftener, though only in unfinished speculations. Lenin, when not busy with practical tasks, turned more willingly to economics or philosophy than to history, and Trotsky's history of the Revolution was a polemic, though also far more. Gramsci sketched a good many programmes of historical study; he could carry none of them out. No one has laid more stress on history as the accompaniment or vehicle of all thinking about human affairs. Marxism was for him 'absolute "historicism" . . . an absolute humanism of history' (p. 465). His word 'humanism' is significant: he gave much more thought to man himself than Marxists content with facile phrases about 'the broad masses' — always with a hint of Stalinist indifference to the individual human being — have often done. Between political history, the statistical study of mass behaviour, and social psychology, the study of how and why men behave as they do, he had exceptional endowments for tracing the links. Man is 'essentially "political" ' because he realizes his nature by influencing others (p. 360) — words akin to those of Shakespeare's Ulysses to Achilles. Individuality is important, but the individual is not the enclosed being portrayed by religion: he is 'a series of active relationships'.[10] Human nature is not immutable, as again religion would have it, but is the sum of 'historically determined social relations', and alters with them (p. 133). At this point Gramsci sees a question facing him. If man is 'the *ensemble* of social relations', how can a historian compare the people of one age with those of another (p. 359)? To this the answer must surely be that social relations have nowhere changed out of recognition: mankind has performed numberless variations on a few primary themes, within a very small number of radically distinct modes of production. Between officer and soldier, mistress and maid, there must be some common attitudes whether in Carthage or in Prussia. If moreover we take account of what we have inherited from prehistoric and prehuman ages, we must expect to find more resistance to change, less ductility of conduct, than an optimistic earlier Marxism supposed.

Gramsci may have been an early 'Western Marxist', but it would be wrong to bowdlerize him into a liberal. His belief in discipline was firm, and though he hoped to see this evolving into self-discipline, it might have to be imposed in the first place by external authority. This applied to education, and to industrialization; and in the political context, thinking no doubt of the Soviet Union but also of Italy, he declares that for classes with no long 'cultural and moral development' of their own 'A period of statolatry is necessary and indeed opportune' (p. 268). In other words dictatorship of the proletariat in a backward country must mean respect for the state as a thing in itself, not only as an instrument, and the date for its withering away must be a distant one. But it was not the socialist state alone that he had in mind when he queried Lassalle's view of the state as a mere 'nightwatchman' or policeman, and credited it with a moral character (pp. 262–4). As a Sardinian, in his youthful days a separatist or home-ruler, Gramsci came to his own Italian State a stranger, with enquiring eyes; it is the more noteworthy that his estimate of the state in general came to be so high.

Authority ought, on the other hand, to be as little bureaucratic or 'commandist' as possible. Occasionally he pondered on parliamentarism, about which he felt some puzzlement. Is a lively parliament 'a part of the State structure', or, if not, what is its real function (p. 253)? Its critics condemn it as a clog. But 'even allowing (as it must be allowed) that parliamentarism has become inefficient and even harmful', abandonment of it might lead backward, to something worse (p. 254); to the 'bureaucratic centralism' for instance that he noted in nineteenth-century Piedmont, growing from 'lack of initiative and responsibility at the bottom', from 'political immaturity' (p. 189). Gramsci thought often about bureaucratism, and about the recruitment of bureaucracies from particular social strata. This was a subject of obvious interest for an Italian – or Spaniard – because competition for state posts has been so heated in their retarded economies, by contrast with a country like England where officialdom was a late and slow growth. He thought of the middle and lower rural bourgeoisie as the groups most addicted to government service (p. 212), a classification more pertinent to southern Europe than to most of the continent. He noted that the transformation of politics since 1848 has included a proliferation of bureaucracies, unofficial ones of parties or trade unions as well as those of the state (p. 221). To these might be added the higher personnel of big corporations, and altogether they have not been given the place they deserve in political history. Very likely in each region the 'private' hierarchies have formed their habits and mentality a good deal on the model of the regular Civil Service, and this has helped to promote a common climate, always more conservative than not.

Gramsci viewed the state as a highly complex phenomenon, and raised points about it which Marxists have too seldom considered; for example 'the organic relations between the domestic and foreign policies of a State', and the question of which determines the other in certain contexts (p. 264). As an illustration one might ask whether the absolute monarchies were chronically at war because of their intrinsic nature, or whether on the contrary absolutism arose because countries had serious grounds for being chronically at war. Gramsci warns us, above all, against conceiving the historic state too mechanically in terms of class power. Remarking that the concept of the state has been impoverished by the growth of sociology and the delusion that society can be studied by the methods of the natural sciences, he goes on: 'The State is the complex of practical and theoretical activities with which the ruling class not only justifies and maintains its dominance, but manages to win the active consent of those over whom it rules' (p. 244). A ruling class holds sway by virtue of intelligence and character as well as by force (p. 57). A corollary must be that it is in jeopardy when it loses its moral ascendancy, as the French aristocracy lost it long before 1789 to the bourgeoisie.

It matters very much to a ruling class, Gramsci writes in another pregnant adage, that the state, which the public looks up to as an independent entity, 'should reflect back its prestige upon the class upon which it is based'. From this point of view it may be better for this class not to stand forward obtrusively, but to leave the sceptre in other hands: that of a monarchy, as in bourgeois Germany, or an aristocracy as in England (pp. 269–70). We may suppose that the German chimney-barons, with Bismarck for whipper-in, accepted this arrangement more willingly because they knew how smoothly it was working in England. When the French bourgeoisie ventured, or after 1870 was virtually compelled, to wield power directly, and this without the blessing of religion, it had to assert itself from time to time by violence, as in 1848 and 1871 and periodically in its colonies. It must be set in the other scale that a ruling class which hides behind the façade of another is bound to contract weaknesses, short-sightedness; these were very marked in the German bourgeoisie, which left far more real authority to the Hohenzollerns and Junkers than was entrusted to Tory landlords in Britain. In more recent times, with upper classes everywhere converging, the British plutocracy has preserved something of the aristocratic spirit, with the drawback of some inefficiency in industrial management. In countries where the ruling class lacks this spirit and is less self-reliant, it has often been nervously in haste to hand over the business of government to generals or dictators.

In the United States the state presented exceptional problems, Gramsci pointed out, because there the industrialists had succeeded in 'making the whole life of the nation revolve round production', and exercised their sway through the factory itself, with small need of 'professional political and ideological intermediaries' (p. 272). Since then salesmanship has been taking precedence over manufacturing, and the state too has had to 'sell itself' to the public, vastly expanding its apparatus in order to keep the country in good humour even more than for purposes of coercion. Another case that Gramsci saw as exceptional was old Russia. 'In Russia the State was everything, civil society primordial and gelatinous' (p. 238). This seems to overlook the far from indefinite relations between the landowners and the peasantry which they pushed down into serfdom; it was only on this foundation that the tsarist state could take its rise. One may dissent too from his aphorism, stimulating though – like so many of Gramsci's – it is, that a new class comes to power with some rough sense of a harmony of interests between itself and the masses, and conceives of its state as 'a continuous process' of eliminating disagreements (p. 182). He has in mind French history from 1789 to 1871; his words may seem more appropriate to England, where the modern bourgeoisie took over power by slow degrees and where consequently haggling and bargaining have been taken to be the essence of politics, than to France where revolutions were likelier to foster illusions of finality, of problems settled once and for all by the perfect Constitutions which first began to be drawn up in 1789.

Any class is an entity distinct from the sum of its members, evolving more freely than most of these, tied as they are in many ways to their prehistoric past, but less freely than the more gifted or mobile individuals among them. Of social classes, and their history and special features, in his own Italy most of all, Gramsci was a penetrating observer. It was one of his objections to vulgar historical materialism – the adulterated form in which as he said Marxism had chiefly circulated – that it takes account only of sordid self-regarding motives, forgetting the wider motivation of class (pp. 162–3). This fits into a thesis he advanced in the same passage, that economic forces are decisive only in an ultimate sense, and that men experience social conflict far more as a struggle of ideas or beliefs than directly as competition for shillings and pence. We may accept this as true for most of history, while wondering whether it still holds good of the advanced societies which in Gramsci's day were only entering on maturity. In Britain nowadays, or the United States – clearly not in Ireland – class struggle would seem to have resolved itself into a realistic, but well circumscribed, competition over 'shares in the national cake', as we have been taught to think of it, a squabbling over shillings or dollars quite free from illusion or ideal. But through the long ages of triangular conflict among lords, towns-people, peasants, the antagonists were too far apart, too little combined by any collective rationality of production, to feel their disagreements in so unromantic a style, or reduce them to vulgar fractions. They fought instead over the succession to the early Caliphate, or the procession of the Holy Ghost. They could compete for material stakes only by combining into classes, but these classes had their own life and thoughts, along with much miscomprehension of themselves with respect to other classes, and all this might overlay and obscure their essential nature. In nations – whose consciousness, varying from class to class, in an idealized (or inebriated) version of class-consciousness – we come on the same phenomenon, still further magnified: nations have continually fought wars whose ultimate purpose was gain, but they have seldom if ever done so confessedly or consciously. If they did, the secret that only a small minority of citizens are going to gain would soon come to light.

Gramsci places class and nation side by side when he speaks, very suggestively, of an 'educational relationship' between all hegemonic classes or nations and the rest (p. 350). An obvious example would be France's intellectual leadership of eighteenth-century Europe. He puts valuable stress too on the part played by international influences, those of ideology among them, in the moulding of class-consciousness (p. 182). This begins, he reminds us, at the social apex. Those lower down lack a clear sense of their collective identity, and 'can only achieve self-awareness via a series of negations', by contrasting themselves with the classes above them (p. 273). It is in the minds of intellectuals that the idea of 'the People' takes shape, not in its own, and in the tug-of-war of classes the higher ones, if not too decadent, have the advantage of longer traditions and memories. As Gramsci notes, unmistakably with recent Italian events in view, in times of crisis and dislocation the ruling class adapts itself more promptly, while the masses are prone to falling under the spell of 'violent solutions' offered by ' "men of destiny" ' (p. 210). We may indeed take failure by a ruling class to adjust itself to a novel quandary as proof of its obsolescence; such as that of the French nobility which in the two years before the Revolution so completely misconceived the situation facing it, and then for the most part collapsed so nervelessly, taking its seat unresistingly in the tumbrils or at best running away to beg for foreign help.

Gramsci stands as a classical exponent and philosopher of the party, that grand invention of modern Europe, its secular version of the old sect. Looked back on from a later day than ours the party, or its established forms at least, may seem to have been in his day on the verge of leaving its grand epoch behind. He saw from the inside a great deal of one party, and of others, including the Bolshevik during his year in Moscow, from not far away; and his idea of psychology as well as his political acumen helped to make him a discriminating, often a disconcerting, commentator. If his compass does not always seem to point unwaveringly to its true north, it is the fascination of the *Notebooks* that in them we wander over the whole range of the socialist movement of that volcanic time, listening to its doubts and mistakes as well as its hopes and inspirations.

That 'Every party is only the nomenclature for a class' (p. 152) must seem too stringent a dictum, though we can more easily agree that at critical moments scattered political groupings will rally in a single class organization (p. 157). It leaves parties in the United States as anomalous as the state. It leaves us to wonder also how many authentic parties there can be in any political bullring, since Gramsci regards all those of 'radical' cut as having no single class foundation, but as being manned by the same miscellaneous petty-bourgeois elements that were turning in his day to Fascism (p. 156); while he considers the big bourgeoisie as usually employing no party of its own, but making use of others according to convenience (p. 155). There is much force in this, and the more mature the ruling class, as in Britain or the United States, the more likely it is to be the case. Still more significant is Gramsci's conception of the party as standing in a sense above the class, as the class stands above the bulk of its members. 'Parties are not simply a mechanical and passive expression of these classes, but react energetically upon them' (p. 227).

Leadership is to Gramsci a matter of the highest priority, and what he says about it has a bearing on past history as well as actual politics. He thinks of it constantly as depending on a correct interplay between leaders and rank and file, just as the party's health depends on an interplay between it and the class it rests on. Left to themselves leaders suffer a besetting temptation to rely on authoritarian methods. 'Parties may be said to have the task of forming capable leaders', through whom in turn classes can be 'transformed from turbulent chaos into an organically prepared political army' (p. 191). 'The active politician is a creator, an initiator; but he neither creates from nothing nor does he move in the turbid void of his own desires and dreams' (p. 172). Gramsci speak more than once of 'the science and art of politics', though here as elsewhere we find him admonishing himself not to take his own phrases too literally: 'Only by metaphor does one speak of the art of politics'. What does a leader's 'intuition' consist in? Not in 'knowledge of men', but in 'swiftness in connecting seemingly disparate facts, and in conceiving the means adequate to particular ends' (p. 252). It would be interesting to study the affinities between practical reason, so understood, and abstract thought: the scholar or philosopher too is in quest of unnoticed connections, as the poet combines unlike things by imagery. 'Correct political leadership is necessary even with an army of professional mercenaries.' In a prolonged struggle it requires great skill to hold the people together by playing on its 'very deepest aspirations and feelings' (p. 88). It must surely be confessed that Hitler and Goebbels as well as Lenin and Stalin displayed this skill.

How high an estimate Gramsci sets on the qualities of leadership may be gathered from his epigram that the loss of an army is more easily repaired than that of its generals (p. 153). In prison he must have been preyed on by the thought that the party he helped to found and lead had, after all, failed disastrously. After every failure, he writes at one point, the responsibility of leaders must be rigorously scrutinized. Yet his conviction of their indispensability is unshaken, and if the other side of this thinking is left out he can sound quite an elitist. He defends democracy against the criticism that it reduces everything to mere counting of heads, by the unexpected argument that votes simply measure the persuasiveness of 'the opinions of a few individuals, the active minorities, the élites, the avant-gardes, etc.' (p. 192). Here again it is likely to strike the reader that this could as well be said of a Fascist as of a progressive movement. Gramsci tries to forestall such a comment by seeing the essence of a Fascist movement not in any elite but in masses of people manipulated by hidden interests and 'kept happy by means of moralising sermons, emotional stimuli, and messianic myths of an awaited golden age' (p. 150). It must surely be admitted that the leading cadres of the Nazi party (if not of Mussolini's) were an 'elite' of a kind, and of remarkable if evil calibre: not all the 'chosen' of history are chosen for good purposes. Gramsci is ready to acknowledge that progressive leadership may fall into some of the ways of its loathly opposite. One may be led astray by 'one's own baser and more immediate desires and passions . . . the demagogue is the first victim of his own demagogy' (p. 179).

Gramsci and his generation were confronted more urgently than the authors of *The Communist Manifesto* with the question of how the working class was to succeed to the position of ruling class, and use it to remake society. Classes evolved only hesitantly, he saw, towards 'integral autonomy' – one of his abracadabra terms, signifying class consciousness and ripeness for intervention in politics. Ruling groups realize their unity through the state and its bonds with society, whereas subordinate groups 'cannot unite until they are able to become a "State" ' (p. 52). If so, how can any of them acquire sufficient unity and resolve to take over the state? Of a modern bourgeoisie, at the level it was attaining in eighteenth-century France, we may say that it is close enough to the levers of power to see them within its reach, and how they can be utilized for its benefit: it itches to supplant its predecessor. To a labouring class, rural or urban, such an aspiration will not come so naturally; its instincts are defensive. A peasantry thinks of liberation from feudal burdens, a proletariat at first of liberation from the factory, then of bettering its conditions inside the factory. It would never be likely to imagine a dictatorship of the proletariat by itself, and Marxism in planning this road may have been confusing its own 'subjective' requirements with the objective power of the working class to build it.

Or if a working class really may be imbued with revolutionary instinct, contempt for niggling reform, it is perhaps only briefly, in an early phase of industrialism, when the windows have not yet all been shuttered and sunlight exchanged for electric lamps; and only in countries like Italy or Russia with still-fresh legends of resistance to oppression. Gramsci in Turin was a fledgling intellectual and leader, throwing in his lot with a fledgling proletariat, to which the Fiat works served for training-school as the Putilov factory did to the workers of St Petersburg. These men and women of Turin, as we see them through Gramsci's ardent young eyes, had the same romantic daring as those of St Petersburg, as we see them through Isaac Deutscher's. In August 1917 during the War they attempted an insurrection, after the War they rejected the directors' proposal to turn the Fiat enterprise into a co-operative. Such a breed may not find it strange to think of its own strength, as young Marx thought of it, as the charmed sword, the Siegfried-weapon destined to destroy all monsters. Some touch of Quixotic idealism, thirst for a new earth and a new heaven, may be needed to kindle the revolutionary mood which no economic grievances by themselves can produce. In terms of money the Turin workers were so well off by contrast with the ordinary poverty of Italy that peasant conscripts could regard them as an upper class, and cheerfully obey orders to fire on them.[11]

Gramsci was all the same well aware of the gap still to be crossed between the mass of the workers recognizing themselves as a class with common interests to defend, and their aspiring to take power and build socialism. He attached great value to the experience of industrial life in itself, to the rational factory organization promoting a sense of participation in collective effort: the Turin 'factory movement' he defines as an effort to bring this mutual reliance into consciousness (p. 202). It would follow that capitalism can hardly help incubating the socialist mentality that is to bring it to an end. Experience unhappily shows that workers in a factory may soon come to view their manager or boss as taking part in the collective effort. A shining example of this for generations was the Krupp enterprise, and the Nazi doctrine of the boss as 'leader' of his employees was only a theatrical rendering of it. In 1972 the most militant of Clydeside workers rejoice, not at their shipyards being socialized, but at American capitalists being bribed by the British tax-payer to come and take charge of them. So strong hitherto, nearly everywhere, has been the hunger for work, so weak the hunger for power, of the working class.

Gramsci had no thought of leaving it to history to do things by itself, however. Speculation about economic crisis or general strike conjuring up a tempest and transforming men's minds overnight he dismissed as 'out-and-out historical mysticism' (pp. 233–4). Only Marxist parties could perform the task, and for him it was axiomatic that their function was to crystallize a socialist feeling in the working class, and guide it towards power. They become necessary, he held, at the moment when in any country conditions are ripe for power to be taken over (p. 152). The working class could come to power only by putting itself at the head of other sections of the people in need of change, in Italy primarily the peasantry. But it has everywhere found it hard to do this, or has baulked at the attempt almost as completely as at that of giving a lead to the masses in its country's colonies. In either case its assumption of leadership would probably require a certain abnegation or postponement of its own economic demands: it would be a matter of class-consciousness having to learn – as national consciousness has never learned – to rise above self-asserting egotism.

Gramsci's great hope for Italy was of the northern working class banding round it the southern peasantry, but he recognized how much of colonialism there was in the relation between industrial north and agrarian south, and his grand alliance would have been a hard one to build, even if it cannot be ruled out – like an alliance of Lancashire weavers and Indian peasants – as an impossibility. A second point which arises is that Gramsci's concept of the mission of a socialist party may seem to neglect an alternative, defensive function of protecting the working class, instead of leading it to power. This has been the real business of all left-wing forces in England since the Chartists, and increasingly in all the developed countries. Further progress may more likely follow roundabout courses than a straight line to outright victory. Even compelling capitalists to give us jobs may, over decades, force some appreciable change in capitalism. We shall at least be educating our masters.

For Gramsci the ultimate problem of history as well as of political strategy was the problem of change, and how it comes about, though he did not like many Marxists overlook history's too frequent failure to change. It is one of his list of complaints against Bukharin's manual that it does not come to grips with the question: 'How does the historical movement arise on the structural base?' (pp. 431–2) He himself supplies no systematic answer; he takes his stand repeatedly on the parallel sayings of Marx – he calls them 'the two fundamental principles of political science' (p. 106) – that humanity only undertakes tasks for the solution of which the material conditions are already present; and that an old order does not perish before its productive potentiality is exhausted. Each of these laconic but far-reaching statements may be open to closer scrutiny than Gramsci subjects them to. People and classes evolve so unevenly that the material conditions for change may be present (as they have now been for generations in western Europe for transition to socialism) without this fact impinging on the majority mind. Many social structures have been put an end to from outside, while others, and modern capitalism above all, seem capable of protean adaptation, if allowed time. Taken together Marx's two contentions may almost verge on economic determinism, which to a certain degree he leaned towards when engrossed with pure economic phenomena, and leaned away from when he was exploring the far more intricate phenomena of history.

Gramsci even finds in them 'the scientific base for a morality of historical materialism': when a task is practicable, its performance becomes a duty (pp. 407–8). One may feel some further doubt about this, which seems to imply that it was a duty to work for abolition of slavery when, but not before, slave plantations became economically superfluous. At what date this happened would be hard to say now, and would have been harder for a contemporary to know. Active campaigners against slavery had motives to which it was irrelevant; and just as bourgeois revolutions are not made by the bourgeoisie, good causes are not fought for by the economic interests which may ultimately benefit by them, as capitalists might do by the abolition of slavery or serfdom. Marx himself was trying to get rid of capitalism when it had, as we can see now, scarcely got into its stride.

Gramsci's emphasis, however, is the reverse of determinist; it is on the fact that economic conditions hold out only a possibility of progress, not a guarantee. Progress only takes place when it is made to take place. He finds in the average man, long divorced from any real part in control of public affairs, a 'fetishistic' attitude towards all institutions, whether of state or party, a taking for granted that they will somehow go on functioning whether *he* does anything or not; and 'the passivity of the great popular masses' is the reason why 'A deterministic and mechanical conception of history is very widespread' (p. 187). (In the light of this remark historical determinism can be seen as, like nationalism and theology and most other ideologies, a formulation by philosophers of an inbred mode of thought of common people.) Gramsci finds this fatalistic tendency infecting Marxism itself, representing, he thinks, a lingering religious habit of mind. Because of the immaturity of the masses it has been for a certain time necessary, like a drug, but the time has come now to dispense with it.[12] This admission of illusion or error as a necessary ingredient in historical advance at certain stages is interesting, and is one of a number of issues on which Gramsci and Nietzsche can be heard saying the same thing. In any epoch some rays of light from the same source will make their way into even the most oppositely facing minds.

To Marx or Lenin themselves, a conviction of the inevitable downfall of capitalism may have had something of the stimulating quality of a drug. Looking back to the age of religion, Gramsci observes mechanical determinism, in the Calvinist guise of pre-destination, furnishing a movement on the defensive with 'a formidable power of moral resistance'.[13] But it may also lead to an obstinate, suicidal rejection of compromise. He might have taken an example of this from Scottish history, in the Covenanters. In his own Italy there was the defeat of a sectarian Left by Fascism, one cause of which, he came to feel, was its being blinded by an obstinate belief that historical necessity was fighting on its side: this led men like the dogmatist Bordiga to assume that all that was required was to take up a theoretically 'correct' position, confident that sooner or later the masses would come round to it, as the sun will rise at its appointed time in the east.

To assume in this spirit that History is always right was not much less fatuous than the Fascist credo that 'Mussolini is always right'. Gramsci as a leader had been accused of 'voluntarism', and he was careful to disclaim any notion, the antithetical error to determinism, that people can make events as they please, if they only want them to happen badly enough. But the bounds he sets to the operation of humanity's free will are far from narrow. He conceives of history as rising by steps from the plane of accident to that of choice, or from necessity to freedom. History-writing of the kind that can be done by statistical method, he observes, is valid only so long as the people remain inert.[14] (For conservative historians the people is always inert, except for odd bursts of futile violence.) Revolutions are not made, in any immediate sense, by economic crisis: in support of this Gramsci argues that the general economic situation in France towards 1789 was good (p. 184), a view which may underrate the precipitating effect of bad harvests, hunger, trade depression just before 1789, and just before 1848. He is more clearly right in saying that nothing happens purely spontaneously: there are always leaders, initiators, though these may be nameless figures who leave no trace (p. 196).

His most exemplary of all leaders are the Jacobins, with their motto of audacity. We can identify them as the professional intelligentsia of a bourgeoisie made up of distinct strands not yet spliced together by industrialism; they could find common ground with the sansculottes of the urban democracy as well as with that politically dull herd of pachyderms, the financiers and manufacturers, who as in England and everywhere else had to be pushed and prodded into power. 'Bourgeois revolution' is a phrase which obscures more than it illuminates. As Gramsci says, these Jacobins 'literally "imposed" themselves on the French bourgeoisie, leading it into a far more advanced position than the originally strongest bourgeois nuclei would have spontaneously wished to take up', even though in the end they could not transcend the limits of the bourgeois dispensation. He adds a sparkling comment on the international factors that help to mould national tendencies: 'The Jacobin spirit, audacious, dauntless, is certainly related to the hegemony exercised for so long by France in Europe' (p. 84).

Seeking to calibrate history's two scales, one recording the accumulation of combustible materials, the other the human endeavour needed to supply the spark, Gramsci often turned to survey the Italian national movement. He might well have recalled in this context his remark about French hegemony and Jacobin daring. Italian artists and musicians dazzled Europe for centuries, but Italy – like Germany – was insignificant; whereas Jacobinism owed a great deal to its homeland's political and military, as well as intellectual pre-eminence. Without Louis XIV and Turenne and Fontenoy there would have been no Jacobins in France to chop off the head of Louis XIV's descendant, but only the sort of 'ideologues' or armchair reformers whom Bismarck was able comfortably to despise in Germany, or Cavour in Italy, with a sprinkling of men like Mazzini brave enough to risk their own lives but not audacious enough to summon the people to arms. Or – to look back another century – there would have been no regicides to chop off Charles I's head if Elizabeth and her sea-captains and Britain's *terrible surges* had not routed the Invincible Armada.

Gramsci effectively criticizes Mazzini and the party of action for failing to emulate the combination of urban and rural mass energies which he regards as central to Jacobin strategy, and which he thinks can be detected in Machiavelli's calculations too.[15] At another point he writes, somewhat contradictorily, that no Jacobin party grew up in Italy because the bourgeoisie was economically unready – but also that the bourgeoisie 'could not for subjective rather than objective reasons' draw the masses behind it – yet that 'Action directed at the peasantry was certainly always possible' (p. 82). Cavour as spokesman of the bourgeoisie, and himself both capitalist and landowner, may have felt by an intuition correct at any rate with reference to the early stages of industrialism, that a poor, subjugated peasantry was preferable to an emancipated one like that of France. The Jacobins were not after all trying to build industrial capitalism, and this developed after their revolution only very haltingly. Still, the distinction between the objective and subjective capabilities of a class which becomes a candidate for hegemony is important. In France the bourgeoisie *could* have got rid of the monarchy far earlier, in Britain the working class *could* have got rid of capitalism long ago. It seems curious to find Gramsci saying that 'The so-called subjective conditions can never be missing when the objective conditions exist' (p. 113), which suggests the one mechanically accompanying the other. We are nearer to his true opinion when he writes that there are times when a certain development may, but need not, occur, and the outcome 'depends to a great extent on the existence of individuals of exceptional will-power' (p. 152). But we are left to ask whether these situations are common enough to make historical 'laws' at best very approximate, and how the leader at the time or the historian later on can be sure that an opportunity has been missed or not.

At all events, any triumph is the outcome of subterranean changes long at work, or what Gramsci often dwells on as the *molecular* process going on in people's minds. We can only dig coal up because geology has slowly laid it down. Mazzini's insurrectionist tactics were bound to fail, in Gramsci's view, because they were not preceded by 'the "diffused" and capillary form of indirect pressure . . . long ideological and political preparation' (p. 110). Transforming influences, operating slowly or less slowly but always obscurely, set limits, more directly than the material condition of society, to what action initiated by resolute groups can achieve. In communities which are pioneering a new path, as Britain was during its Industrial Revolution, conscious adjustment to a new epoch lags behind the material facts; in communities seeking to repeat what others have already done, as in Africa today, awareness may travel far ahead of them. In either case the task of speeding molecular change, in other words the teasing of ideas out of the tangle of experience, and the conversion to these ideas of other minds, is crucial; and it is impeded by manifold safety devices that history has implanted in our minds to keep them from conscious recognition that the world is not as our elders and betters have told us.

History's great men appear to – or pretend to – bestride their narrow world and impose their own laws on it. Gramsci was elaborating one of Marx's ideas when he wrote of 'Caesarism' as arising when political forces balance each other 'in a catastrophic manner' – in such a manner that further competition must destroy both. It was capable of some varying degree of progressiveness; Caesar and Napoleon were progressive, Napoleon III and Bismarck reactionary (p. 219). Gramsci does allow that Napoleon III represented some energies still latent within the existing order (pp. 221–2). Both he and Bismarck did much, in fact, to forward industrialization; though with all this quartet their imperialistic proclivities have to be set on the debit side. Gramsci makes another significant point, that the rival forces held in check by Caesar or Napoleon were not too far apart to be able to amalgamate, 'after a molecular process', later on

(p. 221). Here this phrase covers the development of common social and financial interests, promoted by intermarriage, between an old and a new ruling class, such as took place in England after the Restoration. It could happen the more easily because in Rome, England, France, there was always differentiation within the earlier ruling order between older and newer nobility, blue-blooded aristocrat and parvenu; so that the gap between the old order and its successor was only one of degree.

Inclusion of a Ramsay Macdonald in the category of Caesarism (p. 220) is one of those odd-looking quirks that are to be found in the *Notebooks*. England's contemporary situation was a very different one, and Caesarism without a heroic or pseudo-heroic figure seems out of court. But our century has had many plausible aspirants, with Gramsci's antagonist Mussolini in the van. They have been imitators, approaching their hero Napoleon only in destructiveness, yet representing none the less a portentous new devepment. Claiming to stand above the contest of haves and have-nots, they were aping the Napoleonic pose, impartially above both aristocracy and bourgeoisie, while in reality exercising a dictatorship of the haves against the have-nots. Marxism was slow to take the measure of Fascism after 1918, and has been slow ever since in providing a satisfactory analysis of it. Marxists have indeed seen the basic class situation, whereas most other historians have been obstinately unable to see the wood for the trees; but they have not on the whole seen very much else of a very complex phenomenon. As devious historical combinations are required to bring about regression as to produce progress.

Gramsci meditated in prison on Fascism; his tentative reflections do not neglect the complexity of things, and still deserve attention. But the Fascism he knew was only a fore-sketch of the real thing, Nazism. In Italy the relative weight of archaic social elements was much greater, and hindered Fascism from being either as innovatory and successful, or as monstrous, as in Germany. Gramsci was inclined to think that it was not the deliberate choice of the capitalists, who were seduced into it by their feudal landlord allies.[16] They had to seek ways of restoring their ascendancy after the First World War, but they were not really confronted by any class capable of ousting them (p. 228). In Germany a decade later a bigger capitalist class faced a deeper economic crisis and a better-prepared left-wing challenge, with the now much stronger Soviet Union in the background. Here therefore the old ruling groups had to go much further in adapting themselves to the requirements of Fascism as a torrential movement of demagogy, and the outcome was a regime incomparably more potent.

Gramsci is thinking transparently of Mussolini when he writes that leadership by 'inspired' individuals only suits times of emergency, when critical faculties are submerged: they can originate nothing with any 'long-term and organic character', their true function is to give the reigning powers a breathing-space, a period of 'restoration and reorganisation' (p. 130). Like others of his political concepts, Gramsci's idea of 'restoration' periods is subtle, and not always clear. It meant much to him because he thought of Italy as passing through such a time. A crisis may last for decades, he says, while an old order strives to pull itself together, and in the end the necessity of its supersession will only be demonstrated 'if the forces of opposition triumph' (p. 178). This is another of his hard sayings. Was the right to survive of tsarism vindicated by its overcoming the Revolution of 1905? Or that of Prussian militarism by Bismarck's defeat of the Liberals? In any single arena the ratio of forces will depend on local circumstances, though what is at stake may have a far more than local importance. In Germany the forces of opposition have never triumphed. Yet the national structure has been vastly modified. Bismarckian Germany is indeed the classic example of how one type of 'restoration' in Gramsci's sense works, providing 'sufficiently elastic frameworks to allow the bourgeoisie to gain power without dramatic upheavals' (p. 115). Despite Liberal timidity change went ahead, thanks to the novel factor introduced by industrialism, which has brought in technology as the fourth player at every table. Conservatism could not keep things standing still, if only because of the requirements of its own military machine. History advanced crabwise, or as they say on Wall Street *sideways*.

In a case like this 'molecular change' is clearly involved. It is difficult not to associate it also with another recurrent theorem of Gramsci's, which sometimes appears along with it (for example, p. 109) – that of 'passive revolution'. This it must be confessed is exceptionally puzzling, because he does not use the term regularly to denote what the words suggest: radical change brought about by indirect pressure of circumstances instead of by assault. Gramsci borrowed it from his early nineteenth-century countryman Cuoco, who meant by it something oddly different from this: an attempt at revolution as at Naples in 1799 by an elitist group without local roots or means of winning mass support.[17] For this some adjective like 'exotic' seems more appropriate. Gramsci attaches the label of 'passive revolution' to Gandhi's tactics in the Indian national movement (p. 107), but oftenest and most comprehensibly to those of Cavour in the Italian. (In Cuoco's sense it would better fit Mazzini's.) Tactics like Cavour's could obviously not be a model for socialists in any position. Yet their position now, as it appeared to Gramsci, had something in common with that of the Italian patriots blocked by the immovable obstacle of the Austrian army.

At some point quite soon after 1917 repetition of the Russian Revolution further west became, in anything like the same form, an impossibility. Gramsci believed that Lenin before his death was coming to accept this as a fact, while Trotsky continued to be 'the political theorist of frontal attack in a period in which it only leads to defeats' (pp. 237–8). Gramsci was fond of discussing military matters, such as trench warfare in the Great War, and he did not forget that 'Every political struggle always has a military substratum'; though he reminded himself that political and military reasoning must not be jumbled up (pp. 230–1). But he may have been choosing words for the benefit of the censor when he spoke of the turn from revolutionism in the style of 1917 to something different as a transition from 'war of manoeuvre' to 'war of positions'. He looked upon it as 'the most important question of political theory that the post-war period has posed' (pp. 237–8). Also, of course, of political practice. Hoping against hope, it may well be, he tried to see the 'war of positions' not as relinquishment of revolutionary struggle but as its culminating and most intense phase, with the old order concentrating all its resources for a final desperate resistance (pp. 238–9). But this was to underestimate very gravely the solidity and permanence of Fascism and the popular assent it could command. Neither in Italy nor anywhere else was it destined to be overthrown from within. Some painful inkling of this was bound to visit Gramsci's mind as the prison years came and went. He fell back on conjectures about Fascism as a new type of 'restoration', which might represent, in however distorted a manner, a kind of progress – even a kind of 'passive revolution'.

It might not, he wrote, turn out to be 'entirely reactionary'; it was at least shaking up an ossified state (p. 223). He thought it implied some real turning against the old order 'with all its train of parasites', under compulsion of 'problems which are disturbing the old European bone-structure' (p. 287). Italy like Germany had been inducted into the capitalist era by foreign war instead of by class conflict, without any true bourgeois revolution; hence much lumber from the past still littered the ground, and we looking back may agree that it was part of the 'mission' of Fascism to clear away some of it, in order to carry out its main task of exorcizing socialism, by seeming to provide an alternative path of reform. Gramsci expected the modernizing tendency to include expansion of industry, urged on and directed by the state (p. 115). He counted on the weight of a United

States industrially as far ahead of Europe as intellectually it was behind, to help to compel Europe, and Italy in particular, 'to overturn its excessively antiquated economic and social basis' (p. 317). 'Fordism' intrigued him because he saw it as an effort, inescapable for any modern society, 'to achieve the organisation of a planned society' (p. 279).

All this line of thought led towards an idea which Gramsci took from Vico, and frequently returned to: the idea of things sometimes happening through a 'ruse of providence', a situation bringing about what has to be brought about despite the wishes of those who thought themselves its masters (for example, p. 293). It is an idea well worth pondering in many connections, though patently it could lend itself, just as much as Bordiga's determinism, to a habit of waiting for history to do our work for us like a robot. We may link it with another problematical question, that of *error*, to which makers of history have been as liable as its writers. That leaders fall into many mistakes can only be doubted, Gramsci declares, by mechanical materialism, which 'assumes that every political act is determined, immediately, by the structure' (p. 408; cf. p. 399). We may be compelled to go further than this, and recollect the profound dictum of Engels that what emerges in history is something willed by none of the participants, but the product of all their conflicting wills. Error, it follows, is universal. Even when a goal is proposed and reached, those who reach it have only dimly been able to foresee the consequences of their success. Bismarck made history with more apparent success than almost any leader of modern times, but the Germany he created was not the Germany he desired. Lenin made his Revolution in order to throw a torch into the powder-magazine of Europe, whose powder proved too damp to ignite. What he achieved, and the most that any drastic action can achieve whether in public or in private life, was to bring about a new situation, a new complex of relationships, in which a variety of new possibilities emerged. Mankind's sense of the tragic lies close to this disparity between intention and consequence. What makes tragedy is not failure in action, but the impossibility of foreseeing its results, so that every tragedy is a tragedy of errors; and if tragic drama ends on a note of acceptance, of turning away from past to future, this only epitomizes human experience that through storms and stresses, the strife of wills and its unguessable outcome, new beginnings are at last reached.

In modern times what has hampered guidance of events in a progressive direction is not any omnipotence of material forces, but the reverse – their not being powerful enough to overcome the inertia of men's minds. They push modern man towards socialism, antiquated ideas hold him back. Gramsci expresses this by saying that 'mass ideological factors always lag behind mass economic pheno-mena', and act as a drag on their impetus (p. 168). It may seem to follow as a gloomy consequence that the time for radical social reconstruction never arrives, because when the material conditions are right the mood is not yet ready, and while it is getting ready the possessors of power are at leisure to prepare to deal with it. What is called for, then, is an acceleration of thought, a more rapid spread of ideas, enabling them to keep up with the facts of collective life instead of lagging behind them. Invention of printing brought about such an acceleration, and with it the Reformation, before conservatism had time to rub its eyes and get ready its Index Librorum Prohibitorum and all the rest of its entrenchments. Newspapers had a like influence at first, before they were brought firmly under conservative control, as all later means of communication have been from the start.

Gramsci fixed his hopes, in this regard, on the intelligentsia, but an intelligentsia of a new type. In all his vista of history the intellectual had a very important place. There are times when his estimate of leading thinkers, as well as of political leaders, almost makes him a subscriber to the 'Great Man' theory of history; when for instance he speaks of 'those thousands or hundreds or even dozens of scholars of the highest quality which are necessary to every civilisation' (p. 37). To intellectuals collectively he gives a stature which comes out in a casual remark that the working class cannot build socialism without enlisting the support of the majority of them and of the peasantry[18] – these two bracketed as equally indispensable. It is better, he writes, to start peasant movements through intellectuals than to let them start spontaneously (pp. 74–5). He wonders whether educated Negroes from the United States might go back to Africa and transform it (p. 21): this has not happened, but students returning to Africa from European colleges have done a great deal towards its transformation, as some are doing today through the revolutionary movements in the Portuguese colonies. He considers that for various reasons French intellectuals stand closer to the public, and make more effort to advise it, than in most countries (p. 421).

Intellectuals not anchored to any class, he observes, instinctively think of the state as an absolute (p. 117); and because they take part in so many of its activities, 'Many intellectuals think that they *are* the State' (p. 16). But today they are detaching themselves from allegiance to the state they have helped to erect, and are thereby 'marking and ratifying the crisis of the State in its decisive form' (words at least as true now as then) – but they have no organization of their own to fall back on, such as in the Middle Ages they possessed in the Church. He thinks therefore that the international union of intellectuals proposed by Croce at an Oxford meeting 'undeniably might become an important party with a considerable role to play' (p. 270). He would expect Italians to respond to such a call, for he frequently discusses their traditionally cosmopolitan outlook, the result of Italy's political fragmentation, which it in turn helped to perpetuate (for example, pp. 17–18). One might say much the same of Germany, which became the homeland of modern philosophy and socialism. Gramsci notes that the Kantian ethic was 'linked to the philosophy of the intellectuals as a cosmopolitan stratum' (p. 374). That eighteenth-century mentality was in many ways superior to the nationalism which usurped its place, and socialism has had the duty of keeping it alive. By Gramsci's day intellectuals who were still identifying themselves with the nation-state were being dragged down with it in its decline, or its diseased hypertrophy, into pessimism, or Fascism.

Gramsci has a wealth of instructive footnotes on the intelligentsia in history, principally in Italy. 'Southern Italy is an area of extreme social disintegration', he tells us, and this stratifies the educated as well as the peasantry: there have been leaders of thought — individuals or groups — as there are big estates, but no 'average culture'.[19] Referring to the conferences that helped to enrol men of letters in the Risorgimento, he remarks that 'through spirit of caste' the lower grades of an intelligentsia tend to follow the lead of their superiors (p. 104) – which might be said also of a feudal hierarchy, or that of modern business where the petty trader takes a cue from the multi-director. There are frequent allusions to the religious species of scholar. Churches, notably the Roman Catholic, keep their intellectuals under watch and ward, for fear of their intellectualizing the common people.[20] Following this hint we can account for the scholastic straw-threshing which has so largely occupied the clerisy of all religions, a harmless outlet for mental energies forbidden any serious use. All through history society has taken at least as many pains to prevent its intellectuals from thinking too much, as to train them to think.

Quite often Gramsci may be open to a charge of supposing that the hand that fills the inkpot rules the world. This would, all the same, be a travesty of his position, which is that ideas can be everything when fused with objective forces, nothing by themselves. Every philosophy, he surmises, has addressed itself in one way or other to the problem of theory and practice and how to combine them, most obsessively in periods of rapid change (pp. 364–5). Nowadays cerebration for its own sake has come to be seen as futile (p. 350). Abstract ideas are mere moonshine, 'typical of pure intellectuals (or pure asses)' (p. 189). They blossom in minds cut off from the universe of ordinary people, so that knowing is divorced from feeling: (the intellectual can reach true 'understanding' only when he enters into the problems of the people, and feels them as his own (p. 418). The identity, or the common roots, of authentic thinking and social feeling is a principle deeply ingrained in Gramsci, himself a born scholar yet also a man of action.

But if it is only morbid social arrangements that have pushed the two things apart, it must be admitted that not much has been done as yet towards reconciling them. Minerva's owl has continued to fly only after dark; action in history has been blindly emotional or instinctual – thought has been solitary, enabling individuals partially to understand what masses of people before them have done, not what people are doing now or why they themselves are thinking as they do. Gramsci's way out of this dilemma is the fusing or interweaving of the two processes which he calls 'creative philosophy', or purposeful thinking impelled by will – 'a rational, not an arbitrary will' bounded that is by objective conditions yet possessing a relative freedom by virtue of which it 'modifies the way of feeling of the many and consequently reality itself' (pp. 345–6).

In all this range of comment Gramsci has been discussing the intelligentsia more or less as traditionally viewed, with prominence given to humane letters and philosophy, or any broad interests distinct from contracted specialism. This has been the mainstream of learning and thought of the less utilitarian cast, where concern over human destinies, or what might be called social eschatology, had been chiefly found. It is here too that most would look for the element of disequilibrium, the faculty of mutation, needed to start new currents. This traditional intelligentsia has been from several points of view a distinct 'class' or 'estate'. What Gramsci says of its often cosmopolitan outlook, and its collective importance, seems to bear this out.

Yet when he comes to grapple with the practical issue of the progressive intellectual's place in the strife of present-day society, Gramsci draws a very different picture. He denies any corporate self to the intelligentsia, any continuity. Each fresh epoch, he asserts, throws up its own intellectuals. There has been more continuity than this allows, even though Gramsci is certainly right to expose the intellectuals' fond illusion of themselves as an uncommitted body, 'independent of the struggle of groups' (p. 113). He makes another acceptable statement when he says that those representing the most progressive class draw the others along with them, and so 'create a system of solidarity' among them all (p. 60). This is what took place in the Enlightenment of the eighteenth century: it has not yet taken place in the twentieth, as Gramsci had hoped to see it doing, with Marxism in the lead. But on the contemporary scene Gramsci's emphasis is all on the fragmentation or dispersedness of intellectuals. Instead of their forming any sort of corporation, every section of a complex modern society necessarily develops a specialized intelligentsia of its own.[21]

There is a great deal of obvious truth in this view. A Prussian staff officer was an intellectual in his way, suffering perhaps with all such artificial, inbred types from a streak of morbidity. On the other hand a technician helping to construct bombs is putting his mind to purely manipulative uses. A racing tipster lives by his wits, not his hands, and may qualify as an intellectual if the line is drawn liberally enough. Gramsci broadens the term to include some unexpected meanings. He regards the old aristocracies, kept on as political managers in England or Germany, as the 'intellectuals' of the bourgeoisie (p. 83). He includes bureaucrats, the swarm infesting southern Italy for instance, though down there his chief type of intellectual is 'the pettifogging lawyer', intermediary between peasantry and landlord or state. In the north he includes the factory technician or overseer (pp. 93–4), and all members of any party – paradox though this, as he admits, must sound – are to be reckoned as intellectuals (p. 16). It is through their brains that a class thinks. We may acknowledge that, in so far as conservatism in England can be said to think, it is the Tory Party through which it performs this uncongenial operation, and that even a Tory MP may shine mentally by comparison with most of those who sit on the constituency platforms.

On the Left, in his Italy, Gramsci saw a very practical need for a well-grown intelligentsia, as vital for engineering an alliance between working class and peasantry.[22] It may always, in fact, be among its crucial functions to enable a working class to form alliances with other classes, and emerge from isolation. Intellectuals can or should be able to perform this, Gramsci holds, because the Marxist party enables them to ally themselves with the working class, and so escape from their own isolation. State service cannot bring them into genuine contact with the people; they find this through the party, where they merge with what Gramsci calls the organic intellectuals of the working class. The horizon he sets before them widely different from the old-fashioned duty of a progressive intellectual – to give the people good advice from his own higher level. It was in that older spirit that Shelley's Irish pamphlet of 1812 put out 'Proposals for an association' of men of liberal education and views who would join to give common folk the guidance they so sadly lacked during the French Revolution. As a latter-day caricature of this we have the story of Gramsci's humorous indignation at a young professor expatiating on his noble resolve to help, instruct and direct the workers *gratis*.[23] Gramsci wants intellectuals to integrate themselves with the workers. They cannot do so, he sees, indiscriminately, with the whole mass, only with fellow intellectuals from within its ranks. These are, in the first place, working-class members of the party. They should be more than merely honorary or ex officio intellectuals. They are to be 'cadres of intellectuals of a new type', with the responsibility of raising the mental activity of the entire class, 'giving personality to the amorphous element of the masses.'[24]

But intellectuals who – like Gramsci himself – join them from outside will always, or for very long, be indispensable, because the formation of this 'new type' will be a very arduous undertaking. Peasants, he remarks, produce no intelligentsia of their own, though they supply many individual intellectuals to other classes,[25] and he appears to take for granted that they can never do so. Even in the most favourable conditions it is a hard enough thing to rear intellectuals: they 'develop slowly, much more slowly than any other social group, because of their own nature and historical rôle'. For the proletariat, which he regards as 'poor in organising elements', the task will be very arduous.[26] It will have to learn to develop intellectuals of all levels, 'including those capable of the highest degree of specialisation', and it has not yet acquired the needful adaptation, mental and physical, to learning (p. 43). With his own experience in mind Gramsci never underrates the sheer grind of learning, and its rigours and strains. These rigours help indeed to explain why intellectual activity has always been so largely a hereditary profession, and why its practitioners have always been looked on by 'normal' people as freaks. By comparison with these hurdles Gramsci seems to feel very few misgivings about whether working-class intellectuals are likely to keep their allegiance to their own class and its party, or will use their new wings to fly away to other perches.

Gramsci's vision – the birth of a labour intelligentsia, instead of (revealingly feudal English phrase) an *aristocracy* of labour – was a splendid one. That its realization would be 'a long and difficult' task,[27] he saw more and more clearly; and this meant that the road leading to a socialist society would be also long and difficult, beyond the strength of a working class in its old shape with no more than elemental weight of numbers to rely on. Before becoming able to make a new society it must first set about remaking itself, and discovering its allies. Another four decades of West European experience have confirmed the lesson. It was to this toilsome sluggishness of the historical movement that Gramsci was painfully accustoming his mind as he toiled on in his solitary cell, while Fascism covered Italy with the grandiose monuments whose grandiloquent inscriptions about the 'Sounding Wheels of History' still vacuously confront the tourist.

Postscript

Gramsci's writings are very discontinuous, though only more so than some of Marx's. In its present condition Marxist thinking in general has a similar quality. This may do good by stimulating efforts to fill gaps, and little harm so long as Marxist navigators are steering by the same compass. This can only be depended on while there is enough political magnetism in the ether. Lenin's Third International, which soon became Stalin's, was intended to ensure this by organizing a coherent political movement, ready with guide-lines for socialists of all the five continents. It was a brave ambition, but problems were too intricate and shifting for any 'general staff of the Revolution', such as Engels was proud to style himself in the hopeful early days of the Second International, to cope with effectively.

It was all the more incumbent on Marxist theory to preserve a unity of outlook that exigencies of practical politics could not. Official doctrine everywhere did indeed maintain an unbroken front, like a Saxon battle-line facing the enemy with shields locked each to each. But there was need of ideas both genuinely Marxist and creative, instead of mere repetitions of old ones, and of new ideas the Comintern was always suspicious. Bukharin at Moscow was critical of the national parties for their weakness in Marxist theory; Gramsci in prison in Italy was critical of Bukharin's textbook. These two men's ways of thinking were symptomatic of divergences inescapable in a world movement; nowadays they have a counterpart in discords within the still more monolithic Catholic Church.

A generation later, awareness of a still-spreading lack of uniformity among Marxists must have helped to inspire Althusser's attempt at a regular schema or scientific chart for their guidance. Its failure to maintain its ground may suggest anew that Marxism cannot be reduced to a set of ten, twenty, or any other number of rules, or that this will be impossible at least until after the main conflicts of the age that gave birth to it have been resolved. People will then be able to look back on them from the vantage-ground of a new era, of whose inheritance of ideas Marxism will have bequeathed an important part. There is justification here for the preference of British Marxism for concrete history over abstract philosophy.

Gramsci was orthodox enough in his emphasis on class, and on the action of the masses on events. There is a warning against a fashion of today, of 'quantifying' history or turning it into statistics and graphs and computer models, in his dictum that statistics can only be substituted for real, all-round history so long as the People is inactive. True, it may appear to have been inactive most of the time, but only when we forget the multiplicity of small-scale local struggles, many of them unrecorded. To Gramsci the past and its doings meant all the more because he was so soon cut off from the present. But it has been observed that the Italian Party's theses drawn up under his guidance in 1926 go into the background of the country's economic and political life with 'a historical thoroughness for which there is scarcely a parallel in the programs of other parties'. [28]

A crucial problem for him, as for many of his successors, was the relationship to be hoped and worked for between the working class, as the battering-ram of progress, and other classes with a progressive potential. If we agree with him that Marxist theory must learn from all other modes of thinking, without losing hold of what is essential in its own, we may likewise conclude that practical socialism must know how to collaborate with other movements, without sacrificing its identity. Popular Front tactics were being adopted by the Comintern, in face of the Fascist menace, not long before Gramsci's death, too late to be as effective as they might have been, and not always with much skill.

Gramsci like Marx was fully alive to the significance of the individual, whom he thought of not as a billiard-ball, or self-contained unit, but as the sum of an interweaving of social relationships. From a traditionalist standpoint, formed by the Christian concept of the self or soul as individual possession and responsibility, this may seem to deprive him of reality, somewhat as Buddhist metaphysics dissolved the self into elements not belonging intrinsically to any 'I'. An isolated self is what we each feel ourselves unalterably to be. We ought rather perhaps to see the self as a hibernating creature, or desert seed awaiting moisture and the touch of life. In passivity it consists of inert memories derived from bygone experiences; in activity it shows itself as a complex of relationships and influences, vital and stirring; not a simple cumulation of these, but a unique confluence of them in the setting of the individual's whole past and inherited being.

Gramsci's estimate of the duties of political leadership was a very high one. More habitually he was concerned with intellectual leadership. If an intelligentsia can in some respects approximate to a class, it differs from others in the degree to which its members are individualistically self-conscious, a degree often infuriating to a practical man like Lenin. Ideas may be in the air, as an exhalation of the social climate, but to extract them from the atmosphere and make them available there must be individual minds receptive enough to catch them. Gramsci could reckon on factory foremen as 'intellectuals', because they did not work with their hands, but he evidently thought of a widely graduated scale, as his allusion to the need for first-rate scholars indicates.

Welcoming Croce's call for an international association of intellectuals, Gramsci held that many of them were detaching themselves from the disintegrating modern state, and that this was of 'incalculable historical significance'.[29] Since then the state may have seemed to revive, but most stridently in Fascist guise, which has discredited it further; its inner vitality, even with the help of welfare policies, can scarcely be said to have recovered. Morally though not externally, the withering away of the state foretold by Marx is already well advanced.

3

State and Nation in Western Europe

In the seventeenth century there began that diffusion of ideas and technology from a corner of north-western Europe which is still continuing. Before that date, this decisive area may be seen gradually condensing or crystallizing out of Europe as a whole, or advancing further from a common starting-point. A more or less amorphous earlier medieval Christendom changed by the end of the Middle Ages into a continent where the western lands, primarily those of the Atlantic seaboard, were in the lead. Within another century or two the southern part of this region had dropped out, as Spain and Portugal sank into hopeless decadence, and the northern area – corresponding fairly closely with the one dominated or most strongly affected by Protestantism in its more active forms – went far ahead. This is how it has come about that in nine contexts out of ten today, when the world talks of something as 'European', it means something that originated in this one small area, or growing-point, of Europe. The immense significance for good and evil of this area to the whole human race is in some danger nowadays of being obscured by the pressure, in itself extremely desirable, towards recognition of the political rights and cultural achievements of all peoples everywhere.[1] All men are equal; but only a spurious egalitarianism can reduce the share of all earth's regions in its grand historical advance to one and the same flat level.

Among the various components making up the unique amalgam of modern north-western Europe, none was more important than its political component, the loosely named 'nation-state'. Of the two elements included here, it was the state that came first and fashioned the mould for the nation – but a state, or political organization of society, of a kind distinct from any other in history. What specific factors, then, went to form the west-European state in such a way as to enable, or compel, it at a certain stage to translate the vague sensation of nationality, recognizable in one degree or another in old Persia or China as well, into conscious nationalism? Neither economic nor ideological influences can by themselves explain the appearance of this political mutant; gunpowder, one of its fairy godmothers, was present also at the cradle of the radically different Ottoman State.

Absolute monarchies were, as Kohn says, 'the pacemakers of modern nationalism'.[2] It was a state built in their image whose towering shape so impressed itself on the generations living in its shadow: the Leviathan of Hobbes, the irresistible power with which Shakespeare's Menenius tries to overawe the rebellious citizenry

> . . . whose course will on
> The way it takes, cracking ten thousand curbs
> Of more strong link asunder than can ever
> Appear in your impediment.

But in the East, monarchies equally or more despotic were always ten a dinar. A state can be of real significance, can act in some degree formatively on the society over which it presides, only when it becomes something more than a man or men exercising personal authority, however acquired. It must possess an existence and a continuity of its own, and therefore a fairly complex machinery of administration, distinguishable from a mere swarm of palace flunkeys and flatterers. Monarchy does not easily rise to this level, though it may be most likely to do so when it starts from humble beginnings and has to work its way up – as it did in western Europe, by contrast with the Islamic lands where rulers had from the outset a ready-made, invariable tradition of theocratic authority to step into.

Absolute monarchy in the West grew out of feudal monarchy of a particular sort, corresponding to a particular sort of feudal society. Most historians interested in the classification of societies are Marxist, and these have been much more concerned to stress common denominators among pre-capitalist economics than to observe divergences in other respects. This has led towards a concept of feudalism so extremely generalized as to be of limited utility.[3] It is true and important that both mice and rhinoceroses are mammalian quadrupeds, but that is not the end of the matter. In terms of patterns of social life, and capacity for growth and change, the differences between the 'feudalism' of France, Bengal, Bokhara, Zululand, are enormous.

A rough general distinction may be drawn between feudalism (in an institutional sense) growing up 'naturally' from below, or planted from above. West-European feudalism seems to belong in the main to the former type. Peering with due caution into the mists of time and expert witness, one may associate this fact with the long Dark-Age struggle of its region of origin against the pressure of worse barbarism from outside. Whereas feudal military complexes elsewhere took shape habitually in and for movements of conquest, here the function was, in some considerable measure, defence rather than, or along with, expansion. For centuries the struggle was carried on mainly with local resources, and this was possible because the attackers came in small bands, not in the sudden irruptions of whole peoples that were endemic in Asian history – clans united by war-leaders like Genghis into primitive 'nations', irresistible before firearms were well developed. To strike a balance for any ruling class between its prime business of exploitation and its secondary – protective and organizing – role, is a delicate matter: but the west-European ruling class was somewhat less parasitical than many others. It made for social solidarity also that the alien assailants were regularly pagan, while the defenders, high and low, belonged to one exclusive faith. More often than not, by comparison, the barbarians who continually attacked Islamic civilizations were Muslims from the waste places,[4] or fresh converts – Turk, Mongol, African – more zealous for the faith than the faithful themselves.

In the West some rude integration of society came to bind together all classes, and each manor might be seen as a miniature state with its own 'custom' or unwritten law.[5] This integration extended upwards to the monarch, as well as downwards to the peasant. But monarchs had to cope with a ruling class firmly entrenched in a territorial power which it did not as a rule owe to them. Typical of it were the great nobles of Aragon who called themselves *ricoshombres de natura*, noblemen by intrinsic quality and not by royal creation;[6] and it was no great extension of this to claim, as all Aragonese nobles did, the right of *desnaturalización*, withdrawal of allegiance from a sovereign who displeased them. By contrast, the Muslim equivalent of knight or baron was the Ottoman *timariot* or the Mogul *jagirdar*, holding an assignment, temporary at least in principle, of land, or more exactly of land-revenue, in return for his services;[7] and it was seldom that the ruler was confronted by an aristocracy with an independent basis, except when a regime was as far gone in decay as the Mogul empire after Aurangzeb.[8] The military-feudal organization of the Mameluke State in medieval Egypt and Syria[9] must have owed much to imitation of the Franks. In the West it was very largely in the course of long efforts to assert themselves against their baronage that kings constructed an administrative and coercive apparatus of their own. Friction between ruler and ruling class is something distinct from friction between these two combined and the masses at whose expense they live; and, viewed as a stimulus to political evolution, a healthier as well as less primitive one, productive of greater sophistication of method and outlook. Such an experiment as that of the Norman kings in England of maintaining a Saxon militia as a counterweight to their own nobility would be hard to imagine in most other regions, where strict dichotomy between 'active' and 'passive' citizens – in the language of 1789 – was the norm.[10]

Conversely the baronage was in a fashion a useful buffer between ruler and ordinary people. Winwood Reade's no doubt too-sweeping censure of the political infantilism of the East culminated in the charge that '*Property is insecure*. In this one phrase the whole history of Asia is contained'.[11] From this general insecurity of property western Europe was saved by the solidity of feudal property in land, the corner-stone of all property; and with this, it was saved also, as time went on, from Asia's accompanying insecurity of all other rights, including that of life.[12] As one consequence, European justice was more fully embodied in laws, which might on occasion be harsher than Eastern usage or equity, but were at least fixed and precise, and less dependent on the capricious honesty or benevolence of a magistrate.[13] The resulting growth of a body of professional lawyers was one of the characteristic singularities of western Europe, and has been a weighty factor in its political evolution down to our own day.

Another feature of the west-European situation was the emergence of a congeries of states, in close contact and claiming the same status. Geography helped here; the sea spreads round and into western Europe (as it does also with eastern China and Japan, the two most solid political entities in Asian history) and, besides facilitating trade, provided rough-and-ready 'natural frontiers'. Such a coexistence of more or less equal and stable units, with competition among them accelerating growth and change, is quite a rarity in history at any level above that of city-state or Highland clan. Both Rome and China, once mature, suffered from the absence of any comparable neighbour or rival. Among the scattered valleys and oases of Islam there could be little contiguity of independent powers;[14] the political idea did not escape from a vague religious universalism, and except for Turkey, with its European involvements, there was no real state because there were no states.

The transmutation of any kind of feudal society into any kind of modern state would be impossible to explain if there had been no other ingredients. One such was the Church. If the feudalism of western Europe was unique, so even more markedly was the medieval Church; a highly centralized, disciplined, monopolistic corporation, with an intense *esprit de corps* of its own, which had grown up inside the bureaucratic empire of Rome and still preserved its hierarchical cast. Paradoxically the presence of this body, which often collided with and seemed to injure the feudal state, in the long run, and by a complex process of interaction, doubled and trebled its strength. The absence alike from China, from India, from Islam, of a Church of this order, and therefore of any similar conflict and interplay of Church and state,[15] is of an importance that can scarcely be overestimated in any study of why western Europe was drawing apart from the rest of the world.

Equally specific to Europe was the city: the city, that is, as *civitas*, a body politic, wholly or partially autonomous, with its own political life, memory and habits − the city-state of antiquity surviving or reborn after the disappearance of the Roman Empire. Asiatic monarchy did not by any means prohibit towns, trade and urban commodity production; on the contrary, the earliest European travellers in the Far East were astounded by its numerous and immense cities,[16] while Muslim civilization has always been far more urban than rural.[17] But the town in Asia was politically neuter, part of the feudal-bureaucratic establishment. Over it stood not bishop or baron, but theocratic monarchy, and it felt no impulse towards a demand for self-government.[18] In medieval Europe this impulse was powerful enough to make the towns fight their way into political existence through centuries of heroic struggle. The often-repeated phrase about their 'existing in the interstices of feudalism' may be correct enough in statistical and economic terms. But it does no sort of justice to this struggle, one of world history's genuine epics, or to the human faculties and aptitudes it engendered; and it misses the significance of the towns as an alien, active leaven in the inert feudal mass.[19] Their grand contribution to the slowly forming amalgam of the west-European state was less economic than moral, intellectual and political.

It was not on the western rim of Europe that urban independence blossomed most fully. From Spain to Scotland, the early growth of fairly strong feudal monarchies prevented towns from acquiring complete independence, while it allowed and stimulated them to struggle for their rights within the feudal kingdoms. In east Europe the town tended to be a garrison centre or colony planted by monarchs, dependent on them and often too alien in speech and character from the surrounding population to interact fruitfully with it. It was in between these two zones – in northern Italy, western Germany, the Netherlands, the Baltic – that the town had its freest evolution: in Germany separating itself fully from the neighbouring principalities, in Italy actually bringing the nobility under its control and becoming the dominant political entity. But, great as the commercial and cultural achievements of these city-states were, politically they were in a blind alley. The Hanseatic League, the Lombard League – like the *Hermandad* or Brotherhood of the Basque ports[20] – could not grow into genuine federations. Italian cities turned into petty monarchies, partly because of the disturbing aristocratic element they absorbed; but these were precarious, unstable despotisms, with no national character. Venice and Genoa remained republics, but devoted themselves to building up little empires, mostly outside Italy and likewise incapable of evolving into 'nations'. Only in the Netherlands, marked off from the Holy Roman Empire at large by greater economic activity and closer involvement with the affairs of adjacent countries, was the necessary amalgam of urban and feudal elements consolidated, first by the fifteenth-century Burgundian overlordship and then by the four decades of struggle against Spanish domination.[21]

During the later Middle Ages all sorts of interactions and intermediate forms between urban and feudal can be recognized; and these mutual influences were not confined within the limits of any region. Towns grew less democratic and took on more of the colouring of their aristocratic ambience. But at the same time, the character of the feudal states and their Church was being modified by the cities – by contact, conflict or absorption. Altogether there was an interplay between the two opposite principles, impossible in Asia with its lack of sharp social differentiation above the level of peasant and artisan. Italian city despots, themselves aping the feudal rulers of other lands, were precursors of the absolute monarchs, and urban tradition, especially in Italy, had much to contribute to the drift of thought and feeling towards modern nationalism, a drift much stronger in the western lands than in Italy itself. Florence was a *patria* to its inhabitants before there were patriots in England or France. A strong sense of community can originate only in small units like town, canton, clan, though it can then be taken over by larger ones. Again, in its early days the nation-state (unlike new nations today) had no antecedent model to emulate, except the city. An idealized memory of Rome, the archetypal city of cities, and of Roman public spirit, was to haunt Western patriotism for many generations; and in England

and France the individual as member of the community has come to be called 'citizen'.

Altogether western Europe had acquired a greater richness of forms of corporate life, a greater crystallization of habits into institutions, than any known elsewhere. It had a remarkable ability to forge societal ties, more tenacious than almost any others apart from those of the family and its extensions, clan or caste; ties that could survive from one epoch to another, and be built into more elaborate combinations. But along with fixity of particular relationships went a no less radical instability of the system as a whole. Unlike Chinese society with its limpid simplicity and logic (especially as contemplated from a higher-income vantage-point) and its reflection in a calmly rationalistic philosophy, west-European society was a blend of too many discords to be free from chronic tension. Its ideology was, revealingly, permeated at every graduation of income by those mystical sensations that in China were abandoned to popular Taoism and the illiterate peasant.[22] Asiatic politics might revolve through a simple, self-perpetuating cycle; in the West there was a constant tendency for the structure to evolve into something different and new.

In the late Middle Ages the structure was clearly altering, or even breaking down, fundamentally no doubt under the strains of a developing money economy. A long lull in the pressure on Christendom from outside, in the interval between the Crusades and the coming of the Ottoman Turks, had helped to relax social cohesion. There was a drift towards total separation between upper and lower levels of society, noble and non-noble, armed and unarmed – a symptom threatening social revolt and, even if this could be put down, the long stagnation that awaited central and eastern Europe as it had already overtaken most of Asia. The noble class itself was coming to be perilously bifurcated between a few magnates at the top and a swarm of gentry, often impoverished and discontented.[23] Any ruling class runs the risk of being weakened by this kind of fissure, a truth that twentieth-century capitalism has had more than one occasion to ponder. In situations like that of the Hussite War, the smaller gentry, alienated from the lay and clerical plutocrats above them, were an undecided force which might make common cause with the people below.[24] It was lucky for the higher aristocracy in Germany that the revolts of knight and peasant broke out not quite, though almost, at the same moment, and failed (thanks partly to Luther) to coalesce.[25]

During the prolonged crisis of feudalism there are discernible attempts to reconstruct society on two lines: one, emancipation of the small producer, the peasant and artisan, from the higher classes in Church and state; the other, reorganization of the higher classes, moral rearmament, pruning of excrescences, concentration of power. Attempts of the first kind found most opportunity in central and east-central Europe, because of the weakness of state power there; though in the more easterly part of this area they were crushed with comparative ease because of the poverty of urban life, and the absence of a large class of urban poor as allies of the peasantry. Far the most challenging revolt of the masses came in economically advanced Bohemia. It had a strong tinge of at least elemental nationalism, provoked by hatred of German lords, prelates or patricians inside Bohemia and German interference from outside; it was simultaneously the opening scene of the Reformation.[26] But while the Taborites displayed remarkable proficiency on the battle-field, and their victories sounded an alarm to feudalists all over Europe, they were never able, and indeed never really tried, to take over and remodel or supplant the state power. Among the peasants and artisans who bore the brunt of the fighting, there was the same inclination of a primitive democracy towards anarchism that expressed itself in the next century in Anabaptism with its principle of voluntary church-membership. The Swiss, having thrown off Austrian rule, remained a loose group of cantons with scarcely any bond of association.[27]

Further west, where state resources and prestige were already adequate to keep mass revolt (of which there were plenty of symptoms in all countries) within narrower limits, there took place the complex transformation of feudal monarchy into 'new' or 'absolute' monarchy. This meant a resumption, after the dislocations of the fifteenth century, of the process of state-building on which rulers had long been engaged. They had an easier task now because the propertied classes, especially the big landowners who had most to lose, were frightened into acceptance of drastic reform and of very real sacrifices: the disgorging of Crown lands they had embezzled in Castile, for instance, after the meeting of the Cortes at Toledo in 1480.[28] The fact that the absolute monarchs were not simply 'freezing' a status quo was underlined by their being themselves, to a great extent, new men. There was a general dying out of dynasties towards the close of the Middle Ages, even if their successors usually claimed some connection with them. Various founders of the new order came to the throne, like Isabella in Castile and Henry VII in England, more or less unlawfully.[29]

All the same, these newcomers were building on old foundations. They were able to enforce the necessary rationalization of the feudal order, and thus save its higher classes from themselves, only because monarchy in the West had already achieved, in a fairly integrated society, that relative autonomy, that institutional character, which marks the government of an authentic state, and which cannot be improvised. For the same reason they were strong enough to take control of the Church, and subject it to a carefully regulated reform from above which might or might not pass over into an official, restricted version of Reformation. It is hard to think of any regime in Asia in recorded times that could have imposed on a ruling class so drastic a political and ecclesiastical reorganization. Perhaps Akbar was aiming at something comparable when he sponsored his synthetic cult, the 'Din Ilahi', to rally Hindu and Muslim together round the Mogul throne; but his success was meagre.[30]

While the biggest men, or those of them willing to fall into line, were the biggest beneficiaries, smaller men had to be taken into account – particularly the small gentry, for whom the expanding state could provide much employment in its officialdom and in its standing army. The appropriating classes at large were linked much more closely with the administration. They obtained part of their income from the people independently, as before, in the form of feudal rents, but another part collectively, through the medium of taxation. Such a dovetailing may be said to make for a firmer state structure than either of the alternatives: the appropriation of wealth only or essentially by means of rent, as in eighteenth-century Poland; or by taxation, as in Islam. Capitalism, in its late stage of close interlocking between state and big business, again supplies an analogy.

Even to the less privileged sections, the new state had something to offer. The goodwill of the towns was required, and that of the lower classes was not altogether despised. In Germany and further east, plebeians were reduced to submission by naked brutality, so ferociously in Hungary (1514),[31] Germany (1525)[32] and Croatia (1573)[33] that it was centuries before they, or their countries, could stir again. But in the west, social conflict was on the whole less ungovernable, except in Spain where the lines of class partly coincided with those of religion and where tension could be relieved by the crude surgery of the expulsion of Jews and Moors.[34] The west was after all moving away from serfdom (it was acquiring fresh serfs or slaves in its overseas colonies), while central and eastern Europe were moving towards it. Part of the function of the new monarchy was to conciliate as well as to coerce, and to bridge the too-wide gulf between rich and poor. Rulers such as Henry VIII of England or Henri IV of France acquired a popularity which could 'rub off' to some extent on to the established order as a whole. Something of the confused popular aspirations of the late Middle Ages, impregnated with mysticism and millennarianism, attached itself to these 'most sacred majesties'. The German peasant of 1525, in arms against lord and prince, was ready for the leadership, had any been offered, of a vaguely imagined emperor, a 'little father'.[35] Each rising dynasty inspired the same dreams of social salvation that Horace wove round Augustus, or that our century has woven round its dictators. Each monarch was, in eastern phrase, the Asylum of the World. The hopes these 'new Messiahs' aroused were, of course, most often disappointed, but they themselves, standing now above and beyond the rest of the ruling class, were seldom blamed. They did at least provide order; and though it should not be hastily taken for granted that order is always better for the poor than disorder, most of the poor do seem to have been grateful for it – in Spain pathetically and incurably so.

In spite of all this, the antagonisms within the system were being only very imperfectly eliminated or reduced. It was necessary to turn many of them outwards for relief; and the new monarchy, like the feudalism out of which it grew, bore an essentially warlike character that it was never to lose. For the new monarchy, war was not an optional policy, but an organic need. The aristocracy had to be induced to give up its suicidal feuds; how this could be done most effectively is illustrated by the anecdote of those two quarrelsome Andalusian potentates, the Marquis of Cadiz and the Duke of Medina Sidonia, fraternizing at a heroic moment in the war against Granada.[36] Each ruler saw himself first and foremost, as Machiavelli advised him to do,[37] as a war-lord. He figured in tournaments, and might even lose his life in them. Ability to defeat foreign rivals impressed on his own subjects, both insubordinate grandee and mutinous peasant, his power to deal with them likewise. Wars served as a reason or pretext for stiffening and regularizing taxation. The whole state apparatus that rulers were putting together piecemeal was largely a by-product of war. During its adolescence, the sixteenth and seventeenth centuries, fighting was almost continuous;[38] later on it grew rather more intermittent.

It was not yet, or only by fits and starts, that kings fought their battles as patriotic leaders. Some of them were themselves foreigners, or half-foreign; their standing armies were crowded with foreign mercenaries, and in other respects too each dynamic state can be viewed as a joint-stock enterprise attracting ambitious individuals from far and wide into its service.[39] However, this mobility was less in evidence in the west proper, with its already considerable fixity of political outline, than in the states that developed by imitation further north and east: Sweden (a surprising proportion of whose aristocracy is of Scottish origin), then Prussia, then Russia – whose 'rise' was more properly a *fall* into the greedy hands of a swarm of foreign adventurers. Even there, cosmopolitanism was less unbounded than in the Islamic theatre, where the Ottoman and Mogul Empires represented confluences of fortune-hunters from all over middle and western Asia.[40]

Western monarchies inherited from their medieval forerunners an already established connection with particular areas, their main bases or strongholds. In France the region round Paris constituted this nucleus or heartland; in Castile the original province of Old Castile; in England, London and the home counties. Such regions had enough homogeneity of language, tradition, sentiment, to feel a special corporate interest in the ruler and his fortunes. Very gradually the pattern of personal loyalties within the feudal hierarchy, blending now with the other pattern of civic loyalties, could expand so as to attach an increasing proportion of the population here to its sovereign.

This special relationship between heartland and throne stood out the more because even these western states, except little Portugal, were linguistic conglomerates, with one nationality predominating over others. Scotland had large Celtic and small Norse elements; England had a string of Celtic dependencies; Castile incorporated Basque- and Portuguese-speaking groups as well as its Moorish population. The prime aim of the new rulers in their expansionist effort was to bring under their sway all territory not already theirs within the 'natural frontiers' dimly coming to be perceived. Other small nationalities which had failed to develop as states were now swallowed up: Brittany (1491), Granada (1492), Navarre (1512), Ireland. Their languages and cultures persisted nevertheless;[41] and none of the governments succeeded fully in its programme of unification. England strove in vain to absorb Scotland; Spain was only briefly able to absorb a reluctant Portugal. Frontiers thus surviving helped by mutual irritation to generate a corporate sentiment on both sides. By the seventeenth century an Englishman who did not look down on a Scotsman would have been only half an Englishman; a Scotsman who did not hate an Englishman would not have been a Scotsman at all.

In this way too, by contrast with the invertebrate dominions of the east, these western states had more internal coherence. A good many of their people, especially in or close to the capital, were coming to think of themselves as the king's own particular subjects, with something like the status of what would today be called a *Staatsvolk*: that of the Czechs in the Czechoslovakia of 1919, or of the Serbs in

Yugoslavia. It may have been for want of an adequate nucleus of this kind that the late-medieval principality of Burgundy failed to establish itself on the map. No newcomers, indeed, came forward successfully in this period; all the successful states had already long traditions, potentialities waiting to be turned to account by enterprising rulers. Between these rulers and their chief territory the relationship was of course complex, and affected different classes variably.[42] A monarch struggling to bring over-mighty subjects under control could balance against them the middle classes, but could also hope to achieve that purpose by expansion, outflanking the feudalism of the home province by mastering outlying ones. Possession of rich Catalonia helped the Aragonese kings to tame Aragon proper.[43] Later on the same process might be repeated against the middle class in its turn. The failure of Tudor efforts to incorporate Scotland and Ireland was part of the reason (as well as part of the consequence) of the limited growth of absolutism in England; once Ireland did fall under English sway, it was promptly turned – or so the bourgeois opposition alleged – into a bastion of royal power against England.[44]

A region politically dominant might be economically backward, as both Old Castile (which had no real capital) and Aragon proper were by comparison with the fertile coast and flourishing seaports of Iberia.[45] Expansion might bring such a province more loss than gain. For Castile, or most of its inhabitants, empire proved a crushing burden: it was bled half to death by taxation, while many of the Crown's less favoured possessions got off much more lightly.[46] In France and England, political and economic ascendancy went together and reinforced each other. There the home province and its burghers knew how to profit by the wealth pumped into the metropolis by government and court nobility. In these conditions, in fact, may be seen the matrix of modern capitalism: like nationalism, less the creator than the creation of the modern state. It had many antecedents, but its full emergence required a conjunction of political and moral as well as strictly economic factors. This emergence could take place within the intricate framework of one type of western state then evolving; it may be doubted whether it could have done so under any other circumstances that we know of in history; at any rate it never did.[47]

The new state might be expected to move automatically towards nationalism. Capitalism bound the component parts of a country more closely together. But even in its absence, as in Spain, the struggle for colonies and colonial tribute promoted a further sense of community of interests, real or fancied, between government and people against outsiders. Religion did the same in another way, for each country was cemented by a religious cause, the upholding of some church or other against its satanical enemies at home and abroad. Both forces helped to ensure that the growing readiness of ordinary people to identify themselves with their governments had from the first a chauvinistic character. Men impressed by their ruler's prowess abroad came by degrees to feel that they had a share in it, that his 'glory' was their glory too. There was an element of psychological compensation here, a need to escape from the pressure of despotic rule. Frustrated at home, Frenchmen could console themselves with being the 'great nation' of Europe, as they did long before 1789.[48] Napoleon exaggerated, but not absurdly, when he declared that the victory of Fontenoy gave the Bourbon dynasty an extra forty years of life.[49]

In the coming of nationalism with this peculiarly hysterical cast may be recognized a distortion – as in religion, in all the official reformations and counter-reformations – of something simpler, more genuinely popular, that was dawning in the late Middle Ages. Taborite 'nationalism' had been healthily internationalist. In this early mood, the nation was the 'people', the disinherited mass, rising against oppressors. It lingered on in the semi-mythical forms expressed by the 'Norman yoke' idea[50] among the more radical supporters of the English seventeenth-century Revolution, and by the eighteenth-century French notion of a third estate of Gauls oppressed by a Frankish aristocracy.[51] But within the state, rich and poor, Norman and Saxon, had to be brought to feel as a single community confronting its rivals. Much of the mass-feeling that slowly gathered round the nation-state consisted of class resentment artifically diverted into xenophobia.[52]

No dynasty set out to build a nation-state; each aimed at unlimited extension – Francis I (1515–47) wanted to be overlord of Italy and head of the Holy Roman Empire – and the more it prospered the more the outcome was a multifarious empire instead of a nation. The nation was the empire *manqué*. It had to be large enough to survive and to sharpen its claws on its neighbours, but small enough to be organized from one centre and to feel itself as an entity. On the close-packed western edge of Europe, any excessive ballooning of territory was checked by competition and geographical limits.[53] Even imperial Spain remained a firm unit, distinct from its possessions; most of these lay at a distance from it, and its foreign rulers learned after the revolt of the Comuneros in 1520[54] that they could only have Spain in their empire by making it a Spanish empire, and turning themselves into Spanish Habsburgs. Charles I had arrived in Spain from his native Netherlands totally ignorant of the country: his son Philip II scarcely set foot outside Castile. It was their Austrian cousins who were free to follow their natural bent and amass a purely dynastic, cosmopolitan empire, an amorphous thing in which the original Alpine heartland round Vienna was almost lost. It was a hybrid, half western in character and half akin to the older type of east-European state represented by Poland and Hungary, a type doomed like the city-state to fall by the wayside of history. There too the raw material had been a corporation of feudal landowners; but ease of expansion in a vast frontierless area with no urban tradition fostered little concentration of royal leadership, little emergence of a heartland province, little internal change. Later on a new type of eastern state rose, Prussia and then Russia, owing a great deal to the example and equipment, especially military, of the well-established western states; a barbarized version of absolute monarchy which persisted into the present century.

In its original habitat the monarch, the 'corporation sole' of the English lawyers, was still one corporation of many, embedded among privileged orders, chartered towns, Estates. However sweeping his pretensions, the monarch was still far from the irresponsibility of power, dangerous to king and subject alike, of the 'Oriental despot' who had to deal only with a swarm of individuals. A Spaniard living under Philip II and his decrees thought of the Government as limited by some sort of rule of law, not as an incalculable tyranny.[55] Though the prime function of the new monarchy was to rescue feudal society from being swept away, its composite character and ancestry implanted in it possibilities of further development. Still more was this true of the society it presided over. Indeed from a long-term point of view absolutism was useful only where it was a brief, transitional form, superseded as soon as it had served as a dam or reservoir to collect the social energy necessary for a fresh move forward. Naturally it, and the vested interests that clustered round it, did not want to be superseded; and external success, the winning of as many Fontenoys as possible, was their elixir of life. Spanish kings were able to go on and on, and rule with a minimum of change and reform. They had an army undefeated for more than a century, and they were aided by their special windfall of colonial tribute. The discovery of America and of the sea-route of the Indies powerfully affected the politics of all western Europe, but in very different ways, by accentuating the diverse tendencies of diverse regions. In Spain it fortified conservatism; all the more because it also fortified the Catholic Church, which shared the profits in cash and prestige and which regained as a world religion the self-confidence it had long been losing in Europe. Formerly this Church had been often inclined to side with baron against king as well as serf or burgher. But now it needed a strong central authority to back its crusade against critics and heretics, and the alliance between it and absolutism became so close that it helped to immobilize both.[56]

Spain sank into a rigidity which there was no longer public energy to resist. Though the seventeenth century was one of revolutions in Iberia as elsewhere, movements of protest there were merely centrifugal, confined to the outlying areas, Catalonia and Portugal; apart from food riots, there was no trouble in the heartland of Castile, quiescent since the failure of the Comuneros in 1520. The seventeenth century was an age of decadence for other parts of Europe too; perhaps, as has been argued, on balance for Europe as a whole.[57] Over most of the continent various elements that had enabled the west to make the advance represented by absolute monarchy had been lacking. On much of it the negative consequences of absolutism were imposed by Spanish hegemony and the support it gave to the Counter-Reformation, and absolute monarchy was itself costly and burdensome, as well as being intrinsically a barrier to, or a substitute for, progress: progress, that is, in the sense of social emancipation. Its wars, culminating in the Thirty Years' War, were unprecedentedly wasteful and destructive, and were often kept going irrationally long by rulers for whom it was easier to be at war than at peace.

While Counter-Reformation Europe made its economies largely at the expense of towns and middle classes, Protestant Europe made them, less damagingly for the future, at the expense of the Church, and of the poor so far as these had benefited by monastic charity. By plundering monasteries, rulers and ruling classes gained an immediate advantage at the cost of seriously weakening religion as their great insurance against further change. Since moreover it was in smaller, hard-up countries that this happened, they could seldom dazzle their subjects with triumphs abroad. A Henry VIII might look imposing enough at home, but when he showed himself on the Continent, trotting about in search of Poitiers or Agincourt, he was a laughing-stock. It was in the Protestant lands of the west that capitalism – an alternative kind of 'progress' to what the Taborites had fought for – developed rapidly; and it was only there, in Holland and England, followed at a very long interval by France when French Catholicism had had time to atrophy, that the 'natural' or 'logical' line of evolution from absolute monarchy to bourgeois revolution could work itself out.

Capitalism is as protean as feudalism. It took on the imprint of the mould in which it grew; most important, it carried over from absolute monarchy a pugnacity, a disposition to think of war and conquest as the best way out of all difficulties, which its own inner laws might not otherwise have dictated to it. Conversely, the bourgeois revolution owed much to the old incoherent revolt of peasant and artisan, dammed up by absolutism but continuing under cover of religious sectarianism, which came to the surface again among Anabaptists in the Netherlands and left-wing Independents in England. It was frustrated once more; but it did not disappear without leaving its mark on this north-western part of Europe where so much of the continent's vital energy had by then come to be concentrated.

4

Foreign Mercenaries and Absolute Monarchy

When Alexander invaded Asia in 334 BC his army included 5,000 mercenaries, and the Persian army that faced him at Issos contained 10,000 Greeks.[1] The foreign soldier enlisting for pay is a ubiquitous type in history. One of the epochs in which he may be seen most hard at work is the one that links medieval and modern Europe when absolute monarchy and the modern state were taking shape. Underlying this political development was a reorganization – rather than a transformation – of the social structure of Europe. The feudal order, the rule of the landowning aristocracy, was in the later Middle Ages divided and demoralized. It was meeting with growing resistance from below, and its military resources for coping with both internal and external challenges were obsolescent. In the fifteenth century the knight on horseback who had dominated Europe for a millennium was being driven to shut himself up inside a load of armour that made him clumsy and ineffective. Under the auspices of absolute monarchy, by what might be described as a sort of 'managerial revolution', the aristocratic order achieved a remarkable recovery, though it had of course to undergo important changes.

The new state rested on a new kind of army, and to this the foreign mercenary contributed so much that his services can be regarded as an indispensable condition of all that happened.

'A prince ought to have no other aim or thought', said Machiavelli, 'nor select anything else for his study, than war and its rules and discipline.'[2] A good army was the *summum bonum*, the vehicle of salvation. The awkward problem lay in finding the soldiers to fill it.

Every ruler would have echoed Henry V, who wished his yeomen to imitate the action of the tiger when abroad, and to be quiet and docile at home. It was a difficult combination of qualities for any martial breeder to produce, in an age when popular jingoism had hardly begun to stir; he was more likely to have to complain with Coriolanus that his men were mutinous at home, timid on the field. Recruitment from the mass of ordinary peasants and burghers might have for the Crown the advantage of counterbalancing the strength of the nobility. Norman kings had thought of preserving a Saxon fyrd. For this very reason, however, it would be obnoxious to the nobility, without whose participation no army could be put together. In Castile, for instance, the nobles objected strongly to an ordinance made by Ximénez, when Regent in 1516, on military training for the burgher class,[3] and rulers could not fail to share this reluctance to put arms into the hands of the people. The state was growing out of conditions of civil war – often violent class warfare, as in several provinces of Aragon under John II, Ferdinand and Charles V in turn. Four years after Ximénez's ordinance the burghers of Castile were in rebellion against their king.

Of military thinking about the end of that century Hanotaux writes: '*Tous les contemporains sont d'accord pour déclarer, qu'en France, on ne donnait plus d'armes au peuple, de peur qu'il ne se soulevât contre ses oppresseurs.*'[4] Often, it may be added, the common man was positively unwilling to be armed. Many detested the senseless wars in whose fires new chains were being forged for them. One of the leading principles of Anabaptism was refusal of military service. A vast amount of popular feeling in Europe was distilled by Shakespeare into the great scene in which his English soldiers argue about war on the night before Agincourt. Recruits of a less disputatious sort were no doubt available. With feudal society cracking and crumbling there was a plentiful human debris at every level. In a later period the 'scum of the earth' would be effectively handled by the drill-sergeant. But that could only be after army cadres had been organized and habits of command and obedience evolved. The problem was where to begin. A further objection was that drumming up volunteers had to be left, until the growth of the state was far advanced, to nobles who might turn it to their own political as well as pecuniary ends. Even Richelieu, well on in the seventeenth century, might prefer on this account to look for an army in Germany rather than in France.[5]

A glance at the French army of the fifteenth and sixteenth centuries will illustrate the problem. In 1445 towards the end of the Hundred Years' War Charles VII took the first step towards a standing army by embodying out of the old feudal mass that had answered the *ban* and *arrière-ban* the *compagnies d'ordonnance*: each company made up of 100 'lances', units of one heavy-armed horseman (gendarme) with two or three footmen or mounted infantry. Of the original fifteen companies the first in order and precedence was composed of Scots;[6] otherwise the gendarmes of this picked force were normally French, all (until 1584) were gentlemen, all were permanently in the royal pay. Technically they suffered from a certain aristocratic conserv-atism,[7] and politically the civil wars of the late sixteenth century revealed the instability of the class from which they were drawn. In their day they were the finest heavy cavalry in Europe; but no cavalry could make an army by itself now that the longbow was being followed by the pike and the harquebus. A reliable infantry was needed as well. In the fourteenth century employment of footmen from the town militias had been hindered by 'the sharp new hostility of the feudal nobles towards the lower social strata from which infantry was recruited'.[8] Only sporadically, under pressure of critical circumstances, did the monarchy now try to form bodies of soldiers out of ordinary Frenchmen. In 1448 the *francs-archers* were raised in the countryside, each parish having to find and equip one man. By this time the longbow was getting out of date, and these rustic reserves, practising at their targets on Sundays, soon dropped out of sight.[9] Political hesitations on the Government's part may have helped to keep the experiment futile, as well as the similar ones planned by Louis XII in 1513 and by Francis I in 1534. The fear that the people inspired in the King was, as Lot remarks, a hindrance to any success with infantry.[10]

Only along the troubled and shifting frontiers were regular French infantry formations slowly taking shape, beginning with the *Bande de Picardie*, first of the 'old four' regiments of the later army, and that of Piedmont. But most of the *aventuriers* recruited from these border-lands in the sixteenth century were a mere mob of pilferers. They came from populations mostly more poverty-stricken than those of France proper, and only half French. Gascony, which with Picardy and Brittany furnished a high proportion of France's infantry, was the old 'Vasconia' or Basque land, and had been under English rule until the mid-fifteenth century. Brittany was an autonomous duchy until 1491; Commines mentions a large contingent of Breton gendarmes in Louis XI's service a little before this date, who deserted him at an awkward moment, and Bretons were to be found in the service of Burgundy too.[11] Picardy extended into the Netherlands, and Picards fought for Habsburg as well as Valois.[12]

Frenchmen were seldom eager to serve their king, and their king was not eager to employ Frenchmen. Despots have often chosen to surround themselves with bodyguards of aliens: we see Byzantine emperors with their Varangians, French kings with their Scots and then their Swiss Guard, Napoleon with his Poles, Franco with his Moors. In this spirit Charles the Bold of Burgundy 'entertained strangers rather than his own subjects', of whom he felt 'strange jealousies', in his army.[13] Sixteenth-century France came to depend to a very remarkable degree on foreign mercenaries. A patriot like Fourquevaux might lament this,[14] and Machiavelli had condemned the practice;[15] but the Florentine was often anything but a realist. Use of foreign troops, while it suffered from various drawbacks, had the great merit of being politically safe. It had several secondary advantages. Since as a rule only the king could afford to hire mercenaries in bulk they strengthened him against his nobles; they strengthened both king and nobles against the people, with whom they had no ties of sympathy. While much more expensive than native troops, they left no troublesome widows and orphans; and at the end of a campaign they could be sent away, unlike a country's own men coming home from the wars. Professional fighting-men competing for employment were more likely than others to keep up with technical progress.[16] Experts from the industrially advanced regions played a leading part in spreading the use of fire-arms. In England the first hand-gun soldiers were Flemings and Germans hired for the Wars of the Roses.[17]

Long before absolute monarchy arose, soldiers offering themselves for hire had constituted a major export trade of the Middle Ages, and one of the first to establish a European market. Byzantium, the Crusades and the rich cities of Italy and Flanders had all helped to set it going. It had been, in its way, as vital to the formation of the feudal state as it was now to the new monarchy of the sixteenth century. Feudal rulers had made use of foreign troops both at home and abroad, up to the limit of their purses. John Lackland leaned so heavily on his Flemish mercenaries that Magna Carta prohibited their employment. Flemings assisted in the conquest of South Wales and then of Ireland.[18] Capetian kings imitated their Plantagenet rivals.

Like the 'Brabançons' of the thirteenth century, the 'Armagnacs', 'Ecorcheurs', and similar professionals in the disorderly Companies of Adventurers of the fourteenth and fifteenth were largely pauperized or bastard gentlemen, offscourings of feudality.[19] Not so the men who wielded the longbow, the weapon which revolutionized warfare for a century. They came from Wales. 'It was the South Welsh archers of Strongbow and his fellow-adventurers . . . who made the Norman Conquest of Ireland possible.'[20] With the North Welsh spearmen they 'gradually became famous all over Europe for their courage and skill', while their removal from Wales made that country more easily governed by its foreign masters.[21] Of 12,500 foot in the army Edward I led to Scotland in 1298, 10,000 were Welsh.[22] Wales was only one of a series of recruiting-bases lying outside the settled limits of feudal Europe; and these held far more significance for the future than feudal Europe's internal sources of supply. Besides the Welshmen, Henry II and Richard I of England had hired Basques, Navarrese and Galloway 'kerns'.[23] Most of the 'Genoese' crossbowmen who served everywhere from London to Constaninople, and were the staple infantry of medieval France, must have been drawn from Genoa's possessions, the Ligurian hills and Corsica and Sardinia. Venice got many of its best men from Dalmatia.[24] Altogether, a striking number of these recruiting-grounds lay in mountainous regions on the fringes of Europe, inhabited by alien peoples such as Celts or Basques. In an age when the cultivators of the settled plains had been disarmed by their noble 'protectors', and ravaged by famine and pestilence, these sturdy, needy hillmen were still ready for war.

One may find analogies in the reliance of Byzantine rulers on Anatolian mountaineers, or in the armies of the Persian kings, always until the nineteenth century drawn from the nomad hill and desert tribes of neighbouring Kurdistan, Luristan or Makran.[25] The absolute monarchs followed the same policies, though on a grander scale than in the Middle Ages, for they needed more men, for whom they paid out of the increasing output of the central European silver mines in the late fifteenth century, and even more, out of the stocks of gold and silver which reached Europe from the Americas in the sixteenth.

Salvation for paymasters came from the Andes; for recruiting-officers from the Alps. A new race of hill-folk was coming to market, the Swiss, for two centuries the mercenary soldiery of Europe *par excellence*. It is a striking paradox that the old ruling groups were now, in great measure, saved by the mountaineers who had most resolutely defied feudalism in their Alpine strongholds, and whose revolutionary example had not gone unnoticed in central Europe. 'They want to become Swiss' was the proverbial expression in Germany for all those who wished to throw off allegiance to their lawful lords.[26] Luckily for their aristocratic neighbours the Swiss were as poverty-stricken as they were liberty-loving – 'No people in the world could be poorer', Commines says of them in 1476 when they put an end to Charles the Bold and his ambitions and they found offers of pay and plunder irresistible.[27] A nation of armed peasants, afflicted with the chronic over-population of the barren uplands, numerous enough to form massive columns of pikemen, they acquired by incessant practice the 'extraordinary perfection of skill and discipline' demanded by their system of warfare,[28] and they did this at home in their valleys, at no cost to their employers. True, they were too democratic to be easily handled, and if the pay-chest gave out they changed sides or marched off home. *Pas d'argent, pas de Suisse.* While money lasted they fought like Trojans, local and professional pride giving them a high morale. Altogether they gave their employers the benefits without the drawbacks of a free citizen army.

These Swiss set new standards to Europe's martial classes, and in doing so inaugurated a new epoch. Naturally rulers sought for equivalent mercenaries. Towards 1500 the Emperor Maximilian began to recruit their neighbours, the Swabians, who came from an area with many trading towns and few big territorial princes, which retained a large number of free peasants, at any rate until the aftermath of the Peasants' War. Modelled on the Swiss formations, and intended for use against them, the Swabians were never quite equal to them as soldiers and soon merged into the ordinary mass of German mercenaries or *Landsknechts*.[29] While the Swiss had a special link with France, *Landsknechts* served everywhere indiscriminately, and may have been preferred by some employers because, having less solidarity among themselves, they could be got cheaper and cheated more easily. However, Germany was industrially more advanced than Switzerland and therefore produced professionals who took to firearms more readily, such as the mounted harquebusier and the *Schwartzreiter*, a mounted pistoleer.

Soldiers from Germany, which had no national army, helped to build up almost every organized state in Europe, acquiring meanwhile the conscientious ferocity of modern German warfare long before the first Prussian drill-ground was laid out. Italy was also without a national army. Unlike their fourteenth-century predecessors, the mercenaries of fifteenth-century Italian cities, whose elaborate shadow-boxing Machiavelli derided, were mainly Italians. Yet men of their nationality were to make very respectable cut-throats in the service of foreign and strong governments. Absolute monarchies also utilized much other cannon-fodder in their long series of wars. After their defeat in Bohemia, the Taborites straggled over Germany and into Poland as mercenaries, often armed with the hand-guns in whose use they had been pioneers;[30] they were to be followed in later days by many others who, defeated in the struggle for freedom at home, had to earn their bread by fighting against freedom abroad. By way of the Venetian possessions swordsmen came into circulation from the

Balkans, where the collapse of Byzantium and the turmoil of Turkish conquest coincided with the crisis of the medieval order in the west. Albanians fled in large numbers to Venetia. Old followers of Scanderbeg were the first *Stradiots* or *Estradiots*, a wild type of light cavalry that figures largely in sixteenth-century annals; another type was represented by the *Argoulets*, originally Greek horsemen from Epirus. Most of these military trade names were soon borrowed by men of other nationalities.[31]

In France, whose example was decisive for Europe, Louis XI inaugurated a system destined to survive down to the Revolution when, in 1474, he enlisted Swiss auxiliaries by treaty arrangement with the cantons. From now on Switzerland, conveniently close at hand, was to the French kings what Wales had been to the English. Sluggish in social evolution compared with England, France had hitherto been unable to make effective use of such auxiliaries. More than once on the battlefield the haughty knights had ridden down their own Genoese crossbowmen, as contemptible plebeians. The Swiss were ostentatiously plebeian, but the bluest-blooded gendarme could not fail to respect their prowess, all the more perhaps because they fought hand to hand, not with long-range missiles like the Genoese. To a Louis XII they were barbarians, but they provided an almost ideal answer to the problem of how to build a solid French infantry without the Frenchmen.

Within a few years after the treaty of 1474, a certain number of Swiss came to form part of the new permanent army of the French monarchy, along with its gendarmerie and artillery; while much bigger numbers were imported in wartime. Charles VIII started the Italian Wars in 1494 with 10,000 Swiss and Germans in his army, whose native infantry was merely 'a hastily raised force, poorly armed and equipped . . . there was still the fear of arming the people'.[32] At Ravenna in 1512, during a brief estrangement from the cantons, Louis XII had 5,000 allied Italians (partly under Scots officers), 6,000 Germans, 8,000 Gascons and Picards, some Flemish archers, miscellaneous light horse and 1,200 'lances' of gendarmerie.[33] In 1543 there were 19,000 Swiss in France.[34] They were the backbone of the infantry; and from Francis I to Henry IV they and the gendarmerie were brigaded together and fought in close co-operation.[35] Vacancies in the French ranks were filled up with smaller numbers of English, Scots, Italians, Corsicans, Poles, Greeks. A body of Albanians first enrolled by Charles VIII became 'the nucleus and foundation of the French light cavalry'.[36] Ships and crews were often hired from abroad, especially from Genoa.

In Spain several factors combined to give the army a more

'national' character than any other of the sixteenth century, and this undoubtedly helped it to dominate the battlefield from about 1520, when the Swiss pike by itself ceased to carry all before it, down to the battle of Rocroy in 1643. For one thing Castile — and more particularly the Basque provinces — had been less rich and less heavily feudalized than France, and a gentleman could serve on foot without derogation. For another, Spain's many dependencies required permanent garrisons; this fostered the growth of the *tercios* regiments with a continuous tradition and with the special morale of occupation forces. What also counted was that Spanish troops stationed far away in Sicily or Flanders would not cause their government the same uneasiness that they might have done at home in Spain. None the less, foreign ingredients were needed here too, from the conquest of Granada (1481—91) onward. In the campaigns of Naples, Gonzalvo de Córdoba began operations in 1496 with a very small army including some Germans, as well as many Basques, and he had to hire Italian heavy cavalry.[37] For the battle of Cerignola in 1503 he acquired another 2,000 Germans, making about one-third of his total; there is a symbolic touch about the anecdote of the Great Captain himself riding to the field with a German behind him on the crupper.[38] As the century wore on the Spanish army, much the greatest part of it stationed abroad, was increasingly diluted with non-Spanish elements, until in the end only five out of the twenty infantry regiments at Rocroy were Spanish, five being Walloon, five German, three Italian and two Franc-Comtois.[39]

Henry VIII of England relied on foreign mercenaries throughout his adventures on the Continent: German or Burgundian pikemen, Netherlands or Burgundian heavy cavalry.[40] In 1545 he gave offence to Charles V by enticing into his service a body of some 700 Spanish harquebusiers who happened to land on his coasts (Spaniards and Frenchmen seldom served in other armies), and sending them up under a notable Basque *condottiere* named Pedro de Gamboa to strengthen the garrisons along the border, where the Scots, says the Spanish chronicler, 'were very frightened when they got to know them'.[41] Also stationed on the border were Albanian horsemen and a company of Italians under the Marquis Palavicino:[42] nearly as heterogeneous an array as Rome had once sent to this frontier to defend the Wall. Elizabeth, unable to multiply taxes or plunder a wealthy Church as her father had done, could not make war in this high-spirited style, and her army was in general a mere wretched militia. Of the pressed men sent with Leicester to the Netherlands many deserted: 'The Spaniards had a whole regiment of English renegades under William Stanley.'[43] In the conquest of Ireland liberal use was made of cheap but very unreliable Irish mercenaries: 'kerns', the lowest sort of foot-soldiers, and 'gallowglasses' or 'bonaghts' who had long been coming into Ireland from the Scottish Highlands as mercenaries in the pay of tribal chiefs.[44] For Scotland the Highlands were a valuable if turbulent reservoir of manpower. At Pinkie in 1547 8,000 High-landers, along with 4,000 Irish archers, made up a considerable part of the Scots army defeated by Somerset with the help of his Spaniards and Italians.[45] In 1640 Leslie marched into England with forces which included a large contingent of 'Redshanks', or Highlanders.

European governments thus relied very largely on foreign mercen-aries. One of the employments for which they were particularly well suited was the suppression of rebellious subjects, and in the sixteenth century, that age of endemic revolution, they were often called upon for this purpose. 'Where are my Switzers?' was the cry of many a harassed monarch besides Claudius. Military technique has always evolved in response to the requirements of internal pacification as well as of external war. Thus firearms, which were improved into practical weapons during the crisis of feudalism, were essential to the rise of the modern state, not only because cannon could batter feudal strongholds, but even more because firearms could deal with peasant revolts more effectively than any earlier equipment. Also such arms (like crossbows earlier) were more safely entrusted to foreign than to native troops. France was the last country to adopt hand-guns for its own troops,[46] though it had led the way with artillery. It is thus not really as 'curious' as Oman suggests 'that among the many results of the growing importance of fire-arms was the fact that popular risings became progressively more impotent against trained soldiery'.[47]

Faced with internal rebellion, local regular troops or tenants collected from noble estates might be unreliable, as the King of Spain found in 1520, when the revolt of the Comuneros in Castile and the Germanias in Valencia and Majorca broke out. Governments thus had to look either to backward areas for honest, simple-minded fellows untainted by political ideas — as to the hills of Aragon and the Basque provinces in 1520–1 – or to foreigners. Charles V, who had been caught with few troops in 1520, learned the lesson. When he returned to Spain in 1522 it was with 3,000 or 4,000 Germans and seventy-four guns. 'Foreign soldiers and foreign cannon were hence-forth often employed by Charles V to forestall and put down rebellion in his different dominions.'[48] Gueldrians, Italians and bloodthirsty Albanians and Stradiotes crusaded against the rebels of 1525 in Alsace, under the pious Duke of Lorraine;[49] Czech, Croat and Magyar soldiery against them in Upper Austria, Styria and Carinthia.

Three hundred Italian harquebusiers and some hundreds of *Landsknechts* under Lord Grey de Wilton were sent to reinforce Lord Russell in Cornwall in 1549; 1,000 Welsh hillmen were also drafted. At the fight at Sampford Courtenay the Government side could hardly have carried the day without its artillery and foreign professionals.[50] In Norfolk, Italians and 1,000 German matchlockmen were also thrown in. Warwick was saved, and the battle in August decided, by the arrival of the Germans.[51] Their very foreignness ensured their loyalty, for 'Every foreigner who fell out of rank was instantly killed';[52] a strong inducement to the mercenaries *not* to fall out of rank.

Naturally professionalism cut both ways. In the insurgent areas of Austria and south-west Germany during the Peasants' War many peasants had seen military service, and were thus much better armed and organized than in Thuringia, where there were few ex-soldiers. 'The Allgaeu peasants counted in their ranks a host of foreign soldiers and experienced commanders and possessed numerous well-manned cannon.'[53] (On the other hand much of the 'demoralization' among the peasants may be traceable to the infection of habits learned while fighting and plundering abroad.) Rebellions headed by moneyed men could hire their own mercenaries. If the Huguenots in the French Wars of Religion were worn down by government forces composed largely of Swiss, Germans and Italians (including Protestants), they themselves, mostly gentlemen-cavalry, hired *Landsknechts* and others to make up infantry, as well as numbers of the disorderly *Reiter*. In the decisive year of 1590, when Henry IV won the battle of Ivry, he owed his success to the loyalty of the 13,000 Swiss in his camp.[54] However, in general, governments could outbid rebels at this game. Only in the exceptional case of the Netherlands did mercenaries turn the scales *against* absolutism, because the rebels were the better paymasters. They fought Philip II throughout with a force as polyglot as his own. William of Orange's first attempts in 1568 and 1572 were made with riotous bands sharked up in Germany.[55] The new element contributed by the thrifty Dutch as the war went on was regular pay and careful accounting, rather than native soldiers. It was in the sea-fighting that authentic Dutch glory was won; apart from heroic defence of some besieged towns, 'The warfare on land, with the foreign auxiliaries, the innumerable foreigners even in the States' pay, the foreign noblemen surrounding the princely commander, could never create a really national tradition – not during the whole period of the Republic's existence.'[56] Much the same had been true of Venice, and was to be true of England.

However, the mercenary system also militated against revolution in a subtler way. The reservoirs of mercenary recruitment remained politically stagnant, compared with their neighbours, somewhat as Nepal and the Punjab, two great recruiting-grounds for the British army, long did. For Switzerland the three centuries of symbiosis with despotic France had evil consequences. Cantonal politics were corrupted by the fees received for licensing the export of soldiers, and rings of patricians increased their power at the expense of the common people.[57] In vain had Zwingli tried to put an end to the traffic along with prostitution and adultery. For Europe as well as for themselves the corruption of the Swiss was a misfortune. As Alfieri was to remark bitterly, these free men of the hills became the chief watch-dogs of tyranny.[58] European history might have taken a different turn if the Swiss had still been as revolutionary a force in 1524, when the Peasants' War was fought, as fifty years earlier. The German rebels had close contacts with Switzerland, and were hoping for help from across the border. Many of the *Bundschuh* agitators of previous decades had fled there. But already the old democracy was in decay; a century later the Swiss peasants in their turn were goaded into rebellion and crushed by the united strength of the cantonal governments; and professional rivalry had stirred up violent animosities between Swiss and Swabians. Altogether the mercenary system had a considerable share in diverting the danger that might have threatened the aristocratic order of society from popular forces outside the limits of feudal Europe.

Inside those limits, moreover, it provided a safety-valve, drawing away from social revolt unnumbered multitudes who, like the murderer hired by Macbeth, were so incensed by the vile blows and buffets of the world that they were reckless what they did to spite the world. The common soldier was almost the first proletarian. He had his wage disputes, his strikes and lock-outs. A Swiss contingent, especially, was a trade union, and one that would not put up with any breach of contract.[59] But this haggling over pence, compared with the old epic struggle for Swiss freedom, was a sad falling away. The social conflicts of the age were in part transmuted and diluted into such professional disputes. Even the New Model was a craft union of skilled workers with grievances, though it was much else too. War had become the biggest industry in Europe. Every officer, collecting recruits for a government and making what he could out of their pay, was an entrepreneur, a businessman great or small. Profits and pickings from war – still in the sixteenth century including ransoms – helped the gentry to recoup the deficiencies in its feudal income.[60]

All these tendencies reached a disastrous climax in the Thirty

Years' War. In one sense we can think of this as a mechanism diverting the energies of common men who, on the sixteenth-century Continent as in seventeenth-century Britain, would have 'fought for religion' as rebels or revolutionary soldiers, into pillage and the strengthening of absolute monarchies. Peasants still revolted, as in Upper Austria in 1626, with many old soldiers in their bands, but they were easily put down by the now swarming armies, composed of men for whom war was the alternative to poverty or starvation. From each ravaged area the common man drifted along the well-worn path to the camp, to prey on others in his turn. Women also found the vast baggage trains their most accessible refuge.[61] The demoralization, already visible in 1525, grew to enormous proportions; the German people never fully recovered from it. The War got out of hand – but it never seriously imperilled the governing classes. On the contrary, they emerged from it with a new and powerful political and military implement: the 'standing army' composed of mercenaries, but permanently attached to a given government.

The Thirty Years' War thus brings us from the discussion of mercenaries as weapons against rebellion to consideration of the more general problem of mercenaries and the growth of the modern state apparatus. We must first look at western Europe, for, as we shall see, eastern Europe followed a rather different course. In the west independent mercenary forces were still, at the outbreak of the Thirty Years' War, essential to governments which had not yet built a regular army framework of their own. Mansfield, Tilly, Wallenstein, heirs of the sixteenth-century *Landsknecht*-contractors, were indispensable to states like England, Bavaria and above all Austria, whose hotchpotch of territories only really coagulated into an empire under the pressure of this war; while even France and Sweden, which possessed the foundations of national armies, used foreign professionals to build on them. Wallenstein in particular brought the freelance private subcontract army to its point of highest development, after which nothing remained but for it either to disintegrate or to be permanently attached to some state. His army, which, with its camp-followers, was comparable in numbers to a good-sized modern city, was the biggest and best organized private enterprise seen in Europe before the twentieth century, and its structure mirrored that of contemporary society. All the officers had a financial stake in it, and counted on a rich return on their investment; the rank and file, dredged up from all over Europe and incapable of solidarity, were poorly and irregularly paid, which resulted in a rapid turnover of the 'labour force'.[62] But the commander himself claimed unlimited authority, as though in virtue of a Hobbesian social contract. The day of the free democratic Swiss phalanx had ended, that of the modern regular army was about to begin. 'Midway between them Wallenstein introduced the principle of unconditional military obedience that made possible the construction of the modern type of command.'[63] So vast a force could no longer sell itself to all buyers, for few could afford it. It could either attempt to become the basis of a state itself – as Wallenstein was accused of wishing – or pass to the paymaster by whose support it had grown, and who had grown by its support. Austria inherited what Wallenstein had built up.

As usual it was France which perfected the new type of national-mercenary army organization. Louis XIV and Louvois set on foot an army which found more room than before for native recruits, though it drew its volunteers from the least 'national', most nondescript types, the dregs of the poorest classes. Because foreign troops had by now given France a solid military framework and tradition, this 'scum' could be put to reasonably good use. Military tactics could be based largely on an infantry force, though the riff-raff was officered by gentlemen. Even now, bullying or deception were often needed to persuade the humblest Frenchman to join the colours; paupers, convicts, drunkards, boys of fifteen had to be accepted and desertion was rampant.[64] In 1677 the Maréchal de Vivonne found that 4,000 of his 7,000 men had absconded. Hence an extremely high proportion of foreign stiffening was still requisite. 'Les victoires de Louis, XIV seront souvent dues autant à des soldats d'autres nations qu'á des soldats francais.'[65]

These foreigners were now being incorporated into standardized units of the army, some of them kept permanently on the list. Once more the Swiss stood first, though not in France alone for in other lands too they were 'the lineal ancestors of the modern regiments of Europe'.[66] In France they, unlike the common run of mercenaries, retained their own rights of citizenship and worship.[67] One of Louis XIV's first acts was to raise four more permanent Swiss regiments.[68] Twenty-five thousand Swiss, including Protestants, took part in the invasion of Holland.[69] Another source of raw material that could be turned to good account was the mass of refugees flooding Europe after the religious wars. Prominent among them were the Irish. At the battle of the Dunes in 1658 Turenne's army contained a Scottish regiment previously in Swedish service and one of Irish driven out of their homes by Cromwell; the Spanish army he was fighting contained one Scottish, one English and three Irish regiments.[70] After the battle of the Boyne in 1690 about 14,000 of the defeated Irish came over to France to join the 6,000 already in Louis's service. With no homes to return to they were in a poor bargaining position, and were only paid the same 'petite solde' as the French soldier, less than the Swiss or Germans got.[71] From 1693 down to 1789 an Irish brigade formed a part of the French army.

The first permanent regiment of Germans in France was enrolled in 1654, and survived to 1789. More nationalities than ever before had been laid under contribution by Richelieu and Mazarin; and Spanish, Italian, Corsican, Walloon, Swedish, Danish, Polish, Hungarian and Croat regiments could all be counted on the payroll of Louis XIV. In 1748 foreign troops totalled 52,000. Still more exotic ingredients were being added to the mixture: Turks, Wallachians, Tartars, even a brigade of Negroes drawn from various parts of Africa and Asia. Germans fought in America for France as well as for England in the War of Independence; and vacancies in foreign regiments tended to be filled up with German-speaking volunteers from France's eastern provinces.[72]

This Bourbon army, not less multifarious than Napoleon's, was available for police work as well as for war, in an age when revolt was always smouldering among the French masses who had to pay for all the glory. When for instance the peasantry of the Boulonnais broke out in 1662, the infantry section of the force concentrated by the Governor of Picardy consisted of ten companies of French and five of Swiss guards.[73] In the later years of Louis XIV's reign Swiss troops were among those fighting the Camisard rebels in the Cevennes. During the eighteenth century the Government looked on its foreign detachments as among its chief props, and took pains to keep them contented and loyal.[74] In May 1789 the monarchy mustered them round Paris in an attempt to cling to power. Even in 1830 Swiss troops made the last stand for the restored Bourbons.

Sweden's army, for a brief spell the best in Europe, came to the forefront in alliance with the French. It was also to verify the lesson learned by Machiavelli from the fate of the Italian communes: 'It is more difficult to bring a republic, armed with its own arms, under the sway of one of its citizens than it is to bring one armed with foreign arms.'[75] Gustavus Adolphus started with a provincial militia; as soon as foreign conquests and French subsidies gave him the means he went into the market for foreign troops. Only a little more than half of the men with whom he entered the Thirty Years' War were Swedish or Finnish — part of Finland being Sweden's first colony.[76] War losses were made good chiefly with Germans, and as the military machine and the Baltic Empire expanded, the Vasa dynasty, originally put on the throne by the people, lost its fear of antagonizing its subjects. War burdens pressed the mass of the people down, while the landed nobles, now prosperous generals and ministers of the

Crown, achieved an ascendancy over the peasantry they had never had before.

War is an equalizer, and Holland and England, whose seventeenth- and eighteenth-century evolution led far away from absolute monarchy, differed from France in their methods of recruitment much less than might have been expected. Holland's commercial oligarchy after the struggle for independence had no more taste than its anointed enemy at Paris for a citizen army. Independence had been born out of intense class struggle, and divisions between rich and poor were still bitter. Besides, it was more profitable for rich Dutchmen that poor Dutchmen should work for them than fight for them. Out of the profits foreign muskets could be hired. In 1629, for instance, there were three British regiments in service, with Dutch, French and German officers, and 'a mixture of deserters and out-casts from all nations' to fill up gaps.[77] A Scots brigade was retained down to the French Revolution.[78] It was a system that at times set national security in hazard, but was always good for the security of the governing class. England was working meanwhile on even more Carthaginian lines. At the height of the Civil War the parliamentary leaders (much like the Regent class in the revolt of the Netherlands) looked askance at enrolment of armed Saints, and preferred to subsidize a less disturbing army from Scotland. After the Restoration the memory of the Ironsides lingered on as a bogy to England's rulers as well as enemies: the plutocracy wanted soldiers, but not soldiers who read pamphlets and debated affairs of Church and State. William III fought the battle of the Boyne with a gallimaufry of Englishmen, Ulster-men, Dutchmen, Scots, Huguenots, Danes, Swedes and Prussians,[79] an army whose ideology, at any rate, left nothing to be deplored. A splendid new vista opened about the end of the century when Hesse-Cassel began jobbing off troops to foreign governments, chiefly to England, for whom Hessians became the counterpart of France's Swiss. They were sometimes useful inside Britain. In February 1746 the Prince of Hesse landed at Leith with 5,000 men. Not many years later the Hessians were on their way to uphold law and order in America. In 1701 Frederick IV of Denmark had similarly disposed of 20,000 soldiers to England, including 6,000 Norwegians.[80] After the 'Forty-five' a very important recruiting-ground was opened up in the Highlands. During the Napoleonic wars all comers were welcome to the British ranks;[81] as late as the Crimean War a foreign legion was enrolled.

Eastern Europe after 1648 followed a rather different path. Unlike the west, it developed not voluntary but conscript service (though England had her Hessian conscripts, her press-ganged sailors, and

Highlanders who were often volunteers in name rather than in fact).[82] Volunteers were linked with personal freedom, conscripts with serfdom. In the west the reorganization of feudal society by absolutism involved the disappearance of most serfdom. Eastern imitators of Versailles, however, could only come by the military resources they needed by abetting their nobles in imposing serfdom on their peasantry, often for the first time. When the people had been made accustomed to this it became safe to force guns into their hands and conscript them into standing armies for life – a very different system from the old casual militia service of the west.

But in the east too the foreign mercenary, a familiar figure long before 1648, still had an important part to play. Often he was the first bearer of firearms; gunpowder helped to destroy peasant freedom as it spread eastward. An illustration of some earlier phases can be found in Estonia. Here from the early thirteenth century German feudal lords were confronted by masses of Russian and Lithuanian footmen, and needed infantry support more urgently than did the chivalry of the west. For this purpose the Teutonic Order had to utilize its conquered Estonian peasants, and allow them to retain arms. Thereby it also allowed them to go on rebelling, as they did on a great scale in 1343. When firearms came in it would have been too dangerous as well as costly to supply them to the rank and file, and in 1498 the Diet ended peasant service in the army and replaced it with a tax designed to meet the cost of mercenaries from Germany. From 1507 peasants had no right to bear arms. 'This made them completely defenceless against their masters, and their legal and economic welfare began to deteriorate rapidly.'[83]

The next stages can be traced in the story of Brandenburg-Prussia. Stretched out between Poland and Holland, this state combined the military systems of east and west and drew from the fusion its peculiar strength. Beginning his reign in 1640 with a scanty 2,500 mercenaries, the Great Elector left 30,000 at his death in 1688. Nursing this force carefully, with the aid of revenues from their richer western provinces, he and his heirs were able to coerce their Estates into paying more taxation, and at the same time to join hands with the nobility in subjugating the peasantry. By 1713 it was safe to impose regular conscription.[84] Mercenaries, however, continued to form a good proportion of the army, where they provided a countercheck to the native serfs. As late as the eve of Jena Prussia was paying 80,000 foreign – mainly German – troops.[85]

If Prussia combined the strength of east and west, Poland ended by falling between two stools and having neither.[86] For a very long time, and very closely, Polish military evolution paralleled French; until

Poland's political and economic structure diverged so far from that of France that her army had to seek another path. In the Middle Ages its backbone was the feudal cavalry of the *szlachta*, which in the sixteenth century became a paid force like the gendarmerie; but from as early as the thirteenth century the kings had looked for soldiers more dependent on themselves, and found them by hiring men from outside. Moravians and Bohemians, Lithuanians, Ruthenians and Tartars, fought in the Polish ranks at Tannenberg in 1410. Germans, Hungarians, Serbs, Wallachians were gathered in; Cossacks were first enlisted for the defence of the south-east in 1524.[87] Precisely as in France there were sporadic attempts at times of crisis to form a national infantry. Stephen Bathory (1575–86), the King imported from Hungary, started a system of recruiting peasants from Crown estates, and there was a vain effort to expand it just before the great catastrophe of the invasions of 1655. But with a social order moving steadily in the sixteenth and seventeenth centuries towards the reduction of the peasantry to serdom, reliance on mercenaries was easier and safer. Wladislaw IV (1632–48) hired Cossacks to fight Russia and Sweden; later he planned to use a Cossack army against the Sejm, exactly as Strafford may have planned to use an Irish army against Parliament.[88] He instituted a permanent division between 'Polish' and 'foreign' units; in the latter, though some of the foot might in fact be Polish, the drill and word of command were German. The fatal debility of government and treasury however prevented further development of a professional army. A change-over to a conscript army was also out of the question. Living comfortably off the labour of the peasants, and finding no need for an army to keep them in order, the nobles refused to allow the state either to tax or to conscript their serfs. Poland came to an end – Polish aristocracy went on.

It was in Russia that the east-European system came to full flower, producing the only army capable of standing up to Revolutionary and Napoleonic France on something like equal terms. Russia's long-continuing poverty and backwardness limited the possibility both of an armoured feudal cavalry in the Middle Ages and of a strong professional force in the sixteenth and seventeenth centuries. Originally soldiers were drawn from the small gentry, and from the poorer townsfolk who came to provide the semi-regular body of *streltsi*, one easily infected with the political grievances of the class to which it belonged.[89] In addition to these national contingents, foreign mercenaries were employed here too – Lithuanians and Tartars, for example.[90] In the last years of Boris Godunov (1598–1605) it was noticeable that his small guard of Germans stood by him to the end when all his other supporters had gone over to Dmitri and the Poles. This hint was not lost on the Romanovs, who now mounted the shaky throne. Like many other rulers, they made good use of the prodigious glut of soldiers of fortune produced by the Thirty Years' War, and presently it was realized that a still stronger as well as much cheaper alloy could be produced by mingling foreign professionals with native peasants conscripted for life and drilled by German officers or on German lines. The Romanov army, while enabling Russia to intervene in Europe, found, as Pokrovsky points out, its first and fundamental task at home.[91] During the seventeenth and eighteenth centuries serfdom was being imposed on a steadily expanding area, and the nobles accepted the necessity of a strong state and army to crush the strong resistance they met. As the peasants of each province were cowed, they could be enrolled and used to break resistance in others. The Tsarist Empire's size and heterogeneity, characteristic of all the states that survived in eastern Europe, facilitated this.

By the close of the seventeenth century one small corner of north-western Europe was committed to a new road of change and progress; but taking Europe as a whole, far more of its people were serfs than at the end of the fifteenth century, and its landlords were richer and more secure. Absolute monarchy had cauterized the Continent with war and famine, and left it exhausted, but safe for the landowning aristocracy. Everywhere kings owed this success at least as much to the services of their foreign soldiers as to those of their own subjects.

Postscript

Foreign mercenary troops were appearing on the European stage, as elsewhere, very early. Feudal levies soon proved inadequate. Lords and their knights could be summoned to serve only for short spells; the reason, it must be supposed, is that in the formative periods of feudal kingdoms, like England after 1066, they had to be on the spot in their fiefs, ready to deal with any risings that might break out. Limits once established would be hard for rulers to break through later on. It has been pointed out that protracted sieges of fortresses, the staple of twelfth-century warfare, required men ready to serve as long as they could be paid, and Henry II of England owed much of his success to his employment and skilful use of mercenaries.[92] In 1389 it was with a force of Germans that a king expelled from Sweden came back in an effort to re-establish himself.

Men were engaged as required, or as funds allowed; their earliest permanent tenure was as members of royal bodyguards, which must have lent tone and respectability to the profession as a whole. A corps of *Landsknechts* came to be regularly attached to the Habsburg rulers, with a status of something like Household troops. In the late seventeenth century it struck a traveller in Spain that only one of the King's four companies of guards was Spanish;[93] the custom lives on to this day in the Papal Guard. The first rank-and-file soldiers from abroad to be put on a permanent footing in France were Swiss. France and England could draw on ethnic minorities, Welsh and Breton and others, within their own frontiers. Norway, rich in seamen, was attached to the Danish Crown; Sweden gained control of Finland and made it a recruiting-ground. Spain and its Habsburg partner Austria enjoyed this advantage more fully than anyone else, the former by being in possession of the Netherlands and most of Italy, the latter of Bohemia and other Slav territories and part of Hungary.

It may be less appropriate to think of the mercenary as a 'proletarian' than as a skilled worker belonging to the era of the independent craftsman who had his own tools and knew how to use them. More akin to the true proletarian was the volunteer regular soldier of later times, wearing his own king's uniform, trained by the king's drill-sergeant and equipped with a musket from the royal armoury. Men like him have in fact come increasingly from the working class, and from an urban background rather than from village or mountain valley like their forerunners. There were always technical tasks which called for individuals of higher status. We know of a 'long line of Italian engineers who worked for the kings of France';[94] a German from Moravia built Henry VIII's citadel at Carlisle.

There are parallels on the Turkish side. A Neapolitan renegade, one of the numerous Europeans attracted into Ottoman service, directed the reconstruction of the fleet after its defeat at Lepanto in 1571, with harquebuses instead of bows, and more cannon.[95] Turkish armies abounded in adventurers from many Muslim lands; the special corps of janizaries were Europeans captured or levied as tax in early life, and thoroughly indoctrinated. There had been numerous older experiments in the use of slave-soldiers, the easiest to inure to discipline and obedience, and not in the Islamic world only. Tiberius II of Byzantium in the sixth century set on foot a corps of 15,000 'heathen slaves', as the nucleus of a standing army; among other virtues they would be devoid of any sympathy with popular feeling.[96]

In Ulster the O'Neill chieftains relied on mercenaries from the Scottish Islands;[97] Irish failure to resist the English invaders may be seen as a consequence. Finding Ulster full of footloose swordsmen, the English tried to get rid of some of them, at a profit, by shipping them off to fight in the Baltic.[98] Governments plagued with similar surpluses were not sorry to see their own lieges taking service abroad. From the Cevennes as well as other ill-nourished hill areas went recruits to diverse European armies.[99] Other Frenchmen might be found more exceptionally under foreign flags. In 1572 there were 2,000 at Venice; in the previous year there had been French sailors in the Spanish fleet at Lepanto, a victory made possible as Braudel says by a lull in hostilities elsewhere, which brought a flock of soldiers of fortune southward.[100] Gustavus Adolphus is said to have had 10,000 Scots in his employ, and the number may have been even higher.[101] Happy as their country was to see them go, there might be trouble when they came home to roost; Scotland's rebel army in 1639 had seasoned troops to hand, and it may be guessed that Huguenot resistance to Louis XIV in the Cevennes found similar reinforcement.

It was partly because there were always fighting-men seeking jobs that Europe was nearly always at war. A foreign reservoir encouraged royal irresponsibility; and peasants were less reluctant to pay taxes than to hand over their sons as tribute. The system lingered on into the nineteenth century; it was a symptom of decay when in 1794, with Spain at war with Revolutionary France, officers of the Walloon Guards in Spanish service formed a club at Madrid where very pro-French sentiments were aired. But there was a protest among Spanish liberals in the 1820s against the use of foreigners, as both unreliable and a menace to freedom.[102] In the Kingdom of Naples they were kept until the unification of Italy. By the time that only such vestigial remains were left, a new page had already been turned with the recruitment of Asian and African troops, sometimes conscripts but oftener mercenaries. They were being made use of now on a very large scale, not only for colonial wars and policing but at times (during 1914–18 especially) in Europe as well;[103] and it was in the building of the French Empire that the Foreign Legion did most of its work of killing and being killed.

5
Nationalist Movements and Social Classes

'What ish my nation? Who talks of my nation?' peevishly exclaimed Captain Macmorris, at Fluellen's innocent allusion to the Irish. In Shakespeare's Europe, nationalities were coming more in contact, often painful contact, and growing more conscious of how they were thought about by others. What they felt was only at the beginning of turning into a political idea. A 'nation' meant those born of a common stock, and sharing a common character. Fluellen's own Welshmen could be panegyrized by Milton as 'An old and haughty nation, proud in arms', but they had never been a state, and he certainly had no wish to see them one. Today there is a Welsh nationalist movement, one of a bewildering variety of such movements sprawling over modern history. A paradoxical difficulty in the way of any effort to unravel them is that they could only fully develop after national states and nationalism were established facts in a certain number of countries. Nationalism was a creation mainly from above, the outcome of state power exercised over long periods in the special conditions of early modern western Europe.[1] Yet among these conditions was the prior existence of national feeling, rough and half-formed like Captain Macmorris's though it might be. State and nationality constantly interacted, each requiring the other for its full development towards the point where they could help to inspire nationalist movements in other lands, further and further afield.

Medieval society and its jarring classes were held together, so far as moral cement was wanted, by religion, as in Asia. But towards the end of the Middle Ages a number of feudal monarchies were acquiring something of the quality of the true state, as an entity felt to be somehow representative of all its subjects collectively, and entitled to an allegiance different from mere submission to a ruler of the moment. England led the way, and helped to provoke a similar spirit in France by repeated attacks on its neighbour, as France was to do in turn with Germany. In the sixteenth and seventeenth centuries when the strengthened state of the 'absolute monarchies' took shape, it sometimes coincided, if never more than approximately, with the boundaries of nationality or language. In this case, centralized authority and quickening currents of economic circulation made for a closer linkage between state and public feeling. In all this process urban middle classes figured prominently. Patriotic feeling could bolster their self-esteem and confidence, and by identifying themselves with it they could the better aspire to a leading place in a changing pattern of society. A national revolt like that of the Netherlands – or, less conclusively, that of Scotland about 1640 – was at the same time a kind of bourgeois revolution. Conversely, the bourgeois revolutions in England and then France had a markedly nationalistic tone.

Modern capitalism came into being in western Europe very slowly indeed.[2] Tools and techniques, and ideas too, often lay long unused. We can reckon four centuries of preparation for the big leap of the Industrial Revolution. Nationalism can be seen growing up along with it, also very gradually and fumblingly, and linked with it in many complex ways. By dissolving traditional social structures and substituting fresh ones, the national market that capitalism made for itself brought classes into sharper confrontation, requiring a potent ideology as well as a firm administrative apparatus to keep it within bounds. More and more functions or services of a positive kind had to be undertaken by the state, which enmeshed all classes in its activities. Always a big employer, it became far the biggest employer. Given this increasing involvement, growing cities were a fertile breeding-ground for national feeling; this, with religion declining, was the readiest emotional compensation for the strangeness of urban and industrial life to the first generations of incomers from the countryside. At the same time, newspapers and other means of spreading the nationalist spirit proliferated.

Renan called the nation '*une grande solidarité*', a communion of memory and purpose.[3] It was also, however, a combination of classes, and the state was built not on the nation as a community but on the divisions within a community which it was itself welding into a nation. It learned to do so increasingly, as time went on, by deliberate indoctrination, through mass education especially. Haydn is said to have thought of composing a national anthem of Austria because of the influence he saw exercised in England by *God Save the King*. Full-blown nationalism was worked up out of old elemental ties of neighbourhood and dislike of strangers, much as rival religions have been organized by Churches out of man's plastic primitive religious sense. Nothing can be further from the mark than the oft-repeated maxim that nationalism is natural and proper, whereas communism is unnatural and improper.

Prophets of nationalism have usually been 'very remote from the economic and class interests of the period'.[4] This abstraction was part of what made their ideas acceptable to all classes within established states, but with diverse meanings for each class; and similar diversity of meaning was to show itself in nationalist movements endeavouring to set up new states. On the whole, nationalism was least congenial to the highest and lowest strata. From the aristocratic point of view it was an invasion of the sphere of public life by plebeians. John Chester, the cynical man of the world in Dickens, prided himself on his aloofness from its 'intensely vulgar sentiments'.[5] When such men 'loved their country', they were thinking of it as a glorified private estate owned by themselves and their friends. About most of its inhabitants, and their wants, they preferred not to think: instead they idealized the 'sacred soil', the territory inalienable as an entailed patrimony. A landowning peasantry could share this sensation in its own way. In the towns it was the lower-middle-class groups, made up (like the peasantry) of a mass of individuals with little corporate organization, to whom the thought of nation as 'family' had most appeal. Industrial working classes, far more antagonistic to those above them, and busy building their own forms of organization, had much less emotional need of it, and shared in it chiefly because the state touched their life at more and more points.

In a few countries state nationalism was already old by 1789, but this date may be taken as a starting-point for modern nationalist movements of opposition. They were ushered in by a flurry of revolts in the Habsburg Empire, provoked by the bureaucratic reformism of Joseph II. These were, in the main, conservative regional reactions against change, though in both Hungary and Belgium their social composition and temper were very mixed,[6] their affinity was with the aristocratic intransigence of 1787–9, the initial phase of the French Revolution. In 1808–14 the Spanish War of Independence against Napoleon was prophetic of many later ones in containing another jumble of class ideas and interests, with clerical conservatism dominant but two tendencies opposed to it emerging, a middle-class Liberal programme and peasant discontent against landlord exactions. It was the hope, quickly dashed, of seeing patriotism wedded to progress and reform that made Wordsworth so enthusiastic about the Spanish resistance, and inspired his *Convention of Cintra*, as profound and imaginative a eulogy of the Nation as any ever written.

Within Spain, not long after the Napoleonic Wars, there was reviving an old regional separatism of Catalonia. It is instructive as displaying what has been repeated in the history of many lands, a shift from an earlier stage of conservative withdrawal to a later, more progressive one, introduced by industrial growth and then pushed on by the contradictions this brought with it. At the time of the first Carlist War (1833–9) rural Catalonia, along with the inner Basque area, was the mainstay of the reactionary Carlist cause. These areas were turning away from the alien modernity, the new-fangled administration and the secularism, of Liberal Spain, and fighting to regain or preserve old local rights. But their coastal fringes, with the stimulus of French nearness and capital, were before long becoming Spain's chief workshops, very unlike Brittany in France or Ireland in the British Isles. After the middle of the century a new, less archaic, though still socially conservative *Catalanismo* was developing, to the accompaniment (as in all such cases) of a cultural revival.

Simultaneously, industrial growth was generating acute conflicts of capital and labour. Spain had been little touched, but was none the less alarmed, by the revolutions of 1848; and these had made men of property everywhere look to 'national unity as a miracle worker which would prevent class warfare and a popular rising'.[7] A Home Rule movement was encouraged by employers as a means of diverting working-class resentment away from them and against Madrid. Several right-wing groups coalesced in 1901 in the *Lliga Regionalista*. It won electoral successes, as did a broader combination formed in 1906, the *Solidaritat Catalana*, which in 1914 secured a regional authority of its own, the *Mancomunitat*, with very limited powers. All this could not exorcise class conflict. Barcelona's lower-middle strata remained faithful to their old Liberal tradition, travestied now by the anticlerical demagogy of Lerroux and his Radical Party. Because this was also antiseparatist, Madrid winked at its inflammatory talk.[8] More serious, the workers persisted in organizing militant trade unions and waging a chronic warfare of strikes and sometimes bullets against their employers. After the Great War many of these were in a mood to welcome the right-wing dictatorship of General Primo de Rivera, who in 1925 abolished the *Mancomunitat*. On his fall, and that of the monarchy, the Catalan movement resumed its advance, but with the Left now in the lead, and the workers marshalled in their own *Esquerra Republicana*.

Just a century earlier, in 1831, Belgium gained its independence from Holland very largely by dint of foreign backing. Industry was coming in, sufficiently to stimulate the country and to make the national rising, in part, a bourgeois revolution; it had not gone far enough to set up too many class contentions, and it was monopolized by the Walloon half of the country and gave this a certain solidarity as against the economically backward Flemish half – today strongly autonomist, and insisting on its belated fair share. Norway, transferred in 1814 from Denmark to Sweden, moved during the century from an insulated peasant society's resentment of change towards a modern national consciousness. Economic growth here took the form of world-wide shipping activity, ideally suited to promote a sense of distinct national interests without causing too much class division: after the days of wooden sailing-ships, Norway was buying most of its vessels from abroad, not setting up a big shipbuilding industry at home. It was after universal suffrage came in 1898 that a demand for independence became insistent. Class solidarity in support of it was not tested too severely, because the Swedes – especially their trade unions – were too civilized to try to preserve the union by force.[9]

Ireland, that museum collection of historical miscellanies, went through many experiences before the later 1870s when the Home Rule movement led by Parnell sought a mass social basis by joining hands with a militant peasant movement. It could afford to do so because the landlords were so largely Anglo–Irish and (like Parnell) Protestant; for the same reason the British Government could not afford to go on relying on them for support, as it could in some other colonies, but had to quieten the agitation by buying them out. Nationalism recovered, with underemployed urban lower-middle strata for its chief carrier. There was no big industrial bourgeoisie as a counterweight, and the small working class played little part, in spite of the Socialist Republican Party founded in 1897 by James Connolly.[10] England paid a penalty for its policies in earlier days of hindering industrial development: a bigger Irish bourgeoisie would have seen its interest, sooner or later, in an English partnership against its workers, and (like the Scottish) in a share of empire profits – an important consideration for Catalan businessmen too, so long as there were any Spanish colonies left. Ireland, unlike Catalonia, thus escaped the Scylla of capital-and-labour deadlock, though not, later on, the Charybdis of an undeveloped economy and a sterile social outlook. This sterility was worsened by the movement having too much of a religious complexion, and, like sundry others, too many of its roots abroad. Irish–American sympathy and subsidies did much to keep the desire for freedom alive, nothing to kindle a progressive programme.

National ideology, like a theology such as Calvinism, could take shape only in a very specific social environment, but could then be adapted to a wide variety of others. Middle and eastern Europe entered the post-1815 age shaken by the recent political upheavals, and now by the accelerating march of the Industrial Revolution, as an odd medley of large multinational entities and small fragments of divided peoples. Much of the time from then on was to be devoted to rectifying these anomalies, and establishing the national state, by revival or fresh creation, as the common norm. Britain and France by their success had raised its prestige very high. The endeavours of the rest of Europe to emulate them were to be very often a pursuit of red herrings hidden in holy grails. Still, history has never moved in straight lines, and the more complex and contradictory European society became, the more devious its advance was bound to be, and the fuller of illusions and delusions.

East of the Rhineland, industry was making its appearance only spasmodically, here and there. But while successful risings could take place in regions still pre-industrial,[11] it is to be remembered that capitalism exerted novel pressures even on districts still agricultural; on Romania, for instance, where demand for food in the urban west offered bigger profits for landlords, and incited them both to desire greater autonomy from Turkey and to take away land from their peasants while exacting all their dues from them in full.[12] They were not averse to taking land away from their neighbours as well. Widening horizons, geographical and technological, made for aggressive self-assertion as well as progress, and a climate in which nationalism meant a claim not only to exist, but to expand. Acquisitiveness as well as romantic irrationality often helped to fix a people's ambitions on a territory larger than itself, though arguably belonging to it once upon a time. Again, as in industrialism, Britain set the example. Its own 'nationalist movement' was imperialism, to which patriotism came to be so closely tied that 'Little Englander' was a term of reproach. Tolstoy lamented that small oppressed peoples were catching the infection of nationalism from their oppressors, and were ready in turn 'to perpetrate on other peoples the very same deeds'. He saw realistically how this perversity was fostered by all privileged classes, because their position depended on the possession or favour of state power.[13]

For the outcome of a nationalist movement and the quality of its future state, the vital question was the extent to which different classes participated in it. There was no simple equation between mass involvement and success, since classes once aroused might collide; moreover, foreign opinion always counted, and foreign governments or respectable publics abroad were always averse to the common people taking the bit between their teeth. As a rule only quite small minorities were actively engaged, though they might have the approval, warmer or cooler, of larger numbers. At one end of the scale, in Russia, it might be said that the Tsar himself was the standard-bearer: Nicholas I, 'the policeman of Europe', was in some ways, and prided himself on being, very Russian, and his official version of Russian nationalism[14] was only a caricature of what the Western state taught its citizens. At the other end, support was nearly always forthcoming from the loose bundle of lower-middle-class groupings – teachers, small traders, artisans and many more – which have been lumped together as the 'petty bourgeoisie'. This clumsy as well as un-English term fails to express what is most characteristic of the sector it covers, namely that it is made up of unattached, unanchored individuals or clusters. They are not *individualists* by nature or choice, though they may be made so by circumstances. An individualist requires a firmer footing in society, to sustain as well as to repel him. As a rule these irregulars of history ask nothing better than to be relieved of their non-attachment, incorporated into some union, whether body politic or *corpus mysticum*. They improvise all kinds of minor fraternities of their own; they cannot invent the nation, but they welcome it more emotionally than any other class. To their scattered ranks have belonged most of the intellectuals who have done the work of adapting and spreading nationalist ideas and illusions – both ideas and illusions being, more than with other people, a part of their daily bread.

'Un nom devenu terrible, le nom du prolétaire':[15] so a student of the new working class wrote, two years before *The Communist Manifesto* and the June days of 1848 in Paris which displayed it as a rebel against the social order, not against any mere government. No peoples had yet gained their freedom except the Belgians, and, less completely, some in the Balkans, and in all these cases foreign assistance counted for much. Other movements had mostly lacked mass participation, but their revolutions in 1848–9 failed largely because, now that the masses were beginning to be aroused, their class divisions were more evident; a dilemma equally fatal to the bourgeois revolution needed, above all, by Germany. After the collapse nationalism persisted, and often achieved its aims, but not by force of popular enthusiasm as idealists had hoped; it was being taken up by governments and shepherded into safe conservative ways. National states were again, as previously in the West, though more rapidly now with the aid of modern administrative resources, being built from above.

Germany's first patriots, in the late eighteenth century, often looked forward to a peaceful nation taking its place in a free and fraternal Europe.[16] They were men of the Age of Reason, which was very much an age of amiable fancies, nowhere more than in such blindness to the Manichaean dualism of the Nation. Twenty years of war, ending with the Prussian army recovering its laurels at Leipzig and Waterloo, deepened a harsher note which had been audible from the first in the admiration felt for Frederick the Great.[17] In a country with few industries and many governments, the educated middle class was more than usually addicted to official service. A considerable part of it was made up of semi-hereditary bureaucrats and clergy; a multitude of malcontents failed to find places, and might – until their luck changed – be very loud on behalf of the twin causes of Liberalism and nationalism. The intelligentsia was too weak to challenge aristocratic privilege; it could find consolation in calling on fellow Germans to rise and take their rightful place as masters of Europe. In the cloudy bombast and megalomania of German nationalist ideology can be recognized the frustrations and aspirations of all these plebeians.

In this ideology there was from an early date a note of economic nationalism and capitalist method amid romantic madness. Germans dreaming of a united Fatherland were dreaming also of building up their industries and challenging a hated Britannia on the seas.[18] Economic growth, quickened by the *Zollverein*, strengthened the bourgeoisie and its claim to a share of political power, but it also sharpened class tension lower down, as the rioting of hungry Silesian weavers in 1844 revealed. More perilous in the long run, industrialism was bringing with it that fatal Siamese twin of capitalism, the proletariat. French events in 1848 sounded a thunderous warning against any stirring-up of the masses: there was no foreign oppressor in France to unite the classes, but Germany's foreign oppressors were more imaginary than real, and the bourgeoisie now spreading across the continent was always highly sensitive to the European atmosphere.

Industrial expansion continued, and with it the Liberal threat to autocracy in Prussia; but as Bismarck – in power from 1862 – was shrewd enough to observe, the working-class and socialist threat to the bourgeoisie grew at the same rate. His solution for the difficulties facing conservative rule and its institutions was to give Germany the unification it hankered for by force of Prussian arms. Instead of Prussia being merged in Germany, as Frederick William IV – temporarily reduced to demagogy – proclaimed in 1848, Germany was merged into Prussia. The capitalist wing of Liberalism was relieved at getting so much without a hazardous appeal to the masses, and from now on was content to cultivate its industrial garden, leaving state affairs to the conservatives. Economic growth had already gone so far that political unification scarcely seems to have been necessary for its further increase. It was needed rather for political and social reasons. The function of the new Reich was to provide means of harmonizing or holding in check the animosities of rival classes, as the Western state had done, but as now required to be done far more hastily and forcefully because industrialism was growing so much more rapidly. Chauvinist and militarist indoctrination accompanied by universal military service was an essential part of the process.[19]

Gramsci's mind was always coming back to the problem of the Risorgimento and its hollowness or inconsistencies, thanks to which his Italy had succumbed so easily to Fascism. Regional particularism, attachment to Venice or Sicily more than to Italy, was one of the most palpable obstacles. Devotion to Italy came easiest to small groups of enthusiasts, many of them exiles like the old Garibaldians in South America who dreamed nightly of their native land and were buried with their faces towards it. Distance has often lent enchantment to a patriot's view of his fellow countrymen. One of the earliest and most determined struggles for liberation was that of Corsica against Genoa, only defeated when the Genoese sold the island to France in 1768. Ordinary Corsicans were emboldened by hatred of outsiders, an elite leadership by desire for power or by literary patriotism. General Paoli explained his motives to Boswell by quoting Virgil – 'Vincet amor patriae.'[20]

Paoli was anything but a leveller, as another remark recorded by his admirer shows: 'A diffusion of knowledge among the people was a disadvantage, for it made the vulgar rise above their humble sphere.'[21] His words were ominous of too much Italian nationalism of the next century, and class division was a much more deep-seated impediment than regionalism. In poverty-stricken Italy a social programme to reinforce the romantic dream of union and independence was all the more requisite because religion was both powerful and anti-national, Rome and Vienna as thick as thieves. But any pledge of concessions to the masses, to draw them into the struggle, would mean sacrifices for those who lived at their expense. Ardent young men of the middle classes might be ready for periodical conspiracies and risings, but they were likely, as in Asia, to have too many ties with the landowning system to dream of invoking the land-hunger of the poor cultivator.

Commercial enterprise was damped by the rooted preference for investment in land,[22] in a country where land – in the north at any rate

– had always been a market commodity. In the north some industrial development was taking place by the 1840s, and in Lombardy, where it attracted an active younger section of the aristocracy as well as the wealthier middle class,[23] it was the business interests that suffered from Austrian rule, acceptable enough to most of the big landlords and to the peasantry under clerical tuition.[24] It was complained that the tariff system sacrificed local industry to the interests of Austria and Bohemia, and with Mediterranean trade expanding it was felt that Italy ought to have a better place in it.[25] There was very little revolutionary fervour among the businessmen however. Liberal publicists, so far from representing 'an aspiring and self-conscious bourgeoisie', were often landowners or intellectuals with upper-class connections, 'exerting themselves to rouse a timid and lethargic bourgeoisie to a consciousness of its interests'.[26] Whatever capitalist development took place, in Lombardy or Piedmont, added, as always, to bourgeois timidity about any breach of law and order that might endanger property as well as government.

Of social and economic facts, Mazzini, living on coffee and spinning his pipe-dreams and plots in London, understood very little. Workmen did themselves no good by clamouring for their rights, he told them, and ought to think of their duty instead. All he had to offer as a social programme was that a free government would welcome 'labour associations . . . of proven morality and capacity', and turn unused common lands into smallholdings.[27] Cavour knew all about economics, but from the angle of a landowner and business man, and with him as with Bismarck national unity was a secondary considera- tion. His concern was to fortify established interests in Piedmont, where he took office in 1852, which could only be done by enlarging the principality. It could then beat off the peril of 'red republican' anarchy sweeping Italy, a peril he made use of to frighten European governments and win their approval.[28] Piedmont's army was too small to play a Prussian role; a French army was brought in instead. Napoleon III wanted prestige and scraps of territory, but he also wanted to forestall social agitation in Italy which might infect his own kingdom.

He was disappointed by the few volunteers who came forward in 1859, and by his army's poor reception in rural Lombardy.[29] Realities lurking under the tinsel phrases of patriotism showed themselves in the harsh suppression of peasant mutiny during and after the unification, chiefly in the south.[30] A nation's duty lies in 'supporting and not hindering the actions of the elect minority',[31] as Croce, a true representative of the elite, was to write. A very inorganic Italy emerged, which its rulers set to work to mould into a national state, as in Germany but less successfully, by compulsion. Young men would be made to feel Italian by being made to wear Italian uniforms; jingo propaganda would usurp the place of the fraternal relations with other peoples that Mazzini had looked forward to. Thus speeded up, the state-building which in the west had been the slow work of centuries could not hide its artificiality. Poverty continued to drive swarms of Italians abroad in search of work. When a gang of these labourers were asked by a traveller whether they loved their native land, one of them smiled and said 'Italy is for us whoever gives us our bread.'[32]

In the west, nationalism had an urban habitat, close to the traditions of the old city-state or chartered town. In eastern Europe it was taken up − like the Reformation earlier − in default of an energetic burgher class, by the landed gentry, that 'middle class' of feudal society. An archaic body like the Polish nobility could acquire some degree of moral justification by leading the defence of a subjugated country, and deflect social discontent away from itself. Only a minority of the gentry ever took up arms, and a good proportion of those who did may have been younger sons or men of broken fortunes, although the number of estates confiscated by the Russian authorities is proof that not all were so. Whatever their individual motives, their sacrifices conferred merit on the whole body. Religion supplied a buttress, but also a further blockage against progressive social thinking. Poland, not the Polish people, was the theme of patriotic rhapsodizing, and served to keep social realities out of sight. Mickiewicz, the poet in exile, carried the theme furthest with his mystic concept of Poland as the martyred Christ among the nations.

Mysticism usually means mystification; the real martyr was the Polish peasant, his persecutors the patriotic gentleman. 'Congress Poland', the separately administered kingdom under the Tsar Alexander I after 1815, was free of serfdom, which had been abolished there in the Napoleonic era, but agrarian relations in their essentials were little altered. Gentry patriotism, moreover, was strongly tinged with the feudal imperialism which had ruined Poland in former times: its demand was not for simple freedom within Polish ethnic limits, but for the old eastern marches as well, with their non-Polish inhabitants and Polish landlords.

Agitation in 'Congress Poland' burst out in the Revolution of 1830–1. This was initiated by secret societies and students who seized control of Warsaw. Women took an active part, a symptom as in so many other national movements of new ideas reaching a depressed stratum. Not many peasants, and not all districts, joined in. Tsarist reprisals fell heaviest on the gentry, while the province lost its constitution and was incorporated in the Russian Empire. Another rising was quelled in 1846, and in Galicia, the Austrian share of Poland, the Government gave a demonstration of how easily the tables could be turned by allowing a peasant *jacquerie* against the landlords. This hint was not thrown away, and in 1848 most of Poland was quiet. It was time for a new class to come to the front, and by mid-century a fairly strong bourgeoisie was present, with industry (besides coal-mining), sprouting at Warsaw, Lódź and other centres, impoverished peasants providing the labour force. Industrial depression helped to launch the second big revolutionary outbreak, this time in 1863. All classes were represented in the long-drawn, mainly guerrilla struggle, but unevenly; there was still no united front of the whole nation.[33] Warsaw workers and artisans were prominent. There were divergent views as between progressives, who wanted to set the peasantry in motion by promising it land, and landowners, who demurred. They and the bourgeoisie pinned many of their hopes on foreign intervention, which did not come. Sometimes peasants profited by the confusion to rise against their landlords, as they had been doing on and off all the time, and handworkers to smash machinery.[34] Indirectly the peasants did benefit when the Russian Government, after regaining control, carried out a partial agrarian reform in order to draw the gentry's teeth.

Industry went on growing in the later nineteenth century, but politically speaking it was growing up too late, when the Commune had sounded its tocsin to capitalists everywhere, and the German Liberals had taken refuge with Bismarck. It benefited too by the large Russian market for its goods, as Catalan production did by the Spanish. For the working class there was likewise an alternative, between nationalism as presented by Pilsudski's 'Polish Socialist Party' and class alignment with the workers of Russia. This latter, and eventual federation, was what Rosa Luxemburg, a very much more genuine socialist than Pilsudski, advocated; she maintained – forgetting, Kautsky objected, the intelligentsia – that no class in Poland now identified itself with the struggle for independence.[35] Some other 'unattached' strata may have been exceptions. It has been shown that in eastern Europe generally national feeling was strongest not in industrial zones but where artisans carried on small-scale production for township and village requirements.[36]

At the time of the 1905 Revolution in Russia, the Polish propertied classes came to terms with the weak Russian Liberal Party, for fear of being swept away by the tide of social revolt. This may have helped to push the workers in the opposite direction. In 1913 Stalin was lamenting that a good many of them were 'still in intellectual bondage to the bourgeois nationalists'.[37] When the latter got power after the First World War they made a temporary discreet pretence of socialist sympathies,[38] until it was safe to throw off the mask and seize the disputed eastern lands from Soviet Russia. How the better-off classes really thought of socialism, and of their poorer compatriots, can be judged from the White Terror in Finland when it gained independence under German auspices in April 1918, and a quarter of the working class may have been massacred or jailed.[39]

'The nobility was bound to be everywhere the principal champion of Hungarian nationality',[40] as of Polish; a landowning gentry, or middle nobility, with some distinct qualities, being partly Calvinist, and having along with its dour religion a more tenacious political tradition and hold on local institutions than the Polish gentry. Down to 1848 the peasants, unlike the Italian and most of the Polish, were still serfs, and by agreeing to emancipate them, as the progressive leader Kossuth advocated, the nobles could make an impressive-looking sacrifice which cost them little. Serfdom was out of date and dangerous, as had been shown very recently in Galicia: to abandon it was to deprive Austria of a weapon.[41] With some overstatement an English admirer of Kossuth asserted that this gesture gave the country 'a greater unity of class than any other in the world'.[42] It did at any rate facilitate an alliance of gentry, peasantry and urban middle class, and enabled Hungary to set on foot a regular army – as the Poles were never able to do – and offer a prolonged resistance. Aristocratic officers, it is true, could not conceal their dislike of Kossuth as an upstart – he belonged to the poorest gentry by birth, to the professional middle class by vocation.[43] On the other hand, these nationalists, like the Poles, were not prepared to renounce their claims on borderlands inhabited by other nationalities, where the landowners were often Magyar. They had therefore to fight their Slav underlings as well as their Austrian overlords.

Hungary was finished off by a Russian army instead of being rescued by a French army. Revolutionary ferment went on, and might have broken out afresh in 1866 when the Habsburg Empire was being defeated by Prussia, if Deak and Andrassy, two spokesmen of the nobility who fought in 1848, had not held their friends back.[44] They preferred to accept instead the *Ausgleich* or 'Compromise' of 1867. They may have shrunk from summoning to action again peasants whom emancipation had left still land-hungry. They undoubtedly realized that only by agreement with Vienna could they win back control of their non-Magyar borderlands. To the misfortune of Magyar peasants and workers, and of the national minorities, the empire was turned into the Dual Monarchy. Down to 1918 all the Hungarian wing was lorded over by the Magyar oligarchy.[45]

Slavs in the Empire were peasant peoples, within which evolution of classes had been cut short by foreign dominion and alien landlords, Magyar or German. Modernity reached them mostly at second hand, furnishing them as time went on with spokesmen who were often teachers or other educated middle-class individuals. Railways, newspapers, wider markets and their ups and downs, all did their work in shaking up old habits of mind. National and class-consciousness could then be very close together, as in the Croat Peasant Party founded by Stepan Radic in 1904. Countryfolk were going to the towns in search of work, and very often working for employers of alien stock,[46] the same underlining of social by national antipathy took place as in the countryside, but in the hothouse urban atmosphere. It is in the town that the newcomer finds he has been talking prose, or feeling patriotic, all his life.

It was the Czechs who were proving the most energetic and hopeful. They too were mostly peasants, ever since the Habsburg conquest of Bohemia in 1620 and the replacement of much of its old nobility with Germans. Besides landowners and officials there was a considerable German minority in Bohemia, and in Prague, and a nationalist mood takes on a special character when there is an intrusive population to be envied and resented, with reason or without. Industry and commerce were to a great extent in German hands, so that government service was the first ambition of the burgeoning Czech middle class, whose championing of its own language was at the same time a scuffle for jobs.[47] Control of, or access to, the state machine is all the more vital to a class or community lacking economic strength. But it is from their enemies or rivals that nations learn most, for good or ill, and Czechs had lived side by side with Germans long enough to develop talents for business and practical organization as well as for music. They were pushing their way now into modern economic life, and a Czech bourgeoisie was coming forward, desirous of a national market of its own. The fact that so many employers were German must have done much to avert or soften the collision of interests between Czech employers and workers. Here again *émigré* patriots, in western Europe and the United States, led the way in aspiring to full independence.[48]

In the Balkan peninsula Romania was exceptional in its feudal structure, akin to that of Poland or Russia. Its largely absentee nobility had always enjoyed an autonomous status under the Turks. Elsewhere the situation was akin to that of the Habsburg Slav lands. Towns were chiefly Turkish garrison centres, and in the countryside conquest had eliminated native landlordism, except where, as in Bosnia, owners of estates turned Muslim in order to keep some of their acres, or, as in Greece, the district headmen through whom the rude administration was carried on acquired small properties. A barbarous Turkish feudalism grew up to fill the gap, and oppression was compounded by the weakening of central authority, which allowed an anarchic mode of local misrule and extortion to flourish. By the later eighteenth century the peninsula was coming to look more like a region undergoing foreign invasion than one under settled foreign occupation – which comes in time, like home-bred class rule, to be submitted to as part of the order of things.

What might grow into national rebellion, and was always likely to be mistaken for this by westerners, was usually at bottom agrarian revolt. Social relations, most democratic in the Slav-speaking areas, could give this the strength of tribal simplicity, and draw in the masses far more than any movement in a divided society like Italy's. Resistance which broke out in Serbia in 1804 was a protest against local conditions with no sort of 'national' intention in view.[49] In its ranks, however, were some men with wider horizons, village headmen or dealers engaged – as the partisan chiefs Karageorge and Obrenovich both were – in the country's principal trade, export of pigs. Such individuals were in contact with Serbs outside the fighting area, traders belonging to prosperous colonies in neighbouring Hungary, smaller groups further afield. It was among them that newspapers, modern commerce and town life, could kindle national ideas, which would find their way, along with material aid, into the homeland. Much the same can be said of the Bulgars later on: their homeland contained only peasants, but their migrants in towns like Bucharest and Odessa sprouted a merchantry and an intelligentsia. In such a dislocated social structure, classes in the making were scattered about instead of being perched one on top of the other; a state of affairs helpful in lessening class friction during the struggle for independence, but making for lack of equilibrium later on.

Far the most complex structure was that of the Greeks, whose national rising was correspondingly confused. Something of Byzantine power had survived under the Ottoman aegis. The Church was prompt in rendering to the Sultan what was due to Caesar, and its Greek hierarchy held sway over religious life in both Serbia and Bulgaria until they won their freedom: in fact a desire for native prelates was one of the focal points of Bulgar peasant nationalism. Greek traders and tax-farmers held a big place in Ottoman affairs, particularly the wealthy Phanariot community of Stamboul, members of which had been for a century the well-hated governors of the

Romanian provinces. Greek revolt began at the top, instead of as elsewhere at the bottom. Greek shipping and trade had windfall opportunities during the Revolutionary and Napoleonic Wars,[50] but all business activity in the decaying empire suffered from arbitrary exactions and general insecurity. Merchants who sent their sons to school in Paris, and were in touch with Greek traders all over Europe, were bound to feel the stirrings of the national idea. Characteristically, those who were willing to run the risks of challenging authority, in the first phase at any rate, were not the most prosperous, but those whom success had eluded and who were ready to blame the Turks for their disappointments.[51] This very fact may have lent their schemes a touch of extravagance; they dreamed of something like a restored Byzantium, as the Polish or Magyar gentry aspired to the recovery of their colonies as well as their freedom.

It was in the narrower theatre of the Morea, or Peloponnese, that the real battle had to be waged, and in the islands with their shipping fleets. Shipowners too wealthy to be eager to risk their possessions were pushed on by their militant seamen. Tensions between the two were frequent, but there was something to draw them together in the co-operative arrangement by which a crew as well as a capitalist held shares in a cargo and benefited by the success of a voyage.[52] As the contest went on, the merchant class gave important support, more than the propertied classes on terra firma where lives as well as goods were at stake. These were owners of estates, few by comparison with the Turk feudatories; 'primates', or district headmen; and the higher clergy. They had little fault to find with Turkish rule, except that those with land wanted more, and as things were could not hope to get it.[53] Village priests were ardently on the popular side, as village priests unlike prelates so often were in olden days in the west. Another gulf separated agriculturists from hillmen, half shepherd and half brigand. Very much as in the Spanish War of Independence not long before, there was only bad and quarrelsome leadership, or none at all, but this reflected not only personal faction but a chaos of jarring social interests. Such a war, against an opponent almost as undisciplined, could only lead to stalemate, until foreign intervention grudgingly established in 1833 a small Greek state, furnished with a Bavarian king. In the century and a half since then it has grown in size, but has proved quite unable to reconcile the internecine hatreds that accompanied it into the world.

Of the two Romanian provinces Moldavia, closer to Russia, was the more purely feudal and inert. In Wallachia, which included Bucharest, there was more of an urban middle class, and in 1848 a rising and a provisional government.[54] This quickly ran aground on antagonism between progressives who wanted agrarian reform and recalcitrant nobles, and the Russian intervention was far less needed to restore 'order' than in Hungary. Romania slid into independence in 1858, when both Russia and Turkey were crippled by the Crimean War, and the two provinces united. It was the only Balkan country to start its career with a ready-made ruling class, one of the worst imaginable. To the peasants whose efforts counted most towards freedom in the other lands, the notion of a ruling class, or of a state, was incomprehensible. What they wanted was to be left in peace in their villages; the Serbs, for instance, whom their first ruler Milosh Obrenovich had to dragoon heavy-handedly into acceptance of regular government.[55] The elites which could provide a civil and military apparatus were a motley and unsatisfactory set: expatriates returning from abroad, local vested interests, others thrown up by the struggle itself. All these could savour the prospect of a state of their own, with patronage to be dispensed and power to be wielded. Obrenovich's rise from pigsty to palace left him with an unquenchable greed for money as well as power. In Greece during the fighting the bigger men were amassing land and plunder;[56] when it was over they were ready to coalesce with the merchants and shipowners and form a dominant bloc. Foreign enterprise was active in setting an example of greed, under cover of the monarchies supplied by the Concert of Europe to three of the new states – royal families themselves keenly interested in dividends, and in saving up for a rainy day.

A good deal of territory was still Turkish at the end of the century, and ethnic boundaries were indistinct. Everything conspired to make the Balkans a hotbed of irredentism. Bad governments were in chronic need of alibis; army men were prominent in politics; exporters wanted access to the Black Sea, the Aegean or the Adriatic. Calls to liberate downtrodden brethren met with a ready response from peasant peoples with strong ties of family and clan. They could be set against each other as easily as against the Sultan, and their naïve patriotism was soon inflamed by the ruling groups into a peculiarly vicious chauvinism. Many other governments with little taste for social reform and progress were finding a convenient alternative in irredentism. A fresh bout of tub-thumping about Alsace-Lorraine was one of the most effective expedients of French conservatism before 1914, faced with the socialist menace.

Patriotism was becoming the last refuge of reaction, and nationalist labels were favourites with right-wing parties. They were to be utilized most grotesquely by Franco's 'National' movement, conquering Spain with Moorish, Italian and German forces, and Chiang Kai-shek's 'National' government, retreating before the

Japanese and then trying to reconquer China with American guns. Irredentism and Fascism both owed their names to Italy. The latter represented right-wing nationalism in intensified form, and carried furthest the false simplification of class society into a community of *Volksgenossen*. There was implicit in the nation from the outset, it has been said, a recognition of society's responsibility for all its members.[57] But if so, this has far oftener been its 'recessive' than its 'dominant' characteristic. Once harnessed to the state, national feeling was distorted, and its prime function was to obscure class issues instead of finding healthy solutions for them. With Fascism the cycle was complete.

Beyond Europe, nationalism continued to prove itself an idea adaptable to very diverse needs. Western goods, machines and books were subverting old patterns of life, and making a vacuum. Communism has spread in Asia, it has been pointed out, thanks not only to poverty but to the groping of bewildered multitudes for new ideals.[58] In many ways nationalism too has met this need, inadequately by itself, but the two creeds have often converged, as in Europe they could very seldom do. Hence nationalism in this century has proved a more constructive force in Asia than in its European homeland, where its mission has long been exhausted. Outside Europe it has had the freshness, the inspiration, of a new faith, and by coming later it has been able to profit by Europe's later and better social thinking. China, far bigger and more slow-moving than Japan, was fortunate in the long run in taking so much longer to assimilate modern nationalism, but imbibing it in the end in a far more mature and progressive form.

Any social stratum resembling the old Western bourgeoisie – a political as well as economic construct – was even harder to find in Asia than in eastern Europe. What could be found everywhere was some kind of urban middle-class intelligentsia, becoming acquainted with Western thought and serving as a *conductor* for it. What more powerful sponsors could be enlisted depended on the environment. In the Ottoman Empire, where trade had been left to non-Turks as an inferior concern, only the army was available to deputize for a bourgeoisie. For a few years before 1914 its leaders were seduced by the pan-Turanian fantasy, which constituted a stepping-stone at least between the old Islamic outlook and a Turkish national one. This came to life suddenly when defeat in the Great War swept away the Sultan-Caliph and the rebellious Arab dependencies. With Allied occupation and partition looming before the country, a successful general, Kemal Pasha, raised the banner of national defence, and patriotic enthusiasm swept the towns where Turk and non-Turk lived side by side on chronically bad terms. But the new idea had to be forced on the sluggish rural masses, whose mentality was still Islamic, not Turkish. Only foreign invasion compelled it to accept the new leadership, much as it was compelling the Russian masses to accept that of the Bolsheviks.

Kemal's utterances during the conflict reveal much of the thinking of his party, with its somewhat mystic image of the nation, the half-digested foreign idea, and its highly elitist attitude towards the illiterate commonalty. In his opening address to the Congress at Erzerum on 23 July 1919, he declared that centuries of torpor had blunted the Turkish mind. 'Therefore, those who had penetrated into the inner depths of human affairs and had recognised the truth, must regard it as the highest duty on earth to enlighten and educate the people as far as possible and guide them on a path that leads them to their goals.'[59] In all such pronouncements echoes of older religious axioms can be heard. Kemal's goal was an equivocal one, for Turkey like Asia at large was trying to throw off European shackles in order to be free to Europeanize itself, or its whole outward life at any rate. In non-Communist Asia this meant an equivalent of bourgeois revolution, with a bourgeoisie taking shape during the process and cornering most of the gains. Turkey's village masses have been left to stagnate, and the nationalist cycle from progressive to reactionary has been gone through rapidly. Today, with semi-military rule, there is a right-wing 'Nationalist Front' bloc, and a neo-Fascist 'Nationalist Action Party'.

At the other end of Asia the Far East is a continent by itself, as distinct as Europe is from the rest of the Eurasian land-mass, and cut off from it by sea, mountain and desert far more definitely than either Europe or Asia is divided from Africa. Islam, that obliterator of nations, scarcely reached it, and all its historic states were, to some degree, 'nations' many centuries before European ideas arrived. Even China's early stage of primitive mass protest against Western intrusion, culminating in the Boxer Rising of 1900, was more than mere xenophobia. Clearly the Boxers had a sense of China as a fatherland, of belonging to Chinese tradition and civilization; it came to them through the favourite tales and dramas that were always the conduit between upper-class and plebeian culture.[60] This was confusedly mixed up with a far older, still lingering, anti-foreign feeling against the reigning dynasty, descended from Manchu conquerors of the seventeenth century. Attachment to the memory of the old native Ming dynasty was an example of how men at odds with the present, but unable to envisage a better future, will idealize a vanished past. In Peru as late as the 1920s the Amerindian peasantry struggling to regain the communal fields that once belonged to it went on rebelling in the name of the long-defunct Incas.[61]

Among younger sections of the intelligentsia and what may roughly be termed China's middle classes, especially in the more volatile south, Western civilization was having by 1900 its familiar attractive as well as repellent effect. A nationalist movement sprang up which was also a pallid, prematurely born bourgeois-revolutionary movement; the 'foreignness' of the dynasty and its subservience to foreign imperialism made a linking factor. As with so many stirrings further west, its earliest vantage-points were abroad, among Chinese emigrants under Western rule who gave considerable aid to the rebels at home. This always had its drawbacks; reliance on aid from outside may have made Sun Yat-sen's party less eager to look for popular support at home. There were some contacts with the sporadic mutinies of peasant and worker,[62] but the fall of the monarchy in 1911 found the progressives still few and isolated.

After the First World War, the 'August 4 Movement', starting among the students, found a broader basis. Years of war-lord anarchy and then Kuomintang tyranny and corruption had the happy result of compelling Chinese nationalism to remain in opposition, instead of being imprisoned in an official cage as in Japan or Europe. It had to identify itself with the cause of reform, progress and modernization deeper than any technological change. United action against foreign pressures, with Japanese invasion in the 1930s for climax, was impossible. Rather than share with the masses, the propertied classes preferred collaboration with, or virtual surrender to, the outsiders, like the Manchu regime earlier. It fell to the Communists to organize national resistance. Their recruits came from the humbler ranks of the intelligentsia, artisans, petty bourgeois – those familiar 'unattached' elements, electrons easily detached from their social nucleus, that have so often furnished the priming for mass movements.[63] They had done so already in modern China's two biggest outbursts, the Taiping Rebellion and the Boxer Rising.[64] Through these recruits Communism had access to the masses. It could not rely on the working class, which was small and concentrated in coastal areas where the Japanese hold was strongest. Apart from this, modern weapons and conditions of warfare have been everywhere unfavourable to urban revolutionary forces – as Engels was recognizing near the end of his life.[65] Instead there was the peasantry, goaded into action by indiscriminate Japanese brutality.

There is much in the thesis that the peasants came under Communist guidance because they had to wage a guerrilla struggle against the invaders, not because they wanted to be led against the landowners and their Kuomintang government.[66] But it leaves out of account the agrarian protest, the egalitarian sentiment, that were part of the peasant mind all through the ages. By disrupting the old order, silencing the claims of legitimacy, the war set the peasantry free – like the intelligentsia before it – to follow its natural bent. In the northern regions where Communist strength was greatest and most of the guerrilla fighting took place, numerous landlords and officials absconded, or fraternized with the enemy. It was hardly to be expected that they would be allowed to return and resume their sway when the war was over. It must be recalled, too, that in north China a surprising proportion of peasants, as many as three-quarters perhaps, were not tenants, but had somehow managed to hold on to their small ancestral farms.[67] This had formerly made the north, like the countryside of northern Spain, conservative and loyal, but now as in the time of the Boxers gave it added readiness to stand firm against foreign attack. So too northern Spain had done, but the Chinese resistance had vastly superior political direction. Victory would fulfil not only the present aim of expelling the intruder, but age-old dreams of expelling hunger and oppression as well. By an odd freak the same thing was happening in a corner of the Balkans, Yugoslavia, where the old revolt of the countryside was being repeated, but now on a far higher plane.

India had no past as a nation, and had to grow into one for the first time under the spell of Western ideas and institutions, more firmly implanted here and over a lengthier period than anywhere else in Asia. The National Congress, founded in 1886, represented a standard blend of idealism with the desire of educated professional groups for entry into higher government posts.[68] Within the nationalist ranks were members of subcastes which in past times served the Mogul government, or, like the Chitpavan Brahmins, administered the Maratha Empire. To these latter especially, with their instincts of a hereditary governing class, memories and myths of bygone days, and a more conservative attitude than that of the westernizers, were congenial.

It was not long before wider public support was found necessary to put pressure on the British, and disarm their stock argument that only a few self-seekers and cranks were concerned. Regional and caste barriers hindered the formation of *classes* as understood in Europe. But there it was the poorer urban middle strata – petty traders, lower government employees, discontented clerks – that were the most ready to react to changing times, and to join in. Linking them with the higher grades were the students, a swelling host with diminishing prospects of a livelihood, and a swarm of lawyers – a race ubiquitous in the politics of Europe, unknown in Asia until called into being by British rule. One of these, Gandhi, with a background of struggle for Indian rights in South Africa, worked out a philosophy to meet the needs of a country striving towards advance, but still heavily entangled in the past and all its ways. It diluted cautious reformism with old-world religious views: it allowed conservatives to be mildly progressive, and restrained radicals from being too progressive. It admitted that India must fit itself for independence by some degree of social reconstruction for the benefit of the unprivileged, including women and Untouchables, but insisted that traditional Indian life and thought contained treasures not known to the materialistic West. Under Gandhian tuition, in short, a hesitant India could take up its bed and walk without having to feel that it was leaving home.

This made Gandhi acceptable also to the small body of industrial capitalists, self-preserving men who did not mean to get into trouble with the Government but were prepared to give subsidies and newspaper backing to Congress. In return they stood to gain by its pressure on the British, which compelled London step by step to concede tariff autonomy.[69] Nationalism was stimulating industry more than industry was stimulating nationalism. Indian mill-owners in the epoch of the Third International were more nervous of their workers than querulous about the Government, and had a common interest with British business men in strong police protection. But to hoist the patriotic flag, at half-mast if no more, might shelter them from some opprobrium, and Gandhi with his theories about the rich being trustees for the poor could be a mediator, or buffer, between them and the working class.

On its side the working class, desperately poor and exploited, could see little advantage in a transfer of power to a Congress hand in glove with its masters. More often than not these were men of different speech as well as class: in Bombay mills, Maratha and many other workers were employed by Gujarati capitalists; in Calcutta, Bengalis and Biharis worked for Marwaris. On the whole, labour was little drawn into the national struggle, but fought its own industrial battles, though through these, and harsh experience of the British-officered police, it was coming to a national consciousness of its own. In the countryside the big feudal landlords were solidly pro-British,[70] but Congress could not attack them squarely, or call out the peasantry against them, because too many of its own adherents had an interest in the soil. This was above all the case in Bengal, with its peculiarly morbid agrarian structure, the outcome of the Permanent Settlement.[71] Here the educated Hindu groups which were the first in India to absorb Western ideas, and pioneered the opening phases of the national movement, dropped out of the lead after the First World War, because they were too deeply embedded in the rotting countryside.

There was the danger also that agrarian agitation would invite Communism into the countryside, and might worsen unrest among mill-workers whose ties with the village were still close. Gandhi's trusteeship principle, or fable, which he extended to landlords and princes as well as capitalists, could reassure them that they had little to fear from Congress, even if Nehru's radical talk gave them uneasy moments. Gandhi's religious phraseology could impress rustics, but talk of 'Ram Rajya', the coming reign of God on earth, was better calculated to keep them away from the socialist-inspired Kisan Sabhas, or peasant unions, than to draw them actively into the national movement.[72] During its spells of civil disobedience, Congress thought of summoning peasants to refuse tax payments, but boggled at the proposal. Refusal of taxes might too easily lead to refusal of rents, and a general breakdown of social discipline.

Altogether Gandhi might be said to be pursuing united-front tactics, and superficially with success. But the result left British power intact, though at times embarrassed, able to go on running the country by means of officials, soldiers and policemen, most of whom were Indians. It is a commentry on nationalism at large that Britain could rule India and Ireland through Indians and Irishmen, Russia ruled Poland through Poles and so on, and a reminder that nationalism is only fully itself when stiffened by state power. Congress members and office-holders came from the same circles, the same families, and got on very well together after India gained independence. It owed this to the enfeeblement of British power in Asia by the Second World War. Independence was accompanied by partition, and the breakaway of Pakistan – one consequence of the shallowness of the national movement and its reluctance to draw in the masses except as a stage army of 'extras'.

This left the Muslim masses vulnerable to religious propaganda. Jinnah and the Muslim League after 1936 maintained that Indian Muslims met all criteria of nationhood,[73] but religious passion was what really counted, along with the economic grievances that fed it. In the consciousness of the more genuine zealots, nearly all belonging to the urban lower-middle classes, the two things were fused. Muslims resented Hindu economic and educational superiority just as Hindus resented the British ascendancy, and pride in a superior religion was both compensation and protest. More gradually, League propaganda could penetrate the countryside too, and in fact achieve more success there than Congress, because it denounced tangible enemies of the Muslim peasantry in the form of Hindu usurers in the north-west and Hindu landlords in East Bengal. Of Muslim landlords it had no criticism to make.

Once again the roots of separatism were partly external. The word 'Pakistan' was invented by a student at Cambridge, and the campaign got its start among the Muslim minorities in regions like the United Province only later gripping the Muslim majority areas which eventually formed the national territory. When this happened, a Muslim bourgeoisie, lacking in those areas, flitted from Bombay to Karachi and set up as an industrial-financial oligarchy, in partnership with the feudal landlords of the western Punjab. Their flimsy ideological backcloth, the Muslim League, promptly disintegrated. Pakistan was a hotchpotch of nationalities each better able to meet Jinnah's tests of nationhood, and one of them has already broken away. It has been observed that the separatist movement in East Bengal followed precisely the same lines as Jinnah's,[74] under stress of the same middle-class and petty-bourgeois anger at being kept out of a due share of loaves and fishes, and at being looked down on as inferior.

In other colonial regions the counterpoint of class and nationality was repeated with endless variations. Where no elite was ready to take the lead, a national movement could not start, but where classes were well developed they were liable to cancel each other out. During the inter-war years the new Third International was always scratching its head over the choice of tactics, and generally inclined towards the united fronts prescribed at the outset by Lenin and challenged at the outset by M. N. Roy.[75] National freedom was to be won first, like bourgeois democracy in Europe, social revolution to follow – though the Left, Lenin insisted, must preserve its own distinct organization.[76] But as in Europe (in Marx's Germany of 1848 for instance) mass participation could only be secured by pledges of social reform going beyond what the propertied classes were willing to endorse. They were always nervously aware, even without studying *The Communist Manifesto*, of an executioner standing at the door. Communist parties were so much more likely to divide than to unite subject nations that it was foolish of colonial governments to be so anxious to suppress them. Their search for a 'national bourgeoisie', ready to join in a struggle for independence and fight it out with its left-wing allies later, proved elusive. On their side the masses, wherever they were sufficiently aroused to turn against foreign dominion, were apt to be in a mood to turn against their own parasites as well – 'the Eaters', as they were expressively called in Burma. While people of property often made common cause with foreign power against their own people, the masses might rejoice, as a Puerto Rican nationalist has said, to see their masters knocked about by the more powerful foreigner.[71]

The collision of empires in the Second World War liberated a great part of Asia, and led towards liberation (or promotion to neo-colonial status) for Africa. Elites were ready to take over in Asia; in Africa, as in the more primitive Balkan countries, they developed very much in and through the national movement, and after independence were further built up by foreign interests and influences.[78] Tribal or regional discontents have been rampant, and seem to turn very easily into 'movements' of a sort wherever two or three job-hunters are gathered together.[79] These are men of some education, often Christian converts. Intellectuals of all grades have regularly oscillated between nationalism's two poles, the ideal and the sordid, under the sway of a complex of historical circumstances. Where imperialism refused to withdraw after 1945, Marxism was often on the scene, able to supply guidance as it had lately done in China, and local intelligentsias were among its first adherents. Of all social types the intellectual has it in him more than any other to be a man of action, but only when history compels him.

'A nation is not merely a historical category, but a historical category belonging to a definite epoch, the epoch of rising capitalism.'[80] Stalin's formula appears in many ways close to the mark, but it applies much better to the handful of original nation-states in the west, and their nearest neighbours, than to their imitations further afield; it applies far less well still to the majority of nationalist movements, as distinct from nations. Marxism has often slurred over the distinction between these two things, and made modern national-ism, as well as the classical nation-state, an *alter ego* of capitalism.[81] Capitalism required a homogeneous population, a single language, for its market, Lenin wrote: 'Throughout the world, the period of the final victory of capitalism over feudalism was linked up with national movements.'[82] In the world at large 'final victory' for capitalism has been as rare as for socialism; Lenin was thinking too schematically in terms of a universal advance from feudalism to capitalism and thence to socialism – though it was he who excised the stage of full-blown capitalism from Russian history.

In effect, Marx, Engels and Lenin wanted to see national states established, as good for economic development, but had no liking for nationalism. Like religion, however, or any other great emotive force, nationalism is ambivalent, and can escape very completely from a prescribed political channel. Even in its origins it was a complex phenomenon, deriving both from the solidarity and from the divisions of society. It would have astonished Marx to see socialism owing so much to partnerships with nationalism, in Afro–Asia and in the Soviet Union during the Second World War, but this was a nationalism in which the populist element, instead of the class complex, was uppermost. It may be said indeed that just as the national state of the nineteenth century led logically, by way of the sovereignty of the nation and people, towards bourgeois democracy or republicanism (and hence underwent pathological strains in a country like Bismarckian Germany), nationalism in opposition in the twentieth century has led logically towards socialism.

Postscript

Nationalist movements sprang up in the era when capitalism was spreading eastward across Europe, touching one region after another, with a light finger at first, an influence more cultural than economic, that could only stir vague aspirations among idealists, or 'ideologues'. Their visions of national freedom might remain floating in the air for long, like Mazzini's in the blue Italian sky. When it came to fighting, religion was often called on for its blessing, especially by conservatives, as the easiest way to enlist popular support. General Paoli made much use of priests to fan fervour for Corsican independence, Gibbon heard on his travels in 1764.[83] Poles counted on Heaven being on their side, almost as unquestioningly as if it were one of their lost provinces.

In our overcrowded world today, where newspapers and television allow us all to look over our better-off neighbours' shoulders and count their blessings, there is a more down-to-earth preoccupation with jobs, perquisites, a 'share of the cake'. Resentment at not getting a fair share may find readier expression in terms of nationality than of class; and while material interests come more and more to the front, religion continues to figure. Lands as retarded as Tibet have not yet got beyond it; governments like Pakistan's find it a convenient tool, for such purposes as fomenting anti-Indian feeling in Kashmir, and irredentism at home. In Ulster, where sectarian grudges have always been made the most of to divide the workers, Catholic economic grievances have been handcuffed to patriotic Irish daydreams from another century, which the rest of Ireland has forgotten. The vendetta seems destined to go until the Greek Kalends, or the conversion of the Revd Paisley and the Irish Republican Army to Christianity.

In Tibet clerical-feudal opposition to the Chinese occupation has had popular backing thanks to high-handed Chinese behaviour. The masses were badly in need of liberation from superstition and oppression, but treatment as a colony could bring little progress, as Peking has half acknowledged. In Palestine there has been no pretence of liberation, only plain expropriation or subjection; no class of Arabs has profited, hence all classes feel alike, though they may not think alike about tactics, and religion, though an obvious factor, has been far less needed as a rallying-cry. This can probably be said also of the Tamil revolt in Sri Lanka, where religion has been in evidence chiefly in the form of Buddhist intolerance and its appeal to Sinhalese nationalism against the minority.

A more complex situation is to be seen in the Punjab. Here a rich province, wanting to be richer still, complains of being held back by the central government from adding industrial wealth to agricultural supremacy. It is hard to believe that this argument by itself could lead to a separatist movement. There is good reason to suspect that dis-affection has been incited by the bigger landowners and business-men who have reaped most of the harvest of Punjabi prosperity, and may fear discontent among those who have fared less well, cultivators with little land or none. It has been easy for agitators, among them holy men utilizing up-to-date propaganda methods and equipment, to identify Punjabi nationalism with the Sikh faith, especially since Delhi's act of folly in assaulting the Golden Temple instead of being content to besiege it.[84]

Not much is left of the old romantic-liberal sympathy with nationalist movements abroad. Western statesmen view them with an eye as cynical as Metternich's, most undisguisedly as regards Palestine, each calculating their own interests. Even in older times public opinion followed national predilections. Englishmen felt for Italy, Americans for Ireland. Pakistan feels for the Sikhs, its old foes. Contests far away are increasingly overshadowed by the great divide between East and West. Armed resistance has usually been remote enough to be ignored, as in Nagaland, or Kurdistan. The Kurds have suffered (though also at times benefited) by having three oppressive governments to fight, all of which the West has usually wished to conciliate and sell arms to. Kurds are still a tribal people, with mountain fastnesses to defend, but incipient social differences among them must deepen by degrees. In Timor, the old Portuguese colony, there were sheltering forests, but no national tradition and no equipment to face the Indonesian invaders, backed by Western arms and investors. A third of the indigenous population is said to have been wiped out.[85] Tamil guerrilla resistance has been exceptional in taking place in broad daylight, and being able to look to India for sympathy. There have been extremists in the Tamil community, and moderates less eager to take up arms; distinctions both of class and of historic origins in the island, medieval and modern, have to be taken into account.

'Bourgeois' and socialist (usually Communist) nationalist organizations were seldom able to collaborate; when the former was missing, or discredited, socialism might come to the front, as in China or Vietnam, and champion both patriotic and social aims. To fuse the two, the fires of the battlefield were needed. But the process was a very intricate one, owing much in Vietnam to the willingness to join in the struggle of a literate elite, a great part of it resident in the countryside, where it formed the repository of memories and legends of patriotic resistance to foreign intruders in the past.[86] Ho Chi Minh came from this class, and himself composed poems on historical themes to sharpen peasant determination.

Since those heroic days socialist leadership or participation has been less in evidence. Circumstances have not always made much room for it. But there have been contexts in which whole peoples, however internally divided, or at least considerable sections of all ranks, have been able to feel like a class badly treated by an economically stronger one. (Women, who have played an increasing part in nationalist movements, have begun to discover that they have always been something like an inferior class.) The outcome then depends on how their complaints are received. In a more secular and rational style than the Muslims of India before 1947, Scots have cherished jealousies against England, and at times have talked of breaking away. North Sea oil ignited a patriotic mood livelier than ever before; many socialists, including Marxists, hailed it as a means of advancing their own ideas by linking them with the national cause. But the experiment of a Scottish Labour Party was a speedy failure, and there has been a return to the normal confrontation of classes, except that the Tory party has lost ground from being the most unfriendly to Scottish Home Rule. Separatists had watched and drawn confidence from a parallel movement in French Canada; but this, accompanied by a belated throwing-off of the old asphyxiating clericalism, won rapid economic gains for Quebec province, with the result that the election of September 1984 saw the nationalist party almost eliminated.

All 'free-enterprise' countries are ruled now as much by multi-national capital as by their own governments, and both these mentors want to see their subjects united in the great cause of anti-socialism. The realities of Class are undergoing changes as deep as those of Nation. Which will have more meaning for the twenty-first century is an intriguing question.

6

Conscription and Society in Europe before the War of 1914−1918

Between 1870 and 1914 industrial capitalism was establishing itself decisively over major areas of Europe. In the same period military preparations were being based, more widely than ever before, on compulsory service for all citizens, the principle of 'the nation in arms'. There may be good reason to surmise that these two things were not occurring together fortuitously, but that the great transformation could take place so smoothly − with no serious upheaval in any big industrial country like those of 1848 or 1871 in Paris − because the mass armies buttressed society with a firm framework. Like their predecessors they represented a reserve of armed force for maintenance of order; more novel and more important, they counteracted social discontents by 're-educating' youth, year by year, by taking over the strength of the masses and enlisting it on the conservative side. Like the often painful initiation rites of tribal life, or the young Buddhist's term of austere monastic duty, a spell with the colours became the introduction to manhood and membership of the community.

Conscription appears and reappears in world history in protean forms, and is always a significant index of the society where it is found: to view it solely as a method of conducting wars is to see very little of it. In modern Europe it developed in the eastern lands, after an earlier reliance on foreign mercenary troops, in association with serfdom. In the west the great nation, France, was converted by the

patriotic ardour of the Revolutionary wars from professionalism to a
general levy of all citizens. Austria emulated the example after its
defeat at Austerlitz in 1805, Prussia after Jena in 1806. This country
was the hybrid between western and eastern Europe; it was catching
the germs of patriotism from the one just as it began to mark itself off
from the other by emancipating its serfs. Later on it held more
steadily to the principle of universal service than France, which by
allowing those who could afford it to buy themselves off – as Austria
and most others also did – reverted in effect during the Second
Empire to an army of long-term professionals. It was this army that
was defeated in 1870 by Germany, now a 'nation in arms' on the
Prussian model. Defeat left the French in a mood to borrow Prussia's
system, as Prussia had once borrowed theirs. Italy followed suit in
1873 and Russia in 1874, by way of prelude to a war with Turkey
two years later.

What was happening was acceptance of a rule in appearance
egalitarian, so that it could seem a concession or accolade to
democracy; but if democracy was being legitimized it was also being
adulterated. These new arrays were very unlike the popular militias,
the Swiss pattern, advocated by Rousseau[1] and a great many
nineteenth-century progressives (J. S. Mill among them),[2] as providing
for defence without peril to freedom and without temptation to
aggression. When Bismarck, Roon and Moltke were preparing
Prussia for war they thrust the *Landwehr* or militia into the
background and concentrated on the regular army. It was the same
Bismarck who, after his wars, gave the vote to all German men but
took precautions to render it harmless; in the same spirit Alexander II
had lately emancipated the Russian serfs, with due care to ensure
that no great loss was suffered by their masters. There were some
departures from equality in the armies themselves, apart from the
obvious class demarcation between officers and privates. Avoidance
of service by a money payment was abolished in France in 1872, later
than in Germany or Austria, but continued in Belgium for another
generation. Reduction of the term of service for those with higher
education was abolished in France in 1905, but continued in
Germany. Everywhere a very large proportion of men liable to the
call-up proved physically unfit; here it was the ill-nourished poor who
escaped rather than the better-off.

Subject to these various qualifications, it can correctly be said that
'Conscription, compulsory education, and the right to vote formed
three pillars of the democratic state.'[3] Though within the armies
anything democratic was firmly ruled out, the hope could still be
indulged that there would be a more cautious and responsible

approach to international relations when a big war would draw in the manhood of Europe instead of a few regular soldiers. To a fire-eater like General von Bernhardi, indeed, this seemed so probable that he feared it would lead to decadent thinking about war as barbarous;[4] the new militarism suffered from sundry inner contradictions like this. There really was a long peace among the great powers, from 1871 to 1914, favourable to the economic expansion in progress, which must have owed a good deal to this factor. As time went on mass involvement came, like atom bombs with us, to be familiar and taken for granted. But there was at first much uncertainty among governments about how their subjects would react to a declaration of war.

There were misgivings among the respectable about the whole plan of training everybody to arms. Their grand watchword, Order, might be said to find its apotheosis in a country's transformation into an armed camp; on the other hand, this meant putting weapons into the hands of the poor, and the shadow of the Commune lay for long across respectable Europe. A pessimist in Belgium argued that to let the poor compel the well-off to serve beside them in the forces would be to invite further pressures in the direction of collectivism; to which a war minister replied that it would be ruinous if the well-off went on buying exceptions and left the forces to be filled with proletarians.[5] One argument of Bloch, the anti-war Polish banker, was that conscription made war too grave a risk: working classes under socialist influence would be mobilized *en masse*, and there would be no knowing how to disband them again at the end – worse cataclysms than the Commune were to be expected.[6] He must have been expressing what many of his class felt when he wrote of 'the long service of the professional soldier' as a safer insurance.[7] Europe was shooting Niagara when it embarked on this policy, more dramatically than England when it gave votes to Demos.

Yet Bloch felt that, by the 1890s, the opinion had come to prevail everywhere except in Britain 'that great armies are the support of government, that only great armies will deliver the existing order from the perils of anarchism, and that military service acts beneficently on the masses by teaching discipline, obedience and order.'[8] Armies were offering themselves, some more seriously than others, as Europe's teachers and guides, as well as defenders. Needless to say, the ordinary conservative thought of their teaching as a process of breaking in. Countless men of property must have said to countless young men, as the landowner in Pavese's novel says to the argument-ative carpenter's son: 'I'd like to see how you get on when you're called up. They'll knock some of the nonsense out of you in the

regiment.'[9] More subtly too, where schools were capable of indoctrination, as in Germany, the army could round off their work;
where they were not, it could make up for some of the deficiencies,
and also for those of the churches. Britain's industrial, like its
'bourgeois', revolution came very early and could take place under
religious auspices. Churches were still powerful in the peasant
purlieus of Europe, but even there diminishingly, and in the rapidly
swelling industrial areas they were impotent. Mass conscription
supplied them with a captive congregation and numerous posts for
chaplains, and allowed all the jarring creeds to take their first steps in
ecumenism.

Peasants everywhere continued to provide the bulk of recruits; in
the industrializing countries, ostensibly because of their better
physique, though it may be surmised that there was also at work a
preference for rustics as more tractable. They, it could be hoped,
would be ready to let themselves be used, if need arose to overawe
mutinous towns. For the peasants, even in darkest Russia, the change
from long service for a few to short service for all represented an
amelioration. In less benighted lands army service could be seen as a
means of civilizing the yokel, just as the otherwise abominable
conscription of Indians in the Peru of that age could be credited with
giving them a sort of introduction to the modern world.[10] Von Papen
drew a picture doubtless idealized but not altogether false in his
reminiscences of army life at Düsseldorf. 'The families of the Rhenish
and Westphalian peasants, who made up most of our strength, were
glad to let their sons serve in the Army. They were taught habits of
punctuality, good behaviour, cleanliness and a sense of duty, which
made them better members of the community.'[11] By this cluster of
virtues both their parents and their employers might benefit.

But the critical new force in the developing regions was the
working class. Army service may be supposed to have acted as one of
its recruiting agents, by helping to shake young men loose from their
villages and leading them to settle in the towns, and the experience
both of handling modern equipment and of being handled by the
drill-sergeant would make them more welcome to industrialists.
Likewise, where there was a competently organized military system,
the new race of industrial workers might, in spite of their more
sophisticated mentality, fit into it more readily than the peasant. They
were more accustomed to being away from home. Regiment and
factory were each other's counterpart, each with a daily routine based
on an exact timetable and a hierarchy of command, in a combination
specific to Europe and unapproached by any other civilization; in the
United States it was being carried further still on the industrial side,

with the Ford conveyor-belt running parallel to the Schlieffen Plan. All recruits had the experience of working a couple of years for nothing but their keep, the zero wage that was every employer's ideal standard. After this, very modest pay might look more acceptable. Above all, they were accustomed to obeying orders. For the nervous bourgeoisie, chronically uneasy lest the factory proletariat it was creating should prove a Frankenstein's monster, this was a great reassurance.

Regimentation of the factory on quasi-military lines was a pipe-dream of many philosophers of pessimism, Carlyle, Nietzsche, Spengler, as well as of entrepreneurs like the elder Krupp.[12] Conversely, the more industry grew the more its rationality and organizing talent permeated the army. In Germany Bernhardi could assert what could not be said, for instance, in Spain, that army life did wonders for a townsman's health.[13] It was reckoned indeed that two years with the colours could add five years to the German working man's life,[14] on this basis it might even be calculated that conscription did more to prolong the sum of German existence than the First World War to reduce it. Bernhardi wanted the workers fit and well to do their jobs as well as to fight; he was against shorter factory hours, declaring that work is 'the greatest blessing which man knows'.[15] How pervasive was the spirit of the age may be seen, at an opposite pole, in Trotsky's scheme for organizing trades unions and labour in Red Russia on military lines.

Thanks to the Revolution the French officer corps was mostly middle-class and professional, with an oil-and-vinegar admixture of aristocracy. In the other big armies the aristocratic contingent still kept the upper hand. In control of the army it had a bastion of class power; for the more earnest-minded a truly national army offered also the satisfaction of regaining a valid social function, of being integrated once more with the nation: a nation refined into the *corpus mysticum* of the army, a partnership, like Burke's State, in every virtue. Universal service by multiplying the number of officers required brought a gradual infiltration of the corps by newcomers from the middle class: in Prussia this was happening from 1860, and in Germany by 1913 reduced the noble share from 65 to 30 per cent.[16] At the same time, however, bourgeois Germany was under-going the curious 'feudalization' that has struck historians. There and over most of the Continent the middle classes had abandoned any direct struggle for power and turned to the roundabout mode of building a golden bridge, of piling up money. Any social group that allows itself to be turned aside like this from its historical path is denatured and liable to succumb to ideas foreign to it.

It was in great part by coming forward as educator of the masses in respect for order and property that the army was winning the esteem of a bourgeoisie formerly hostile to it. In striving to convert the masses it was aided by its aristocratic outlook, enabling officers to affect, and in some degree to feel, an impartiality between rich and poor. Altogether these new-style national armies could be practical exercises in class collaboration, as champions of universal service seem to have reckoned from the start. In England the ritual of sport performed a similar function: its symbolic figure was Edward VII leading in his own Derby winner, amid applause of high and low. In the more advancd countries on the Continent the classes met under the colours, like well-chaperoned young men and women at a ball. This applies best of all to Germany, the classic land in Europe, as Japan was in Asia, of headlong industrialization contained within a framework bequeathed by a feudal past. Only in these two countries and in France (apart from Switzerland with its militia) did universal service become a truly national institution, an essential part of public life; for eastern Europe it was too modern, for Britain and Scandinavia, as for the United States, too archaic.

'Anybody could rule this country,' said George, '*I* could rule it.' Jerome's three men on their bummel were impressed by the way that, even when back in civil life, the German remained a soldier, looking up to the policeman as his officer and mentor; and they noted how the schoolroom paved the way for the camp by its 'everlasting teaching of duty', in other words 'blind obedience to everything in buttons'.[17] In 1906 the man who was ruling Germany discoursed lengthily to a British diplomat on 'the advantages of militarism to the youth of the country and on its popularity in Germany'.[18] It sounds as if William appreciated clearly enough that the system was at least as vital for keeping the people quiet as for keeping the frontiers secure. This meant in the first place keeping Germany secure for Hohenzollerns and Junkers. Against the corrosions of industrial society, its 'wide-sweeping inanimate agencies and mechanical procedures', an injection of warlike ideas was, as Veblen pointed out, the best safeguard.[19] Francis Joseph instinctively protected himself against modernity by scarcely ever in his long life appearing except in uniform, like a knight of old never laying aside his armour.

In the second place the army had to extend its patronage and protection to the new capitalist class; and it could do so more successfully because it stood, or seemed to stand, outside the realm of capitalist greeds and offered an alternative to them. A concept of the army as a school of national virtue went back to the early nineteenth-century reformers and now, as then, but on a far greater scale, the country was undergoing transformation, amid which the army had a reassuring fixity like Wordsworth's mountain 'familiar with forgotten years'. Nowhere else had civic and private qualities been so closely enmeshed with it as in Prussia, which unlike Rome had no senate as an alternative focus. 'The voice of our national conscience', William's toady Prince Bülow could unctuously write, 'tells us what German militarism really is: the best thing we have achieved in the course of our national development as a State and as a people.'[20]

Nowhere else, correspondingly, did army service and industrialization fit more closely together, each reinforcing the other. By damping down class tensions the army conferred a gift on the bourgeois Liberals that did at least as much as his unification of Germany to reconcile them to Bismarck, and turned them into National Liberals as socialists were later to be turned into National Socialists. In Prussia serfdom had been abolished from above, by reformist aristocrats, not from below by revolt. Ever since 1525 Germany had known no such fundamental class conflict as France in 1789, 1848, and 1871; and this left open a broad ground for Hohenzollern and Junker to occupy as arbiters. They could in some practical measure fulfil what in England was only a Carlylean or Disraelian fantasy of aristocracy coming forward to befriend and lead a bewildered mass of workers. Conscription and Bismarck's welfare programme were two sides of the same flag: one showed the young man how powerful was the state and how limitless its claim on him, the other showed him how much the state could do for him.

Bülow was drawing a very rosy picture of the officer corps and bestowing heavy flattery on bourgeois self-esteem, when he described it as a meritocracy, 'formed from members of the intellectually superior classes'.[21] But his picture was not altogether fanciful especially if one looked back at the victors of 1866 and 1870, at a time when their class, the smaller nobility or gentry, was still untouched by the contact with plutocracy which bred Mammon-worship in the army later on. In those days they really were 'a military community of a very unusual kind'.[22] They had some affinities with the Teutonic Knights, Prussia's first crusading founders. A Guards officer of the bluest blood might dine for sixpence and deny himself a penny cup of coffee.[23] Such an army could present itself as a truer version of socialism than any preached by the agitators outside.

'The contact between officers and other ranks was very close', von Papen wrote of his early army life, 'and although discipline was strict, a human relationship was built up that lasted all our lives.'[24] It was only with soldiers, or servants, that his class – like the British in India – could find a 'human relationship' now. Reality was of course often less idyllic, and tyrannical officers of the type common further east were by no means unknown. In 1892 Engels hugged himself over the appearance in the socialist press of a royal corps-commander's condemnation of ill-treatment of privates.[25] On the eve of the First World War the Prussian Minister of War, General von Falkenhayn, had to stress that recent episodes of the same sort had 'brought the Army and its institutions under heavy attack'.[26] Yet there was a sufficient number of more responsible men to give these institutions a strong flavour of paternalism; an attitude still more marked in the Japanese officer caste, and quite absent from a British army whose privates were merely odds and ends from the poorest working class, or from the Irish peasantry, enlisted for pay.

'Belief in a mission of popular education may be ascribed to the German officers' corps as a general conviction.'[27] It was a regular duty, General von Eichhorn reminded officers of his Eighteenth Corps in 1909 in a highly revealing circular, to conduct political instruction, to mould their men into 'loyal subjects'. 'The young soldier's mind', he urged, 'is normally like a piece of wax on which every sort of impression can be made. Many, of course, have already been infected by Social-Democracy before they were called; but they are young, their sickness is only superficial, and their service with the colours must work like a healing spring, and wash the sickness out of their system.' What was paramount, he added, was the need to win their confidence. 'The men must be convinced that the officer is their best friend, and that what he says is true and right.'[28] A quotation from *Hamlet* follows; this commander was far from illiterate, in spite of his mixed metaphors. But here, as in many other ways, the implications of this whole epoch can be seen carried to their grotesquely logical conclusion in National Socialism.

It was the consensus of respectable opinion 'that the habit of obedience to constituted authority acquired in the army . . . formed the best possible guarantee against the undue spread of socialistic doctrine'. In uniform men learned 'the hopelessness of armed resistance', while later they learned 'the substantial advantages that accrued to them personally from their previous connection with the services'. When, during the 1880s, the army intake was allowed to drop, it was found that men who had not been through the ranks were less acceptable to employers, tended to be unemployed, and hence to turn socialist. To remedy this it was decided in 1893 to shorten the term and increase the number.[29] Yet in 1911 Bernhardi was bitterly complaining that only about half the able-bodied men available were being called up and that the big towns were being neglected; universal service was being abandoned to the French.

'Opinion oscillates between the wish to enforce it more or less, and the disinclination to make the required outlay.'[30] Dislike of tax burdens must have been a real obstacle. Some of the wealthier may have been coming to feel by this time, after decades with none of the dreaded workers' outbreaks, that insurance against socialism could be obtained more cheaply. The army's own sense of its educating mission is likely to have been weakened by the dwindling of the aristocratic element, still more of its old Spartan standards. Besides all this there was the fact that nobles, still holding many key posts in the army, were unwilling to have the officer cadre further diluted by middle-class entrants, as would inevitably happen if the army were brought up to full strength. This feudal prejudice may have cost it three corps, and with them perhaps the failure to reach Paris in 1914.[31] Here is another glimpse of the many contradictions besetting the task of turning a class society into an armed nation.

In France the bloodthirsty suppression of the Commune made a rift hard to overcome. It was carried out by the old professional army, whose triumph over the people added to its failure against the Prussians made it so obnoxious that something else had to be put in its place. The new army set up in 1872 was more egalitarian than the German; happily for France, there was nothing paternalistic about it. This was a bourgeois country, dedicated to rugged individualism, yet at the same time one of inadequate industrial development. Barrack conditions were rough and ready; so, when the First World War came, were medical services, as in Napoleon's day. Habits of colonial conquest and of drilling or dragooning native troops helped to fix the army's character; though it was to the more intelligent officers familiar with colonial problems, such as Lyautey, that the thought of the officer as educator was likeliest to occur.

To the young Frenchman, by contrast with the German, his spell with the colours was commonly a mere blank, or interruption of life, a disagreeable duty to be got through as best might be. To the propertied classes the masses remained for long an unknown quantity; at the outset many must have distrusted general military training as much as Thiers did, regarding it as a rebirth of Jacobinism, a desperate expedient forced on them and other ruling classes by the necessity of not seeming less patriotic than the German. Uncertainty about how a swollen factory proletariat would behave may explain in part the sluggish growth of industry, the preference of capital for foreign investment. For straightforward use as an armed police the new army could not be reckoned as reliable as the old one. It was favourite doctrine with the Kaiser that the soldier must be ready to fire on his closest relatives at the word of command. But when, at

Fourmies in 1891, French troops were ordered to fire on a crowd in the market-place, some officers refused to repeat the order, most of the men fired in the air, some did not fire at all: one, Lebon, 'because his mother might have been in the crowd', and his captain upheld him.[32] There was all the more need to make the army a support to order by the other, more oblique means of using it to fill the public with fear and hatred of the national enemy, pride in empire and thirst for glory.

In nineteenth-century Spain when Liberals were in power a National Militia, where all were supposed to serve, existed side by side with a force of conscripts serving for a fairly long term (eventually eight years). Democrats wanted to abolish this regular army altogether; conservatives when in power suppressed the militia. Selective conscription, with substitution allowed to those who could afford to pay, was restored after the stormy days of the First Republic in 1874. It continued to do well enough for a repressive government as a gendarmerie, but the army could acquire no national appeal because its purpose was too blatantly obvious: except for colonial rebels there was no external enemy in sight. As to shepherding the new working class into the national fold, it faced the special disadvantage that industry was located chiefly in the national minority regions, Basque or Catalan, where conscription was a further goad to regional feeling. It was a special levy of conscripts for Morocco in 1912 that provoked a general strike at Barcelona and Spain's 'Tragic Week'.

When Italy went in for general conscription in 1873, it was by way of a facile substitute for the nation-building programme needed to turn its formal political unification into a living reality; soldiers from different provinces were put together in the same units. In the industrializing north military service could have some of its normative influence; for the most part it was simply one more burden on the peasantry, and the south, to which Piedmontese rule was foreign rule, could not be roused to much indignation against either of the indispensable 'national foes' dangled by turns before it, Austria and France. The rational reluctance of Italians to fight for their rulers in either of the two world wars was foreshadowed by their inclination to evade military training, by desertion or emigration. It required 'superhuman efforts', a senator lamented, to get conscription established in Sicily, and then it was largely undone by so many Sicilians flocking abroad.[33] A law of 1888 sought to prevent men below the age of thirty-two from leaving Italy; it had little success.

'That the English have no universal military service is one of the shortcomings of English culture,' wrote Treitschke, finding fault with their vulgar addiction to games and athletics instead of to 'noble arms'.[34] There were some demands for conscription from army men, others from conservatives whose motives seemed transparent to one of their critics: 'They do not mention the foe within; but he is in their minds much more than the foe without. A drilled and disciplined proletariat is their hope against an insurgent democracy.'[35] Long after that date, in April 1970, a local survey of opinion reported a majority in favour of a return to conscription, chiefly on the ground that a spell of strict discipline would do young men good. Here the social calculation can be seen long outlasting any argument of military utility.

By imposing conscription on Italians and Germans Napoleon did much to turn Europe against him; when Britain had to adopt conscription in 1916, Irish bitterness was redoubled. In general, if the system helped to counteract socialism in the advanced countries, it helped to worsen one of the gravest problems of the more backward, that of national minorities. In Russia this was displayed on a vaster scale than in Spain and more intensely than in the Habsburg Empire. The Ottoman Empire, which counted its subjects by religion, not nationality, was safer while it adhered to its time-honoured usage of conscripting only Muslims and making others pay an extra tax. Backward Turkey was ahead of Europe in treating army duty as a badge of honour instead of a hardship. When the Young Turks seized power in 1909 and in the name of equality and fraternity extended the privilege to Christians, they only made their Christian subjects more eager to see the end of the Empire.

Elsewhere in eastern Europe the practice had for a long time been selective conscription of peasants, for very long terms: in the Russia of Nicholas I twenty-five years, or virtually for life. The longer soldiers were kept away from their old homes and ties, the more blindly obedient they became and the more easily employed on their chief business, keeping the people down. Where a peasantry was being reduced to serfdom, or otherwise broken in, conscription had punitive uses in place of educational. A recalcitrant peasant would be disposed of by being drafted into the army, in much the same way as in Russia his lord might have him removed to Siberia. In Sweden in the seventeenth century the lord's power to rid himself of an individual in this way was a valuable means of subduing the whole class, by depriving it of leaders.[36] In Denmark, for half a century from 1735, peasants were chosen for the militia by their landlords; this was far less onerous, but extremely unpopular nevertheless, so that here again a strong weapon was placed in the landowner's hand. In

Austria the government or its local representatives were empowered to put any suspected trouble-maker on the army roll without more ado; service was perpetual. Good use was made of this in 1790 when there was peasant agitation to be dealt with.[37] So good an idea was sure to strike other masters far away. During Venezuela's wars of independence we hear of a Negro slave sent into the army because he was too independent for his owner's liking.[38]

In Russia links between conscription and the spread of serfdom were close, and hatred of army enrolment helped to fan peasant resistance. To the non-Russian peoples of the Empire it was a special grievance, most of all when they did not share the Orthodox religion which gave the tsarist army most of its moral cement. This was especially the case with the Jews, for whose benefit conscription took the highly educational turn of an attempt to Christianize and Russify them.[39] For a regime so primitive as the tsarist, the change to a modern national army was bound to be, as for Turkey, a hazardous experiment. 'The Russians . . . have adopted a system of universal liability to service for which they are not civilised enough,' wrote Engels.[40] 'And then, where to find officers for so many in a country without a bourgeoisie?'[41]

Russia in fact possessed neither a mature middle class, such as gave the French officer corps its professionalism, nor a genuine aristocracy, such as gave the German its paternalism. With class conflict smouldering in the countryside, landlord officers and peasant recruits were unlikely to meet in brotherly harmony. For winning over or neutralizing the discontented workman this army was even less well qualified; high-handed treatment of workmen in the ranks, and in the navy where more of them were required, by their *high-well-born* officers only exasperated them further. One of the Tsar's reasons for proposing a peace conference and reduction of armaments was that more artillery would call for more skilled craftsmen in the army, whose loyalty could not be relied on.[42] This clumsy, inert force could still be massively employed, as the French and probably the German could not, for crushing internal revolt, as in 1905–6; but it was as ill-equipped for anything like 'moral rearmament' as for fighting artillery battles. In 1917 the weakest link at which the chain of tsarist authority snapped was the army.

Resistance to conscription was everywhere on a small scale. It was proof of the power the modern state had built up that it could enforce what Tolstoy called a condition of slavery with 'a degree of humiliation and submission incomparably worse than any slavery of the ancient world'.[43] Defiance needed the convictions of a group to nerve it; this was nearly always a religious body, and in a series of countries there were small sects whose members refused to serve. In Russia the Doukhobors, spiritual descendants of the old Anabaptists, did so; the Government retaliated brutally.[44] Tolstoy made himself the mouthpiece of protest, and conscription became one of his main indictments against tsarism. He argued that the way to prevent war was not any artificial device such as an international tribunal, but a simple refusal to put on uniform.[45]

Tolstoy tried to demonstrate that even the physical risks incurred by refusal were smaller than those of army life and war. He may have been right, but it was not an argument that would embolden many individuals to challenge their rulers. For this a strong positive faith was needed. Religion being overwhelmingly on the side of Caesar, the alternative was socialism, which however was not prepared, like some of the religious minorities, for direct action against conscription, but relied on the gradual effect of its anti-war campaigning. Tolstoy and the socialists may each be said to have seen some weaknesses of the other's approach. He taxed the workers with 'participation in murder', because they 'either consent or pay the taxes for the army or become soldiers themselves, regarding such action as quite normal'.[46] The time to oppose general conscription may have been when it was new and unfamiliar. But in Prussia it was much older than socialism, older than the working class itself, which was born inside its prison; and the longer it went on anywhere the more mechanically it came to be identified with patriotism and civic duty.

Socialist inaction early on must be explained partly by illusions about its 'democratic' nature, its resemblances to the 'national militia' type of defence force. It might again be hoped that, by being subjected for only a year or two to army control, the masses would be inflamed by it, not tamed; that the ruling groups of Europe were digging their own graves by teaching their subjects how to fight. At the end of 1888, when Boulanger seemed on the verge of power in France, with no visible programme except a march on Berlin, Paul Lafargue wrote to Engels: 'War today means the people in arms; and that is what Conservatives of every kind dread.'[47] Three months later he added: 'Perhaps the declaration of war will usher in the revolutionary era. War means the people armed. In Paris and in many other towns there will be uprisings.'[48] This looks in retrospect a romantic vision. Yet his expectations must have been nervously shared by many of the bourgeoisie, and may have been less unrealistic then than they were later. If so, Europe's rulers were well advised to postpone their rupture for so long, until another quarter-century of the drill-ground had done its work.

'The army has become the main purpose of the State', Engels wrote in *Anti-Dühring*, 'and an end in itself.'[49] It was not quite this, if we allow for its social utility. But Engels suffered from no illusion about war being a godsend to socialism. Weighing the chances in 1889, the certain horrors 'against what slender hope there is that this ferocious war results in revolution – this is what horrifies me'. If revolution broke out in France, Russia would join with Germany to crush it.[50] The mass armies stood ready to 'restore order' in other lands, not only in their own, as they were to attempt to do in Russia after 1917. Engels wanted a militia instead of a regular army, quoting with approval a dictum that the Republic in France, or democracy, 'will always be in danger so long as every worker does not have his own Lebel rifle and fifty cartridges'.[51] This became the standard socialist thesis. In 1891 Kautsky and Bernstein admitting that at present 'The disbanding of standing armies is utterly impossible', proposed 'conversion of the standing armies to citizen armies'.[52] In France Jaurès, ardent advocate of peace as well as – unlike the Marxian socialists – ardent patriot, made himself the spokesman of the idea. In 1907 it was endorsed by international socialism at the Stuttgart congress.

It may not have been altogether beside the point to ask whether citizen armies or militias would really be immune from the infection of chauvinism, as enthusiasts like Jaurès believed.[53] The experiment, in any case, was not tried by any big country. In the meantime, Engels may have set an example of being too hopeful that a rising tide of radicalism would exorcise the spirit that the armies were seeking to instil in their men. Jubilant over some successful demonstrations in France, he wrote: 'These bloodless victories are an excellent way of accustoming the soldier to the supremacy and infallibility of the popular masses.'[54] This was allowing too little for the moral or psychological influence of the drill-ground. Engels was one of curiously few leading socialists, in that militarizing age, to have worn uniform himself, but that was long ago and he had been out of personal contact with his compatriots for many years. He was impressed by the more favourable aspect of army training, the methodical habits it helped to impart to the German workers' movement. 'Our organisation is perfect – the admiration and despair of our opponents . . . our military training and discipline is invaluable.'[55] These are qualities any serious movement demands (just as a factory does, and Engels had been a mill-owner as well as a soldier), and he was always critical of inefficiency, of which he observed a great deal in French left-wing activity. Ultimately, however, the beneficiary would be the employer, yearly receiving a contingent of workers ready for factory routine, instead of socialism – not Spartacus but Noske.

Tolstoy had a clearer sense of how young men, 'thanks to artful discipline, elaborated during centuries – are inevitably transformed in one year into submissive tools in the hands of the authorities'.[56] Conscription was, as he said, a form of slavery and shared its *infantilizing* impact, most extreme on those of stunted mental growth like the East Prussian or Russian peasantry. 'No man, whatever his political convictions, who is serving in the army, and has been subjected to that hypnotic breaking in, which is called discipline, can, whilst in the ranks, avoid obeying commands, just as an eye cannot avoid winking when a blow is aimed at it.'[57] Training, mostly drilling and marching, had as its cardinal aim the total absorption of the individual in the uniformed mass, a submission akin to the blind faith exacted by religion. Carried over from the past into an epoch when new weapons were rendering it obsolete, it was justified by its social function of licking a whole male population into shape as professional armies had been.

In most recruits, in the more developed countries, there would be a more positive, emotional response as well. It is hard for the individual to go on feeling at odds with the life round him, and the more so when this is as close and all-enveloping as an army's; the most reluctant would be impelled to come to terms with it. He would learn to hug his chains, if they were as decently gilded as they were in Germany, so as not to feel galled by them or go through his term chafing at the drudgery and despotism to which he was subjected. Once he accepted his lot he could let himself be drilled into a warrior, into a collective *raptus*, as the savage dances himself into ardour for the fight or the hunt, or a dervish into a fit of mystic rapture. Mimic battle could take on the quality of a game. Annual manoeuvres in Germany, presided over by the All-Highest and wound up by his favourite *coup de théâtre* of a grand cavalry charge, might be poor preparation for actual warfare, but excellent for the results on participants. One of the young soldiers we meet early on in *All Quiet on the Western Front*, seated on their commodes out in the balmy summer air, is not quite sure whether the Kaiser ever has to visit the lavatory.

If on common days of the week a man suffered from his army boots (which were playing havoc with Europe's feet), his easiest consolation was grumbling at the villainous foreigners whose fault it was that he had to go clumping about in them. Thus army life intensified that diversion of discontents outwards against foreign bogies that was so large a part of Europe's adaptation to this traumatic period of social transition. Altogether, the average individual would come out of it more firmly integrated in the national collective. It would be of interest to know how many socialists whose faith remained militant had, for medical or other reasons, been spared the brainwashing of the barracks. Of those young men who most feared or resented the prospect of service, a good many avoided it by emigrating, as Italians did in such numbers. Emigration, temporary or permanent, was a more ingrained habit in Italy than anywhere else, and socialists of Mussolini's generation often turned to it on principle. It was to escape conscription that many of the Russian Jews who poured into England in the late nineteenth century left home.[58] An enquiry among 131 immigrants in the United States showed that 18 of them – 5 Russians and 13 Greeks – had crossed the sea for the same reason.[59] Several states besides Italy sought to prevent this by legislation; but it probably did more to ease the system by providing a safety-valve than to make the men who stayed at home less willing to go through the mill.

'A really national army unites all the citizens of the country', wrote Treitschke.[60] It was a security against class war, that is, but sooner or later the price might have to be a foreign war. When 1914 duly came it was naïve of those who approved of the military system simply for its peacetime benefits to feel astonished and indignant. Lichnowsky accused an irresponsible Hohenzollern of perverting 'militarism, which by rights is an education for the people and an instrument of policy', to purposes of aggression.[61] It always had to have international tension to sustain it; as Tolstoy said, governments could have no wish for their quarrels to end and would invent fresh ones if the old ones vanished, because there was no doing without them as 'a pretext for keeping up the army upon which their power is based'.[62] Those issues, looked back on today, often seem ludicrously trivial; under cover of them aggressive aims, older or newer, were developing which had nothing to do with the basic function of the military system, the preservation of social order.

As Chekov noted, there was a type of officer, common in the home of Russian roulette, who craved for war as a distraction. 'The idle, so-called governing, classes cannot remain long without war. When there is no war they are bored.'[63] To the more earnest type, far commoner in Germany, army life could be fully satisfying in itself. It was a German, Colonel von Schwarzhoff, who undertook the defence of the spiritual values of militarism at the first Hague Conference.[64] Yet any officer corps must be conscious, like Napoleon, of the need to *chauffer la gloire*, to win fresh laurels, from time to time. It ceases to command respect if it never does any fighting, wears no medals earned under fire; to say nothing of the sluggishness of promotion. The peace before 1914 was already embarrassingly long-drawn and made at least sabre-rattling obligatory. Moreover, while the middle class learned to ape the warlike deportment of its superiors, the Junker caste was acquiring a relish for bourgeois fleshpots. Two social elements were mingling in a compound far more combustible than either by itself. With Treitschke's disciples preaching war as the only antidote to national decay, and Bernhardi pressing the views of the more bellicose soldiers, the chimney-barons' imagination – notably but not only in Germany – might well be fired and set them thinking of their own growing strength and that of the army, wondering what windfall gains of markets, materials and empire the two together might not yield.

Ironically, national antagonisms were being fanned in order to justify the existence of armies of a type poorly suited to fight the war they were likely to bring about. There was some half-comprehension of this among professional officers, who were nowhere genuinely eager to have to deal with all the manpower offered them. Their talk of 'nations in arms' was more rhetoric, designed to keep the people in the right frame of mind, than sober planning. In particular the French generals, with their smaller population and greater fear of civilian criticism, were (as Jaurès complained) banking on a short war, to be fought chiefly with the 'barracks army', the troops immediately available, whose term was extended in 1912 to three years.[65] They must have expected these to be more docile, as well as in better trim, than recruits called back after years of exposure to the contagions of civil life. To the extent that the public was aware of this design, universal service would become a far lesser deterrent to war. Each age-group in turn took its risk of war breaking out while it was with the colours: after that it could expect to be well away from the firing-line. When the war turned out to be quite literally a conflict of peoples in arms, in the more modern countries the long decades of drilling proved their worth by leaving the millions ready conditioned to endure the ordeal, if they also dictated in advance its primitiveness. The more worm-eaten political structures collapsed. Capitalism survived and flourished where it was already strong, but its hinterland of eastern Europe was lost.

Postscript

More than fifty old English ballads sing of plough-boys who won the love of rich men's daughters, only to be got rid of by being press-ganged into the navy or sentenced to transportation on a trumped-up charge.[66] In such cases conscription was useful to individuals as a means of dealing with poor men who forgot their place; in its full-blown shape it performed an analogous service for the upper classes collectively. Foreign mercenaries had been a vital adjunct of state power at one stage, conscription was their successor, with its culminating point in the universal liability to service of the decades before 1914.

Karl Liebknecht, the German Social Democrat leader murdered in 1919, underwent a prison term for a book against militarism published in 1907.[67] He had much to say of conscription as a political weapon against socialism. Universal service provided the type of army most appropriate to capitalist society, he wrote, one which although drawn from the people was 'not a people's army but an army hostile to the people'. He showed how it was designed to cut young men off at an impressionable age from family and class, and subjected them to every means of playing on weaknesses or vanities and gaining control of their minds. Bullying and indoctrination in the ranks was followed by pressure from old soldiers' associations to keep their members from having anything to do with any activity displeasing to their war-lord the Kaiser.[68]

Armies never mobilized all the manpower available, for mixed reasons, among them nervousness about 'democratic, or even worse, perils',[69] if the drill-sergeant failed to achieve his object. Meredith's socialistic officer, Nevil Beauchamp, tells the wealthy heiress Cecilia that her father the colonel may toy with the notion of compulsory service in England, but his real motive is to turn it against agitators, and he distrusts the workers too much to risk the experiment. Nevil's own view is also revealing: he would not like to see the middle classes armed, because then they would have no fear of the workers, and hence no further willingness to extend voting rights.[70]

When Napoleon was King of Italy his conscript army there formed a meeting-place for Italians and a nursery, for the more literate, of patriots. When Mahmud II disbanded the old janizary corps in 1826, in Turkish style by turning his artillery on it, all Muslims in the Ottoman Empire were made liable to service. In practice only Turks were called to the colours, and the experience was a strong binding force; what was created was 'not merely a national army but a nation'.[71] In the West nationalism was being harnessed, by the later nineteenth century, as a conservative force. But if conscription could be a nation-building mechanism, it might make national minorities more instead of less refractory. A useful precaution was to station recruits from minority areas far away from their homes; this however became more difficult as the practice had to be accepted of basing units on a territorial area of their own, for the sake of speed in mobilization.

Austria–Hungary was the chief sufferer. With its acute problems of nationality as well as class, the prime function of its army, more than in western countries, was to buttress internal order.[72] When the test of war came in 1914 it showed that short-term conscripts had imbibed far less of loyalty to the dynasty than the longer-serving cadres who quickly became casualties. Thus, as M. E. Howard says, the military system helped to break down the social structure it was designed to uphold.[73] As the war went on German-speaking and Magyar recruits had to be mixed in with other regiments as a stiffening.[74]

Reaction to the Militia Acts of the 1790s in England 'demonstrated that country folk were not incurably passive or deferential'.[75] In later years there was seldom organized resistance anywhere; instead, multitudes sought a private escape by migration. Norman Angell quoted a dictum of 1910 that German emigrants were less affected than anyone else by homesickness – 'Their one idea is to evade conscription'.[76] West Berlin nowadays contains numbers of young Germans who have moved there with the same incentive. Others grumbled but submitted, and rustics might gain from their spell in uniform some needed adaptation to modern life. In Lower Austria about the end of the century, railways, primary education and conscription were the three chief factors transforming rural life.[77]

Opposition to the system came from the Social Democrats, who wanted standing armies to be replaced by citizen militias. Engels wrote a set of articles in 1893 calling on Germany to lead the way, and arguing that there was nothing to be lost from the point of view of national security. Privately he pointed out the force of some professional criticisms; a militia might be better able to defend Switzerland than a larger country.[78] All the same, in 1896 the London congress of the International came out in favour of citizen soldiers and courts of arbitration to settle disputes that could imperil peace.

In R. L. Stevenson's Ruritanian novel *Prince Otto* (1885) an adventurer who has become chief minister of the small state of Grünewald, and is planning a war, reconciles the Liberal conspirators he is in touch with to a decree of army service by telling them that learning to use arms is 'a necessary preparation for revolt'.[79] Some European socialists were thinking on the same lines. Marx's son-in-law Lafargue was accused of telling French workers publicly that they had a big lead over the British, in knowing how to handle rifles – 'And I have no need to tell you against whom you should use those rifles: the employers, they are the enemy.'[80] No one was more convinced of this advantage than Lenin. 'Disarming is a reactionary-Christian jeremiad', he jotted down in some notes. The more militarization, especially if it was extended to women, the sooner could war, when it came, be turned into civil war.[81]

This forecast contrasts sharply with Engels's conviction in his late years that a war would be an immense set-back for the socialist movement, and Liebknecht's warning that a workers' revolution was going to be more difficult now than any revolution of the past.[82] Both views were to prove correct; Engels and Liebknecht were thinking of German conditions, Lenin of Russian. One difference, vividly brought out in a novel by Kuprin, from first-hand experience, was that recruits in Russia were treated with far more than the usual brutality, and by officers of very inferior quality.[83] Loyalty survived the upheaval of 1905, but it could not withstand the military and social strains of the First World War.

On the other side of the world the same opposite calculations were being made. Australia adopted compulsory training in 1911, for boys of fourteen, as the most malleable material, and most in need of being taught discipline and respect for authority as 'part of good citizenship'.[84] Socialists agitated against conscription of any sort, but after 1919 the Marxists dropped out, hopeful that a citizen army could 'one day be "jumped" by the workers, and used to forward the revolution'; a hope still alive in the Second World War.[85]

Engels believed that mass conscription and novel weapons had kept the peace since 1870, by bringing about 'a complete revolution in all warfare', and rendering the outcome of a conflict 'absolutely incalculable'.[86] Short-term service, he observed, must take a long time to produce a nation in arms; sixteen, even twenty-five annual levies would be needed to provide a sufficient trained mass.[87] But this could not ensure peace for ever. We must even ask whether any government ever expected to use the whole weight of its manpower in war. France extended its term of service in 1912 in order to have the maximum number of men ready for immediate action. It was widely held that no country's finances could sustain a long-drawn struggle, and in 1914 there was general expectation of a quick finish, a knock-out blow. But if the millions taught to fight were not really intended to be used on the battlefield, there is all the more cause to look elsewhere for the true motives of the system.

7

Working Class and Nation in Nineteenth-century Britain

'The workers have no fatherland.' For the Marx of *The Communist Manifesto*, born in a Germany which had only a dozen years before ceased to be the Holy Roman Empire, this was a necessary condition of their historic task; it meant emancipation from the past and all its trammels. In Britain the factory working class started existence doubly segregated, morally and physically shut off in its smoky towns from the rest of the nation. Yet it was being born into a land where the spirit of nationalism had flowered, along with nascent capitalism, earlier than anywhere else. England's most remarkable traveller listened with deep indignation to the King of Brobdingnag's ridicule of his noble country – 'the mistress of arts and arms; the scourge of France; the arbitress of Europe; the seat of virtue, piety, honour, and truth; the pride and envy of the world'.

Gulliver spoke for the middle classes, but many things combined to give those below them a concern with the national greatness. In a heterogeneous labouring population with little in common except poverty, seamen and shipwrights and their dependent trades were always affected by any foreign quarrels. French wars loaded Britain with tropical islands and slave plantations which supplied the man in the street with cheap sugar, tobacco and rum, creature comforts very helpful towards keeping all quiet and contented. Less agreeably, there were always immigrants trickling or pouring in, most of them poor folk coming to compete with native workmen, and arousing the same 'nativist' resentment as newcomers in the nineteenth-century United States. It was an anomaly of the world-wide British Empire to include one colony close at hand, and the great influx from Ireland, the most bitterly resented of all, coincided with the Industrial Revolution. But English as most English might feel, few of them possessed citizen rights. Defeat of the popular forces in the Commonwealth debarred the majority from participation in the public life of their country. This was a deprivation against which urban masses might react morbidly; Tory mobs and Church-and-state demonstrations were a pathetic attempt to claim a place in the nation by those pushed down or in danger of being pushed down into the limbo of exclusion.

While the new working class was in its formative years Britain was involved in further long spells of conflict abroad. The onset of the Industrial Revolution came a few years after the victorious Seven Years' War, and a few years before the less glorious war of the American Revolution, quickly followed by the contest between 1793 and 1815 with Revolutionary and Napoleonic France. So much fighting, with France always the chief enemy, and with the national energies more and more heavily drawn on, could not fail to have its effect on most minds. When the sailors mutinied in 1797 their manifesto boasted how often they had 'made the British flag ride triumphantly over that of our enemies': all they asked for was the same increase of pay and pensions lately granted to the army and militia. Prudent Tories found ways to confirm the common man in his allegiance. Scott describes in a letter of 1812 how in honour of the battle of Salamanca he treated his labourers to 'an ocean of whisky-punch' and an all-night dance on the banks of the Tweed.[1] He had lately been busy breaking up combinations of workers in nearby Galashiels; now he had a chance to play a more benign part.

Scott's workmen were semi-rustics, easily brought under gentry influence, whereas the factory proletariat which he dreaded was an unknown, inaccessible force, a Frankenstein monster as Kingsley was to call it.[2] It was multiplying in its grimy lair at the same time as the long-drawn wars were intensifying national consciousness among the upper and middle classes and their appendages. Seldom have two such opposites been growing side by side. Social strife smouldered, breaking out at times in Luddite violence and reprisals. But in the post-war years there took shape the movement for parliamentary reform which in 1838 took the form of Chartism. The 'Charter' was devised in London, by representatives of the old type of skilled craftsmen, familiar with England's constitutional traditions. These were as remarkable and unique as its precocious nationalism, and interwoven with it; between them they fostered a conviction that in England man is born free, whereas everywhere else he is in chains. Dickens was to be a spectator at an elaborate London working-class entertainment which included a pantomime depicting the Spirit of Liberty.[3]

Freedom as an English birthright might be illusory, yet it could stimulate efforts to bring reality into line with the ideal. Only in England would a mass movement of workers think in terms of an enlargement of constitutional rights, and only there would it be allowed to run its course. Lovett and his London Workingmen's Association were trying, under the pressure of changing times, to secure their status in society, and to this end had to enter into an always uneasy alliance with the northern mill-workers.[4] Chartist leadership was taken over by men like Feargus O'Connor, a lawyer but an Irishman, from outside the English pale, and ready to talk of force. In between these two camps were the cottage industries scattered about in villages and townships. Hand-weavers, unlike many other craft-workers, were being crushed by the new machines. Hitherto politically null, these men had some share of culture, unlike the uprooted mill-workers whom they were inclined to look down on but with whom they now often felt compelled to make common cause. Collectively all Chartists were claiming a place in the national life, guaranteed by votes; but the factory-workers, most restless and radical because newest, most ambitious because of the sense of strength brought by concentrated numbers, wanted – if dimly – more than this, and would use their power to transform society as well as government.

With Chartism by 1850 virtually at an end, the failure of the new working class to enter and remould the national life left it shut up in the 'labourism', the self-absorption and political apathy, from which it has never really recovered. Mill life was by now familiar and accepted, but those living it were still cut off from other other sections of the labouring classes, as well as from the rest. Marx expected a fairly rapid dissolving of the middling strata of society into the proletariat, which would thus come to constitute the bulk of the population: it would be the People, confronting as in 1789 a small class of exploiters. In fact industrialism, and the proletariat with it, were growing fairly slowly. While hand-weavers disappeared many other craftsmen in old, small-scale trades survived; new skilled occupations emerged, bringing a new, successful type of trade union and leadership; these were capable of bettering their position, and so 'ceased to be estranged from society'.[5] There was the fact also that the country's political and intellectual metropolis lay far away from its main industrial areas. In France the two were closer; in Germany each region had always been more self-contained, though there too the distance between the Ruhr and Berlin may have had some harmful effects. This division immunized the industrial north of England from some metropolitan infections, but deprived it of much political stimulus, and both it and the London working class suffered through lack of the mutual reinforcement that Chartism had given.

'There is really no bond of union amongst the working men of England,' *The Beehive* wrote in 1872. 'There is no determined well-defined thought as to any necessary work. . . . They originate nothing; have no hearty faith in any understood policy'.[6] But the instinctive desire of any class or group to feel that it belongs to a wider community is a deep-rooted one, and if not satisfied in a healthy, positive way is likely to find partial substitutes of a worse kind. Carlyle's or Ruskin's conviction that the masses were longing to be ruled and guided by their natural superiors had some corroboration in the rise of the Tory working man, or 'deference voter', and above all in the conversion of a once fiery Lancashire to Toryism. This seems to have happened largely under religious suasion,[7] aided by the gulf between English and Irish. It was a bizarre re-creation in a new environment of the acquiescent torpor of the cottage-workers of old. 'A member of the aristocracy,' Bright wrote disgustedly in his diary in 1857, 'or anyone willing to act with the aristocracy and *for them*, is accepted by the people as if he were the friend of the people.'[8]

As part of Tory demagogy's design to content the workers with an illusion of citizenship, in an old society varnished over, flourishes of drum and bugle figured prominently. Warlike distractions came promptly on their cue: the Crimean War in 1854–6 was closely followed by the second Opium War with China, and in 1857 by the Indian Mutiny. As an organization combining all classes the army made a suitable emblem of national unity, of the nation as a big family. All imagery or ideology of nation and state has derived a great deal from the family; in the factory districts it must have had more persuasiveness as family life there recovered from its disruption in the early days of industrialism. No one felt the link more warmly, or could better embody the 'motherland', than Queen Victoria. During the Crimean War, for the first time in English history, soldiers of all ranks were collected to shake hands with their sovereign and receive their medals from her. As she wrote lyrically to her uncle Leopold, it was an exalting experience to feel 'the rough hand of the brave and honest private soldier. . . . Noble fellows! I own I feel as if they were my own children; my heart beats for *them* as for my *nearest and dearest*'.[9]

Most of the Chartist papers had faded away, though for 'the thinking section of the working class' *Reynolds' Weekly* still upheld the old cause and was also well primed on foreign affairs.[10] David

Urquhart, with a mixture of the Russophobia he shared with Marx and the current myth of a constitututional golden age in Anglo–Saxon times, was able to reach the radical artisans of the west midlands and north-west during the Crimean War, and his Working-men's Committees proliferated.[11] Straightforward jingoism found it easiest to reach London labour, always within earshot and with a considerable *lumpen* ingredient. Music-halls growing up in London suburbs and the provinces were patronized by better-off workers, and might purvey on a more modest scale the exhilaration the Covent Garden audience got from 'The Fall of Sevastopol', music imitating 'the deafening noise of exploding mines . . . the shrill sound of the trumpets, the ships blown in the air, the cries of the fugitives and the shouts of the victors'.[12]

But it has been noticed that music-hall gatherings were apt to applaud any stirring or striking song or spectacle, whether its political moral meant anything to them or not. What happened in the wide world was outside their sphere. For the solid bulk of the working class 'Labourism' served to muddle all ideas from outside, bad as well as good. Perhaps indeed an Indian crowd's enjoyment of any *tamasha* or show, which has misled both Viceroys and Communists, has been typical of common folk everywhere. It stands out all the same that when the electorate gave Palmerston's China war a vote of confidence in 1857 Bright lost his seat at Manchester – and he was bottom of the poll in every ward, despite the fact that Manchester and Salford at that date were supposed to muster a fifth of all working-class votes in the country. This was in late March. Immediately afterwards the Indian Mutiny broke out and threw Britain into another fit, worsened this time by rabid racialism. Common soldiers and sailors putting down the rebels displayed the same revengeful temper as their superiors. An inbred contempt for the Irish among English workers must have predisposed them to take an arrogant view of other colonial races.

This and the China war were scarcely over before there was fresh sound and fury about an invasion that England's late ally Napoleon III was alleged to be plotting. Out of it came the Volunteer movement. There was little ground for the scare,[13] and it must be suspected that it was welcomed and made the most of by those who still thought the workers dangerous. Of the something like 100,000 serious recruits, most were middle-class or rural[14] and would furnish a reliable National Guard in case of social disturbance. Significantly there was nowhere more keenness to enroll, or readiness to work under the army authorities, than in Manchester and other Lancashire towns.[15] Carried away by detestation of Louis-Napoleon and love of soldiering, Engels threw himself into the drilling and training with immense ardour and, one must think, an odd lack of realism. In one of his many articles on the subject he complains of the 'shameful' behaviour of some in a crowd watching a review, who threw stones and tried to break it up.[16] They may have been hooligans, but it seems as likely that they were old-fashioned radicals. In general the effect of this stir and bustle would be to draw the classes closer: these amateur warriors were protecting rich and poor from the dreadful French, and their parades were animating spectacles. When the Scottish Volunteers were reviewed by the Queen in Holyrood Park at Edinburgh on 7 August 1860, while the royal standard of Scotland floated above the summit of Arthur's Seat, a crowd of 100,000 'made the welkin ring with their reiterated cheers'.[17]

Britain is still sprinkled with public houses entitled Volunteer Arms. The movement continued, on broader lines, with the Government taking over more of the costs and direction, until it became something like an army reserve. By the later 1870s there were 200,000 on the rolls, of whom three-quarters may have belonged to the working class, almost entirely to its better-off categories.[18] This meant that these upper strata were being brought under strong conservatizing influence, an important antidote to the voting power conferred on the workers by the second Reform Act in 1867. As to the regular army, it offered young men an alternative in bad times to unemployment. They came mostly from the lowest levels of casual labour, and were often illiterate.[19] Ex-servicemen drew small pensions; they usually found themselves unemployable, and were numerous among 'the homeless and the inhabitants of common lodging houses.'[20] But civic receptions for home-coming troops, the attraction of uniforms to young women, so frequent a theme for banter in *Punch*, and regimental associations, particularly active in martial Scotland, helped to invest army life with a certain glow.

All this beckoned in the direction of empire, which many were eager for many reasons to popularize. In retrospect there may appear to have been no deep social crisis in Britain in the later nineteenth century, but there was quite enough social tension to make imperialism a useful as well as profitable diversion. Two politicians very conscious of this tension, first Disraeli and then Chamberlain, took the lead in promoting imperial sentiment. There were fears that the working class now being enfranchised would prove indifferent, if not hostile, to empire and its costs and risks. They were expressed in 1887 by an American proponent of the idea, fashionable on both sides of the Atlantic, of an 'Anglo–Saxon' league. In a fresh conflict with Russia, he wrote, Britain might be compelled to abandon Asia, because its domestic problems were so urgent and its workers took little interest in remote possessions and frontiers. 'The cry of "Perish India" is sometimes heard.'[21] During the eastern crisis of 1878 the two biggest peace meetings, in Hyde Park, drew the bulk of their attendance from radical working-men's clubs.[22] But most workers' notions about all such things beyond the narrow horizons of daily life continued hazy and unstable, symptomatic of a class half in and half outside the nation. It has been remarked that the average workman was not religious, but did not like to be dubbed an atheist; his patriotism may often have been of the same order.

Poets of the people, like Capern and McGonagall, tuned their lyre to the same conquering themes as poet laureates like Tennyson, sometimes not much more feebly. Willingness to back the Government against colonial rivals had primitive precedents in crowds of workers brawling with one another at election-time to get their respective employers into Parliament. Another parable of the common man drawn into his betters' quarrels may be found in a story from Lakeland of a fight between gangs of labourers employed by two landowners at odds over a right of way.[23] More rationally, some workers as well as capitalists could benefit from the captive market provided by a colony, most bountifully by India for Lancashire cottons. In the late nineteenth century two-fifths of the county's cloth exports were going to India, and this was all the more satisfactory in view of the prevailing depression.[24] Even though not the prime cause of Lancashire's political stagnation, this advantage must be supposed to have deepened it. Perhaps as time went on it may have helped to bring English and Irish mill-hands closer together, as well as labour and capital.

There was little in the equipment of the ordinary labour spokesman to enable him to resist the insidious appeal. He came into politics by way of his trade union, grew dependent on it as a career, was always immersed in petty detail.[25] He was easily induced to regard an empire as a good thing for his rank and file, so long as they got their share of the proceeds. There were indeed labour spokesmen of a very different calibre, such as Tom Mann, and those through whom the British working class played its part in the formation of the First International and the development of the Second. On the level of articulate debate, however, the Fabians supplied a prophylactic against Marxism by adapting socialism to the capitalist outlook, 'especially to the new Imperialist phase of that outlook'.[26] Meanwhile a wealth of propaganda resources were being mobilized on its side. Chamberlain dismissed any talk of 'manufactories of political opinion, where zeal and unanimity are produced to order', an observer remarked in 1902, but they were in fact busily at work.[27] A new-style cheap press was one; another, of course, primary education. At a Suffolk village school when Empire Day was celebrated in 1907 'Her Ladyship kindly lent 20 flags and the children were taught to salute the Union Jack. Lessons were given on the Union Jack and the "Growth and Extent of the British Empire". Several patriotic songs were sung.'[28]

There is no doubt a problem of psychology as to what hold ideas put into heads artificially can have over them. Images of tropical colonies were necessarily superficial, not rooting and growing in the consciousness. A recent analyst speaks of 'the almost total lack of impact made by colonial matters upon the lives and interests of the British populace'; surveys in 1948 and 1951 showed that more than half could not name a single British possession.[29] Nevertheless, even very blurred impressions can be persistent, and affect behaviour potently, at least at moments of excitement. Religion has swayed multitudes ignorant of the latitude and longitude of heaven. Beery euphoria might deposit a gradual sediment of loyalty.

Moreover, empire feeling was buttressed, in a way not shared with any other country, by the colonies of white settlement, to which legions of workers had migrated. They wrote to their relatives at home, and described their new lives;[30] many must have sent home remittances, as Irish emigrants did. In a Jubilee poem Tennyson evoked, side by side with Canadians and others,[31]

> . . . the hardy, laborious,
> Patient children of Albion

part of an imperial family, brought out for the occasion like well-washed children at a party, and looking more respectable than the working class usually did in his poetry. There was also of course that former colony, the United States. To the workers their facility of emigration was far the best of the 'crumbs' bestowed on them by imperialism, and the real aristocracy of labour was to be found in Toronto and Chicago and Melbourne.

A test came in 1899 with the Boer War, whose advocates were anxious to draw labour into a united front, and felt they were succeeding. 'Great Britain,' the *Scotsman* with somewhat fatuous logic pronounced, 'is not expanding because it is greedy of territory; it is expanding because it must find outlets for its teeming population and employment for the workers at home.'[32] One of its staff reported complacently that pro-Boer speakers were appealing to labour in vain, and 'discovering that the British working man whose name has been taken in vain contributes his quota to the discussion by means of brickbats.'[33] Brickbats are all right when thrown in the right direction. 'Some of us,' Norman Angell wrote a few years later, 'have seen a pro-Boer aristocrat running for his life before a howling mob of working-class "patriots".'[34]

But in all such cases, part of the incentive is the plebeian's relish of being licensed for once to mob his superiors. In Britain generally workers showed far less frenzy about the War than the middle classes. On the other hand, organized labour made no attempt to oppose it. Working-class newspapers were mostly critical of the War, and had much to say about soldiers' hardships and their officers' incompetence; on the other hand workers could not be got to believe that the soldiers, their fellow-toilers, were behaving barbarously.[35] In Scotland at any rate no pro-war songs were heard in music-halls;[36] working-men's clubs everywhere had a tolerant ear for anti-war talk, yet they were quite prepared to join in celebrations like Mafeking night.[37] Inconsistency, non-Euclidean logic, is very far from being confined to any single class; but Price has good ground for stressing its part in working-class attitudes to the Boer War, and for pointing out that historians are less familiar than anthropologists with how 'What appear to educated minds to be two seemingly contradictory opinions can be held at the same time about one event'.[38]

One channel through which the working class was being accosted was the chapel: Rosebery courted Dissent on behalf of Liberal Imperialism, and the *Methodist Times* succumbed readily, but the average Nonconformist minister was faithful to his pacific past.[39] It would be worth while to ask how much of the working class's deafness to any abstract principle, good or bad, might be ascribed to the fact of most of it having little or no religious grounding; in a negative sense a fact not to be regretted, since most religion was Anglican, very Tory and jingo, or Catholic. In the long run, in any case, it seems that flag-waving was only effective when accompanied by more tangible inducements. Unionists had been talking, as Halévy says, of social legislation to avert socialism, even if Chamberlain's 1895 proposals were much less comprehensive than their Bismarckian model. In 1897, to cover up the Jameson raid fiasco, he pushed through a workers' compensation measure; but having managed to light his South African fire he felt no need to fulfil his pledge of old-age pensions. Altogether the social legislation of this Unionist government was unimpressive.[40] Disappointment with it must have assisted the landslide victory of the Liberals in 1906.

Pensions now made their appearance. Conditions remained bad enough. Prices rose gradually between 1904 and 1914, wages barely kept pace with them. On the eve of the First World War 'It was stated on high authority that there were eleven million people living on the verge of starvation.'[41] Once again some friends of order detected a whiff of revolution in the air. It is only when two halves of a ruling class each feel that the other is mishandling the masses that they hate each other as acridly as Tories and Liberals did in the years just before the First World War. But unrest was still elemental, little transformed into socialist thinking. Levels of literacy were as low as standards of living. In 1907 an inquiry into reading habits among 200 households in Middlesbrough – during the War a big armaments centre – found only twenty-five individuals reading any sort of serious book; cheap papers and novelettes were the usual pabulum.[42] On trade-union and bread-and-butter issues the working class was an increasingly solid, firmly anchored force; politically it might be as volatile as the small middle classes, because it had so little of a political tradition to orient it. Brailsford remarked that it could be swayed by speeches about fraternity with workers abroad, but equally by anti-foreign claptrap.[43]

Germany had suddenly become the country to be hated. Unlike France it was not an old antagonist, and there were no time-honoured memories to play on; but to make up for this there were now means of indoctrination which could be brought to bear in all sorts of ways. A rising politician, who looked upon war with Germany as a historical inevitability, treated his company of Territorials to a visit to the theatre to see a play which expounded a suitable moral.[44] Not all such propaganda sank in. Blatchford, preaching a combination of socialism and patriotic preparedness, was not making much impact with either; he met with a 'continued mass indifference to the growing threat from Germany and its navy'.[45] What may have sunk in far more than prophecies of a German invasion was the bogy of Germany bent on ruining Britain by cut-throat competition. Britons had no experience of being invaded, but loss of jobs in some corner of the economy because other people were making the same things cheaper was familiar enough.

We hear one of Tressell's workmen, a reader of the Tory *Obscurer*, grumbling about the country being beggared by foreigners. 'Just go to a shop to buy something; look round the place an' you'll see that more than 'arf the damn stuff comes from abroad.'[46] Foreign competition had not stimulated British capitalists to keep up with the times, but it had long inspired them to eloquent calls to labour to realize that they were both in the same boat. That Britain deserved to be the workshop of the world, and British workmanship was the best in the world, was comfortable doctrine for both. Without much success William Morris tried to warn labour that 'desperate "competition" ' might soon turn into 'desperate war': that talk of the necessity to prepare for a fight was 'no longer confined to the honour-and-glory kind of old Tories, who if they meant anything at all by it meant that a Tory war would be a good occasion for damping down democracy'.[47]

On the eve of the War labour unrest was acute. 'In this respect we started the War under a heavy handicap,' Lloyd George was to confess.[48] Yet this quickly seemed to be vanishing amid a rush to enlist; at Middlesbrough, for instance, where employers were helpful and families were given half-pay, with the other workers contributing a levy.[49] It was much the same nearly everywhere. H. G. Wells thought he heard the host of volunteers saying to themselves: ' "Thank God! we can serve our country at last instead of some beastly profiteer".'[50] Some such vague but uplifting sensation there must indeed have been, a substitute for the socialism which had failed to blossom. In a more earthy vein a farm labourer recalled in afteryears: 'We were all damned glad to have got off the farms', away from grinding toil and callous treatment.[51] But these men were also staunchly patriotic, being more directly exposed than the industrial workers to thought-control by the society which exploited them. Gallacher surmised that his fellow-Clydesiders were joining up under yellow-press hypnotism, but even more from a craving for excitement, 'the illusion of wonderful adventure', escape from 'the deadly monotony of working-class life'.[52] This too must account for a great deal.

It is only fair to the peoples of Europe, working classes and middle classes alike, to say that they all believed themselves, however deludedly, to be engaged in a defensive war. It is only fair to the British people in particular, so long deluged with imperialist propaganda, to remember that it thought it was going to war in defense of a small neighbouring country barbarously invaded, not in pursuit of any fresh colonies or markets. In this atmosphere it might appear as if a whole estranged class was suddenly finding its way out of limbo into the national fold. Before long several labour leaders were entering the Government. Ben Tillett's visits to the front to promote morale were 'a task he greatly enjoyed and carried out superbly'.[53] By contrast with the French wars a century before, integration seemed to have been achieved. Reality was far more complex. Not all labour leaders were prepared to take the war at its face value, and as it dragged on this face value grew less and less convincing. In South Wales at first well-known militants from the mines could be heard making recruiting speeches.[54] But when Mrs Pankhurst was there before the end of 1915 she found the Welsh very unresponsive: 'They are sulky and difficult to handle, and will not sing the national anthem.'[55]

Out of ten million men of military age only six million were physically fit for 'general service'.[56] Most of the unfit must have belonged to the working class, which thus got some recompense for the crippling existence it was condemned to. Before conscription began to be introduced in January 1916, two-thirds of the six million had joined up. Men in reserved occupations were exempted; again these were mostly workers, miners and gun-founders and the like, especially numerous in Scotland. When comb-outs had to be resorted to they proved awkward; there was an obstinate feeling that if labour was to be conscripted, the same must happen to capital. Dilution of labour too was bitterly disliked. A left-wing union activist like Thomas Bell, himself anti-war, has scarcely anything to say in his record of the war years except of trade-union stands over grievances like this.[57] The workers' whole equivocal place in the nation was finding the sharpest possible expression; the class was divided, to a considerable degree emotionally as well, between the men at the front and those at home, painfully defending their own trenches, the small collective rights painfully won by generations of struggle. Meanwhile outside their dugouts empires crashed, revolutions erupted, history took giant strides.

Milner wrote at the end of the War of 'the lurid picture of approaching Revolution, in which critics of the Labour Party usually indulge'.[58] In reality the Party, despite its nominal adoption in 1918 of a socialist programme, came out of the War patriotically conformist instead of radicalized.[59] There was enough radical impulse to inspire – with the aid of war-weariness, no doubt – the Hands Off Russia campaign, and the founding of the Communist Party. The General Strike might be viewed as a belated epilogue to the War, an outburst of all the smothered feeling it and its profiteering had stirred up; a swing from integration to the opposite pole of secession. As against this, something of the working-class dichotomy of the war years was perpetuated by ex-servicemen's organizations, under conservative guidance. Those who have made sacrifices for a cause seldom find it easy to admit to themselves that the cause was worthless, the sacrifices made for nothing.

It is moreover a fact of developed industrial societies that war can bring social progress on some lines, or accelerate it more than any peacetime effort is likely to do. During the First World War health in Britain improved and mortality was reduced;[60] it was agreed that more care had to be taken of mothers and children, because so many were left on their own, or if only to ensure that there would be enough soldiers for future wars. The Second World War brought a much bigger, but again fortuitous, advance. Since then, with the dwindling of empire and navy, and the entry into the European Economic Community, the old siren-songs have faded almost into silence. More and more, governments and capitalists are compelled to provide, or appear to be providing, material benefits for voters, instead of rhetoric. On these benefits labour has strenuously insisted; but little of a more rational social consciousness and purpose has grown up to replace the old half-accepted false consciousness.

England's proletariat was recruited from a countryside where the degradation of the farm labourer had destroyed the old folk arts. Its lack of any culture of its own has been a permanent factor in helping to keep it *incommunicado*. In place of it, since Nature abhors moral as well as other vacuums, there has been a growth of the cult of sport which would have astonished Marx and Engels even more than the rise of nationalism in the world; though it was already in their time an important go-between of the classes. In Manchester on 22 May 1977, a thousand people collapsed in the press when three-quarters of a million thronged the streets to cheer a football team which had defeated Liverpool, and a few days later there was as ecstatic a reception for the Liverpool team returning from Rome with the European Cup. This naïve hero-worship is of course not to be mistaken for the sum total of working-class allegiance or aspiration. In itself it may be said to represent a sturdy independence, deserving of respect in a world of increasingly machine-made values. These crowds might have been filling the streets to applaud far worse men than a football team. Symbolically they were turning away from the higher collectivities of nation, state, Church, always artificial and in part fraudulent, to the simpler spirit of tribalism. It would not be hard to find a parallel between this and the relationship of women to the man-built world they have lived in, seldom positively challenging it and its ideologies or laws, but equally seldom, perhaps, whole-heartedly accepting them. Women in Nazi Germany offered no collective resistance, but neither did they identify themselves with the Third Reich in the way a strenuous indoctrination sought to make them do.[61] German women proved less malleable than German men. In Britain, in the course of the long interaction between a new class and an old nation, each has, but only very limitedly, transformed the other. From this imperfect incorporation, this autonomy which the working class has preserved, negative as it may often seem, fresh beginnings can always be looked for hopefully.

8

Revolution

'Revolution' in its fullest sense should mean a vital transformation of society, something far beyond any ordinary shaking-up, a decisive transfer of power both political and economic. This can happen very seldom. But Europe has known many lesser eruptions, resembling it in some measure. Overt class conflict has been only occasional, disharmony among classes or social groups has been ubiquitous, and in all these collisions its presence can be traced. They have been of many species; and with Europe's always uneven development growing more and more uneven, forms of revolt belonging to distinct stages of history might be going on in different regions at the same time.

Europe's mutability must be traced to fundamental features of its make-up. Underlying them has been its duality, the discordant nature it derived from its Roman-Christian and Germanic-feudal ancestry. Both strands made for close interweaving of state and society, in most of Asia joined by mechanical, external clamps. Both gave rise to a wealth of political or politically relevant institutions of all kinds, which forces of change could work on and through, even if often obstructed by them. In Europe also, unlike most of Asia, many autonomous polities packed close together meant that exterior factors were always liable to intensify internal frictions.

In medieval times movements of revolt included those of peasants against landowners, towns against lords, urban workers against employers in centres of nascent capitalism, peoples against foreign domination. Most strident of all was the example set by the dominant class itself, the feudal lords. It could take opposite forms, one that might be called 'constitutional', the other, in times of ruling-class disintegration, anarchic faction fighting. All these types of rebellions continued into the sixteenth and seventeenth centuries, forming new combinations and sometimes reaching higher levels; this entire era of transition may be termed a single protracted revolution, whose outcome varied from region to region. At the bottom of it was the struggle between the masses, chiefly agricultural, and the upper classes living at their expense and bent on depriving them of what betterment they had gained, a good deal through the lucky accident of the Black Death, by reimposing old burdens or devising fresh ones.

Political and social confusion, before the state could be built up anew, gave opportunity for prolonged though scattered resistance, all the way across Europe. Great peasant revolts broke out in turn, early in the modern epoch before reorganization of the propertied forces had got too far: in Hungary in 1514, in Germany in 1524–5, in Croatia in 1573. As in China's peasant risings, there was an admixture of other social elements, which served as catalyst and might furnish some guidance. Most rebels were trying to defend their small possessions or rights, as peasants or artisans; among some of the dispossessed, and a few idealists, there might be a primitive socialist idea of goods or poverty shared. They were all defeated. Lack of combination was still more marked among the masses than among their superiors. They were weakened by their own numbers, growing afresh and bringing increased pressure on the land and further stratification among the tillers. In Germany these received some, but inadequate, reinforcement from the urban poor; in Valencia in 1520–2 the *Germania* or Brotherhood of the urban lower classes drew too little backing from a countryside where Christian and Morisco were at odds.

Bloodthirsty and massive repression made for quiescence in subsequent times. So, more permanently, did the rise of new state-forms, holding out at times some small protection to the peasants, though protection they had to pay dearly for, but steadily tilting the balance of power in favour of the privileged classes by improved military organization. In France even during the civil wars, in Germany during the Thirty Years' War, mutiny could flare up again in the villages only rarely and briefly. But although the revolt of the masses was subdued, it was not without some share in the long-term remodelling of Europe, if in the oblique fashion that has most often marked their contribution to history. Their aspirations found expression, so far as they had any distinct ideology, in Anabaptism, which, persecuted and driven underground, still helped to push northern Europe into the Reformation. Cramped and half-hearted though this was by comparison, it was nevertheless a kind of revolution, opening the road – if again in very roundabout style – to all later progress. One consequence of schism was to lend a sanction to rebellion, since a ruler who attacked the true faith could be deemed a tyrant, and forfeited his claim to obedience.

Even the boldest were chary of recognizing a right of disobedience in the common people. Althusius was one political theorist who grudgingly admitted it, but he like most others much preferred to leave the right to the 'ephors', the magistrates, spokesmen in other words of solid men of substance.[1] Fear of social upheaval persisted, and hastened the reconstruction of state power. Three main types of monarchical governments were developing. One was the Muscovite, a semi-Asiatic despotism based on a new service-nobility; the others corresponded more or less with the Protestant and Catholic territories, though like their Churches they had much in common. In the northern area more survived of the old 'Estates monarchy': the propertied classes were represented, with a degree of vitality proportionate to their own, by provincial or national assemblies. Southward the 'absolute' monarchy was freeing itself in the course of the sixteenth and seventeenth centuries from the restraint of such bodies, and expanding its civil and military machinery far more rapidly. Once established it would prove very difficult to get rid of, or even modify. By contrast the 'northern' state, looser and less heavily equipped, was more prone to change, revolutionary change though this might be. Attempted revolt anywhere might be bedevilled by foreign meddling; on the other hand rebels might receive encouragement and aid from abroad. Moreover the swelling armies and their chronic wars were undisciplined and unpopular, and instead of bolstering order sometimes helped to disrupt it, while their cost was enough to plunge the richest treasury into bankruptcy.

In general, class conflict in its elemental shape of poor against rich was being relegated to the eastern realms where feudal reaction was going furthest and reducing the cultivators to complete serfdom; principally to the Russian borderlands where there was most room to fight it out. Western countries were moving towards more complex crises, social strife intermixed with political and ideological issues. One was the Revolt of the Comuneros in 1520–1.[2] Urban patriciates were protesting against official encroachments; dislike of taxation brought in the humbler citizenry, who had little or no share in the management of their towns; and they were joined by a good many noble *frondeurs* and churchmen with one motive or another for dissatisfaction. A way forward was what Castile required, but too little political initiative could be mustered, too many supporters wanted to go backward instead. There was no true capital city, and the disturbance remained bottled up in the north. While the leadership fumbled, the commonalty grew self-assertive and obstreperous. There was a riot of wool-carders and other plebeians at Segovia; at Valladolid a democratic committee wielded power in the streets; unrest spread to some of the feudal estates. Before long the united front against an absentee king was breaking up, the nobility changing sides, the wealthier townspeople losing heart; the movement fizzled out.

Some of the same ingredients could be found in the French broils after 1562, complicated by religious hatreds and regional jealousies. Monarchy and old Church kept the upper hand in the capital and its surrounding provinces; the opposition drew most of its strength from frontier areas, less advanced and only half assimilated, with a character and traditions of their own. What should have been the leading social forces were split, because many from the middling or upper-middle strata had been drawn off into government service or a *rentier* existence, as well as by creed and locality. Once the sword was drawn, the Huguenot urban section was overshadowed by the military, men of the gentry class for whose restless energies and hungry wants the Italian wars had provided a safety-valve until the peace of 1559. It was something like an anticipation of the reliance of weak progressive movements in later days on army support, as in Spain.

Also as often later, Catholicism had more success in enlisting popular allegiance, at any rate in some of the towns, Paris above all: the countryside was indifferent, having nothing to gain or lose. Paris however got out of hand, as Valladolid had done, and radical-democratic demands mingled with religious fanaticism. During the long-drawn contest there were stirrings of constitutional theory in both camps, as one or the other faced the prospect of having to live under hostile sway; each in turn was ready to endorse limitations on monarchical power. But the destructiveness of the wars, foreign intervention, fear of the plebs taking the bit between its teeth, compounded by symptoms of rural revolt, made sensible men end by agreeing that order and prosperity could only be looked for under a restored and still more authoritarian crown and bureaucracy. The states general, which had shown occasional signs of reviving and taking the lead, expired.

Even in Muscovy during the Time of Troubles about the close of the sixteenth century it might seem as if the Zemski Sobor was coming to the fore. But it was no more than a recent creation of the tsars, unlike the far older assemblies of cental and western Europe, and the most active party in it was the service-gentry whose grand aim was the final enserfment of the refractory peasantry. There were moments when runagate serfs, free Cossacks from the borderlands, disgruntled small fief-holders of the south, and factious boyars, could be found jostling together in the same rebel army; but nothing could keep them together for long.[3] Here as in several other countries the dying-out of an old dynasty had been the signal for grievances of every kind to boil over; a new one was found, and within a few decades the autocracy was firmer and more rigid than ever.

By taking advantage of the troubles to invade Russia the Poles had stirred up a fever of patriotism, or xenophobia dyed with religion. National consciousness was awakening in many corners of Europe, in its initial forms, and could borrow from and in turn fortify all other turbulent passions. One of the first, and one of the few successful struggles for independence was the Swedish breakaway from Denmark in the 1520s. This was at least in part the divorce of a relatively egalitarian society from a feudal monarchy, and brought on the scene an authentic nation with much internal development as well as external expansion in store for it. Irish resistance to English conquest was more primitive; Ireland had never been a state, and had no national organs. Much the same can be said of the last Morisco rising of 1568 in southern Spain, likewise fiercely religious.

It was typical of revolts both national and social in being provoked by intensified pressure from above. In the next reign but one Olivares embarked under stress of war on a programme of further central control and stiffer taxation of the non-Castilian provinces of Iberia. Out of this came in 1640 the rebellions of Catalonia and Portugal. Both of these had preserved their own institutions, which were unlikely to initiate defiance but, once this was afoot, could give it some leadership, usually poor, and respectability in the eyes of the higher classes and (always important) the Church, and seek to keep the people within bounds. In Catalonia, with more commercial stir and bustle than Portugal, and a peasantry which for centuries had shown readiness to fight against oppression, this was less easy; jarring social interests fanned the agitation, but also fostered disagreements.

Sicilian and Neapolitan insurrections in 1647 were aimed more directly against native oppressors than against Spanish rule: Madrid paid the penalty for a colonial policy based on patronage of the aristocracy, but it was able to recover control because the classes were incapable of uniting against it. In the Neapolitan case however there were signs of rural and urban poor joining forces. This was a menace seldom encountered; in the neighbouring Papal States, for example, endemic disorder and brigandage in the countryside never swelled into serious revolt, because Rome, a city of prelates and prostitutes, could supply no inspiration or aid as Naples on occasion could. Altogether the cluster of revolutionary movements about mid-seventeenth century was very much the result of economic decay accompanied by the political and military running down of Spain, which had made itself the policeman of Europe. While the Spanish Habsburgs went downhill the Habsburgs of Vienna were still endeavouring to plant themselves firmly. They had already got the better of their own Austrian subjects and of the Bohemians, whose joint disaffection ended in the fiasco of 1620 because the nobility was disunited and hesitant, the burgher estate enfeebled and the peasantry, reduced to serfdom by its masters, had nothing to hope for from following them.

In some restricted areas of Europe a more sweeping transformation was being prepared by obscure economic currents and their social and intellectual concomitants. In sum this meant that while the rural masses were being pushed down, some propertied groups were evolving towards a more modern pattern. There are no pure classes in history, any more than pure races, and any 'class' is partly an ideal concept or abstraction. But out of a medley of social fragments, few of them clearly demarcated, there was a gradual drawing apart of two contrasted classes, or congeries: an aristocracy, with the court for rallying-point, 'neo-feudal' by comparison with its forerunners, and a bourgeoisie, still more distinct from the old burgherdom.

This entity, hard to define, was manifestly different from anything that had gone before in Europe, or ever emerged in old Asia. It was a nationwide body, in place of the mosaic bits of one that the citizenry of scattered towns had represented. Its hallmark was an economic composition shifting in the direction of capital involved in production. Wealth derived from finance, trade, colonial booty, could be fairly well accommodated within the social and political order as reconstituted after the late medieval breakdown. More indigestible, and in the long run more significant, was industrial capitalism, which in the Middle Ages had made only small sporadic beginnings. Now it was growing from above, as merchant capital, for instance connected with maritime trade, turned to shipbuilding or ship-owning, or encourged investment in them by others; and at the same time from below, among the petty commodity producers, artisan or peasant, as newer conditions favoured the rise of the luckier or more ambitious into small capitalists or labour-employing farmers.[4] Technological innovation was part of the process, and underpinned all the rest.

In Spain and most of the Counter-Reformation lands impulses towards industrial growth were soon damped down. France was the country fullest of ambivalences; there was far more vigorous growth here, but here too the absolutist state which made it possible also piled up obstacles against it. It was in the Netherlands, under foreign, fairly lax tutelage, and in a not over-governed England, that a really congenial setting was to be found. Aided by the printing-press, far the biggest factor of mutation among all the novelties of the age, the classes most nearly concerned were acquiring each an appropriate ideology or ethos, derived from Protestantism and furnishing some common ground to capital and labour. Calvinism was groping towards social and moral integration in an altering world; and whatever its precise relationship with emergent capitalism, the two, wherever they were together, stimulated and helped to mould each other.

Out of this flux was coming the epoch of 'bourgeois revolutions': events very rare, even counting unsuccessful ones, though their influence has always radiated far beyond their own boundaries. They can be seen as broadened, national repetitions of former struggles of town against feudal overlord, but with a much more complex make-up. Their title is misleading.[5] They were not projected, fought and won by any bourgeoisie, though this class would be their chief heir. Capitalism was as yet embryonic; its presence could give a fresh turn to diverse social strivings and tensions, older or newer; only after these burst out, and transformed the environment, could it fully take shape. There are no revolutionary classes in history, none whose intrinsic nature compels revolt. Bourgeoisies have at most manipulated other social forces, and often have been shoved forward by them.

Nor of course were the popular forces which did a great deal of the fighting eager to establish bourgeois rule, or capitalism. The outcome of any such mêlée could not be foreseen or intended by anyone, with any clarity; resulting from a unique historical compound, it was accidental, though also in another sense inevitable. What the masses were doing when they took part was to recommence on new ground their old struggle against exploitation, the weight of an unjust world resting on their backs. They themselves were undergoing a meta-morphosis, with the coming-up from their ranks of the petty entrepreneur, that mode of formation of capitalism which Marx saw as the 'truly revolutionary' one. This modest pioneer was still close to his workers, and could share many of their feelings; he was not a Manchester mill-owner with swarms of imported hands from Ireland. With such men in the van the people, who had failed in their own battle against the old order, might achieve another kind of vindication.

It was in religious guise that the old spirit had lingered on most tenaciously. Vistas of material progress which the age now dawning could open up were visible at first only to the higher classes, and could only gradually acquire a meaning for the poor. Their aspirations, in harsh unfamiliar conditions, fixed themselves with intense ardour on the hope of a better life in another world. In the Netherlands they were going to the stake by thousands, or fleeing abroad, for many years before the rebellion began. But in this north-western corner of Europe where things were altering most rapidly, Anabaptism was tempered by Calvinism, and fanatical devotion began to be tinged with fresh hopes for the world below as well as the world to come. Together these two urges could inspire a will to fight such as no thought of material benefit by itself is likely to infuse, except in professional soldiers.

'Bourgeois revolution' may be conceived then not as a simple substitution of one dominant class or economic system for another, but more broadly as a whole social organism outgrowing its skin. Any true revolution must be the response of an entire society, though not of all its members equally, to a novel situation pressing on it; not surprisingly it has always, in one degree or another, had a national as well as a social dimension. This holds good most obviously of the first and lengthiest of the bourgeois revolutions, that of the Netherlands.[6] It began as a defensive reaction against the desire of Philip II's distant government to strengthen its hold and increase its exactions; national movements were to be provoked in the same fashion by Charles I in Scotland and George III in America, as well as by Philip IV in Catalonia. But this one was at the same time a convergence of constitutional and religious protest with economic ambitions engendered by growing productive forces in what had long been a focal area of commerce and manufacture, and, along with these, mounting social tensions.

First to come forward were some of the high nobility, resentful of being dislodged from their armchairs in the royal service by the new centralism. Blue blood, more inflammable and readier to run risks, to gamble with life and fortune rather than lose 'face', as well as revenue, made a valuable if paradoxical contribution to this as to all bourgeois revolutions; while the House of Orange provided a rallying-point for the provinces, each too fond of going its own way. For their part the men of money were drawn on by this example, pushed on by pressure from behind. When the fervour of the streets became uncomfortably stormy, and outbursts of religious fury in the south seemed to imperil the social as well as ecclesiastical fabric, rich burghers and landed nobles there equally preferred to retreat to the shelter of the Spanish sceptre. It was the same falling-out of classes as had put an end to the Comunero movement half a century before.

In the south all further advance came to an end, as did Protestantism. Failure there could be redeemed by success in the north, not yet too far gone in class antagonisms to be capable of united exertion, but ready to take over the torch of economic growth. Religious zealotry, though only of a minority, did much to sustain the war effort; but in spite of this and the appeal of patriotism, the Dutch like the Huguenots in their civil wars had often to rely for a field army on foreign mercenaries led by the nobles. Towns could defend themselves, and a host of southern refugees reinforced both determination and industrial growth. Another multitude of fugitives was pouring into England and hastening its evolution. Indeed for capitalism to win supremacy some such windfall addition to the ranks of labour, in areas where conditions were propitious, may have been indispensable.

Gradually a new country was revealing itself to Europe, unmistakably different from any predecessor. Its seven free provinces were a disjointed federation, its institutions showed a marked continuity from medieval times. There was no inclination among the wealthy urban groups now in power to sweep them away. Expanding capitalism might require in principle a unified national market; capitalists wanted, on the contrary, maintenance of the jumble of separate authorities which they themselves, as 'Regents', mostly directed. Unsatisfactory as these arrangements might be in many aspects, political and economic both, they were far less an obstacle to progress than the unyielding framework of the monarchies. The republic looked forward instead of backward, outward instead of inward, very unlike the Portugal which regained independence not much later. Some currents from the tempestuous sea of European popular revolt found entry into its national life, and did something there for the common man and his rights. Here was a 'bourgeois revolution' which was also, to the small extent then attainable, a 'bourgeois-democratic' one, inaugurating a capitalist era not in economic terms alone but with the constitutional and cultural values capable of coexisting with it.

In England, of the bigger countries, the state as a distinct entity was least in evidence, yet conflict between it and the more unstable sections of the nation, when it came, was violent. With no hypertrophied bureaucracy to distort class relations as in Spain or France, political dissensions were more free to assert themselves, while moods of dissatisfaction were fomented by lack of openings for a legion of the educated, younger sons and others, who would elsewhere have been functionaries. Tudor rule rested on a more organic unity of government and ruling class, within which the latter remained very much a governing class also. This was the case in particular with the wealthier gentry, or middle grade of landlords. They had a platform in the House of Commons, where their representatives – a practice very exceptional in Europe – sat with and habitually took the lead over those of the boroughs. England thus shared with the Netherlands the two opposites of political continuity from the past and a revolutionary leap from this base into the future.

A shift of agrarian relations was taking place, in the direction of capitalism, or oftener a hybrid variant of this, nowhere to become predominant except in England, in which the landowner was sleeping partner to a farmer who paid rent and employed labour. It gave such landlords an admixture of bourgeois mentality, while only partially detaching them from their feudal antecedents, and leaving intact much of their collective personality at the same time as the apparatus of manorial law. From the amalgam arose a type very incongruous with any bred by ledger and counting-house, and apter for a challenge to government than any bourgeoisie has been. In the civil wars it was to take some appreciable share in the fighting, not content to fight merely by proxy. All the same, its ties with the urban upper strata were multiplying.[7] Everywhere within range of London the squire-archy felt the magnetic pull of Europe's biggest city and its enormous concentration of riches. All such influences work selectively on individuals, families, groups, not on an entire class, and this one itself, with the rapid turnover of landed property, was in flux. Here is a reason why dividing-lines in the civil wars often appear so erratic and unpredictable.

Bigger-scale manufacturers were on the increase from Elizabeth's later years, profiting by inflation and the influx of refugees and their skills. Cottage industry had been widespread for a very long time, and it helped to extend the climate of capitalist enterprise into the countryside. In early Stuart times difficulties were being encountered, principally of markets, for which the Government was likely to be blamed. It, needless to say, did not know what 'capitalism' was, and had no more notion of systematically obstructing it than of promoting it. On any narrow scrutiny of its policies and of capitalist requirements, whether on the land or in industry, it seems impossible to conclude that the former constructed shackles which the latter were compelled to snap.[8] On a wider view it is far easier to agree that without drastic political change the national development would have been impeded more and more by a regime less and less in harmony with it. More immediately this was out of step with an alliance of classes strong and self-confident enough to aim at managing national as well as local affairs, instead of leaving them in the hands of royal councillors. There was too, as in all such cases, pressure of popular unrest which could usefully be diverted against the court, even though it was aroused by things for which the court's opponents, or their backers, had most responsibility. Riots against enclosures of village lands were still occurring on the eve of the civil wars. Against usury there was outcry from all sides; its morbid proliferation was part and parcel of early capitalism, an evil of a time when one social order was crumbling and another stumbling into existence.

As always, the approaching collision was not a straightforward one, but was taking place very much at a tangent, amid a welter of minor or extraneous issues, calculations, and – at least as important – miscalculations. Crown and Commons, hitherto so close-knit, were moving apart, each side preoccupied with its own needs, and each thinking to safeguard itself by undermining the other, while pro-claiming, and even believing, that it was only defending itself against the other's trespassing. Above all, as in every parallel case, it was shortage of money, the result of inflation and heavier calls on expenditure, that compelled the Government to embark on courses which its opponents would regard as revolutionary, subversive of Magna Carta and that half-real, half-fabulous ancient English constitution on which the parliamentary lawyers took their stand.

Bourgeois revolution headed by semi-capitalist landowners could only be a garbled affair, though an event so momentous, complex and to contemporary eyes so enigmatic, could scarcely come about less confusedly. Most readily felt by the people of the times were the religious contentions kindled by and interacting with social change, sensations not to be contained within the artificial walls of the Elizabethan Church. Heavenly problems are easier to sum up in thirty-nine or some other number of theses, convenient for disputa-tion, than the more intricate and tenebrous concerns of this earth. Calvinism was seeping from town into country, within the radius of the new economy, and taking on its Puritan complexion, as English as England's agrarian capitalism. Entering the countryside in the wake of this, it had a very specific rural middle class to work on, made up of independent yeomen and tenant farmers. It forged links between them and the gentry, and between both and the townsmen. Political parties, destined to play so towering a role in the fortunes of western Europe, were in their infancy; the religious sect supplied a model.

Revolution when it came took the form of protracted civil war, because monarchist ideology was still very much alive, like the conservative social strata it appealed to. Social and regional boundaries largely coincided, and whereas in the French 'wars of religion' the capital and its environs were mostly with the Crown, here they were against it. London's internal politics were complicated, and it went through a municipal revolution of its own, the displacement of an old patriciate by the merchant groups which had been thrusting their way to the front. Its adhesion to the parliamentary side carried immense weight, in spite of the fact that there were no levers of power by which the whole country could be quickly grasped, and there was no army: each side had to build a force from scratch. Possession of the metropolis, and identification with anti-Catholic feeling, lent the parliamentary cause a national flavour akin to that of the Netherlands revolt; royalists could be suspected of plotting to use the Irish against their own country. 'Populist' language was much in vogue; rebellion spoke in the name of the People, who were also God's chosen.

Popular clamour at the outset, loudest in London, had its familiar effect of polarizing the opposition. Some of those who declined to go further with it when it took up arms must have felt that too hazardous a precedent for insubordination was being given to the masses.[9] But in the fields peasant revolt had long since dwindled to no more than haphazard rioting. Landless labourers, such as more and more of the cultivators were becoming, have been surprisingly submissive nearly everywhere, as if the ploughman loses his soul when he loses his patch of land. During the civil wars they remained inert, thereby allowing the fight to go on to a finish. As to the gentry, they had less fear of losing their authority now because they were so long accustomed to laying down the law in their own districts. Yet many of them hung back, as reluctant as their city cousins to fight their own battle for power. Cromwell filled their places by making officers out of plebeian enthusiasts; by so doing he ensured success, but also ensured further strife to follow.

It can be said with some truth that Parliament got a better army because it paid better wages; yet in the New Model a militant elite at least among the soldiers was fired by zeal for the cause, and the less alacrity the gentry displayed the more easily these men could make the cause their own. Many of them were yeomen, through whom the peasantry can be seen making its last stand. Like the small entrepreneur in industry, the farmer employing a few hands was still embedded in the mass he was to rise above. He would still, down to Cobbett's younger days, live in patriarchal fashion with his labourers eating at his own table. It might then be said that these men were fighting on the wrong side. Agrarian capitalism would leave most of them servilely dependent on the landowners for their farms. They were groping; their position and destiny were deeply contradictory; it was the measure of the divergence between the real world, or historical process, and their perception of it, that religion was so much the stuff of their thinking. Leaders like Cromwell would make the most of it to hold their followers together until the enemy was routed.

When victory allowed discords to rise to the surface, the army was at once a big trade union and a miniature republic, its 'agitators' the Parliament of the common man. In their debates with Cromwell and the senior officers at Putney in November 1647 the revolutionary tide reached its furthest point, in democratic arguments astonishingly modern. But though Levellers, like Chartists in days to come, might formulate principles of political democracy, inarticulate longings for social reform could not so well crystallize into a programme out of the cloudy millenarian dreams of the sects. Meanwhile the Levellers' modern-mindedness put them ahead of their times.[10] Revolution more than anything else can only be carried forward by minorities, vanguards, always liable to find themselves too far in front, and impotent. Within the army the elite was not at one with the bulk of the soldiers, more concerned about arrears of pay than about more ideal goals. In the Commonwealth years the army as a whole drifted out of sympathy with the rustic mass, unpolitical and virtually non-religious.

Left free to enjoy the spoils, the winners too were disorientated, uncertain what polity would suit them best. They did not set about framing capitalist blueprints, nor did the economy burgeon as soon as Charles's head was off. Every class, not Marx's peasantry alone, has two souls, and a bourgeoisie 'arriving' has always exhibited more clearly than any other a duality of lofty purpose and sordid greed, not seldom in the same individuals.[11] A messianic sense of mission to humanity, transcending national frontiers, easily degenerated, as in Dutch precedent, into imperialism and slave-trading. In the village, gentry power meant elimination of feudalism so far as this consisted of obligations of landowner to Crown, retention of feudal law which he could take advantage of against the cultivator. 'Bourgeois revolution' could thus include a taking over of antiquated property rights into new hands. From the point of view of humanity's devious future all this might be 'progressive'; for the majority of the peasants, now unmistakably to be reduced to helotry, it was very much the reverse.

It is however an error, to which Marxism has too often succumbed, to view all resistance by the common man to new-fangled property demands as a futile obstacle to progress, to be swept aside by 'history'. In this as in many eras it altered the channel of history, and helped to drive it on – not in a straight line, but there are few straight lines in human annals. Fear among the well-to-do of social revolt, once their Protector was off the scene, was one motive for their decision to bring back the Stuarts; their blatant selfishness had pushed the better aspects of the Commonwealth out of sight, and prevented it from winning any general esteem. Charles II received the throne on their terms. Parliament went on vastly strengthened. It spoke for landowners and the moneyed men, but with it a system of law and convention continued to evolve which in the town if not in the village included some rights for the common man. To this extent, as in Holland, what had happened was a 'bourgeois-democratic' revolution, and it left the way open for further struggles later on. As token of this there remained a circumscribed freedom of religion. Survival of the Nonconformist sects had a positive value: they were not simply blind alleys, but in their way sanctuaries of liberty and civic spirit.

In Scotland in those years, a far poorer and more feudal realm, the swaddling-clothes of religion lay more thickly on the vanguard of the commonalty, and kept social consciousness from breaking through as it did up to a point in England. Patriotism, the commoner's other incentive, was still little more than the xenophobia of the medieval wars of independence, and hindered any learning of the lessons that contact with English Levellers might have taught. Higher up in the scale there was greater enlightenment; lairds and traders of the more far-sighted kind were bent on securing a more profitable partnership with rich England not on sealing themselves off from it.[12] Because of this and the Cromwellian occupation, there was some shift of power from lord to laird, and to laird now more closely connected with burgher. In this light the epoch had for Scotland too something of the stamp of bourgeois revolution.

A Leveller pamphlet was republished in France in 1652, during the Frondes;[13] and after 1688 philosophers wrestled anew with the conundrum of when it might be legitimate for a people to perform the 'sovereign act', as Locke called it, of overthrowing its government. None of them wanted to see this happen often, and on foreign opinion revolution and regicide in England must have had on balance, like all such cataclysms later, an influence more deterrent than stimulating. Louis XIV's feat of restoring absolutism on a yet higher level, and the artificial sunshine of Versailles, must have added to this. In France aristocracy and bourgeoisie could seem to be reaching a point of equilibrium. In 1721 Montesquieu depicted their happy mingling in the salons – 'A Paris règne la liberté et l'égalité'.[14] Only Fraternity was still to join them.

Eighteenth-century Enlightenment derived from the more cultivated aristocratic as well as middle-class circles of western Europe; though the economic recovery which it accompanied was bound to follow the capitalist lines pioneered by Holland and England, and the concept of Progress which it fertilized was more appropriate to social *milieux* whose full unfolding was yet to come. As for the People, as an explosive force it was dwindling in this tranquil interval to Mob. Religion's fierier elements were overlaid by the more soporific: when Christianity returned to active life it would be an adjunct of conservatism, as under Catholic skies it had always been. Russia, further dragooned by Peter the Great, was a partial exception: some schismatic Old Believers, arch-conservatives in theology, figured in the mass revolts led by Bulavin in 1707 and Pugachev in 1773, the last on a grand scale before 1905. Both took place, like earlier ones, in the south-eastern marches where state power was still consolidating itself.

In western as in eastern outskirts the demands of the age met with pockets of recalcitrance: the Highlands, Corsica, later Ireland. North America was more remote still, but quite up to date, with a political philosophy stemming from the English-speaking common stock of 1688. Its War of Independence was fought by colonies free from feudal fetters and hastening towards capitalism. It was not a 'bourgeois revolution' in the sense of marking a transfer of class power. But it was bourgeois-national, and also democratic in creating more equality of civic rights (for white men) than Europe could yet envisage. Repercussions on Europe were considerable, though they are hard to assess. 'The American Constitutions were to liberty what a grammar is to language', wrote Tom Paine.[15] In the Enlightenment there was a pervasive unease between faith in human nature in the abstract and distrust or fear of human beings in the mass; the spectacle of America encouraged the more optimistic view. By this date also monarchy in most of Europe was losing its gloss. Insurrection flared up in the unwieldy Habsburg Empire, from Belgium to Hungary, against Joseph II's bureaucratic centralizing. For this he had some better motives than the Spanish Habsburgs long before, but it aroused similar antipathy; and as then, the privileged sort could divert the ill humour of the poor, now showing itself once more, away from themselves against the alien ruler. Aristocratic circles took the lead; in Belgium they soon had to face radical middle-class competition.

Smollett travelling through France in 1766 had a shrewd inkling of catastrophe in the offing.[16] Half-heartedly the old regime at its last gasp sought to raise its drooping credit by piecemeal reforms, which can be adduced as proof that revolution was 'unnecessary'. This is to suppose the bureaucracy equal to the task of mobilizing enough public support to bear down obstruction from vested interests, its own messmates for ages, without letting public tumult sweep it away with them. When the test came it soon proved that monarchy was no more than a ghost, in which no one really believed. Its dispossession was a revolution pure and simple, only vestigially a civil war like the English.

First in the field, as against Joseph II, was the aristocracy, which for some time had been trying to reassert itelf, and make the most of its archaic feudal rights. With the treasury empty it faced for the first time the ugly prospect of having to pay taxes in earnest. Its demagogy stirred up the excitement that soon overwhelmed it. It then displayed the incapacity, the loss of self-reliance born of lack of any serious duties, by running away. A more intelligent set of nobles had been reading the Encyclopaedia, and understood that things could not stay as they were; these men had a good deal to do with launching the Revolution and propping and guiding it in its opening stages.

The bourgeoisie was a conglomerate, as 'middle classes' always are; but its component parts had sufficient in common for the Jacobin clubs to enrol 'a complete cross-section of them', individuals of the most active, stirring sort from each.[17] During a long era of internal peace and economic advance a shift of the centre of gravity had been taking place, from the more state-affiliated sections – official, tax-farming, *rentier* – towards the more independent and productive. This development must have been retarded by the fate of the Huguenots, by which France lost economically and lost perhaps still more morally or psychologically. Since then the loss had been made good. Financial and mercantile capital increased and multiplied; manufacturing capital had a more obscure growth, still mostly small-scale and in the form of cottage industry. It might well seem time for capitalism from above and from below to merge into a single system, and build a capitalist France. One impediment was the very imperfect record of the monarchy in clearing away the debris of the past and creating the uniformity needed for a national market, in place of a maze of provinces, laws, jurisdictions. Such conditions had not hampered the Netherlands too much in their heyday, but they had fallen behind by now, and with the Industrial Revolution under way in Britain from about 1780 there was need of a new dispensation.

Yet modern capitalism has been remarkably versatile, once in motion, in accommodating itself to varying environments. No necessity of capitalism alone would have conjured up a revolution, let alone a 1789, or driven the Assembly to proclaim on the night of 4

August 'the entire abolition of the feudal system'. An event so apocalyptic, in Hazlett's phrase, could only come from a conflux of angry forces, immense and torrential because it happened so late, when an industrial proletariat had begun to take its place while an old-world peasantry was still in being. Moreover another path to fortune was soon diverging from the harder industrial highroad. On a far bigger scale than in the English Revolution, accessions of private wealth came the way of citizens with money to invest through the selling of Church lands, a windfall not dissipated long ago as in Protestant countries, and of *émigré* and Crown estates.

Every revolution is a 'revolution of the intellectuals', in so far as only they are called on to gather up and codify the press of obscure thoughts, hopes, rancours that such times breed. Those of 1789 were heirs to a long epoch of reforming ideas dammed up. It may not be fanciful to see in the exaggerated devotion of classical French literature and drama to rules of logic, symmetry, regularity, an unconscious protest against the signal lack of these virtues in the national life, and a prologue to the grand endeavour of the Revolution to reorganize and systematize everything, including religion; not merely to standardize weights and measures, but to translate them all into a scientific decimal language. In 1780 the reign of Reason was being inaugurated. It spelled good order, concord, abroad as at home: the Revolution and the applause of watching Europe were, among many other things, a rejection of three centuries of the military follies of kings.

Any prospering class (or nation) and its representatives are too ready to assume that what is good for it is good for all, and must therefore be rational and 'natural'. But an intelligentsia always has far wider horizons than those of the social strata out of which it chiefly sprouts; at history's supreme moments they are startlingly widened, and it can feel itself, with less self-deception than in commonplace times, the conscience or guardian of all classes. In the more idealistic participants, not in socialist revolutions alone, awareness of the miseries of the poor, longing to remedy them somehow, has always been at work. To Wordsworth's enthusiastic officer friend the Revolution was a crusade against pauperism.[18] With such sentiments may be associated the optimism of the Industrial Revolution in its dawn, not yet brooding on satanic mills or iron laws, full of faith in the capacity of science, applied to man's needs, to banish human ills. Tremors of a social earthquake lurked within a revolution dedicated to the sanctity of Property, that anointed successor of monarchy and birth. As Mathiez said, 'The agrarian law which alarmed the Girondins was neither a myth nor a phantom.'[19]

In reply the law of 18 March 1793 pronounced sentence of death on anyone who should tamper with the rights of ownership. Sales of *biens nationaux*, snuggeries in the bureaucracy, buttressed the new regime with material interests, but also enveloped it in a miasma of greed, intrigue, corruption. Between them and any soaring vision of an enslaved world ransomed at last, the gulf was deep. Yet with all its shortcomings this Revolution did promote the welfare of at least some humbler folk, notably the better-off peasants, considerably more than its forerunners had done. Hence it had less recourse to other-worldly promises as substitutes for bread and butter, even if it made great use of will-o'-the-wisps like Liberty and Fatherland. Impatience to ring out the old and ring in the new went with the freedom of the men of 1789 from religious habits of mind; intellect as well as capital had been maturing.

Caged up since the advent of the modern state and its armaments, agrarian bitterness was set free by the crisis of 1789 to erupt afresh. It had been envenomed of late by heavier feudal exactions, and grabbing of village commons by landlords. An indiscriminate jacquerie, such as the *Grande Peur* for a while seemed to be turning into, would have alarmed and alienated all good bourgeois. But the *gros paysan* who came to the front was a respectable figure, a kulak, who would be stolidly conservative once he got what he wanted, liberation from feudal dues and tithes and relief from taxation. Long an avid buyer of futher scraps of land, he himself belonged to a time of capitalism in the making; bourgeoisie and rural petty bourgeoisie were growing up together. From 1793 war, for the first time requiring positive mass support, resulted in sales of government lands in small lots. Content with their gains, the better-off peasantry threw up no separate leadership.

There could be no simple panaceas like these for the grudges long accumulating in town slums, and sharpened now by the bad harvests and distress which hung over the threshold of this as of many revolutions. Had there been a massive factory proletariat straining to break out of its prison,[20] the bourgeoisie would have been thrown into panic as much as by a *levée en masse* of the countryside. Most wage-earners however were employed in small workshops, still close, as always in the preliminary stages of industrial capitalism, to the small masters they worked side by side with. Other workers were artisans on their own, who detested the old order which kept them half-starved, but whose instincts like those of the small masters went against the grain of bourgeois revolution because big capitalism was a threat to their autonomy, as large estates, whether bourgeois or feudal, were to the peasantry. No mutual aid of town and village toilers was possible. Food scarcities and profiteering set urban sansculottes and cultivators with surpluses to hoard at loggerheads, while rural labourers and poor, who also suffered, had no organization and no link with the slums.

Jacobin dictatorship in the 1793–4 climax of revolutionary grandeur and ferocity meant the forcible holding together of class and mass forces and tensions, by a frantic effort, against foes at home and abroad. Even within a single class like the bougeoisie, when most fully determined on a common purpose, individuals cannot be counted on to sink their private advantage for it. In an emergency it must find men to coerce it and its auxiliaries, and these are likely to be drawn from outside its own ranks, or from their margins. A militant vanguard now stood in the same relation to the run-of-the-mill frequenters of Jacobin clubs as these did to the bulk of the social strata they came from. It was more petty bourgeois or professional than bourgeois or commercial, and with a stronger infusion of the intellectual and idealistic, without which action beyond the sphere of routine is impossible. To Robespierre it could even appear that the chief stumbling-block in the way of this revolution was precisely the bourgeoisie: 'pour vaincre les bourgeois, il faut rallier le peuple'.[21]

Gramsci said of these Jacobins that their vision went far beyond the immediate wants of any class, and embraced a long stretch of history still to come.[22] They drew their vital essence not from France alone but from the reservoir of all Europe of the Enlightenment: if a revolution is national, it belongs to Europe or the world as well. For their watchword of audacity they owed a debt to the heroic cult of arms of the French nobility of bygone days, with which the endless wars of the monarchy had infected other classes too. A vortex like that of 1793–4 takes on a demonic power, over and above the wills or feelings of those who serve it, and who may well have the sensation of actors treading a giant stage, instead of men obeying their own volition. Rhetoric and ritual, bizarre costume and self-dramatization, so often remarked on, might descend to the histrionic, but were proper enough to the hour of destiny, the collective fever that chooses certain men to exalt, and before long to exhaust, if it does not physically destroy them.

Jacobin boldness was cemented by close connections with a Paris on which the kings had conferred a primacy now all the more unquestioned because of the erasure of the old provinces from the map. It was thanks to Paris that revolution once set in motion could stride so far and fast, at the cost of leaving much of France behind. But the voice of Paris was for direct democracy, sovereignty of the people assembled in their Section meetings, and with this the Jacobin concept of revolutionary centralism was, before the end of 1793, incompatible.[23] Government by Terror rose above, not from, the masses, and its axe had a double edge; the Commune of Paris was deprived of the status of a parallel authority, the ultra-left leadership was destroyed. None the less, pressure of hunger and hope in the capital pushed the Committee of Public Safety into measures it would not have turned to of its own accord. Prominent among them was the fixing of maximum prices for food and other commodities. Lloyd George's mind went back to that experiment when he told his Clydeside hecklers, at the height of the First World War, that their demand for price-controls was too 'revolutionary'.[24]

Concentration of purpose such as the Jacobins sought to achieve could be no more than short-lived. It depended too much on the synthetic fraternalism of war; peril of invasion deepened the nationalistic flavour shared by all revolutions, and recognizable already in the anti-English tone of sundry *cahiers* of 1789. With this exigency receding, unity flagged, and with it the better impulses it released. In Robespierre was personified the frustration of anticlimax, and the convulsive search for an escape from it by means of the guillotine. When Thermidor brought the turn of the now isolated Jacobin leaders to furnish victims, the bourgeoisie left to its own devices let its stupid greed run wild. What was coming to the top was the froth of financial speculation, instead of capitalism's more constructive self; a not unfamiliar story. Babœuf's 'Conspiracy of the Equals' in 1796 was a hopeless last stand of revolutionary idealism,[25] though it was also the first milestone along an untravelled road. He saw 1789 simply as a rising of poor against rich, an antithesis of urban and rural masses on one side and the propertied minority, aristocratic or bourgeois, on the other. To enlarge civic into social equality, by curbing exorbitant possessiveness, was an idea that had glimmered before the sanculottes; a more novel, more far-reaching idea of collective ownership glimmered before Babœuf and his associates.

Animosities left festering by the Revolution could find relief only in further warfare beyond the frontiers. France's inner contradictions and the energies stored up by them set French armies marching across Europe, reforming and plundering at once as the Revolution had done at home. Things were following the same trajectory as in the earlier bourgeois revolutions, with a fidelity that contemporaries could not fail to be struck by and influenced by. One had ended with Orange aspiring to a populist autocracy; another with Cromwell as would-be founder of a dynasty. Bonaparte fulfilled their ambitions.

Under his aegis all the winners at the gambling-table had their gains legitimized and guaranteed. He styled himself heir of the Revolution, and clearly with much justification, though he inherited far less of its ideals than of its material accomplishments. These provided a fairly broad foundation for his regime; he had no need to rule through the army, like Cromwell. But only in the realm of metrics, removed from the social arena, was the grand aim of renovation realized in full; in law, administration, family and all else, it suffered some or much obstruction. Without a new earth there could be no new heaven, and religion had to be brought back to assist in the winding-up of the Revolution.

Despite this, France had done nearly all that Reason could propose to equip it for a majestic step forward, and this, it was clear as the whirlwind subsided, should mean a step towards industrial capitalism. There was now a perfected administrative uniformity, more congenial than the 1789 design of local self-government to a bourgeoisie with so strong an imprint of state service in its historic formation. There was a national market, freed of all impediments, and a government eager to see it fructify. Napoleon could even talk of wishing to be remembered as creator of French industry. His kingdom was a chamber swept and garnished for the bridegroom. Yet steam-age industry was tardy in putting in an appearance, whereas in Britain, where it enjoyed far fewer modern conveniences, it was forging ahead. Instead the post-1815 years saw government jobs multiplying by leaps and bounds. Democratic principles enshrined in the law of inheritance hindered accumulation of capital. Peasant proprietorship, given a fresh lease of life by the agrarian revolt of 1789, hindered the flow of labour into industry. Entrepreneurs might well shrink from becoming employers of those dour artisans who had carried the Revolution on their pikes. It may then be argued that doctrines of equal rights, and the intervention of demos in politics, had impeded economic progress. On the other side it can be said that the peasants' insistence on their share of the spoils imposed a check on the bourgeois estate-buying, the diversion of investment funds into land, which must be counted as one more cause of industrial torpor. But once again, history was not moving in a direct line. As to the gospel of Reason, there is a fallacy in any expectation of its leading straight on to capitalism, a mode of ordering life which may be rational in its daily detailed workings, but as a historical phenomenon, a compartment of human evolution, is not.

A verb *révolutionner* was coined in 1795, and Englished a couple of years later. Blind accident would give place from now on to deliberate planning. But this was a game two could play at. Burke had warned Europe that 1789 would sour the 'easy good nature' of all kings,[26] and now conservatism was forewarned and forearmed. If the coming age was to be one of insurrectionary parties and movements, it would be one of counter-revolution and White Terror also, enlisting popular forces on behalf of reaction. They got their start in Catholic backwaters like the Vendée and Brittany, and Naples with its San Fede; everywhere they owed much to the heavy-handedness with which bourgeois regimes imposed themselves on a countryside of which they had scant comprehension.

As Lenin was to observe, French historians after 1815 like Mignet and Guizot 'were forced to recognise that the class struggle was the key to all French history'.[27] Marx grew up expecting to see the bourgeoisie in other lands emulate their French exemplars. But a revolution is 'glorious' for its middle-class beneficiaries, like that of 1688, in proportion as it gives them power cheaply, without recourse to the aid of demos, or Caliban. From this point of view 1789 was a far from happy and glorious memory. 'I begin to see they are no great hands at revolutions', Wolfe Tone wrote of the Irish merchantry in 1793.[28] Factories and machines confirmed the primacy of industry within the capitalist family, but economic strength might mean political weakness, for with it went the herding together of multitudes of sullen mill-hands. It may have been illusion that made the new proletariat, that strange race of beings, appear even more menacing than the all too well-known artisans of the Paris faubourgs. At any rate employers were reluctant to quarrel with their government when it meant giving their workers an opportunity to quarrel with *them*. Their ancestors had clung to the apron-strings of monarchy; now after the interlude of revolutionary fits and starts, they would soon be turning to another species of autocrat, a Napoleon III or a Bismarck.

In western Europe it was Spain and Portugal that had least industrial growth and most political turmoil; and in a way the meagre proletarian presence made it seem not too risky, until late in the nineteenth century, to resort to armed force as a lever. Here the bourgeoisie was of a watery consistency, largely made up of speculative financiers, money-lenders, land-buyers, lawyers. Ideas came from outside, far more than from any home-spun thinking. Politics meant first and foremost, as to a lesser extent in France, scrambling for government jobs: this made control of the state a vital object, though the ups and downs of faction left its nature little altered. Land was the other big prize, and seizure of clerical and royal estates bulked far larger among the gains of the moneyed classes than it had done in France, because here there was no question of sharing with the peasantry: on the contrary the village commons were added to the takings. Landlordism was only imperfectly defeudalized. Repression and spiritual blinkers kept the miserable peasantry quiet; its failure to rebel in any strength is, all the same, remarkable.

In the towns artisans and cognate groups were ready enough to work off their restless radicalism in bouts of action, but singularly slow to learn any lessons from experience. They tailed behind Liberal leadership; this however relied more willingly on the army, that is on an officer corps mainly middle class, with professional grievances and ambitions which could for a while attach themselves to the Liberal cause. On this footing the long and murderous Carlist War of 1833–9 performed, clumsily and bunglingly, something of the function of a bourgeois revolution: it crippled the Church and turned a decrepit absolutism into a quasi-constitutional monarchy, with a less rusty administration. Liberals had no desire to mobilize the peasants, except as conscripts, and left many of them to be drawn into the reactionary blind alley of Carlism. Economy and political life continued to limp. It might well seem to onlookers that the more brawling, the less progress, and that Spain offered a salutory object-lesson in the futility of revolution.

In England the bourgeoisie played on working-class discontent to simulate revolution and get what it wanted in 1832, with an adroitness that Ernest Jones was to warn the workers against later on.[29] In 1848 the old bourgeois radical Brougham was staggered by Europe's abrupt plunge into real anarchy – 'Revolutions made with the magic wand of an enchanter – Monarchies destroyed at a blow – Republics founded in a trice – Constitutions made extempore'.[30] Bourgeois revolution was having its ultimate flare-up. Half Europe was drawn into a whirlpool of contending passions, whose origins lay in diverse epochs of history. Paris underwent in February a self-conscious repetition of the prelude to 1789, of only languid interest now, especially to famished workmen. Their rising in June followed this stage-lightning like a real thunderclap; it showed the significance of a living revolutionary tradition, such as England had lost, but in France could be taken over from the middle classes by the proletariat.

Many years later Engels was to declare that British conservatism was saved by the June days in Paris, which frightened the petty bourgeoisie and confused the workers.[31] More obviously on the Continent middle-class radicals were thrown into alarm, and this was redoubled by tumults nearer home, Luddite attacks on mills in western Germany for instance. Of Jacobin resolution there was little display anywhere. In Russia nothing happened; widespread revolt by the peasants on their own had been brought to an end, and no other

class was ready to come forward. In middle Europe villagers seized
the chance to strike a blow at what remained of feudalism, as in
France in 1789, and they came off better than the townspeople
because from now on the old order was obliged to reckon the value of
a contented peasantry as social ballast.

A contented upper-middle class would be even better. Despite the
fiasco of 1848–9, Europe had reached a point where change was self-
sustaining, not to be halted by any conscious will. With machinery for
multiplier, capitalist production took on a qualitatively new
momentum. Formerly it might be useful to rulers, but was not
essential, and could be allowed to decay. Now it was indispensable to
any state ambitious of great-power rank. More and more at the same
time, capital dominated and overshadowed the capitalist, whose
hesitant political claims might well be disarmed if the monster he
served was given a free run. Compromise could be reached, in other
words, on terms amounting to a peaceful transition to capitalism.
Germany was the classic illustration. Its bourgeoisie, Treitschke was
to complain, was too timid and convention-bound for any revolutionary deeds: an aristocrat, a Bismarck, was called for.[32] Every
bourgeoisie, or other class, has its own local character; social
conditioning and psychology, besides more measurable economic
attributes, determine its behaviour. Bismarck learned from Napoleon
III to abandon Metternich's strategy of peace and collective security
against revolution, for one of war to divert bad humours outward
and identify reaction with patriotism. Engels might exert himself to
interpret the unification of Germany as a 'revolution' forced on the
Junkers,[33] and so in a certain sense it was, but it bore only too much
resemblance to Liberal subservience to the army in Spain. Yet at their
own task of industry-building the German chimney-barons, politically spineless, quickly proved themselves the most efficient in
Europe.

Since the French Revolution, Europe has been highly charged with
nationalist fluids, in addition to class antagonisms, and for these too
1848–9 was a climactic turning-point, and a dismal failure. National
and Liberal risings sometimes fell foul of each other, and the
Habsburgs were able to get some nationalities on their side, much as
the Carlists profited by Basque and Catalan regionalism. The
besetting weakness of nationalist movements at all times was that,
glowingly romantic as they looked from a distance, they were riddled
with sordid ill-will of class against class.[34] Only very slowly and
reluctantly did most of them begin to contemplate any social reconstruction. No doubt idealists looked forward to a happier future for
their poorer fellow countrymen, taking it too much for granted that the

fact of independence would ensure this. A social programme capable of rousing the masses would be only too likely to alienate those called on for sacrifices. Parnell showed rare insight and courage when he broadened Irish Home Rule by merging it with the land war, but this was easier in Ireland because so many landlords were aliens as well as absentees.

Poland embarked twice over on a war of independence, but was a glaring case of refusal by the *haves* to give up anything to the have-nots. Foremost in the fight were the gentry, ardent for Polish freedom but with no intention of granting freedom to Polish ploughmen. When industry and its reflexes gained ground, as in Poland later in the century, mill-owning and landowning sectors would be hard to harmonize, capital and labour still harder. In northern Italy a bourgeoisie entering on life rather earlier was desirous of national union and independence, but did not relish the flurry of little plots and risings which were Mazzini's method; still less did it wish to see workers and peasants roused to action. It put itself behind Cavour, and achieved its ends by means chiefly of French intervention. It was satisfied with an Italy which was an enlarged kingdom of Piedmont, conservative and undemocratic, very much as Germans were satisfied with a fatherland made in the image of Prussia. No people in fact (except the Norwegians, who did not have to take up arms) won liberty without foreign help, direct as in the case of Belgium in 1830, indirect as in that of Hungary, with Austria's humbling by Prussia. Like Italy these other countries were spared the need to invoke, and then recompense, the masses. After the Polish defeat of 1863 there was no similar attempt in Europe before the First World War, except in Balkan irredentas.

Meanwhile the revolt of the masses of which respectable Europe lived in chronic fear had evolved little by little from sansculotte to Bolshevik. There was a long twilight when alarmists talked of 'Red Republicanism', loudest in 1848 and at the time of the Paris Commune in 1871; in 1936 the phantom Red Republic, like a Flying Dutchman's vessel, was sighted again through conservative telescopes in Spain. In the background of all this was the rise of socialism, ushered in by the prodigious upheaval of 1789–1815 and the parallel phenomenon of the Industrial Revolution. Between them they constituted one of those rare junctures when men are able to look over the ramparts, outside the three dimensions, of their world of use and wont.

Like Anabaptism three centuries before, socialism could put on either a pacific or a warlike guise. Utopians such as Weitling hailed the speedy approach of a harmonious Communist society, installed

by general agreement. Proudhon, summoning propety and government to vanish simultaneously, was the prophet of another persistent
evangel. Against both of these Marx pitted his thesis of socialism to
be set up and maintained, as the bourgeois order had been, by
organized force. In the factory proletariat he saw the instrument of
destiny. Only a class altogether outside the society built on private
ownership could undertake, and would have no choice but to
undertake, its root-and-branch abolition.

Marx himself designed no revolutionary party, and the workers'
parties committed to his teachings which sprang up before his death
were apt to stifle revolution under the wrappings of organization, or
reduce it to a lifeless fetish. Numerous other movements were in the
field, to say nothing of those individuals already often to be met with
by the 1850s, 'ultra-revolutionaries for whom nothing was radical
enough', nine-tenths of them 'heroes only in words'.[35] After the fall of
the Commune its survivors in exile were torn by recriminations
among a dozen sects. Anarchism in varying shapes continued the
chief rival of Marxism, with the countervailing defect of leaving the
winds of revolution to their own spontaneous devices, unharnessed to
any mill-wheel. Blanqui was a man apart, one of those paladins for
whom 'The act of revolution was almost an end in itself.'[36] He strove
for the social, not merely political emancipation of the toilers, but
relied on chosen groups, in Mazzini's style, for his battering-ram,
instead of rallying the toilers to emancipate themselves. Nihilism in
tsarist Russia was an extreme version of the same trust in violence
exercised on behalf of the many by a few.

In London after the disasters of 1849 the *émigrés* – not Marx, in his
citadel of the British Museum – 'made plans for the overthrow of the
world and day after day and evening after evening intoxicated
themselves with the hashish draught of thinking that "tomorrow it
will begin" '.[37] It is on the whole striking that the century of
industrialization passed off with so little of the working-class mutiny
so vividly longed for or dreaded. An occasional whiff of grape-shot
was one corrective, as musketry had been for mutiny in the fields.
What mattered more, the proletariat and the idea of socialism never
coalesced so completely, so explosively, as Marx anticipated. They
came nearest it at times when, as in 1848 and 1917, big industry,
though dominant elsewhere and striding towards world domination,
was at an early stage in the centres concerned. 'It is the revolutionizing
of all established conditions by industry *as it develops* that also
revolutionizes people's minds', Engels wrote near the end of his life,[38]
scarcely taking account of how much this told against any picture of a
proletariat steadily tempered and fortified in revolutionary conscious-

ness by experience. Rather, as it grew accustomed to the modern scheme of things, it moved towards acceptance, seeking a place in it, like the German bourgeoisie, instead of trying to fashion a better one. With this went the fact that industry was adding rapidly to the stock of wealth, and out of their superfluity the rich could be induced or compelled, slowly and painfully, to part with a modicum to the poor. Facility of emigration to North America was an important sedative, not of working-class disgusts alone.

European institutions, from police to Parliament, tested by long weathering of storm and stress, proved as a rule resilient enough to contain the situation. Russia was far less well equipped, and socialism transplanted there could be more disruptive. But Marxists in so backward a country faced an extremely complex task, which was to be the source of interminable controversy. It was the paradoxical one of pushing on a bourgeois revolution, as the indispensable preliminary to a socialist one, but with more democratic goals than any hitherto, and with socialist-led workers supplying the want of grit among the middle classes and their leaders. All this was what Lenin had in view in the thick of the chaotic Revolution of 1905; but the Russian bourgeoisie, the least Jacobin in Europe, was predestined to stray into the 'Prussian' path of accommodation with autocracy. When this collapsed in 1917[39] the revolutionary spark failed to leap from Russia to the west, too heavily conditioned against it, and left him in something like the isolation of Cromwell and the army after 1649. His gamble did more in the West to benefit conservatism, as the Commune had done, by giving it a target for anti-socialist propaganda, and so assisting the rise of Fascism, twentieth-century Europe's pseudo-revolutionary substitute for the overtly counter-revolutionary movements of the nineteenth.

Russia had remained a reservoir of agrarian revolt because,[40] in the absence of any real challenge from a bourgeoisie, tsarism was not compelled to conciliate the peasantry more than very meagrely. Socialist revolution could hitch itself on to this force, as bourgeois revolution had drawn vitality from the struggle of the small producers against feudalism. In both cases things turned out for the masses far otherwise than they expected. Capitalism levied its tolls from smallholders as greedily as feudalism, if more stealthily; socialism would drive or shepherd them into collective agriculture. A second and related similarity is that socialist revolution also has been closely associated with nationalism. This by itself has seldom or never resorted to force with success; on the other hand class bitterness by itself seems too negative or rejective to raise emotion to the necessary temperature.

Lenin looked to Asia to reinforce or reinvigorate the European spirit of rebellion. Historians may look to the innumerable revolutionary movements of the 'Third World', all making their own use of ideas and methods borrowed from Europe, for some fresh light on the mechanics of change in Europe's own record. Revolutions of all sorts everywhere, like all wars, must share some attributes. They have regularly seen generations as well as classes confronting each other. China has proved afresh how much intellectuals can count for when times are out of joint and classes in disarray.

Edmund Wilson has described the metamorphoses undergone by the French Revolution in the historical writing of the following century, and the emergence from them of the Marxist and Leninist concepts of revolution.[41] Soon after 1917 a sensible scholar could declare that 'the study of revolutionary theories is an essential part of social philosophy.'[42] Social science was slow to grapple with this task, as one of its exponents complained in 1964.[43] Most of them preferred to study 'normal' conditions, as economists have been attracted by equilibrium rather than slumps. Gustave le Bon was content to dismiss revolutionism as a psychological disorder, 'an envious hatred of every kind of superiority . . . Cain, in the Old Testament, had the mind of a Bolshevik'.[44] In recent years the question has been faced more seriously, even if answers have not seldom looked highly academic.[45] An intelligent survey of much of the debate can be found in Wertheim's book,[46] over such issues for example as whether revolutions have been the consequence of spells of exceptional economic hardship, and whether they are likelier to come when governments are harshest or when they have begun to make concessions.

In a remarkable survey of social violence of all types in modern France, Italy and Germany,[47] the Tillys find much reason to doubt two hypotheses which have had wide currency: that revolt is a chaotic symptom of breakdown of authority, and that it is engendered by rapid social change, such as a shift from rural to urban life. They show that, on the contrary, any serious resistance requires forms of organization, not anarchy, and long-held convictions of right and wrong, rather than simple disorientation. These conclusions may be extended to the whole history of popular revolt, fuelled by material distress but never simply 'materialistic', always with its own standards, however indistinct, of justice and human 'brotherhood'. These ideals have been enshrined in the perennial myth of Utopia, as native tradition or in more learned guise. Much Utopian hopefulness has been descried even behind the front of Marx's 'scientific' socialism.[48]

Resentment against exploitation has been the subterranean fire smouldering under the surface of European life. It could break out most effectively in situations where property interests were at odds, not as between individuals or groups merely but between species, historical categories like 'feudal' and 'bourgeois'. Such a rift was more clearly marked in 1789 than in 1642. Moreover, the English Revolution, very unlike the French, had a long prehistory of parliamentary opposition, and started with a political leadership already well seasoned, while in France guidance had to be improvised. Here is a reason why the common people could be kept under firmer control in England, while in France there was more room and more need for their intervention. The sansculottes who put their shoulders to the wheel of the bourgeois revolution were a very mixed lot, agreed only on what they detested. This included capitalism; and they interposed so forcibly that no bourgeois movement anywhere would ever again feel safe in summoning the 'rabble' to its aid. In future it would be oftenest left to military failure, defeats like those of 1870 or 1918, to perform imperfectly the surgery of revolution by getting rid of regimes which there was no adequate internal energy to dismiss.

Of all interpretations of the revolutionary past, the one bequeathed by the middle class in its post-1789 mood to Marx, and elaborated by a long series of Marxists – of revolutions as victories of class over class and of one economic order over another – remains by far the most convincing. All the same, prolonged and minute scrutiny has revealed to adherents and opponents alike its need for very much further refinement.[49] Explorations in this field enrich our understanding of history as a whole. Revolutionary times bring close together and force into intense interaction all those elements, economic, political, cultural and the rest, which ordinarily straggle along far more loosely linked. None of them by itself is capable of explaining fundamentals; it is such times of fusion that provide the historian with the finest laboratory.

Postscript

'One must not talk too loud here', Beethoven wrote one day in 1794: there were rumours in Vienna of revolution hatching, and arrests were being made – 'but I believe that so long as an Austrian has his beer and sausage, he won't rebel.'[50] Successful revolutions, or even serious attempts at them, have been fewer than the theories spun to explain them. In nearly all people a revolutionary mood is very hard to kindle, and does not last long; psychological reaction is no less inevitable than the political reaction that follows revolution. Yet these rare events tower above the flatlands and foothills of history. Of late there has been a search for features common to more than one of them. The Russian and Chinese have an obvious attraction for seekers of 'broader similarities and differences'.[51] More ambitiously, an American scholar has combined these two with a third, the French. One of her themes is the resulting expansion of state power, though this may at the same time have grown more 'popularly inclusive'.[52] Government inherits, or usurps, the mass energy that has suddenly irrupted into public life.

Nationalist revolt is a recovery of lost liberty, though it may, as in the Netherlands, be accompanied by profound social change. As late as Tom Paine, a true revolution might be conceived as a return to immutable natural principles. The parliamentarians who challenged James I and Charles I liked to to take their stand on a perfect constitution enjoyed by their ancestors but since subverted, very much as in their religious garb as Puritans they thought of restoring the Church to a primitive purity. Their good old constitution was partly camouflage, partly illusion, covering uncertainty about what they intended. It is no less true of classes or communities than of individuals that, as Cromwell said, no one goes further than the man who does not know where he is going.

It may not be possible to say anything much more precise about the cause of conflict in England in the 1640s than that a powerful body of opinion felt that the time had come for radical change. Historians have tried hard to supply the explanation that the actors in those events could not. Ideas, religious especially, were the first to suggest themselves. Of the alternatives that followed the most clear-cut was the Marxist. It has proved very suggestive, but *too* clear-cut to fit all the known facts, and many are not known. Recently the concept of an English bourgeois revolution has once more been dismissed, by Lawrence Stone, who can add that its ablest proponent, Christopher Hill, no longer postulates a black-and-white issue between 'feudal and bourgeois ideologies and classes'.[53] Hill now stresses the need to look back much further than the events of 1640–2.[54] The latest and most judicious survey of the question in all its bearings, by G. E. Aylmer,[55] concludes that what happened was less than a 'revolution', less that is than a total reconstruction of society, but far more than a mere 'rebellion'. Of course no pre-socialist revolt can do more than bring about shifts of power, extensive though these may be, within the horizons of private property.

Although 1789 had stood out as the prime example of a 'bourgeois revolution', it has been argued with considerable force that, like the English case, it offers inadequate evidence of a confrontation between an impatient bourgeoisie and an effete aristocracy.[56] One way round this may be to say that the more bourgeois or modern-minded half of an elite drawn from two classes living comfortably side by side found it expedient to sacrifice the other half, in order to placate mass discontent against both. This other, more irresponsible and parasitic section, was engaged from 1787 in trying to dismantle much of the machinery of state built up over centuries for the monarchy, very largely by its bourgeois assistants. Having failed, after 1789 it emigrated and set itself to destroy the Revolution from abroad. In contrast with the English situation, a vast administrative apparatus, with all its perquisites, was itself one of the biggest prizes fought over by the factions of 1789–99; in addition there was the immense wealth of Church and crown, mostly in the form of land. Land-buying on a vast scale would delay the establishment of a fully capitalist economy; but an interval of expanded capitalist agriculture may have been, as in England though more briefly, a necessary preparation.

J. H. Billington has given us a panoramic study of the faith in revolutionary action that caught fire from the French Revolution and burned brightly if fitfully in Europe into the early twentieth century.[57] To understand why it was left to Russia to carry out a socialist revolution, it may be helpful to recall a saying of Burckhardt, long before, that Russia was still free from the morbid Western excess of individual, as opposed to collective, consciousness.[58] There was no previous model for 1917; in the cataclysmic months following the seizure of power Lenin appealed to socialists abroad for critical suggestions, as well as for sympathy and support. The Revolution was made by the people, but in some ways the regime it gave rise to was a new version of the 'revolution from above' that had served, in central and still more markedly in eastern Europe, in place of the west's revolution from below.

This had a further, more distorted prolongation into the colonial world. Marx thought of Asia's succumbing to Western rule as a blundering sort of bourgeois revolution thrust on it from outside, the penalty for having fallen long since into grooves that made independent advance impossible. As a substitute it could have only a limited cleansing or modernizing impact; and there were no appropriate classes ready to step into Western shoes when they became vacant. Nearest to readiness – which cannot be measured in money alone – was the Indian bourgeoisie.

Europe's revolutions were town-made. A peasant revolution, pure and simple, is scarcely possible. China had endless peasant revolts, with fringes of other social elements attached to them (increasingly, it is probable, in the nineteenth century), but they lacked the real guiding force, the new perspective, that only an urban class could supply; and China's cities, like all Asia's, could not harbour a 'political class', because they had no civic character. But 1789 could happen because its leaders, who had little to offer to urban workers, found a powerful ally in the peasants. For them abolition of feudal dues, and then sales of land in small parcels, were a grand reward, at little cost to the bourgeoisie. In China the peasantry was still more indispensable for a Communist revolution, though it seems unlikely now to provide a firm base for socialism. Peasants have, indeed, been a great asset because there are always ready means of rewarding them, with land or with freedom from serfdom, rents, tithes.

For leaders to guide them into uncharted futures the masses began by looking to extraordinary individuals. Masaniello, heading the rising of 1647 in Naples, was treated like a king, ' "a man sent by God" . . .some claimed to have seen a white dove circling his head.'[59] Hung Hsiu-chuan came forward to launch the Taiping Rebellion in mid-nineteenth century China as a brother of Jesus Christ. After 1789 the middle classes could think of themselves collectively as the Lord's anointed, bringing progress to stumbling humanity; their own stumblings in this century brought a new race of 'supermen', leaders from secular cradles now, to the fore. Meanwhile Karl Max had seized on the emerging class of industrial workers as the true Prometheus. This class too has been weighed in the revolutionary balance and found wanting, and for giant-killers people have turned their hopes towards Youth, the 'Third World', women, the intelligentsia. Intellectuals had much to do with the Chinese, as with the Russian, Revolution, only to end too often like engineers hoist with their own petard. But none of these expectations has been more than very imperfectly fulfilled; the lesson may be that humanity can only move onward now by some broader convergence of progressive forces, instead of by following behind a chosen vanguard.

Critics who see nothing very wrong with the world as it is have talked one-sidedly of the destructiveness of revolution, until the epithet 'bloody' has come to be attached to it automatically. Wars have been vastly more bloody, more frequent and more futile. So have counter-revolutions, of which our century has seen many. It can indeed be made an objection to revolutions as a mode of advance that they are apt to provoke as much reaction as progress. Most of the retrograde currents of modern history, as well as most of the progressive, can be traced in one way or another back to 1789, or to 1917. 'The irony of world history turns everything upside down', Engels wrote in 1895. Socialists were thriving on orderly, lawful methods of spreading their gospel; it was the 'parties of order' that were chafing now at 'the legal conditions created by themselves', and would finally have no choice but to 'break through this legality so fatal to them'.[60] His prophecy has been grimly fulfilled by Fascism, and by numberless army coups against elected governments all round the world.

Notes

Introduction V. G. Kiernan: Seeing Things Historically

1 V. G. Kiernan, *The Lords of Human Kind*, rev. edn (Harmondsworth, Penguin Books, 1972); *European Empires from Conquest to Collapse, 1815–1960* (London, Fontana, 1982); *Marxism and Imperialism* (London, Edward Arnold, 1974); *America: The New Imperialism* (London, Zed Press, 1978; new preface, 1980); *British Diplomacy in China, 1880–1885* (Cambridge, Cambridge University Press, 1939; reprinted with new foreword, New York, Octagon Books, 1970); and *Metcalfe's Mission to Lahore, 1808–1809* (Lahore, Punjab Government Record Office, Monograph 21, 1943).

2 V. G. Kiernan, 'Foreign Interests in the War of the Pacific', *Hispanic American Historical Review*, 35, 1 (February 1955), pp. 14–36; 'India, China, and Sikkim: 1886–1890', *Indian Historical Quarterly*, 31, 1 (March 1955), pp. 32–51; 'India, China and Tibet: 1885–1886', *Journal of the Greater Indian Historical Society*, 14, 2 (1955), pp. 117–42; 'Kashgar and the Politics of Central Asia: 1868–1878', *Cambridge Historical Journal*, 11, 3 (1955), pp. 317–42; 'Colonial Africa and its Armies', in B. Bond and I. Roy (eds), *War and Society* (London, Croom Helm, 1977), vol. 2, pp. 20–39; 'The Old Alliance: England and Portugal', in R. Miliband and J. Saville (eds), *The Socialist Register 1973* (London, Merlin Press, 1973), pp. 261–81; and 'India and Pakistan: Twenty Years After', in R. Miliband and J. Saville (eds), *The Socialist Register 1966* (London, Merlin Press, 1966), pp. 305–20. For a complete bibliography of Kiernan's writings to 1977, see the special issue of *New Edinburgh Review*, 'History and Humanism', prepared in his honour: 38–9 (Summer–Autumn 1977), pp. 77–9.

3 Tom Bottomore, et al. (eds), *A Dictionary of Marxist Thought* (Oxford, Basil Blackwell, 1983).

4 See, for examples, V. G. Kiernan, 'Intellectuals in History', *Winchester Research Papers in the Humanities* (Winchester, King Alfred's College, 1979); 'Class and Ideology: The Bourgeoisie and its Historians', *History of European Ideas*, 6, 3 (1985), pp. 267–86; and 'Evangelicalism and the French Revolution', *Past & Present*, 1 (1952), pp. 44–56.

5 See V. G. Kiernan, 'Working Class and Nation in Nineteenth-century Britain' (1978), ch. 7 in the present volume; also, 'Victorian London: Unending Purgatory', *New Left Review*, 76 (November–December 1972), pp. 73–90; and 'Labour and the Literate in Nineteenth-century Britain', in D. Martin and D. Rubinstein (eds), *Ideology and the Labour Movement: Essays Presented to John Saville* (London, Croom Helm, 1979), pp. 32–61.

6 See, for examples, V. G. Kiernan, 'Wordsworth and the People', in J. Saville et al. (eds), *Democracy and the Labour Movement* (London, Lawrence and Wishart, 1956), reprinted with a postscript in D. Craig (ed.), *Marxists on Literature: An Anthology* (Harmondsworth, Penguin Books, 1975), pp. 161–206; 'Human Relations in Shakespeare', in A. Kettle (ed.), *Shakespeare in a Changing World* (New York, International Publishers, 1964), reprinted in Eric Bentley (ed.), *The Great Playwrights* (New York, Doubleday, 1970), vol. 1, pp. 283–300; 'Art and the Necessity of History', in R. Miliband and J. Saville (eds), *The Socialist Register 1965* (London, Merlin Press, 1965), pp. 216–36; 'Civilisation and the Dance', *Dunfermline College of Physical Education Occasional Papers*, 2, (April 1976); and 'Private Property in History', in J. Goody, J. Thirsk and E. P. Thompson (eds), *Family and Inheritance: Rural Society in Western Europe, 1200–1800* (Cambridge, Cambridge University Press, 1976), pp. 361–98.

7 V. G. Kiernan (tr. and ed.), *Poems from Iqbal* (Bombay, 1947); rev. edn (London, Murray, 1955); *Poems by Faiz* (New Delhi, 1958); rev. edn (London, George Allen and Unwin, 1971); *From Volga to Ganga* (Bombay, People's Publishing House, 1947).

8 Harvey J. Kaye, *The British Marxist Historians* (Oxford, Polity Press, 1984).

9 Ibid., pp. 8–18; and Eric Hobsbawm, 'The Historians' Group of the Communist Party', in M. Cornforth (ed.), *Rebels and their Causes* (London, Lawrence and Wishart, 1978), pp. 21–47.

10 Kiernan's article is 'Evangelicalism and the French Revolution', see note 5 above. Also, see the retrospective in the 100th issue of *Past & Present* by Christopher Hill, Rodney Hilton and Eric Hobsbawm.

11 Barrington Moore, Jr, *Social Origins of Dictatorship and Democracy* (Boston, Beacon Press, 1966), pp. 522–3.

12 For example, see V. G. Kiernan, 'The Covenanters: A Problem of Creed and Class', in F. Krantz (ed.), *History From Below: Studies in Popular Protest and Popular Ideology in Honour of George Rudé* (Montreal, Concordia University Press, 1985), pp. 95–115.

13 Perry Anderson, *Lineages of the Absolutist State* (London, New Left Books, 1974), p. 11, and Kaye, *The British Marxist Historians*, p. 229.

14 One cannot help but note once again the biographical relationship between Nonconformism and socialism found in the lives of Kiernan, Christopher Hill, E. P. Thompson and Sheila Rowbotham. See my references in *The*

British Marxist Historians, p. 103. It should be added that Kiernan has for many years kept notes towards a book to be called *Religion in History*.

15 H. S. Ferns, *Reading from Left to Right* (Toronto, University of Toronto Press, 1983), pp. 76–7.

16 See T. E. B. Howarth, *Cambridge Between Two Wars* (London, Collins, 1978). For a recent fictional representation, see Raymond Williams, *Loyalties* (London, Chatto and Windus, 1985). For Kiernan's own thoughts on Cambridge in the 1930s, see his piece, 'Herbert Norman's Cambridge', in R. W. Bowen (ed.), *E. H. Norman: His Life and Scholarship* (Toronto, University of Toronto Press, 1984), pp. 25–45.

17 Ibid. Cornford died fighting for the Republican cause in the Spanish Civil War. Klugmann remained a Party activist and official until his death in 1977. On Cornford, see Kiernan's 'Recollections', in P. Sloan (ed.), *John Cornford: A Memoir* (London, Jonathan Cape, 1938), pp. 116–24; and Peter Stansky and William Abrahams, *Journey to the Frontier: Two Roads to the Spanish Civil War* (Boston, Little, Brown and Co., 1966).

18 Norman returned to Canada to pursue an outstanding career as a diplomat and scholar until his death in 1957, when he committed suicide having been hounded by McCarthyite witch-hunters. See Bowen (ed.), *E. H. Norman*, see note 20 above; also, Reg Whitaker, 'Return to the Crucible – the Persecution of E. H. Norman', *The Canadian Forum* (November 1986), pp. 11–28.

19 Kiernan, 'Herbert Norman's Cambridge'.

20 See note 9. Also, see with regard to Kiernan's work in this area his contributions to Ali Sardar Jaffri and K. S. Duggal (eds), *Iqbal Commemorative Volume* (Delhi, 1980); these are 'Iqbal as Prophet of Change', 'Iqbal and Milton', and 'Iqbal and Wordsworth'.

21 V. G. Kiernan, *The March of Time* (Lahore, Gur Das Kapur and Sons, 1946); *Castanets* (Lahore, Lahore Art Press, 1941); and 'Brockle' and 'The Señorita' in *Longman's Miscellany* (Calcutta), 3, 4 (1945 and 1946).

22 Hobsbawm, 'The Historians' Group of the Community Party'.

23 See V. G. Kiernan, *State and Society in Europe, 1550–1650* (Oxford, Basil Blackwell, 1980).

24 Hobsbawm, 'The Historians' Group of the Communist Party', p. 24.

25 For examples: in Britain, David Cannadine, 'The State of British History', *Times Literary Supplement*, (10 October 1986), pp. 1139–40; and in the United States, Thomas Bender, 'Making History Whole Again', *New York Times Book Review*, (6 October 1985), pp. 1, 42–3.

26 Dominick La Capra, *History and Criticism* (Ithaca, Cornell University Press, 1986).

27 E. H. Carr, *What is History?* (New York, Vintage Books, 1961), p. 69. A recent assertion of the conservative position is Alan Beattie, *History in Peril* (London, Centre for Policy Studies, 1987).

28 V. G. Kiernan, 'Notes on Marxism in 1968', in R. Miliband and J. Saville (eds), *The Socialist Register 1968* (London, Merlin Press, 1968), p. 182.

29 Kiernan, 'Class and Ideology' p. 268.

30 Kiernan, 'Notes on Marxism in 1968', p. 184.

31 From Kiernan, *The Lords of Human Kind*, p. xiv; and a letter to HJK of 8 June 1986.

32 V. G. Kiernan, 'Problems of Marxist History', *New Left Review*, 161 (January–February 1987), p. 106.

33 Kiernan, 'Notes on Marxism in 1968', pp. 186, 208. Indeed, the opening words of Kiernan's first book, *British Diplomacy in China*, are: 'All abstraction falsifies' (p. xxvii).

34 Hobsbawm, 'The Historians' Group of the Communist Party', p. 31; and Christopher Hill in conversation with the editor in January 1987.

35 Maurice Dobb, *Studies in the Development of Capitalism* (London, Routledge and Kegan Paul, 1946), e.g., pp. 17–18.

36 Keith Tribe, 'The Problem of Transition and Question of Origin', in his *Genealogies of Capitalism* (London, Macmillan, 1981), pp. 19–21, also from papers in the possession of V. G. Kiernan. The Group's 'position' was stated in 'State and Revolution in Tudor and Stuart England', *Communist Review* (July 1948), pp. 207–14.

37 See Kaye, *The British Marxist Historians*, ch. 2, pp. 23–69.

38 See T. H. Aston and C. H. E. Philpin (eds), *The Brenner Debate: Agrarian Class Structure and Economic Development in Pre-Industrial Europe* (Cambridge, Cambridge University Press, 1985); and Philip Corrigan and Derek Sayer, *The Great Arch* (Oxford, Basil Blackwell, 1985). Christopher Hill's own 'bourgeois revolution thesis' has been much revised; see Kaye, *The British Marxist Historians*, ch. 4, pp. 99–130.

39 See Kaye, ibid., esp. pp. 36–40, 51–3. It should be noted, however, that Kiernan's general position on merchant vs. industrial capital has also been revised; see his *Development, Imperialism and some Misconceptions*, (University College of Swansea, Centre for Development Studies 1981), Occasional Paper 13, p. 25.

40 Though, of course, so too have Eric Hobsbawm and E. P. Thompson. For examples, see: Hobsbawm's 'Karl Marx's Contribution to Historiography' in R. Blackburn (ed.), *Ideology in Social Science* (London, Fontana, 1972), pp. 265–83; and Thompson's *The Poverty of Theory and Other Essays* (London, Merlin Press, 1978).

41 'History' (ch. 1 in the present collection); also, see Kiernan's essays in *Marxism and Imperialism*.

42 Kiernan, 'Notes on Marxism in 1968', pp. 178, 183.

43 F. Engels, *The Peasant War in Germany* (New York, International Publishers, 1966). Kiernan, 'History', p. 43 in this collection. Also, see Kiernan's 'Foreword' to F. Engels, *The Condition of the Working Class in England* (Harmondsworth, Penguin Books, 1987), pp. 9–25.

44 V. G. Kiernan, 'Gramsci and Marxism' (ch. 2 in the present collection) and 'The Socialism of Antonio Gramsci', in K. Coates (ed.), *Essays on Socialist Humanism* (Nottingham, Spokesman Books, 1972), pp. 63–86. Also, see his article 'Gramsci and the Other Continents', *New Edinburgh Review*, 27 (1985), pp. 19–23. For Gramsci's writings, see *Selections from the Prison Notebooks*, ed. and tr. Q. Hoare and G. Nowell Smith (New York, International Publishers, 1971); and Lynne Lawner (ed.), *Letters from Prison* (New York, Harper & Row, 1973).

45 Kiernan, 'The Socialism of Antonio Gramsci', p. 75; and 'Gramsci and Marxism', p. 45 in this collection. Related to this, see Harvey J. Kaye, 'Political Theory and History: Antonio Gramsci and the British Marxist

Historians', *Italian Quarterly*, 97–8 (Summer–Fall 1984), pp. 145–66.

46 Kiernan, 'Gramsci and Marxism', p. 73 in this collection.

47 Kiernan, 'Art and the Necessity of History'.

48 V. G. Kiernan, 'Reflections on Braudel', *Social History*, 4 (January 1977), p. 522.

49 This part of the book, which would normally appear first, is situated rather late in the text. This is probably due to the fact that the work was attuned to the requirements of diplomatic history, the latter section added by a young Marxist interested in questions of social and political structure, change and development.

50 V. G. Kiernan, 'Foreword to the 1970 edition', *British Diplomacy in China, 1880–1885*, p. xii. See note 2 above for references to his post-war and later diplomatic studies, though additionally should be noted his article 'Diplomats in Exile', in R. Hatton and M. S. Anderson (eds), *Studies in Diplomatic History* (London, Longman, 1970), pp. 301–21, one of the things which he says he most enjoyed writing.

51 This concern also led him to write 'Britons Old and New', Colin Holmes (ed.), *Immigrants and Minorities in British Society* (London, George Allen and Unwin, 1978), pp. 23–59. This article surveys British historical development in terms of its being a receiver of immigrants and refugees. Also, see Kiernan's pugnacious piece, 'After Empire', *New Edinburgh Review*, 37 (Spring 1977), pp. 23–35.

52 Kiernan, *European Empires*, p. 230. Another similarity between this book and *The Lords of Human Kind* is the style in which they are written. A British reviewer of *The Lords* refers to it as 'historical impressionism'; the reviewer of *European Empires* in the *American Historical Review* (June 1983) describes its form as 'pointillist'. I would agree with the latter, applying his description to both books for, indeed, the two are characterized by numerous 'capsule accounts' of incidents, episodes and battles drawn by Kiernan from the entire geography of imperialism to provide particular pictures of its landscape.

53 For an example of a related article, see V. G. Kiernan, 'American Hegemony under Revision', in R. Miliband and J. Saville (eds), *The Socialist Register 1974* (London, Merlin Press, 1974), pp. 302–30.

54 Kiernan, *America: The New Imperialism*, p. 1.

55 Kiernan, 'Imperialism, American and European', in his *Marxism and Imperialism*, p. 130.

56 Kiernan, *Marxism and Imperialism*, pp. viii, 67.

57 Ibid., p. viii. 'The Marxist Theory of Imperialism and its Historical Formation' is the first essay in *Marxism and Imperialism*, pp. 1–68.

58 Kiernan, *European Empires*, p. 227. Unfortunately, Kiernan provides no estimates here; nor do we know if he is including the African slave trade prior to the nineteenth century (which, admittedly, Africans themselves participated in quite actively).

59 V. G. Kiernan, 'Imperialism and Revolution', in R. Porter and M. Teich (eds), *Revolution in History* (Cambridge, Cambridge University Press, 1986), p. 129.

60 Ibid., p. 121.

61 V. G. Kiernan, 'Tennyson, King Arthur and Imperialism', in R. Samuel and

G. Stedman Jones (eds), *Culture, Ideology and Politics* (London, Routledge and Kegan Paul, 1982), p. 139.

62 Kiernan, *The Lords of Human Kind*, p. xxvi.
63 For example, see Kiernan, *Development, Imperialism and some Misconceptions*.
64 V. G. Kiernan, 'Europe and the World: The Imperial Record', in M. Wright (ed.), *Rights and Obligations in North–South Relations* (New York, St Martin's Press, 1986), p. 38; and 'Tennyson, King Arthur and Imperialism', p. 147.
65 Kiernan, 'Imperialism and Revolution', p. 137.
66 Kiernan, 'Notes on Marxism in 1968', pp. 195, 190–1.
67 Ibid., p. 196.
68 V. G. Kiernan, *Duelling in Social History: A Study in the Aristocratic Ascendancy* (Oxford, Oxford University Press, 1988).
69 For examples of these renewed interests, see Benedict Anderson, *Imagined Communities: Reflections on the Origin and Spread of Nationalism* (London; Verso, 1983); Ernest Gellner, *Nations and Nationalism* (Ithaca, Cornell University Press, 1983); Anthony Giddens, *The Nation-State and Violence* (Oxford, Polity Press, 1986); and J. A. Hall (ed.), *States in History* (Oxford, Basil Blackwell, 1986).
70 See note 23 above. Kiernan himself notes the similarity between his own book and that of Perry Anderson's *Lineages of the Absolutist State*.
71 Kiernan, *State and Society in Europe, 1550–1650*, pp. 35, 6.
72 Kiernan, 'State and Nation in Western Europe' (p. 109 in the present collection); originally published in *Past & Present*, 31 (July 1965).
73 Ibid., p. 114.
74 Kiernan, *State and Society in Europe, 1550–1650*, p. 12.
75 Kiernan, 'State and Nation in Western Europe' (p. 117 in the present collection).
76 See V. G. Kiernan, 'Marx, Engels, and the Indian Mutiny' in his *Marxism and Imperialism*, esp. pp. 227–34.
77 Kiernan, 'Notes on Marxism in 1968', p. 204.
78 V. G. Kiernan, 'Nationalist Movements and Social Classes (p. 139 in the present collection); originally published in A. D. Smith (ed.), *National Movements*, (London, Macmillan, 1976).
79 Ibid., p. 154. Also, see V. G. Kiernan, 'On the Development of a Marxist Approach to Nationalism', *Science and Society*, 34, 1 (Spring 1970), pp. 92–8.
80 V. G. Kiernan, 'Revolution' (pp. 201, 205, 263, n.5, in the present collection); originally published in P. Burke (ed.), *The New Cambridge Modern History*, (Cambridge, Cambridge University Press, 1979), vol. 13: *Companion Volume*.
81 V. G. Kiernan, *The Revolution of 1854 in Spanish History* (Oxford, Oxford University Press, 1966).
82 See Kiernan's 'Introduction' to I. MacDougall (ed.), *Voices from the Spanish Civil War* (Edinburgh, Polygon, 1986); also his review of Ronald Fraser's *The Blood of Spain*, in *New Left Review*, 120, (March–April 1980), pp. 97–107.
83 Kiernan, *The Revolution of 1854*, p. 1.

84 In the 'Introduction' to another volume of Kiernan's writings, to be entitled *Intellectuals, Culture, and History*, I hope to provide a fuller discussion of his work in cultural studies.

85 For example, see Kiernan's review of Raymond Williams's *Culture and Society*, in *The New Reasoner*, 9 (Summer 1959), pp. 75–83, and his review of Christopher Hill's *The Century of Revolution*, in *New Left Review*, 11 (September–October 1961), pp. 62–5.

86 Kiernan, 'History', p. 31; 'Revolution', p. 205; and 'Patterns of Protest in English History' in R. Benewick and T. Smith (eds), *Direct Action and Democratic Politics* (London, George Allen and Unwin, 1972), p. 32.

87 Kiernan, 'Labour and the Literate in Nineteenth-century Britain', p. 47. Kiernan credits this view of the English working class to his friend, Professor John Saville, another former comrade of the Historians' Group, important figure in the development of British labour history and a founder–editor of the annual *Socialist Register*. On this issue, see Saville's 'Ideology of Labourism', in R. Benewick, et al. (eds), *Knowledge and Belief in Politics* (London, George Allen and Unwin, 1973), pp. 213–26.

88 Kiernan, 'Victorian London'; and 'Working Class and Nation in Nineteenth-century Britain' (ch. 7 in this collection).

89 See the bi-annual journal *History Workshop* for samples of such work – along with the volumes they have produced.

90 Kiernan, 'Notes on Marxism in 1968', p. 188.

91 Kiernan, 'After Empire', p. 30.

92 Kiernan, 'Notes on Marxism in 1968', p. 201.

93 Kiernan, *Marxism and Imperialism*, p. 167.

94 Kiernan, 'On the Development of a Marxist Approach to Nationalism', p. 97.

95 V. G. Kiernan, 'The Peasant Revolution: Some Questions' in his *Marxism and Imperialism*, p. 132.

96 Kiernan, 'Notes on Marxism in 1968', p. 200; and *Marxism and Imperialism*, pp. 201, x, 147,

97 For a critical review of this 'new' politics of socialism, see Ellen M. Wood, *The Retreat from Class* (London, Verso, 1986).

98 V. G. Kiernan, 'Notes on the Intelligentsia', R. Miliband and J. Saville (eds), *The Socialist Register 1969* (London, Merlin Press, 1969), pp. 76–7, 81; and 'Notes on Marxism in 1968', p. 200.

99 For example, 'Intellectuals in History' (see note 4 above).

100 See 'Gramsci and Marxism', (ch. 2 in this collection).

101 Kiernan, 'Wordsworth and the People', p. 270. On the attention paid to poetry in the Historians' Group, see Bill Schwarz, ' "The People" in History: The Communist Party Historians' Group 1946–56', in R. Johnson, et al. (eds), *Making Histories* (London, Hutchinson, 1982), pp. 76–7.

102 Kiernan, 'The Socialism of Antonio Gramsci', p. 75.

103 Kiernan, 'Art and the Necessity of History', p. 234.

104 Kiernan, 'The Socialism of Antonio Gramsci'.

105 Kiernan, *The Lords of Human Kind*, pp. xxviii–xxix; and 'The Covenanters'.

106 Kiernan, 'Herbert Norman's Cambridge', pp. 25–6; 'Socialism, The Prophetic Memory', in B. Parekh (ed.), *The Concept of Socialism* (London,

Croom Helm, 1975), pp. 14–37; and 'Christianity', in *A Dictionary of Marxist Thought*, pp. 69–71.

107　Kiernan, 'Patterns of Protest in English History', p. 33; *Marxism and Imperialism*, p. 180; and 'Royal Mysteries', *London Review of Books* (20 January–3 February 1983), p. 12.

108　W. Benjamin, 'Theses on the Philosophy of History', in his *Illuminations* (New York, Harcourt Brace Jovanovich, 1969), p. 257.

109　Ibid., p. 255.

110　Kiernan, 'Gramsci and Marxism', p. 93 in this collection.

1 History

1　F. Engels, *Dialectics of Nature*, (Moscow, 1953), pp. 2–3.

2　See R. L. Meek, *Social Science and the Ignoble Savage* (Cambridge, 1976).

3　V. I. Lenin, 'Marx' (1914), in J. Fineberg (ed.), *Marx, Engels, Marxism* (London, 1936).

4　K. Kautsky, *Ethics and the Materialist Conception of History* (1906), tr. J. B. Askew, 4th edn (Chicago, 1918), p. 14.

5　F. Engels, *Ludwig Feuerbach and the End of Classical German Philosophy* (Berlin, 1886), section IV.

6　K. Marx and F. Engels, *The German Ideology*, English edn of parts I and 3, ed. R. Pascal (London, 1938), p. 38.

7　See, for this view, with a wealth of detail, M. Rubel, in J. O'Malley and K. Algozin (eds), *Rubel on Karl Marx: Five Essays* (Cambridge, 1981).

8　See, for example H. Lefebvre, *Dialectical Materialism* (1938); (London, 1968), pp. 81–2, 86. Cf. J. Seigel, *Marx's Fate* (Princeton, 1978), pp. 320ff.

9　G. Plekhanov, *Fundamental Problems of Marxism* (1908), tr. E. and C. Paul (London, n.d.), pp. 25–6.

10　K. Marx, 'Moralizing Criticism and Critical Morality' (1847), in *Karl Marx: Selected Essays*, tr. H. J. Stenning (London, n.d.), p. 152. See K. Marx and F. Engels, *Werke* (Berlin, 1964), vol. 4, p. 347.

11　K. Marx, 'The English Revolution', in *Karl Marx: Selected Essays*, pp. 202–5.

12　R. Pascal, 'Preface' to Marx and Engels, *The German Ideology*, p. ix.

13　A good exposition will be found in V. Venable, *Human Nature: The Marxian View* (London, 1946), pp. 82ff. Cf. D. R. Gandy, *Marx and History* (Austin, Texas, 1979), pp. 129ff.

14　J. M. Maguire, *Marx's Theory of Politics* (Cambridge, 1978), p. 53; he draws on T. S. Hamerow's account of Germany in *Restoration, Revolution and Reaction* (Princeton, 1966).

15　Cf. M. Evans, *Karl Marx* (London, 1975), pp. 64, 68, 71.

16　Marx and Engels, *The German Ideology*, p. 29.

17　Ibid., p. 10.

18　Ibid., p. 62.

19　Ibid., pp. 10–11.

20　Ibid., p. 13.

21　Ibid., pp. 22–4, 72, 75.

22　Ibid., pp. 59–60.

23 Ibid., p. 60.
24 K. Marx and F. Engels, *Revolution in Spain* (collected articles; New York, 1939), pp. 22–4.
25 Marx and Engels, *The German Ideology*, p. 1.
26 Ibid., pp. 20–1.
27 Ibid., pp. 30, 43.
28 Ibid., p. 14.
29 Engels, 'Preface' to his *Ludwig Feuerbach*.
30 F. Engels, *Germany: Revolution and Counter-Revolution* (1851), (London 1933), pp. 36–7.
31 F. Engels, *The Peasant War in Germany*, (Moscow, 1956), p. 149. For some recent comments on this work, see B. Scribner and G. Benecke (eds), *The German Peasant War 1525: New Viewpoints* (London, 1979). Cf. D. McLellan, *Engels* (London, 1977), p. 27: 'It was in writing history that Engles' talents found their fullest expression.'
32 T. Carver, *Engels* (Oxford, 1981), pp. 33–4.
33 Engels, *The Peasant War in Germany*, pp. 67ff.
34 Ibid., p. 130.
35 K. Marx, letter of 2 September 1854.
36 Marx and Engels, *Revolution in Spain*, pp. 31, 33.
37 Ibid., p. 71.
38 K. Marx, *The Eastern Question*, ed. E. M. and E. Aveling (London, 1897), e.g., pp. 62, 231–6. See generally on Marx's views about right and wrong wars Dona Torr (ed.), *Marxism, Nationality and War* (London, 1940).
39 Marx to Engels, 2 June 1853, and Engels to Marx, 6 June 1853. The letters will be found in the selected *Correspondence 1846–1895*, tr. Dona Torr (London, 1934), pp. 64ff.
40 K. Marx and F. Engels, *The First Indian War of Independence 1857–1859*, collected articles (Moscow, 1959), pp. 150–1.
41 Ibid., pp. 16–17.
42 Engels, *Germany: Revolution and Counter-Revolution*, pp. 55–6, 86.
43 K. Marx, *Marx on China 1853–1860* (collected articles), ed. Dona Torr (London, 1851), p. 7 (June 1853).
44 Ibid., pp. 50–1 (June 1857).
45 K. Marx, 'Preface' to *A Contribution to the Critique of Political Economy*.
46 E. J. Hobsbawm, 'Introduction' to K. Marx, *Pre-Capitalist Economic Formations* (London, 1964), p. 11.
47 K. Marx, *Correspondence 1846–1895*, p. 354. Cf. Evans, *Karl Marx*, p. 73.
48 Marx, *Pre-Capitalist Economic Formations*, pp. 71–2.
49 K. Marx, letter to F. Engels, 30 October 1956.
50 Marx, *Pre-Capitalist Economic Formations*, p. 83; cf. pp. 91–2.
51 Ibid., p. 71.
52 Lenin, *Marx, Engels, Marxism*, p. 12.
53 M. Rubel, pp. 96–8.
54 Marx, *Pre-Capitalist Economic Formations*, p. 111.
55 K. Marx, 'Conclusion' to his *Capital*, vol. I, ch. 32.
56 This essay, published as such in 1892–3, formed the chief part of Engels's introduction to the English edition (1892) of his *Socialism: Utopian and Scientific*, a section published separately in 1880 of his *Anti-Dühring* (full

title: *Herr Eugen Dühring's Revolution in Science*) of 1878. In his letter of 21 September 1890 to J. Bloch, Engels refers him for light on the theory and practice of history to Marx's *The Eighteenth Brumaire of Louis Bonaparte* (1852), parts of *Capital*, and his own *Anti-Dühring* and *Ludwig Feuerbach*.

57 Carver, *Engels*, pp. 62–3.
58 Ibid., p. 38.
59 F. Engels, 'Marx' in Marx and Engels, *Werke*, vol. 19, pp. 96–106; English version in *Reminiscences of Marx and Engels* (Moscow, n.d.).
60 See Meek, *Social Science and the Ignoble Savage*, pp. 1, 31.
61 K. Marx, letter to L. Kugelmann, 17 April 1871. Cf. the objection advanced by G. Leff: 'History is concerned with the contingent'; 'the absence of uniformity from human affairs' is central to it: see *History and Social Theory* (London, 1969), p. 3.
62 Engels, *Ludwig Feuerbach*, section IV.
63 F. Engels, letter to J. Bloch, 21 September 1890.
64 Marx, 'Preface' to *A Critique of Political Economy*.
65 Engels, *Dialectics of Nature*, p. 214.
66 F. Engels, letter to C. Schmidt, 27 October 1890.
67 F. Engels, *The Role of Force in History*, tr. J. Cohen, ed. E. Wangermann (London, 1968), pp. 46ff.
68 As Wangermann emphasizes in his introduction to *The Role of Force*, p. 27.
69 F. Engels, letter to C. Schmidt, 5 August 1890. He writes here that 'The materialist conception of history also has a lot of friends nowadays to whom it serves as an excuse for *not* studying history'.
70 Engels, letter to J. Bloch, 21 September 1890.
71 Engels, letter to C. Schmidt, 27 October 1890.
72 Engels, *Dialectics of Nature*, pp. 208–9.
73 Kautsky, *Ethics and the Materialist Conception of History*, p. 7.
74 Ibid., pp. 110–11.
75 Ibid., pp. 164ff.
76 Ibid., pp. 184–5.
77 G. M. Enteen, *The Soviet Scholar–Bureaucrat: M. N. Pokrovskii and the Society of Marxist Historians* (Pennsylvania State University, 1978), p. 7.
78 G. Plekhanov, *The Materialist Conception of History* (1895); (London, 1940), pp. 12ff.
79 Plekhanov, *Fundamental Problems of Marxism*, p. 25.
80 Ibid., pp. 33–4, 51.
81 Ibid., pp. 36, 40–1.
82 Plekhanov, *The Materialist Conception of History*, p. 32.
83 Plekhanov, *Fundamental Problems of Marxism*, p. 42.
84 N. I. Bukharin, 'Marx's Teaching and its Historical Importance', in Bukharin et al., *Marxism and Modern Thought*, tr. Ralph Fox (London, 1935), p. 33.
85 Ibid., pp. 43, 44; cf. his *Historical Materialism*, (London, 1925), p. xiii, etc.
86 V. I. Lenin, *The Letters of Lenin*, tr. E. Hill and D. Mudie (London, 1937), p. 463.
87 Enteen, *The Soviet Scholar–Bureaucrat*, p. 21.
88 F. Gorochov, 'An Anti-Marxist Theory of History', in *International Literature*, 9, (1937).

89 Lenin, *Marx, Engels, Marxism*, p. 64.
90 J. Stalin, *Dialectical and Historical Materialism*, (Moscow, 1951), p. 23. This was originally (1938) a chapter of the history of the Bolshevik Party.
91 L. Trotsky, *Stalin* (London, 1969), vol. 1, p. 207.
92 Reported by the *Observer* (1 February 1970).
93 M. Shirokov (ed.), *A Textbook of Marxist Philosophy*, English edn ed. J. Lewis (London, 1937). See section II, chs 3, 6.
94 O. Kuusinen (ed.), *Fundamentals of Marxism–Leninism*; (London, 1961), p. 153.
95 Ibid., p. 216
96 Ibid., pp. 167–8.
97 See A. D. Lublinskaya, *French Absolutism: The Crucial Phase 1620–1629*, tr. B. Pearce (Cambridge, 1968).
98 A. Gramsci, *Selections from the Prison Notebooks* ed. and tr. Q. Hoare and G. N. Smith (London, 1971), p. 173.
99 Ibid., p. 399.
100 A. Gramsci, *The Modern Prince and Other Writings*, tr. L. Marks (London, 1957), p. 93.
101 Gramsci, *Prison Notebooks*, pp. 431, 470–1.
102 Ibid., pp. 377–8. Gramsci speaks much more favourably here of Labriola, the pioneer of Marxist thinking in Italy.
103 Ibid., p. 408.
104 Cf. P. Anderson, *Considerations on Western Marxism* (London, 1976), p. 102: in England 'The calibre of Marxist *historiography* has probably been superior to that of any other country.' On theory and the British labour movement, see S. Macintyre, *A Proletarian Science: Marxism in Britain 1917–1933* (Cambridge, 1980), ch. 5: 'Historical Materialism'. Also see H. J. Kaye, *The British Marxist Historians* (Oxford, 1984).
105 See D. C. Price, *Russia and the Roots of the Chinese Revolution, 1896–1911* (Cambridge, MA, 1974), especially ch. 2.
106 R. Browning, in discussion on 'Stages of Social Development', *Marxism Today* (October 1961). Cf. M. I. Finley, *Ancient Slavery and Modern Ideology* (London, 1980), pp. 40ff, 57–8.
107 Cf. W. H. Shaw, *Marx's Theory of History* (London, 1978), p. 138.
108 M. Cornforth, *The Open Philosophy and the Open Society* (London, 1968), pp. 138–9.
109 See, for example, Shaw, *Marx's Theory of History*, p. 81 etc.
110 J. McMurtry, *The Structure of Marx's World View* (Princeton, 1978), p. 219; cf. pp. 157, 214. For an opposite view, see Venable, *Human Nature*, pp. 89–91.
111 F. Braudel, *Capitalism and Material Life 1400–1800*; English edn (London, 1973), p. 116.
112 See R. Brenner's arguments in T. H. Aston and C. H. E. Philpin (eds), *The Brenner Debate: Agrarian Class Structure and Economic Development in Pre-Industrial Europe* (Cambridge, 1985).
113 Bukharin, *Historical Materialism*, p. 78.
114 A. Conan Doyle, *The Sign of Four* (London, 1890), ch. 9. Cf. V. Gordon Childe's remark that to turn statistical laws describing masses of particles into historical laws is too mechanistic: *History* (London, 1947), p. 82.

115 A. Walker, *Marx: His Theory and its Context* (London, 1978), p. 107; cf. G. Leff, *The Tyranny of Concepts* (London, 1961), pp. 153ff.

116 Engels, letter to C. Schmidt, 27 October 1890.

117 F. Engels, letter to F. Mehring, 14 July 1893.

118 Plekhanov, *The Materialist Conception of History*, p. 28.

119 K. Mannheim, *Essays on the Sociology of Knowledge* (London, 1952), p. 184.

120 Braudel, *Capitalism and Material Life* p. 243.

121 Anderson, *Considerations on Western Marxism*, p. 78.

122 D. R. Gandy, *Marx and History*, p. 153. Evans, *Karl Marx*, p. 62, calls it 'an unfortunate metaphor from the language of constructional engineering'.

123 Information from Ian Gow, of Sheffield University.

124 V. Purcell, *The Boxer Uprising* (Cambridge, 1963), pp. 270–1.

125 J. den Tex, *Oldenbarnevelt* (Cambridge, 1973), vol. 1, ch. 6.

126 A. Brewer, *Marxist Theories of Imperialism* (London, 1980), p. 12.

127 L. Althusser, 'Philosophy as a Revolutionary Weapon' (interview, 1968), translation in *New Left Review*, 64 (1970). For a useful critique, see N. Geras, 'Althusser's Marxism', in *New Left Review*, 71, 1972. Cf. Anderson, *Considerations on Western Marxism*, p. 84.

128 I. Wallerstein, *The Modern World-System* (New York, 1974).

129 A. G. Frank, *Capitalism and Underdevelopment in Latin America* (New York, 1967). In both this and Wallerstein's work, Brewer (*Marxist Theories of Imperialism*, p. 264), while recognizing their value, complains of a lack of thorough analysis 'to back up their sloganistic generalizations'.

130 A. Cabral, *Revolution in Guinea. An African People's Struggle* (London, 1969), p. 77.

131 For example, Lucien Rey; Hamza Alavi. Cf. Brewer, *Marxist Theories of Imperialism*, pp. 186–7.

132 A good many of them are represented in the large volume of *Essays in Honour of Professor S. C. Sarkar* (New Delhi, 1976).

133 A. Dirlik, *Revolution and History. The Origins of Marxist Historiography in China 1919–1937* (Berkeley, 1978), pp. 229–31.

134 Ibid., p. 116; cf. ch. 6 on problems of periodizing.

135 Marx and Engels, *The German Ideology*, p. 46.

136 J. P. Harrison, *The Communists and Chinese Peasant Rebellions. A Study in the Rewriting of Chinese History* (London; 1970), p. 20; cf. pp. 190–1.

137 A criticism made in a New Left Club discussion at Edinburgh in March 1961.

138 L. Stephen, *An Agnostic's Apology* (1893); (London, 1931), p. 27.

139 See on this point Kaye, *The British Marxist Historians*.

2 Gramsci and Marxism

1 A. Gramsci, *Selections from the Prison Notebooks of Antonio Gramsci*, ed. and tr. by Q. Hoare and G. N. Smith (London, 1971), pp. xcvi, 483. Besides the long introduction the volume contains a wealth of explanatory notes. About eighty pages of the material, chiefly 'The Modern Prince',

appeared in the English anthology translated by L. Marks in 1957 (see note 3). Page references in brackets in the body of this chapter are to the new volume.

2 Editors' introduction, p. lxviii.
3 A. Gramsci, *The Modern Prince and Other Writings*, tr. L. Marks (London, 1957), pp. 83, 85. This volume is cited below as *The Modern Prince*.
4 Ibid., p. 98.
5 Ibid., p. 82.
6 See editorial remarks by Hoare and Smith (eds), in Gramsci, *Prison Notebooks*, pp. 321–2, 360.
7 Gramsci, *The Modern Prince*, pp. 92–3.
8 Ibid., pp. 96–7; cf. p. 92.
9 Ibid., pp. 99–100.
10 Ibid., p. 77.
11 Ibid., pp. 12–13.
12 Ibid., pp. 69, 75.
13 Ibid., pp. 69–70.
14 Ibid., p. 95.
15 This comes out in much of the discussion on Machiavelli in *The Modern Prince*.
16 Hoare and Smith (eds), in Gramsci, *Prison Notebooks*, editorial note on p. 214, no. 3.
17 Ibid., p. 59.
18 Gramsci, *The Modern Prince*, p. 36.
19 Ibid., p. 47.
20 Ibid., p. 65.
21 Ibid., pp. 123, 126.
22 Ibid., pp. 50–1.
23 Ibid., p. 15.
24 Ibid., p. 73.
25 Ibid., p. 119.
26 Ibid. p. 50.
27 Ibid. p. 67.
28 E. Nolte, *Marxism, Fascism, Cold War* (Assen, Netherlands, 1982), p. 126.
29 Gramsci, *Prison Notebooks*, pp. 270–1.

3 State and Nation in Western Europe

1 'L'Orientalisme en crise', by Abdel-Malek, in *Diogène*, 44 (1963), pp. 109ff., is a well-argued declaration of Afro-Asian intellectual independence from Europe, which does not perhaps altogether avoid the danger referred to.
2 H. Kohn, *The Idea of Nationalism* (New York, 1945), p. 4.
3 A tendency to recognize this showed itself in the discussion in *Marxism Today* during 1961–2 on 'Stages of Social Development'.
4 Like the Wahabis of eighteenth-century Arabia, who gave Islam a powerful revivalist impulse. For a brief sketch of them, see W. C. Smith, *Islam in*

Modern History (New York, 1957), pp. 48–51.

5 Cf. C. Hill, *Society and Puritanism in Pre-Revolutionary England* (London, 1964), p. 442, on the carrying over into modern life of 'some of the sense of communal responsibility which was inherited from the mediaeval manor and borough'. He remarks that Coke and Norden in the early seventeenth century 'still called the manor "a little commonwealth" '. So was the Indian village, no doubt, but this was an isolated unit, not part of a wider political organization.

6 On them, see R. Trevor Davies, *The Golden Century of Spain 1501–1621* (London, 1937), p. 6.

7 On the *timar* or Turkish military fief, see Col. Lamouche, *Histoire de la Turquie* (Paris, 1953), p. 179. On its Mogul equivalent, the *jagir*, see Abdul Aziz, *The Mansabdari System and the Mugul Army* (Lahore, 1945).

8 Feudal decentralization was well under way during Aurangzeb's own reign (1658–1707), as S. C. Sarkar and K. K. Datta point out: *Textbook of Modern Indian History* (Allahabad, 1937), p. 91.

9 On this, see A. N. Poliak, *Feudalism in Egypt, Syria, Palestine, and the Lebanon, 1250–1900* (London, Royal Asiatic Society, 1939), especially chs 1, 2.

10 An 'active' citizen was one entitled to vote and enter the National Guard, under the tests, including payment of a certain amount in direct taxation, prescribed by the Constitution of 1791, titre III, sect. II, art. II.

11 W. Reade, *The Martyrdom of Man* (1872); (London, 1932), 'Thinker's Library', p. 405.

12 It is in this light that Marx's dictum may be considered, on absence of private property in land as the key to Asiatic history: letter to Engels, 2 June 1853, in Dona Torr (ed.), *Karl Marx and Friedrich Engels, Correspondence 1846–1895*, (London, 1934), p. 66. The view is less applicable to China than to the (mainly Islamic) countries he refers to.

13 N. J. Coulson, *A History of Islamic Law* Edinburgh, 1964), ch. 9, makes it clear that the *Shari'a*, or canon law, covered only a restricted part of life, and was no safeguard against arbitrary exercise of authority.

14 The most notable exception may be found in the sixteenth- and seventeenth-century conflicts and alliances among the four Great Powers of Islam – Turkey, Persia, Bokhara and Mogul India – of which there is a good outline in Aziz Ahmad, *Studies in Islamic Culture in the Indian Environment* (Oxford, 1964), pp. 21–47. But these were after all very long-range and intermittent contacts.

15 M. Maruyama, *Thought and Behaviour in Modern Japanese Politics* (Oxford, 1963), pp. 5–6, 138, recognizes the bearing on Japanese history of the absence of anything like the Western antithesis of Church and state. On the absence of a regular priesthood in Islam see E. Lammens, SJ, *Islam, Beliefs and Institutions* (London, 1929), p. 105.

16 For example, Odoric of Pordenone's descriptions of Canton, Fuchow, etc., in Sir H. Yule (ed.) *Cathay and the Way Thither* (Hakluyt Society, 2nd ser., xxxiii, 1915–16), ii, pp. 179ff.

17 There is a valuable discussion of this point in X. de Planhol, *The World of Islam* (London, 1959), ch. I.

18 J. Needham notes the profound effect on Chinese history of the absence

there of any spirit of urban autonomy: 'The city in China was always essentially a node in the administrative network of the Empire': see *Arts and Sciences in China*, 2, (1964), p. 17.

19 Cf. Trotsky on towns as the missing factor in Russian history: *The Russian Revolution*, ch. I. The contrast between the militant burghers of the West, and Russian merchants, often serfs as late as the nineteenth century, is a glaring one.

20 This *Hermandad*, which had sometimes concluded foreign treaties on its own account, was virtually ended by the absolute monarchy in 1490: R. Altamira, *Historia de España*, 4th edn (Barcelona, 1929), vol. 2, pp. 203–4, writes of the lack of any political cohesion among the three Basque provinces.

21 P. Geyl describes the Burgundian rule in *The Revolt of the Netherlands (1555–1609)* (London, 1932), ch. I.

22 See V. Purcell, 'Sects and Rebellions', in *The Boxer Uprising* (Cambridge, 1963), ch. 7.

23 In Poland, for instance, the higher and lower nobility might be found supporting rival candidates to the throne, as in 1574: O. Halecki, *History of Poland* (London, 1942), p. 105.

24 On the wavering attitude of the small nobility in Bohemia, see B. T. Rubtsov, *Gusitskie Voini (The Hussite Wars)* (Moscow, 1955), pp. 74–8, 138–9, 214, 276–7.

25 On Luther's relations with Hutten and Sickingen, the leaders of the Knights' War of 1522 – three years before the Peasants' War – see J. Mackinnon, *Luther and the Reformation* (London, 1925–9), vol. 3, pp. 161ff.

26 Cf. the remark in H. M. Chadwick, *The Nationalities of Europe and the Growth of the National Ideologies* (Cambridge, 1945), p. 110, that English reawakening after the Norman conquest expressed itself in religious ideas like Wycliffe's and in agrarian feeling.

27 See W. E. Rappard, *Collective Security in Swiss Experience, 1291–1948* (London, 1948), part I.

28 See W. H. Prescott, *The History of the Reign of Ferdinand and Isabella the Catholic*, 3rd edn (London, 1841), vol. 1, pp. 242–4. The Duke of Alba found himself the poorer by 575,000 *maravedís* a year, the Duke of Albuquerque by 1,400,000.

29 Isabella, supported by one faction of the baronage, claimed the throne at the death of her half-brother Henry IV in 1474, on the pretext that his daugher and only child was illegitimate.

30 On the *Din Ilahi* or 'divine religion', see for example, V. A. Smith, *Akbar the Great Mogul 1542–1605* (Oxford, 1917), ch. 8.

31 The Hungarian peasant revolt under Dozsa in 1512 was followed by the complete reduction of the peasants to serfdom, and this within a few years by the almost complete conquest of the country by the Turks: see O. Zarek, *The History of Hungary* (London, 1939), pp. 215–9.

32 The Peasants' War of 1525 occupies book 7 (in vol. 4) of J. Janssen, *History of the German People at the Close of the Middle Ages* (London 1910).

33 See Y. V. Bromley, *Krest'yanskoe vosstanie 1573g. v Chorvatii (The Peasant Rising of 1573 in Croatia)* (Moscow, 1959).

34 The Jews were expelled from Spain in 1492, eighteen years after Isabella's

accession and the commencement of the 'new monarchy', and the Muslims from Castile in 1502.

35 Kohn, *The Idea of Nationalism*, p. 333, speaks of the imperial knights and free peasants as 'the last social forces which had linked their aspirations with the fate of the Empire' (cf. p. 335).

36 Washington Irving, *The Conquest of Granada* (New York, 1929), ch. 7.

37 N. Machiavelli, *The Prince*, ch. 14.

38 The 'Italian Wars' went on with intervals from 1494 to 1559; the next four decades saw the French Civil Wars, the revolt of the Netherlands, the Anglo–Spanish War; the Thirty Years' War involved most of Europe between 1618 and 1648; the wars of Louis XIV cover 1666–8, 1688–97, 1702–13, or twenty-eight out of the fifty-four years of his personal reign.

39 One aspect of this is well illustrated by H. R. Trevor-Roper's article, 'Religion, the Reformation, and Social Change', in *Historical Studies*, 4 (1963).

40 One symptom of this is the overlaying of both these empires by the cosmopolitan Persian culture of middle Asia. G. L. Lewis remarks that Ottoman Turkish became a 'fantastic hotch potch', smothered under Persian constructions as well as Persian and Arabic addiction: *Turkey* (London, 1955), p. 97.

41 In some ways it was a stimulus to these small cultures to have to struggle for survival within larger complexes. See H. J. Fleure, *Human Geography in Western Europe* (London, 1918), p. 195: 'The little units reveal spiritual efforts and activities of marked tenacity and scope, and it is no accident that great contributions of genius and of talent from them have been made.'

42 There are some instructive comments on the ambivalent relationship between Paris and the French monarchy in K. Kautsky, *Terrorism and Communism* (London, 1920), pp. 8ff.

43 Cf. R. B. Merriman, *The Rise of the Spanish Empire* (London, 1918), vol. 1, p. 277, on the dynastic union of Aragon with Catalonia: 'The important support of the powerful eastern countship was thus secured against the manifold dangers which threatened Aragon at home and abroad.'

44 On this allegation against Strafford and Charles I, see C. V. Wedgwood, *Strafford, 1593–1601* (London, 1935), pp. 244–5, 284; cf. T. Ranger, 'Strafford in Ireland; a Revaluation', in *Past & Present*, 19 (April 1961). In 1688, just before his overthrow James II did bring troops over from Ireland.

45 This became true of Spain by the seventeenth century, if it was not true earlier. J. H. Elliott considers that in the early period of the new monarchy Castile was more prosperous and 'dynamic' than the periphery; *Imperial Spain 1469–1716* (London, 1963), pp. 31–2, 109. Cf. his article on 'The Decline of Spain', *Past & Present*, 20 (November 1961).

46 C. Viñas y Mey, *El problema de la tierra en la España de los siglos XVI–XVII (The Agrarian Problem in Sixteenth- and Seventeenth-Century Spain)* (Madrid, 1941), part I, ch. 4.

47 Some modern Indian and Chinese writers have suggested that a capitalist order of society was beginning to emerge in their countries when it was interrupted by the Western advent. See P. C. Joshi (ed.), *Rebellion 1857, a Symposium* (Delhi, 1957), p. 139; Ho Kan-chih, *A History of the Modern*

Chinese Revolution (Peking, 1959), p. 2. The view might be more plausible with reference to Japan.

48 Thomas Smollett, travelling through France in 1763, was incessantly struck by the boundless and ridiculous national vanity of the French – 'They are really persuaded, that theirs is the richest, the bravest, the happiest, and the most powerful nation under the sun, incapable of ever losing a battle except through trickery': *Travels through France and Italy* (Oxford, 1907), World's Classics, p. 38.

49 Lord Rosebery, *Napoleon, the Last Phase* (London, 1909), p. 184.

50 See C. Hill, 'The Norman Yoke', in J. Saville, et al. (eds), *Democracy and the Labour Movement* (London, 1954).

51 Kohn, *The Idea of Nationalism*, pp. 206–7.

52 The Boer War of 1899–1902, the climax of jingo nationalism in Britain, reveals this very clearly. It was so popular among the workers that the aristocratic anti-imperialist W. S. Blunt blamed it on them and thought they ought to be made to pay the extra taxation for it: *My Diaries* (London , 1932), p. 421, entry for 19 April 1901.

53 C. de Grunwald, in *Tsar Nicholas I* (London, 1954), p. 45, quotes the remark of Kircevski in 1831 that all Russia's energy had been absorbed by its vast size and rapid expansion: 'Material growth has made spiritual growth impossible.'

54 See H. L. Seaver, *The Great Revolt in Castile (1520–1)* (London, 1929).

55 See for example, J. A. Maravall, *Teoría española del estado en el siglo XVII (Spanish Theory of the State in the Seventeenth Century)* (Madrid, 1944); French tr. (Paris, 1955), ch. 5.

56 This alliance took shape in the long collaboration of Ferdinand and Isabella with Ximénez de Cisneros, who became Archbishop of Toledo and Metropolitan of Castile in 1495, Grand Inquisitor of Spain in 1507. W. Starkie, *Grand Inquisitor* (London, 1940) may, with some caution, be consulted.

57 E. J. Hobsbawm, 'The Crisis of the Seventeenth Century', in *Past & Present*, 5 and 6 (1954).

4 Foreign Mercenaries and Absolute Monarchy

1 P. Jouquet, *Macedonian Imperialism and the Hellenization of the East* (London, 1928), pp. 12–14. Greek mercenaries served as far away as southern India; see Sir M. Wheeler, *Rome Beyond the Imperial Frontiers* (London, 1955), p. 160.

2 N. Machiavelli, *The Prince* (Everyman edn.), ch. 14. K. Brandi, *The Emperor Charles V* (London, 1939), p. 465, reckons that of the Spanish revenue of over two million ducats in 1543, four-fifths went on war expenses. Cf. H. Koenigsberger, *The Government of Sicily under Philip II of Spain* (London, 1951), p. 124: 'Compared with military and naval expenses the charges of the civil administration were relatively insignificant.'

3 W. H. Prescott, *The History of the Reign of Ferdinand and Isabella the Catholic*, ed. J. F. Kirk (London, 1879), vol. 2, p. 516; cf. the militia experiment of 1496, ibid., p. 69.

4 G. Hanotaux, *Tableau de la France en 1614* (Paris, 1898), p. 109.

5 C. V. Wedgwood, *The Thirty Years War* (London, 1938), p. 401.

6 E. Fieffé, *Histoire des troupes étrangères au service de la France* (Paris, 1854), vol. 1, p. 41.

7 R. Doucet, *Les Institutions de la France au XVIe siècle* (Paris, 1948), vol. 2, p. 627.

8 O. L. Spaulding, N. Nickerson and J. W. Wright, *Warfare; a Study of Military Methods from the Earliest Times* (London, 1925), p. 370.

9 See, for example, G. Dickinson (ed.), *The 'Instructions sure le Faict de la Guerre' of Raymond de Beccarie de Pavie Sieur de Forquevaux* (London, 1954), p. xxviii.

10 F. Lot, *L'Art militaire et les armées au moyen âge* (Paris, 1946), vol. 2, p. 436; cf. p. 433. The 'francs-archers' were so called because they were released from various tax obligations.

11 *The Memoirs of Philip de Commines*, ed. A. R. Scoble (London, 1855), book 1, chs 3, 4.

12 See, for example, *The Scandalous Chronicle* of Jean de Troyes, in Scoble (ed.), *Philip de Commines*, book 2, p. 390.

13 Scoble (ed.), *Philip de Commines*, book 5, ch. 1.

14 Dickinson (ed.), *The 'Instructions sur le Faict de la Guerre'*, p. xxxi.

15 Machiavelli, *The Prince*, ch. 12.

16 Doucet, *Les Institutions de la France*, vol. 2, p 229.

17 C. W. C. Oman, *A History of the Art of War in the Middle Ages* rev. edn (London, 1925), vol. 2, p. 229.

18 E. Curtis, *A History of Medieval Ireland from 1086 to 1513*, enlarged edn (London, 1938), pp. 39, 48.

19 Lot, *L'Art militaire*, vol. 1, p. 366; vol. 2, p. 432.

20 Oman, *Middle Ages*, vol. 2, p. 59.

21 E. Inglis-Jones, *The Story of Wales* (London, 1955), pp. 81–2.

22 Oman, *Middle Ages*, vol. 2, p. 77; cf. on Welsh in the Hundred Years' War, Lot, *L'Art militaire*, vol. 1, p. 346; A. H. Burne, *The Crecy War* (London, 1955), p. 34.

23 Lot, *L'Art militaire*, vol. 1, p. 306.

24 B. Dudan, *Il Dominio Veneziano di Levante* (Bologna, 1938), pp. 255, 257.

25 Sir A. T. Wilson, *Persia* (London, 1932), pp. 68–9.

26 W. Oechsli, *History of Switzerland 1499–1914* (Cambridge, 1922), p. 7.

27 Scoble (ed.), *Philip de Commines*, book 5, ch. 1.

28 Spaulding, Nickerson and Wright (eds), *Warfare*, p. 339.

29 Commines defines *Landsknechts* as 'a collection from all the countries upon the Rhine, Suabia, the Pays de Vaux in Sequania, and Guelderland': Scoble (ed.), *Philip de Commines*, book 8, ch. 21.

30 Lot, *L'Art militaire*, vol. 2, p. 209; Oman, *Middle Ages*, vol. 2, p. 366.

31 C. W. C. Oman, *A History of the Art of War in the Sixteenth Century* (London, 1937), p. 41; Dickinson (ed.), *The 'Instructions sur le Faict de la Guerre'*, pp. xxxiv–xl. The name 'Croat' for a type of light horse was similarly made free with; F. Watson, *Wallenstein: Soldier under Saturn* (London, 1938), p. 164.

32 Spaulding, Nickerson and Wright (eds), *Warfare* p. 416.

33 J. C. S. Bridge, *A History of France from the Death of Louis XI* (Oxford

1929), vol. 4: *The Reign of Louis XII 1508–1514*, p. 151; Fieffé, *Histoire* vol. 1, p. 71.

34 R. Doucet, *Institutions de la France*, vol. 2, p. 638.
35 Fieffé, *Histoire*, vol. 1, p. 53, n. 1.
36 G. T. Denison, *A History of Cavalry* (London, 1877), p. 243.
37 Hon. J. W. Fortescue, *A History of the British Army* (London, 1899), vol. 1, p. 97; Oman, *Sixteenth Century*, p. 54.
38 Prescott, *Ferdinand and Isabella*, vol. 2, pp. 239, 250ff; V. R. Burke *The Great Captain* (London, 1877), p. 120; L. M. de Lojendio, *Gonzalvo de Córdoba* (Madrid, 1942), p. 214.
39 Lot, *L'Art militaire*, vol. 1, p. 318; Spaulding, Nickerson and Wright (eds), *Warfare*, p. 489.
40 Oman, *Sixteenth Century*, pp. 288–90 and book 4 *passim*.
41 *Chronicle of King Henry VIII of England*, tr. M. A. S. Hume (London, 1899), ch. 58. See also M. Hume, 'Los mercenarios españoles', in *Españoles e Ingleses en el Siglo XVI* (Madrid, 1903), ch. 1.
42 J. L. Bain (ed.), *The Hamilton Papers* (Edinburgh, 1890–2), vol. 1, pp. 578–80, 592–3.
43 Oman, *Sixteenth Century*, pp. 376, 549. On Elizabeth's financial embarrassments over the hiring of continental troops to aid the Dutch in 1578, see L. Stone, *An Elizabethan: Sir Horatio Palavicino* (Oxford, 1956), ch. 3.
44 C. Falls, *Elizabeth's Irish Wars* (London, 1950), pp. 41, 68–9, 76ff, 84; C. G. Cruickshank, *Elizabeth's Army* (London, 1946), p. 12.
45 J. A. Froude, *History of England* (London, 1872), vol. 4, pp. 291ff; Oman, *Sixteenth Century*, p. 359.
46 Fieffé, *Histoire*, vol. 1, p. 78.
47 Oman, *Sixteenth Century*, p. 288.
48 R. B. Merriman, *The Rise of the Spanish Empire* (New York, 1925), vol. 3, p. 120.
49 E. B. Bax, *The Peasants' War in Germany 1525–1526* (London, 1899), p. 313.
50 Froude, *History of England*, vol. 4, pp. 411–36. At the time of the Pilgrimage of Grace a shortage of matchlockmen had been complained of on the government side (Oman, *Sixteenth Century*, p. 350).
51 Ibid., pp. 445–53; cf. Oman, *Sixteenth Century*, p. 369.
52 Froude, *History of England*, vol. 4, p. 432.
53 F. Engels, *The Peasant War in Germany* (Moscow, 1956), chs 5, 6.
54 Oechsli, *History of Switzerland*, pp. 182–3.
55 P. Geyl, *The Revolt of the Netherlands, 1559–1609* (London, 1932), pp. 107, 117ff.
56 Ibid., p. 235.
57 Oechsli, *History of Switzerland*, pp. 23ff, 62.
58 'E per una strana contraddizione, che molto disonora gli uomini, gli Svizzeri, che sono il popolo quasi il piu libero dell'Europa, si lasciano prescegliere e comprare, per servir di custodi alla persona di quasi tutti i tiranni de essa' (Alfieri, *Della Tirannide*, 1789, ch. 7).
59 See Oman, *Sixteenth Century*, p. 36.
60 'Do you think,' Henry VIII's Spanish captains once said to their general, 'we

are in the King's service for the four ducats a month we earn? Not so, my lord; on the contrary we serve with the hope of taking prisoners and getting their ransom': *Chronicle of King Henry VIII of England*, ch. 56.

61 Armies then conventionally reckoned one woman and boy to each soldier (Wedgwood, *Thirty Years War*, p. 132). On peasant resistance, see O. Schiff, 'Die Deutschen Bauernaufstände von 1525 bis 1789', *Historische Zeitschrift*, 130 (1924), pp. 189–209.

62 G. Pagès, *La Guerre de Trente Ans 1618–1648* (Paris, 1939), pp. 115–6.

63 Watson, *Wallenstein*, p. 161.

64 L. André, *Michel le Tellier et Louvois*, 2nd edn (Paris, 1943), pp. 239–41. See also J. U. Nef, *War and Human Progress* (London, 1950), pp. 206–7; and E. J. Hamilton, *War and Prices in Spain, 1651–1800* (Cambridge, MA, Harvard University Press, 1947), p. 134, n. 58.

65 P. Sagnac and A. de Saint-Léger, *La Prépondérance francaise: Louis XIV (1661–1715)*, 2nd edn (Paris, 1944), p. 232. In 1688 there was another attempt, again of limited value, to form a militia.

66 Oman, *Middle Ages*, vol. 2, p. 236.

67 Fieffé, *Histoire*, vol. 1, p. 284.

68 Ibid., vol. 1, pp. 164–5.

69 Oechsli, *History of Switzerland*, p. 224.

70 Fortescue, *History of the British Army*, vol. 1, pp. 270–1.

71 D. C. Boulger, *Battle of the Boyne* (London, 1911), pp. 288–90; cf. Fieffé, *Histoire*, vol. 1, pp. 176–8.

72 Ibid., vol. 1, pp. 180, 183ff, 278–81, 279, 282, 284, 414.

73 André, *Michel le Tellier et Louvois*, pp. 107ff.

74 Fieffé, *Histoire*, vol. 1, pp. 254, 283.

75 Machiavelli, *The Prince*, ch. 12.

76 C. Hallendorff and A. Schück, *History of Sweden* (London, 1929), p. 238. One odd influx into Sweden's army was of Irish *bonaghts*, exiled by James I's conquest: see Falls, *Elizabeth's Irish Wars*, p. 69.

77 F. Grose, *Military Antiquities Respecting a History of the English Army* (London, 1786–8), vol. 2, App. 6.

78 Fortescue, *History of the British Army*, vol. 1, p. 294.

79 T. A. Jackson, *Ireland Her Own* (London, 1947), p. 63.

80 K. Gjerset, *History of the Norwegian People* (New York, 1927), vol. 2, p. 305.

81 See, for example, C. W. C. Oman, *Wellington's Army 1809–1814* (London, 1912), pp. 220–33.

82 See Earl of Selkirk, *Observations on the Present State of the Highlands of Scotland* (London, 1805), ch. 5.

83 E. Uustalu, *The History of the Estonian People* (London, 1952), pp. 55–61, 62.

84 G. A. Craig, *The Politics of the Prussian Army 1640–1945* (Oxford, 1955), pp. 3–9.

85 W. O. Shanahan, *Persian Military Reforms 1786–1813* (New York, 1945), p. 56.

86 My colleague Mr A. J. A. Malkiewicz was good enough to translate and discuss with me the relevant passages of M. Kukiel, *Zarys Historji Wojskowosci w Polse* (*Military History of Poland*) (London, 1949).

87 'Cossack' was a vague term, at first perhaps occupational. One element among the Cossacks came from the Circassians, who were prominent in Turkish military life after having been so among the Mamelukes in Egypt. See W. E. D. Allen, *The Ukraine: A History* (Cambridge, 1940), pp. 68–9; cf. Denison, *History of Cavalry* pp. 273–5.

88 Allen, *The Ukraine*, p. 105.

89 M. N. Pokrovsky, *Brief History of Russia* (London, 1933), vol. 1, p. 85.

90 Lot, *L'Art militaire*, vol. 2, p. 389.

91 Pokrovsky, *Brief History of Russia*, vol. 1, pp. 85–6, 89. Peter the Great's navy was officered as well as built for him by foreigners. In the Baltic fleet in 1713 only two out of eleven commanders and seven out of seventy other officers were Russians: see M. Mitchell, *The Maritime History of Russia 848–1948* (London, 1949), p. 63. Cf. the picture of foreign officers running away from their own Russian soldiers in A. Tolstoy, *Peter the First* (London, 1956), ch. 3, section 4.

92 R. Barbar, *The Knight and Chivalry* (London, 1974), p. 6.

93 Mme D'Aulnoy, *Travels into Spain* (1960); (London, 1930), p. 227.

94 D. Buisseret, *Sully and the Growth of Centralized Government in France 1598–1610* (London, 1968), p. 128.

95 F. Braudel, *The Mediterranean and the Mediteranean World in the Age of Philip II* (London, 1972–3), p. 801.

96 G. Finlay, *The History of Greece under Ottoman and Venetian Domination* (Edinburgh, 1856), p. 47.

97 C. Maxwell, *Irish History from Contemporary Sources 1509–1610* (London, 1923), pp. 259ff.

98 See *Calendar of State Papers, Ireland, 1608–10*, p. 458, etc.

99 A. D. Lublinskaya, *French Absolutism: The Crucial Phase, 1620–1629* (Cambridge, 1968), p. 183.

100 Braudel, *The Mediterranean and the Mediterranean World*, p. 1105.

101 G. Donaldson, *Scotland: James V–James VII* (Edinburgh, 1978), pp. 253–4, with details of Scots soldiers and noblemen during the Thirty Years' War in Danish, Swedish and (after France's entry) French service.

102 A. Gil Novales, *Las Sociedades Patrióticas (1820–1823)* (Madrid, 1975), vol. 1, pp. 6, 63.

103 See, for example, my article 'Colonial Africa and its Armies', in B. Bond and I. Roy (eds), *War and Society*, (London 1977), vol. 2; and my *European Empires from Conquest to Collapse* (London, 1982).

5 Nationalist Movements and Social Classes

1 See V. G. Kiernan, 'State and Nation in Western Europe', ch. 3 in the present volume.

2 This is emphasized by F. Braudel in *Capitalism and Material Life* (London, 1973).

3 E. Renan, *Qu'est-ce qu'une nation?*, a lecture of 1882 (Paris, 1882), sec. 3.

4 O. Jaszi, *The Dissolution of the Hapsburg Monarchy* (Chicago, 1929), p. 258.

5 C. Dickens, *Barnaby Rudge* (1841), ch. 23.

6　H. Kohn, *The Idea of Nationalism* (New York, 1945), p. 528, remarks that the peasant in Hungary looked to enlightened Austrian rule for protection against his lord. E. Wangermann, *From Joseph II to the Jacobin Trials* (Oxford, 1959), pp. 34ff., points out that patriotism was not monopolized by conservatives: others were hoping that a free Hungarian Parliament would bring progress.

7　F. Fetjö , 'Hungary', in F. Fetjö (ed.) *The Opening of an Era, 1848,* (London, 1948), p. 316. Cf. p. 314: The minor nobility, half of it too poor to count, may have totalled 680,000 in a population of 12 million.

8　G. Brenan, *The Spanish Labyrinth* (Cambridge, 1950), p. 30. See also E. A. Peers, *Catalonia Infelix* (London, 1937), chs 7–9.

9　Karl Liebknecht, *Militarism and Anti-Militarism* (Glasgow, 1917), p. 125.

10　This party was to stand for 'national independence as the indispensable ground-work of industrial emancipation': James Connolly, 'Patriotism and Labour' (1897), in D. Ryan (ed.), *Socialism and Nationalism*, a selection from his writings, (Dublin, 1948), p. 29.

11　As A. D. Smith points out, in *Theories of Nationalism* (London, 1971), p. 122.

12　D. Mitrany, 'Rumania', in N. Forbes, et al. (eds), *The Balkans* (Oxford, 1915), p. 275.

13　L. Tolstoy, 'Patriotism and Government', in his *Essays and Letters*, trans. A. Maude (London, 1903), p. 244.

14　See N. V. Riasanovsky, *Nicholas I and Official Nationality in Russia, 1825–1855* (Berkeley, 1959).

15　Introduction to *Des Prolétaires*, by the author of 'Monde avant le Christ' (Paris, 1846).

16　See Kohn, *The Idea of Nationalism*, ch. 7; and for a summary of the German romantic theory of nationalism, Smith, *Theories of Nationalism*, pp. 16–17.

17　An English traveller writes of 'The pride with which a Prussian throws out his breast and erects his head, when he speaks of the "Liberation War" '; see J. Russell, *A Tour in Germany* (Edinburgh, 1828), vol. 2, p. 55.

18　See J. G. Legge, *Rhyme and Revolution in Germany . . . 1813–1850* (London, 1918), pp. 159ff.

19　See Liebknecht, *Militarism and Anti-Militarism*; and V. G. Kiernan, 'Conscription and Society in Europe before the War of 1914–1918', ch. 6 in the present volume.

20　F. Brady (ed.), *Boswell on the Grand Tour: Corsica, and France 1765–1766,* (London, 1963), p. 174.

21　C. Ryskamp and F. A. Pottle (eds), *Boswell: the Ominous Years 1774–1776* (London, 1963), p. 329.

22　K. R. Greenfield, *Economics and Liberalism in the Risorgimento: A Study of Nationalism in Lombardy 1814–1848* (Baltimore, 1934), pp. 149, 151.

23　Ibid., pp. 56, 58.

24　R. J. Rath, *The Fall of the Napoleonic Kingdom of Italy, 1814* (New York, 1941), p. 207.

25　Greenfield, *Economics and Liberalism in the Risorgimento*, p. 71.

26　Ibid., pp. 299–300.

27　G. Mazzini, *The Duties of Man* (London, 1907), pp. 1ff., 246.

28 A. J. Whyte, *The Political Life and Letters of Cavour 1848–1861* (Oxford, 1930), p. 423.
29 Ibid., p. 319.
30 See A. Gramsci, *Selections from the Prison Notebooks of Antonio Gramsci*, ed. and tr. Q. Hoare and G. N. Smith (London, 1971), pp. 67, 101. Gramsci notes that the right-wing nationalist leader Crispi, a Sicilian, relied on the Sicilian landlords to support the central government after unification, because they needed its protection against their peasants. On Sicilian separatism as displayed in the revolutionary year of 1820, see R. M. Johnston, *The Napoleonic Empire in Southern Italy* (London, 1904), vol. 2, pp. 122ff. On the south in the Risorgimento, see also M. A. Macciochi, *Pour Gramsci* (Paris, 1974), ch. 4.
31 B. Croce, *A History of Italy 1871–1915*, tr. C. M. Adey (Oxford, 1929), p. 28.
32 R. F. Foerster, quoting P. Villari, in *The Italian Emigration of Our Times* (Cambridge, MA, 1924), p. 22.
33 See S. Kieniewicz, 'Polish Society and the Insurrection of 1863', *Past & Present*, 37 (1967). Cf. C. de Grunwald's comment on the 1830 rising, that there was 'something morbid in this political excitement of the Polish leaders: they lived in a world which no longer had any touch with reality' (*Tsar Nicholas I*, tr. B. Patmore (London, 1954), p. 117). R. F. Leslie emphasizes how much dreams of past greatness, as distinct from concrete interests of the present, influenced younger patriots especially: *Polish Politics and the Revolution of November 1830* (London, 1956), pp. 95–6. See also his *Reform and Insurrection in Russian Poland, 1856–1865* (London, 1963).
34 Kieniewicz, 'Polish Society and the Insurrection of 1863', pp. 132, 139.
35 H. B. Davis, *Nationalism and Socialism. Marxist and Labour Theories of Nationalism to 1917* (New York, 1967), pp. 134ff.
36 Hroch, quoted by E. J. Hobsbawm, 'Some Reflections on Nationalism', in T. J. Nossiter, et al. (eds), *Imagination and Precision in the Social Sciences* (London, 1972), pp. 385–406. But this must be seen as the spirit of an old self-sufficient community, resenting interference. The Argentine hinterland, as opposed to Buenos Aires, was content with Spanish colonial rule, resentful of British intrusion, free trade and competition; see H. S. Ferns, *Britain and Argentina in the Nineteenth Century* (Oxford, 1960), chs 2, 3.
37 'Marxism and the National Question' (1913), in Joseph Stalin, *Marxism and the National and Colonial Question* (London, 1936), p. 17. He argued that Marx had been right to desire an independent Poland, but Polish Marxists were now right to reject it because economic and cultural changes had drawn Poland and Russia much closer (p. 21).
38 W. F. Reddaway et al. (eds), *Cambridge History of Poland 1697–1935* (Cambridge, 1941), p. 496.
39 V. Serge, *Year One of the Russian Revolution* (1930), tr. P. Sedgwick (London, 1972), pp. 186–91.
40 H. Marczali, *Hungary in the Eighteenth Century* (Cambridge, 1910), p. 222. Cf. Jaszi, *The Dissolution of the Habsburg Monarchy*, p. 301: In the 1840s the lower nobility, with an ideology compounded of old feudal and French Revolutionary elements, 'became the real *tiers état* of Hungary'.

41 A. Massingberd, *Letter on Kossuth and the Hungarian Question* (London, 1851), p. 12; cf. Jaszi, *The Dissolution of the Habsburg Monarchy*, p. 225.
42 Massingberd, *Letter on Kossuth*, p. 20.
43 Fetjö, 'Hungary', pp. 340–1.
44 K. Tschuppik, *The Reign of the Emperor Francis Joseph 1848–1916*, tr. C. J. S. Sprigge (London, 1930), p. 161.
45 Down to 1914 only 6.5 per cent of the Hungarian population had votes, and voting was not secret: cf. Jaszi, *The Dissolution of the Habsburg Monarchy*, p. 227.
46 Davis, *Nationalism and Socialism*, pp. 143ff. On the Habsburg Slavs, see also A. J. May, *The Hapsburg Monarchy 1867–1914* (Cambridge, MA, 1951), pp. 375ff.; and J. Plamenatz, 'Two Types of Nationalism', in E. Kamenka (ed.), *Nationalism. The Nature and Evolution of an Idea*, (Canberra, 1973), pp. 30ff.
47 Tschuppik, *The Reign of the Emperor Francis Joseph*, p. 312.
48 See R. A. Kann, *The Multinational Empire* (New York, 1950), p. 261.
49 L. S. Stavrianos, *The Balkans since 1453* (New York, 1958), pp. 245ff. Cf. H. M. Chadwick, *The Nationalities of Europe and the Growth of National Ideologies* (Cambridge, 1945), p. 12.
50 Stavrianos, *The Balkans since 1453*, pp. 274–5.
51 R. Clogg, 'Aspects of the Movement for Greek Independence', in R. Clogg (ed.), *The Struggle for Greek Independence* (London, 1973), p. 14.
52 C. M. Woodhouse, *The Greek War of Independence* (London, 1952), p. 59.
53 Ibid., pp. 35–6.
54 M. Roller, 'The Rumanians in 1848', in Fetjö, 'Hungary', pp. 303ff.
55 Stavrianos, *The Balkans since 1453*, p. 252.
56 H. G. A. V. Schenk, *The Aftermath of the Napoleonic Wars* (London, 1947), pp. 136ff.
57 M. S. Anderson, *The Ascendancy of Europe: Aspects of European History 1815–1914* (London, 1972), pp. 188ff. This is a work that may be referred to for many illuminating comments on nationalism and nationalist movements.
58 W. M. Ball, *Nationalism and Communism in East Asia* (Melbourne, 1952), p. 198. Cf. W. Z. Laqueur, 'Communism and the National Minorities', in *Communism and Nationalism in the Middle East* (London, 1956), pt. 8.
59 *A Speech delivered by Ghazi Mustapha Kemal . . . October 1927*, (Leipzig, 1929), p. 309. The speech is a lengthy narrative of the national revolution.
60 See V. Purcell, *The Boxer Uprising* (Cambridge, 1963), ch. 11; and Wu Yung, *The Flight of an Empress*, tr. I. Pruitt (New Haven, Ct., 1936), pp. 24ff. There is a judicious estimate of the 'concept of China in the hearts and minds' of the people, after millennia of national unity, in J. Strachey, *The End of Empire* (London, 1961), p. 128.
61 Hobsbawm, 'Some Reflections on Nationalism'.
62 See Wu Yu-chang, *The Revolution of 1911* (Peking, 1962), ch. 11.
63 C. A. Johnson, *Peasant Nationalism and Communist Power: The Emergence of Revolutionary China 1937–1945* (Palo Alto, 1962), p. 87. Cf. Cabral's discussion of what he calls, for want as he says of a better word, the *déclassés* who 'proved to be extremely important in the national liberation

struggle' in Portuguese Guinea: Amilcar Cabral, *Revolution in Guinea* (London, 1969), p. 48.

64 See S. Y. Teng, *The Taiping Rebellion and the Western Powers* (Oxford, 1971), pp. 54–5, etc.; and J. Chesneaux, 'Preface', to J. Reclus, *La Révolte des Tai-Ping* (Paris, 1972), p. 12; and on the Boxers, see Purcell, *The Boxer Uprising*, pp. 55, 210–11; and J. Chesneaux, *Secret Societies in China*, tr. G. Nettle (London, 1971), pp. 70–1.

65 F. Engels to Paul Lafargue, 3 November 1892, in *Frederick Engels, Paul and Laura Lafargue. Correspondence*, (Moscow, n.d.), vol. 3, p. 208.

66 This is the main thesis of Johnson, *Peasant Nationalism and Communist Power*. Of the Japanese peasantry, B. Moore remarks that it seems not to have been much infected by ultra-nationalism, though this was utilized by the upper classes to keep it docile: *Social Origins of Dictatorship and Democracy* (London, 1967), pp. 307–8.

67 J. L. Buck, *Chinese Farm Economy* (Chicago, 1930), p. 145.

68 See Hira Lal Singh, *Problems and Policies of the British in India 1885–1898* (Bombay, 1963), chs 1, 3. A threshold stage was marked by semi-political bodies representing upper-class vested interests, like the British Indian Association, founded in 1815; see A. Seal, *The Emergence of Indian Nationalism* (Cambridge, 1968), pp. 202–3.

69 On British tariff policy and the Indian bourgeoisie, see Bipan Chandra, *The Rise and Growth of Economic Nationalism in India* (Delhi, 1966), ch. 6; and V. I. Pavlov, *The Indian Capitalist Class* (Delhi, 1964), ch. 11.

70 See Moore, *Social Origins of Dictatorship and Democracy*, p. 316: The British presence, and its reliance on landed interests, 'prevented the formation of the characteristic reactionary coalition of landed elites with a weak bourgeoisie'.

71 Much light is thrown on social structure and national movement in Bengal by Premen Addy and Ibne Azad, 'Politics and Society in Bengal', in R. Blackburn (ed.), *Explosion in a Subcontinent* (London, 1975).

72 Competing national and class appeals to the peasantry are well illustrated in Majid Hayat Siddiqui, 'Peasant Movements in the United Provinces: 1918–1922 (unpublished Ph.D. thesis, Delhi, Jawaharlal Nehru University, 1975).

73 See *Speeches and Writings of Mr. Jinnah*, ed. Jamil-ud-Din Ahmad (Lahore, 1942), vol. 1: *1935–44*, pp. 164, etc.

74 G. W. Choudhury, *The Last Days of United Pakistan* (London, 1974), pp. 55, 133.

75 See 'Theses on the Eastern Question' of the Fourth Congress, November 1922, in J. Degras, *The Communist International 1919–1943: Documents*, (London, 1956), vol. 1, pp. 382ff; as well as other documents in this collection. P. C. Joshi, a former general secretary of the Communist Party of India, reviews the issues between V. I. Lenin and M. N. Roy, from a point of view favourable to the former, in 'Lenin and National Revolution' (Working Paper IV.1 of the Lenin Centenary Seminar held by the Indian Council of World Affairs, February 1970). After the Second World War, Owen Lattimore wrote that nationalism, discarded in Western Europe, was being left to the emergent peoples, and added somewhat over-hopefully, 'It is a heritage that has fallen to whole peoples, rather than to classes': *The Situation in Asia* (Boston, 1949), p. 51. E. Kamenka points to the Mexican

Revolution as the first to combine national with social ideals: 'Political Nationalism – the Evolution of the Idea', in Kamenka (ed.) *Nationalism*, p. 18.

76 See, for example, V. I. Lenin, *Collected Works* (Moscow, 1966), vol. 31, pp. 122–8.

77 J. A. Silén, *We, the Puerto Rican People*, tr. C. Belfrage (New York, 1971), p. 113.

78 See J. S. Saul, 'The State in Post-Colonial Societies: Tanzania', in R. Miliband and J. Saville (eds), *The Socialist Register 1974* (London, 1974), pp. 350–2, 355–6. P. Worsley, *The Third World* (London, 1964), pp. 192ff, seems too optimistic on this question.

79 See V. A. Olorunsola (ed.), *The Politics of Cultural Sub-Nationalism in Africa* (New York, 1972), pp. 220–1, 223, 263, etc.

80 Stalin, *Marxism and the National and Colonial Question*, p. 13.

81 See, for example, Dona Torr (ed.), *Marxism, Nationality and War* (London, 1940), pt. 1.

82 V. I. Lenin, *Collected Works* (Moscow, 1964), vol. 20, p. 396; written in 1914.

83 Edward Gibbon, *Autobiography* (London 1907), World's Classics p. 146 n.

84 Two interesting studies of the Punjab issue and its background are R. Fox, *Lions of the Punjab: Culture in the Making* (Berkeley, 1986); and R. Jeffrey, *What's Happening to India?* (London, 1986).

85 See a review article by Peter Carey, in *Times Literary Supplement*, (27 February 1987).

86 See D. Hunt, 'Village Culture and the Vietnamese Revolution', *Past & Present*, 94 (1982), and T. Hodgkin, *Vietnam: The Revolutionary Path* (London, 1981).

6 Conscription and Society in Europe before the War of 1914–1918

1 H. Kohn, *The Idea of Nationalism* (New York, 1945), pp. 244, 254, 257.

2 M. S. Packe, *The Life of John Stuart Mill* (1954), pp. 437, 478, 483.

3 H. Gollwitzer, *Europe in the Age of Imperialism 1880–1914* (1969), p. 90.

4 General F. von Bernhardi, *Germany and the Next War* (1911), tr. A. H. Powles (1928), p. 9.

5 N. S. de Bohigas, 'Some Opinions on Exemption from Military Service in Nineteenth-Century Europe', *Comparative Studies in Society and History*, 10 (April 1968), pp. 281, 289.

6 I. S. Bloch, *Is War Now Impossible?* abridged edn (1899), pp. 36, 356.

7 Ibid., p. 347.

8 Ibid.

9 Cesare Pavese, *The Moon and the Bonfire*, tr. L. Sinclair (1963), p. 82.

10 See Sir C. R. Markham, *The War between Peru and Chile, 1879–1882* (1882).

11 Franz von Papen, *Memoirs*, tr. B. Connell (1952), p. 10.

12 A. Vagts, *A History of Militarism, Civil and Military*, rev. edn (1959), pp. 428ff, 454.

13 Bernhardi, *Germany and the Next War*, p. 244.

14 *Encyclopaedia Britannica*, 11th edn, see 'Conscription'.

15 Bernhardi, *Germany and the Next War*, pp. 245–6.

16 K. Demeter, *The German Officer-Corps in Society and State 1650–1945*, tr. A. Malcolm (1965), pp. 28–9.

17 Jermone K. Jerome, *Three Men on the Bummel* (1900), ch. 14.

18 Lord Hardinge, *Old Diplomacy. The Reminiscences of Lord Hardinge of Penshurst* (1948), p. 128.

19 Thorstein Veblen, *Imperial Germany and the Industrial Revolution* (1939), pp. 80–1.

20 Prince Bernhard von Bülow, *Imperial Germany*, rev. edn, tr. M. A. Lewenz (1916), p. 147.

21 Ibid., p. 154.

22 W. Gorlitz, *The German General Staff*, tr. B. Battershaw (1953), p. 76.

23 S. Whitman, *German Memories* (1912), pp. 156–7.

24 Papen, *Memoirs*, p. 10.

25 F. Engels to Laura Lafargue, 3 February 1892, in *Frederick Engels, Paul and Laura Lafargue: Correspondence*, (Moscow, n.d.), vol 3: *1891–5*, p. 159.

26 Circular of 25 May 1914, in Demeter, *The German Officer-Corps*, pp. 346–7.

27 Gollwitzer, *Europe in the Age of Imperialism*, p. 92.

28 Demeter, *The German Officer-Corps*, Appendix 23.

29 See note 14.

30 Bernhardi, *Germany and the Next War*, pp. 170–1.

31 Vagts, *A History of Militarism*, pp. 207, cf. 219.

32 Paul Lafargue to F. Engels, 21 May 1891, in *Engels–Lafargue: Correspondence* (1960), vol. 2: *1887–90* pp. 68–9.

33 R. F. Foerster, *The Italian Emigration of Our Times* (1924) p. 490.

34 M. A. Mügge, *Heinrich von Treitschke* (1915), p. 60. England still retained a vestigial obligation to serve, by ballot, in the militia. On the British recruiting system at the end of the nineteenth century, see R. Price, *An Imperial War and the British Working-Class* (1972), pp. 178ff.

35 A. G. Gardiner, *Pillars of Society* (?1915), p. 240.

36 See M. Roberts, 'Queen Christine and the General Crisis of the Seventeenth Century', in *Past & Present*, 22 (1962), pp. 40, 55.

37 E. Wangermann, *From Joseph II to the Jacobin Trials* (1959), p. 69.

38 R. B. Cunninghame Grahame, *José Antonio Páez* (1929), p. 194.

39 See I. Friedlaender, *The Jews of Russia and Poland* (1915).

40 F. Engels to Laura Lafargue, 25 February 1888, in *Correspondence*, vol. 2, pp. 97–8.

41 F. Engels to P. Lafargue, 7 March 1890, ibid., p. 367.

42 Vagts, *A History of Militarism*, p. 399.

43 L. Tolstoy, 'Patriotism and Government' (1900), in H. C. Matheson (ed.), *Social Evils and their Remedies*, 2nd edn (1917), p. 155.

44 A. Maude, *The Life of Tolstoy* (1930), World's Classic series vol. 2, pp. 349ff.

45 L. Tolstoy, 'Carthago Delenda Est', in Matheson (ed.) *Social Evils and their Remedies*, p. 224.

46 L. Tolstoy, 'The Only Means', ibid., pp. 58–9.

47 P. Lafargue to F. Engels, 6 December 1888, in *Correspondence*, vol. 2, p. 171.

48 P. Lafargue to F. Engels, 23 March 1889, ibid., p. 208.

49 F. Engels, *Herr Eugen Dühring's Revolution in Science*, tr. E. Durns, n.d.), p. 194. The passage expresses a belief that 'This militarism also carries in itself the seed of its own destruction', by 'making the people more and more able at a given moment to make its will prevail'.

50 F. Engels to P. Lafargue, 25 March 1889, in *Correspondence*, vol. 2, p. 210.

51 F. Engels to P. Lafargue, late October 1887, ibid., pp. 65–6.

52 F. Bernstein, *Evolutionary Socialism* (1961), p. 169.

53 Such a doubt was expressed, after the outbreak of the Great War, by Jaurès's admirer Margaret Pease; see her *Jean Jaurès* (?1914), pp. 119–21.

54 F. Engels to P. Lafargue, 5 December 1887, in *Correspondence*, vol. 2, p. 80.

55 F. Engels, *Daily Chronicle* interview in *Correspondence*, vol. 3, p. 399.

56 L. Tolstoy, 'Government', in Matheson (ed.), *Social Evils and their Remedies*, pp. 128–9.

57 Ibid.

58 S. H. Jeyes, 'Foreign Pauper Immigration', in A. White (ed.), *The Destitute Alien in Great Britain* (1892), p. 192.

59 J. W. Gregory, *Human Migration and the Future* (1928), p. 86.

60 Mügge, *Heinrich von Treitschke*, p. 45.

61 Prince Lichnowsky, *Heading for the Abyss* (1928), p. 79.

62 Tolstoy, 'Carthago Delenda Est', p. 125. Cf. 'Letter to a Non-Commissioned Officer' (1899), in *Essays and Letters*, tr. A Maude (1903), pp. 230–1.

63 A. Tchekov, *The Notebooks of Anton Tchekov*, tr. S. S. Koteliansky and L. Woolf (1921), p. 30.

64 Vagts, *A History of Militarism*, p. 401.

65 Ibid., pp. 350, 378.

66 A. L Lloyd, *Folk Song in England* (St Albans, 1975), p. 209.

67 K. Liebknecht, *Militarism and Anti-Militarism*, tr. and ed. G. Lock (Cambridge, 1973).

68 Ibid., pp. 17, 32, 71.

69 Vagts, *A History of Militarism*, p. 375.

70 Meredith, *Beauchamp's Career* (1875), ch. 17.

71 D. G. Hogarth, 'Turkey', in N. Forbes et al., *The Balkans* (Oxford, 1915), p. 350.

72 O. Jaszi, *The Dissolution of the Hapsburg Empire* (Chicago, 1929), p. 137.

73 M. E. Howard, 'The Armed Forces', in *New Cambridge Modern History* (Cambridge) vol. 11, p. 214.

74 Jaszi, The Dissolution of the Hapsburg Empire, pp. 15–16.

75 J. Bohstedt, *Riots and Community Politics in England and Wales, 1790–1810* (Cambridge, MA, 1983), p. 183.

76 N. Angell, *The Great Illusion* (London, 1933), p. 207 n.

77 See G. Lewis, 'The Peasantry . . . [in] Lower Austria at the Turn of the Century', in *Past & Present*, 81 (1978).

78 Engels, *Correspondence*, vol. 3, pp. 320ff.

79 R. L. Stevenson, *Prince Otto*, book 2, ch. 2.

80 Engels, *Correspondence*, vol. 3, p. 63, n. 3.

81 V. I. Lenin, *Collected Works*, vol. 39, p. 247.
82 Liebknecht, *Militarism and Anti-Militarism*, p. 74.
83 A. Kuprin, *The Duel* (London, 1916).
84 J. Barrett, *Falling In. Australians and 'Boy Conscription' 1911–1915* (Sydney, 1979), pp. 27, 230.
85 Ibid., pp. 264–5.
86 F. Engels, 'Introduction' (1895) to Marx, *The Class Struggles in France*.
87 F. Engels, *The Role of Force in History*, tr. J. Cohen, (London, 1968), p. 87.

7 Working Class and Nation in Nineteenth-century Britain

1 W. Scott to Lady Abercorn, 2 September 1812.
2 Charles Kingsley, *Alton Locke, Tailor and Poet* (1850), ch. 33.
3 C. Dickens, *The Uncommercial Traveller* (1861), ch. 4.
4 Z. Bauman, *Between Class and Elite. The Evolution of the British Labour Movement* (Manchester, 1972), pp. 39–40.
5 Ibid., pp. 125–6.
6 From *The Beehive* (4 May 1872); extract in J. B. Jeffreys (ed.), *Labour's Formative Years 1849–1879* (London, 1948), p. 127.
7 P. F. Clarke, *Lancashire and the New Liberalism* (Cambridge, 1971), p. 25.
8 J. Bright, *The Diaries of John Bright*, ed. R. A. J. Walling (London, 1930), pp. 224–5.
9 Queen Victoria, 25 May 1855; *The Letters of Queen Victoria*, ed. A. C. Benson and Viscount Esher (London, 1967), vol. 3, p. 127.
10 Kingsley Martin, *The Triumph of Lord Palmerston. A Study of Public Opinion in England before the Crimean War*, rev. edn (London, 1963), pp. 92–3.
11 Olive Anderson, *A Liberal State at War. English Politics and Economics during the Crimean War* (London, 1967), p. 149; cf. pp. 153–4.
12 P. M. Young, *The Concert Tradition* (London, 1965), p. 210.
13 Admiral Sir H. W. Richmond, *The Invasion of Britain. An Account of plans . . . from 1586 to 1918* (London, 1941), p. 65.
14 W. H. Chaloner and W. O. Henderson (eds), *Engels as Military Critic* (Manchester, 1959), pp. 2, 4, 33.
15 Ibid., p. 36.
16 Ibid., p. 37.
17 J. Grant, *Cassell's Old and New Edinburgh* (London, n.d.), vol. 2, pp. 319–22.
18 H. Cunningham, in a discussion on 'Jingoism and the Working Classes 1877–8' *Society for the Study of Labour History, Bulletin*, 19 (1969), p. 8.
19 E. M. Spiers, *The Reform of the Front-Line Forces of the Regular Army in the United Kingdom, 1895–1914* (Ph.D. thesis, University of Edinburgh, 1974), pp. 3–6.
20 G. Stedman Jones, *Outcast London* (Oxford, 1971), p. 79; cf. Spiers, *The Reform of the Front-Line Forces*, pp. 27, 37.
21 W. D. Foulke, *Slav or Saxon* (1887); 2nd edn (New York, 1899), p. 41.
22 Cunningham, discussion on 'Jingoism and the Working Classes 1877–8', p. 7.

23 S. Johnson, 'Disagreements by the Duddon, 1825–1832', *Transactions of the Cumberland and Westmorland Antiquarian and Archaeological Soc.*, (1966), pp. 379–81.
24 Clarke, *Lancashire and the New Liberalism*, p. 79.
25 J. A. Spender, *The Public Life* (London, 1925), pp. 156–7.
26 John Strachey, *What Are We to Do?* (London, 1938), pp. 74–5.
27 M. Ostrogorski, *Democracy and the Organization of Political Parties* (London, 1902), vol. 1, p. 211.
28 R. Blythe, *Akenfield. Portrait of an English Village* (1969); (Harmondsworth, 1972), p. 169; cf. pp. 171, 173.
29 D. Goldsworthy, *Colonial Issues in British Politics 1945–1961* (Oxford, 1971), pp. 68, 399.
30 G. M. Trevelyan, *English Social History* (London, 1944), p. 583.
31 Lord Tennyson, 'On the Jubilee of Queen Victoria', (1887).
32 *The Scotsman* (2 November 1899).
33 *The Scotsman* (25 September 1899).
34 N. Angell, *The Great Illusion* (1908); (London, 1933), p. 264.
35 R. Price, *An Imperial War and the British Working Class . . . the Boer War 1899–1902* (London, 1972), pp. 46, 86.
36 G. Best, in 'Jingoism and the Working Classes 1877–8', p. 8.
37 Price, *An Imperial War*, p. 92.
38 Ibid., p. 4.
39 E. Halevy, *A History of the English People in the Nineteenth Century*, (London, 1951), vol. 5, p. 104.
40 Ibid., pp. 231, 235–7.
41 Viscount Milner, *Questions of the Hour* (London, 1923), p. 64.
42 Lady Florence Bell, *At the Works* (1907); extract in P. Keating (ed.), *Into Unknown England 1866–1913* (London, 1976), pp. 285ff.
43 H. Brailsford, cited by H. B. Davis, *Nationalism and Socialism. Marxist and Labor Theories of Nationalism to 1917* (New York, 1967), pp. 112–3.
44 M. V. Brett (ed.), *Journals and Letters of Reginald, Viscount Esher*, (London, 1934, 1938), vol. 2, p. 438.
45 L. Barrow, in 'Jingoism and the Working Classes 1877–8', p. 10.
46 Robert Tressell, *The Ragged Trousered Philanthropists* (London, 1955), p. 20.
47 W. Morris, *Signs of Change* (London, 1888), p. 6.
48 D. Lloyd George, *War Memoirs* (1934); (London, 1938), p. 1141.
49 W. Robertson, *Middlesbrough's Effort in the Great War* (Middlesbrough, n.d.), pp. 6–7.
50 H. G. Wells, *War and the Future* (London, 1917), p. 200.
51 Blythe, *Akenfield*, p. 42.
52 W. Gallacher, *Revolt on the Clyde* (London, 1936), p. 26.
53 F. Williams, *Ernest Bevin* (London, 1952), p. 64.
54 M. Foot, *Aneurin Bevan* (London, 1962), vol. 1, p. 32.
55 A. J. P. Taylor (ed.), *Lloyd George. A Diary by Frances Stevenson*, (London, 1971), p. 64.
56 Lloyd George, *War Memoirs*, p. 1561; and see J. M. Winter, 'Britain's "Lost Generation" of the First World War', *Population Studies*, 31 (1977).
57 T. Bell, *Pioneering Days* (London, 1941), chs 8–11.

58 Milner, *Questions of the Hour*, p. 109.
59 See R. McKibbin, *The Evolution of the Labour Party, 1910–1924* (London, 1974), chs 5, 6.
60 J. M. Winter, 'The Impact of the First World War on Civilian Health in Britain', *Economic History Review* (1977), pp. 502ff.
61 See Jill Stephenson, 'The Nazi Organization of Women 1933–1939', in P. Strachura (ed.), *The Shaping of the Nazi State* (London, 1978).

8 Revolution

1 J. Althusius, *The Politics of Johannes Althusius*, ed. F. S. Carney (London, 1964), pp. 186–7, 190.
2 See H. L. Seaver, *The Great Revolt in Castile (1520–1)* (London, 1929).
3 See P. Avrich, *Russian Rebels 1600–1800* (London, 1973).
4 Marxism has extended the term 'industrial capital' to agriculture; 'productive capital' seems preferable. Marx did not forget that 'feudal' and 'bourgeois' are only useful abstractions, as R. S. Neale points out in his introduction to E. Kamenka and R. S. Neale (eds), *Feudalism, Capitalism, and Beyond* (London, 1975), p. 11. For a Marxist analysis of the transition, see M. Dobb, *Studies in the Development of Capitalism* (London, 1946). A penetrating review of the literature is given by I. Wallerstein in *The Modern World-System. Capitalist Agriculture and the Origins of the European World-Economy in the Sixteenth Century* (New York and London, 1974).
5 See on this M. N. Pokrovsky, *Brief History of Russia* (London, 1933), vol. 1, pp. 143–4; and I. Deutscher, *The Unfinished Revolution – Russia 1917–1947* (London, 1967), pp. 21–2. In a controversy among British Marxist historians in 1947 I wrote: 'Bourgeois revolutions, like "bourgeois art", are made for the more or less reluctant bourgeoisie by the radical petty bourgeoisie'.
6 Of expert pronouncements on this subject since the standard work by P. Geyl, *The Revolt of the Netherlands 1559–1609)* (London, 1932), a student has remarked discouragingly: 'We find versions so much at odds with each other that only a dyed-in-the-wool historian can continue to put his [sic] faith in the value of history as a serious discipline'.
7 See the essays by L. Stone and A. Everitt on 'Social Mobility in England 1500–1700' in *Past & Present*, 33 (1966); and L. Stone, *The Causes of the English Revolution, 1529–1642* (London, 1972).
8 For a criticism of this hypothesis, see my review of C. Hill, *The Century of Revolution 1603–1714* (London, 1961), in *New Left Review*, 11 (1961).
9 D. Pennington, in *Past & Present*, 6 (1954), p. 87 – replying to B. Manning – lays stress on the fact that more than two-fifths of the members of the Long Parliament took the King's side. But the fact of a nearly unanimous parliamentary opposition before 1642 is more significant than that of so many changing sides when it came to the gamble of civil war.
10 A compendium of their views can be found in D. M. Wolfe (ed.), *Leveller Manifestos of the Puritan Revolution* (New York, 1944).
11 Cf. Belinsky, in a letter of 1847: 'The middle class is always great in its struggle, in the pursuit and attainment of its aims. In this it is generous and

cunning, hero and egoist, for only its chosen act, sacrifice themselves and perish, while the fruits of achievement or victory are reaped by all'. See V. G. Belinsky, *Selected Philosophical Works* (Moscow, 1948), p. 500.

12 See D. Stevenson, *The Scottish Revolution 1638–44* (Newton Abbot, 1973), pp. 314–5, etc.

13 C. Hill, *Society and Puritanism in Pre-Revolutionary England* (London, 1966), p. 207.

14 C. de S. Montesquieu, *Lettres Persanes*, no. 89.

15 T. Paine, *The Rights of Man*, 7th edn (London, 1791), p. 93. Cf. *The Impact of the American Revolution Abroad*, a 1975 Library of Congress Symposium (Washington, 1976).

16 Tobias Smollett, *Travels through France and Italy* (1766), letter 36.

17 C. C. Brinton, *The Jacobins* (New York, 1961), pp. 70–1; cf. ch. 3 generally; and G. Lefebvre, *Quatre-Vingt-Neuf* (Paris, 1939), part 2, 'La Révolution bourgeoisie'. A. Cobban, *The Social Interpretation of the French Revolution* (Cambridge, 1964), maintains that there was no such thing as a revolutionary bourgeoisie in a capitalist sense; cf. a commentary by C. Lucas, 'Nobles, Bourgeois and the Origins of the French Revolution', *Past & Present*, 60 (1973).

18 W. Wordsworth, *The Prelude*, book 9.

19 A. Mathiez, *The French Revolution* (1922–7); (London, 1928), p. 206.

20 The growth of a modern factory working class is overstated by D. Guérin, *La Lutte de classes sous la première République 1793–1797* (Paris, 1946), Cf. A. Soboul, *The Parisian Sans-Culottes and the French Revolution 1793–4*, tr. G. Lewis (Oxford, 1964).

21 P. S.-C. Deville, *La Commune de l'an II* (Paris, 1946), pp. 43–4.

22 A. Gramsci, *Selections from the Prison Notebooks of Antonio Gramsci*, ed. Q. Hoare and G. N. Smith (London, 1971), p. 78.

23 See A. Soboul, 'Some Problems of the Revolutionary State 1789–1796', *Past & Present*, 65 (1974).

24 C. Wrigley, *David Lloyd George and the British Labour Movement* (Hassocks, 1976), p. 120.

25 See *Babœuf et les problèmes du Babouvisme. Colloque international de Stockholm, 1960* (Paris, 1963).

26 E. Burke, *Reflections on the French Revolution* (1910), Everyman series, p. 36.

27 V. I. Lenin, 'Karl Marx' (1915), in Lenin, *Collected Works* (Moscow, 1964) vol. 21.

28 F. MacDermot, *Theobald Wolfe Tone and his Times* (1939); (Tralee, 1968), p. 99.

29 'The middle classes will *speak* ultrademocracy . . . will be glad to see – nay, as they did in 1830 – will incite you to commit violence, from a twofold reason: 1. It will intimidate their rivals into submission; 2. It will afford them an excuse for not giving you what they promised': see J. Saville, *Ernest Jones, Chartist* (London, 1952), p. 170; the words belong to 1851.

30 H. Brougham, *Letter . . . on the Late Revolution in France*, 3rd edn (London, 1848), p. 30.

31 F. Engels in *London Commonweal*, 1 March 1885, cited by J. Bryne in P. C. Joshi (ed.), *Rebellion 1857* (Delhi, 1957), pp. 300–1.

32 G. A. Craig, 'Introduction' to Treitschke's *History of Germany in the Nineteenth Century* (Chicago, 1975), p. xx.

33 F. Engels, *The Role of Force in History* (1887–8); (London, 1968).

34 See my essay 'Nationalist Movements and Social Classes', (ch. 5 in the present collection).

35 F. Lessner, in *Reminiscences of Marx and Engels* (Moscow, n.d.), p. 168.

36 J. Joll, *The Anarchists* (London, 1969), p. 139.

37 Wilhelm Liebknecht, 'Reminiscences of Marx', in V. Adoratsky (ed.), *Selected Works of Karl Marx*, (Moscow, 1935), vol. 1, p. 109.

38 F. Engels, letter to F. A. Sorge, 31 December 1892; Marx and Engels, *Selected Correspondence* (Moscow, 1953), p. 535.

39 L. Trotsky, *The History of the Russian Revolution*, tr. M. Eastman, (London, 1932).

40 This factor, in Russia and a number of regions outside Europe, is discussed in E. R. Wolf, *Peasant Wars of the Twentieth Century* (London, 1971).

41 E. Wilson, *To the Finland Station* (London, 1941).

42 C. Delisle Burns, *The Principles of Revolution* (London, 1920), p. 7.

43 H. Eckstein (ed.), *Internal War. Problems and Approaches* (New York, 1964), p. 1. He adds of this collection: 'There is no use pretending that the essays have achieved the end intended' (p. 5). Cf. P. Schrecker, 'Revolution as a Problem in the Philosophy of History', in C. J. Friedrich (ed.), *Revolution* (New York, 1969), p. 35.

44 G. le Bon, *The World in Revolt. A Psychological Study of Our Times*, tr. B. Miall (London, 1921), p. 179.

45 For example, C. Johnson, *Revolution and the Social System* (Palo Alto, Ca., 1964), p. 10: 'Revolution is the acceptance of violence in order to bring about change'.

46 W. F. Wertheim, *Evolution and Revolution* (Harmondsworth, 1974). See also D. W. Brogan, *The Price of Revolution* (London, 1951), and P. Calvert, *A Study of Revolution* (Oxford, 1970).

47 C., L. and R. Tilly, *The Rebellious Century 1830–1930* (London, 1975).

48 See, for example, F. L. Polak, *The Image of the Future* (Leyden, 1961), vol. 1, pp. 268–71.

49 There is no better way to appreciate this than to go through the relevant contributions to *Past & Present* since it began in 1952. Some of them will be found collected in T. Aston (ed.), *Crisis in Europe 1560–1660* (London, 1965), and D. Johnson (ed.), *French Society and the Revolution* (Cambridge, 1976). For two recent Marxist works, see F. Marek, *Philosophy of World Revolution* (London, 1969); and J. Woddis, *New Theories of Revolution* (London, 1972).

50 L. von Beethoven, letter to Nickolaus Simrock, 2 August 1794.

51 W. G. Rosenberg and M. B. Young, *Transforming Russia and China* (London, 1982), p. x.

52 T. Skocpol, *States and Social Revolutions* (Cambridge, 1979), pp. 226, 231.

53 L. Stone 'The Bourgeois Revolution of 17th-Century England Revisited', *Past & Present*, 109 (1985), p. 53. On this, see Harvey J. Kaye, *The British Marxist Historians* (Oxford, 1984), esp. ch. 4 on Hill.

54 C. Hill 'A Rejoinder', *Past & Present*, 98 (1983), pp. 158ff.

55 G. E. Aylmer, *Rebellion or Revolution? England 1640–1660* (Oxford, 1986).

56 For a recent commentary see G. C. Comninel, 'The Political Context of the Popular Movement in the French Revolution', in F. Krantz, (ed.), *History from Below: Studies in Popular Protest and Popular Ideology* (Montreal, 1985).

57 J. H. Billington, *Fire in the Minds of Men. Origins of the Revolutionary Faith* (London, 1980).

58 J. Burckhardt, *Judgements on History and Historians*, tr. H. Zohn, (London, 1959), p. 200.

59 P. Burke, 'The Virgin of the Carmine and the Revolt of Masaniello', *Past & Present*, 99 (1983), p. 16.

60 F. Engels, 'Introduction' (1895) to *Marx, The Class Struggles in France*.

Index

Page numbers in bold indicate central discussion of the item.

absolutism, absolute monarchy, absolutist state, 8–9, 18–20, 103, 107, **109–17**, **118–37**, 138–9, 201, 205
Africa, Africans, 12, 14–16, 60, 131, 137, 162–3
Althusser, Louis, 59, 76, 99
America, American *see* United States of America
Anderson, Perry, 3, 243
Arabs, 155, 164
Aragon *see* Spain
aristocracy, aristocrats, **17–20**, 97, 104, 108, **110–17**, 134–5, 140, 147, 170–2, 174, 202, 204, 206, 213–14, 222
see also land, landlords
arms and armies, 19–20, **118–37**, 155–6, 164–5, **166–85**, 201–2, 210–11
see also war and militarism
art and artists, 26, 198
see also poetry and poets
artisans, 107–9, 116–17, 136, 144, 149, 187–8, 190, 200, 204, 219–20
Asia, Asians, 4–5, 12, 14–16, 39–42, 104–10, 112, 137, **155–63**, 226, 229–30

Australia, 185
Austria, Austria-Hungary, 36–7, 109, 115, 127, 129, 147, 150–1, 167, 184, 204, 223, 227
see also Habsburg Empire; Hungary

Balkans, 144, 151–4, 158, 223
see also Croatia; Greece; Ottoman Empire; Serbia; Yugoslavia
base and superstructure, 58, 74
Basques, 107, 122, 125, 175, 222
Belgium, 140–2, 144, 167–8, 213
Benjamin, Walter, 27–8
Bismarck, Otto von, 46, 89, 91, 145, 149, 163, 167, 220, 222
Boer War, 193–4, **249**
Bohemia, 109, 123, 134, 147, 151, 204
Bolsheviks, 40, 51, 66, 70, 156, 223, 226
see also Lenin; Russia; Soviet Union
Bonaparte, Louis-Napoleon III, 36–7, 89, 220, 222
Bonaparte, Napoleon I, 68, 89, 114, 140, 176, 181, 183, 218–19
see also Napoleonic Wars
Bourbons, 131
bourgeoisie (capitalists), 8–9, 18–22, 78–9, 88, 113, 145, 149, 151, 170–2, 204–5, 211, 214, 216–22, 225, 263

bourgeois revolution(s), 8–9, 21–2, 116–17, 139, 144, 157, **205–9**, 213, 218, 225, **227–9**
Braudel, Fernand, 11, 58, 137
Britain, British, 11–13, 23–4, 38–9, 79, 132, 142–3, **186–98**, 219
　British Empire, 11–13, 39–40, 158–62, 192–3
　see also England; Ireland; Scotland; Wales
Bukharin, N. I., 50–2, 73–4, 76, 99
Bulgars, Bulgaria, 152
bureaucracy, 78, 97, 202, 207, 213–14, 216
　see also state, nation-state

Calvinism, Calvinists, 143, 150, 205–6, 209
Calvin, John, 87
Cambridge University, 3–5, 161
Canada, 165, 193
capitalism, capitalist development, 8–9, 16, 18–21, 34, 42–3, 113, 116–17, 139, 162–3, 166, 182, **204–6**, **208–12**, 214, 219, 222, 225, 227
　see also bourgeoisie; merchants
Carlism, Carlists, 141, 221–2
Carr, E. H., 6–7
Castile *see* Spain
Catalonia, 141–2, 175, 203, 206, 222
　see also Spain
Catholics, Catholic Church, 94–5, 99, 106–10, 115–16, 201–3, 213
Chartism, Chartists, 85, 187–9, 211, 221
China, Chinese, 11–12, 39–40, 53, 61–2, 64, 67, 103, 105–6, 108, **154–8**, 162–4, 189–90, 200, 229–30
　Chinese Revolution, 62, **228–20**
Christianity, 26, 67, 72, 75, 100, 163, 200, 213
　see also Calvinists; Catholics; Protestants; religion
Church *see* Catholics, Catholic Church
cities and towns, 42, **106–7**, 110, 112, 115, 139, 148, 199, 202, 204, 216–17
class and class struggle, 2–3, 14, 17–25, 32, 56–7, 61, 63–4,

79–81, 83–5, 97–100, 104–5, 114, 116–17, 129, 132
class and conscription, 169–81
class and nationalism, 138–65, 186–98
class and revolution, 199–231
　see also aristocracy; bourgeoisie; middle classes; peasants; working class
class consciousness, **23–6**, 84, 151, **186–98**
colonialism, 12–16, 113, 137
　see also imperialism and European powers
Communist parties, 2–6, 21, 52–3, 60–1, 66–7, 99–100, 157–8
　see also left, leftists; socialism, socialists
Communist Party, British, 2–6, 8–9, 197
　Historians' Group, 2–3, 6, 8–9, 18, 23–8
conscription, **166–85**, 197
conservatism, conservatives, 140–1, 146, 166, 168, 221
　see also Fascism; right, rightists; Tory, Tories
Cornford, John, 4, 235
Crimean War, 38, 132, 154, 189
Croatia, 37, 110, 151, 200
　see also Serbia; Yugoslavia
Croce, Benedetto, 72–3, 95, 147
Cromwell, Oliver, 210–11, 218–19, 225, 228
culture, 23–7, 34–5, 112, 190–5, 198, 207, 215, 239
Czechs, Czechoslovakia, 37, 112, 151
　see also Bohemia

democracy, 26–7, 82, 109, 161, 163, 167–8, 202, 211–13, 217–19
Denmark, 142, 176, 203
diplomacy and diplomats, 11–12
Dobb, Maurice, 9, 263
Dutch (Holland, The Netherlands), 21–2, 107, 127, 132, 139, 142, **205–7**, 210–13

education, 139, 166–9, 171, 173–4
empires *see* Britain, British Empire; colonialism; Habsburg Empire;

Holy Roman Empire; imperialism and European powers; Ottoman Empire; Rome, Roman Empire

Engels, Friedrich, 2, 9–10, 16, 20, **29–46**, 66, 76, 99, 162, 173, 178–9, 184–5, 191, 198, 221–3, 230–1

England, English, 26, 30–1, 89, 105, 107, 109–10, 112–13, 116–17, 125, 131–2, 135, 139, 142–3, 171, 175–6, 182–4, 186–98, 205, 207–13, 221, 227–8

English Revolution, 8–9, 21–2, 31, 114, **207–13**, 227–8

see also Britain; Scotland; Wales

Enlightenment, 212–14, 217

Fascism (including National Socialism/ Naziism), 4, 21, 70, 83–4, 87, 90–2, 100, 146, 154–5, 156, 172–3, 225, 231

see also right, rightists

Ferns, Henry, x, 3–4

feudalism, 8–9, **17–20**, 54, **103–16**, 118–19, 151–2, 170–1, 211, 214–16, 222, 225

Finland, 131, 150

Flanders, Flemish, 121, 142

France, French, 30, 79–80, 87–8, 104, 107–8, 110–17, 119–21, 123–4, 130–2, 136–7, 139, 167, 170, 174, 178–9, 182, 200, 204–5, 212–21

French Revolution of 1789, 15, 21–2, 29–31, 87–8, 137, 140, 166–7, 187, **212–20**, 221–2, 226–9

Franco, Francisco, 21, 154

Gandhi, 'Mahatma', 91, 159–60

gentry, 108, 110, 148–50, 172, 202, 209–11, 223

Germany, Germans, 30–41, 46, 79, 90–3, 95, 107, 109–11, 123–5, 129, 131, 135, 139, 145, 149, 151, 167, 170–4, 180–4, 195, 198, 200, 222–3, 225

Gramsci, Antonio, x, 10–11, 23–5, 52, **66–101**, 146, 217, 255

Greece, Greeks, 152–4

Habsburgs, Habsburg Empire, 36, 114, 136, 140, 150–1, 204, 213

Hegel, G. W. F., 31, 44–5, 58, 67, 73

Hill, Christopher, x, 2, 8, 228, 234, 246

Hilton, Rodney, x, 2, 17

history, historians, historiography, **1–65**, 76–7, 87, 100, 220

Hitler, Adolf, 21, 82

Hobsbawm, Eric, 2, 6, 24, 27

Holland *see* Dutch

Holy Roman Empire, 107, 114

Hungary, Hungarians and Magyar, 110, 115, 126, 134, 140, 150–1, 154, 184, 200, 223

see also Austria, Austria-Hungary

hydraulic theory, 12, 39

ideology, 34–6, 74, 195, 200, 209

see also culture, Fascism; nationalism; religion; socialism

imperialism and European powers, 1, 4–5, 11–16, 162–4, 191, 211

see also Britain, British Empire; colonialism

India, 4–5, 39, 42, 60–1, 104, 106, 110, 158–61, 164, 189, 192, 229

industry, Industrial Revolution, 84, 139, 143, 147, 166, 170, 186–9, 204–5, 208, 214, 219, 223–4

intellectuals, 25–8, **94–101**, 147, 162, 215, 230

intelligentsia, 145, 149, 152, 155, 157, 215

Ireland, Irish, 112–13, 125–6, 136–7, 142, 160, 163, 176, 187, 192, 203, 205, 210, 223

Islam and Muslims, 104, 106, 110, 136, 152, 156, 160–1, 164–5

Italy, Italians (including Genoese, Venetians, Sicilians, etc.), 33, **68–101**, 107, 122, 124, 127 137, 146–8, 154–5, 163, 175, 181, 203–4, 223, 230

Jacobinism, Jacobins, 87–8, 174, 214, 217–18

Japan, Japanese, 12, 15–16, 58–9, 105, 155, 157, 171

Jaurès, Jean, 179, 182

Jews, Judaism, 26, 67, 110, 177, 181

jingoism *see* patriotism

Kautsky, Karl, 47–9
Klugmann, James, 4, 235

labourism, 23–4, 188–90, 239
Labour Party (British), 197
land, landlords, 105, 109, 115, 118,
   135, 143, 146–9, 158, 168,
   176–7, 199–200, 208–11, 216,
   219–21, 229
   see also aristocracy, aristocrats
Latin America, 60, 115, 255 n. 36
law, 105, 208–12, 214–16, 219
lawyers, 97, 105, 158, 209, 220
left, leftists, 26–7, 69–70, 85, 97, 161
   see also Communist parties;
   socialism
Lenin, V. I., 25, 30, 33, 50, 57, 66,
   69–70, 92–3, 161–2, 185, 220,
   225–6, 229, 257
Levellers, 211–12
liberalism, liberals, 38–9, 91, 140–1,
   145, 172, 194–5, 221–2
Luther, Martin, 37, 108
Luxemburg, Rosa, 149

Machiavelli, Niccolo, 52, 88, 118,
   121, 123, 131
Mao Tse-Tung, 57, 64, 67, 70
Marx, Karl, 2, 7, 9–10, 16, 20, 23, 26,
   29–65, **29–43**, 70, 76, 85–6, 89,
   99, 161–3, 186, 188, 198, 205,
   211, 220, 224, 229–30
Marxism, 6–11, 14, 23–8, **29–65**,
   66–101 161–3, 192, 211, 224–31
'Western Marxism', 52, 58, 67, 77
Mazzini, G., 88–91, 147–8, 163,
   223–4
mercenaries, foreign, 19–20, **118–37**,
   166
merchants, merchant capital, 8–9,
   152–3, 204, 210, 214, 236
   see also bourgeoisie; middle classes
Middle Ages, medieval, 17–20, 33,
   102–8, 118, 122, 133–4, 138,
   199–200, 204
   see also feudalism
middle classes, 21, 37, 140, 144–7,
   151, 153, 155, 158, 161, 170,
   174, 182, 194, 196, 209, 213–14,
   221, 227, 230
   see also bourgeoisie

modes and relations of production,
   8–9, 12, 32–42, 74
   see also capitalism; feudalism;
   slavery
Moors, 110, 154, 200, 203
Mussolini, Benito, 83, 87, 90–1

Napoleonic wars, 132, 141, 148, 153,
   174, 187
   see also Bonaparte, Napoleon I
nation *see* state, nation-state
nationalism, 20–1, 80–1, 107,
   113–14, **138–65**, **187–98**, 225,
   228
   see also patriotism
Netherlands *see* Dutch
Nietzsche, Friedrich, 75, 86, 170
Norman, Herbert, 4–5, 235
Norway, Norwegians, 136, 142, 223

Ottoman Empire, 103, 108, 124, 136,
   152–5, 176
   see also Turkey, Turks

Paine, Tom, 213, 228
Pakistan, 161
Paris Commune of 1871, 149, 168,
   174, 223, 225
Parliament (English/British), 31, 192,
   208–12, 228
parties (political), 82, 87–8, 224
   see also Communist parties; Labour
   Party (British); socialism,
   socialists; Tory, Tories
patriotism, 21, 23, 107, 138–65,
   154–5, **190–8**, 212, 249
   see also nationalism
peasants, 21, 25, 37, 61, 64, 85, 98,
   107–17, 119, 127–9, 131, 133,
   134, 140, 148–54, 157–8, 160,
   169, 176–8, 199–200, 203–4,
   210–11, 219, 221,229–30
Peasants' War (German), 37, 44,
   110–11, 127–8, 200
Plekhanov, G., 48–50, 52, 55
poetry and poets, 5, 26, 192–3
Poland, Polish, 133–4, 148–50, 203,
   223, 255
Portugal, Portuguese, 15, 102, 120,
   203, 220
property, 105, 211, 215, 219, 227
Protestant, Protestantism, 102, 116,

127, 130, 201—2, 205—7, 211, 234
Prussia, Prussians, 46, 91, 112, 115, 133, 145, 150, 167, 172, 223, 225
Puritans, Puritanism *see* Calvinism, Calvinists

race, race relations, 12—13
Reformation, 31, 37, 109, 116, 200
religion, 3, 26, 86—7, 109, 113—14, 116—17, 132, 140, 148, 152—3, 156, 162—3, 169, 177, 193–4, 200—2, 205—7, 209—10, 228
revolution, revolutions, 21—2, 36—7, 38—9, 56, 87—8, 91, **198—231**, 1848, 21, 36—8, 141, 144—5, 221—4
see also bourgeoisie, bourgeois revolutions; China, Chinese; England, English; France, French; Russia, Russian; United States of America
right, rightists, 27, 154—5
see also conservatism, conservatives; Fascism; Tory, Tories
Risorgimento, 69, 95
Robespierre, M., 217—18
Romanticism, 164
Rome, Roman Empire, 33, 54—5, 105—6
Rousseau, Jean-Jacques, 68, 167
Roy, M. N., 161, 257
Rudé, George, x, 2, 24, 27
Rumania/Romania, 143, 151—4
Russia, 38—9, 48, 50—1, 70, 79, 112, 115, 134—5, 144, 148—50, 167, 176—8, 185, 201—2, 213, 225—6, 229—30
Russian Revolution, 50, 92, **225—6**, 228, 229—30
see also Bolsheviks; Lenin, V. I.; Soviet Union

Saville, John, 239
Scotland, Scots, 69, 87, 112—13, 120—1, 125—6, 130, 142, 136—7, 139, 165, 191, 206, 211—12
Serbia, Serbs, 112—13, 152, 154
see also Balkans; Croatia; Yugoslavia

serfdom, 41, 110, 133, 134—5, 150, 166—7, 176, 201, 203—4
Shakespeare, William, 4, 5, 18, 29, 77, 103, 119, 138
Sikhs, 5, 164
slavery, slaves, 41—2, 54, 136, 177, 21
Slavs, 150—2
socialism, socialists (including Social Democrats), 23—8, 29—30, 57, 66, 84, 142, 149, 163, 165, 173, 178, 192, 223—6, 230
see also Commmunist parties; left, leftists; Marxism
Soviet Union, 21, 51, 150
see also Russia
Spain (including Castille, Aragon, etc.), 15, 22, 34, 38, 102, 104, 109—16, 124—6, 136—7, **140—2**, 175, 200—1, 203—4, 220—1
see also Basques; Catalonia
Stalin, Joseph and Stalinism, 50—1, 57, 70, 255
state, nation-state, 8—9, **18—22**, 78—83, 89—92, 101, **102—17**, 138—40, 143—4, 151, 155, **166—85**, 207—12
see also nationalism
Sweden, Swedes, 111—12, 130—1, 135, 142, 176, 203
Switzerland, Swiss, 109, **122—4**, 126, 128, 130, 167

Thirty Years' War, 128—9, 131, 135, 200
Thompson, E. P., 2, 24, 27, 234
Tolstoy, Leo, 143, 177—8, 180—1
Tory, Tories (British Conservative Party), 79, 97, 165, 187, 189, 195—6
Trotsky, Leon, 51, 69, 76, 92, 170
Turkey, Turks, 108, 131, 143, 151—6, 176, 183
see also Ottoman Empire

United States of America, 13—14, 79, 80—2, 92—4, 151, 169—70, 181, 193, 213
American Revolution, 15, 31, 131, 187, 206
urbanization *see* cities and towns

Vietnam, 13, 165

Wales, Welsh, 121–2, 138, 196
war and militarism, 19–20, 33, 41,
    46, 55–6, 75, 92, 104–5, 111,
    118–37, 167–85, 189, 193–8,
    216, 218–19, 230
    see also arms, armies; Boer War;
    Crimean War; mercenaries,
    foreign; Napoleonic wars; Thirty
    Years' War; World War I; World
    War II
women, 129, 148, 165, 198, 230
Wordsworth, William, 4, 26, 141,
    172, 215
    see also Romanticism

working class (proletariat), 23–7, 31,
    83–5, 98, 136, 140–1, 145, 159,
    169, 175, 178–9, **186–98**, 199,
    216, 220, 224, 230
    British working class, 186–98
    see also artisans
World War I, 69, 84, 90–2, 137, 141,
    150, 155, 174, 182, 185, 194–8,
    218
World War II, 5, 21, 197

Yugoslavia, 158
    see also Croatia; Serbia